The Olivier S

The Olivier Sisters

A Biography

SARAH WATLING

OXFORD
UNIVERSITY PRESS

OXFORD
UNIVERSITY PRESS

Oxford University Press is a department of the University of Oxford. It furthers the University's objective of excellence in research, scholarship, and education by publishing worldwide. Oxford is a registered trade mark of Oxford University Press in the UK and in certain other countries.

Published in the United States of America by Oxford University Press
198 Madison Avenue, New York, NY 10016, United States of America

© Sarah Watling 2019

First published in Great Britain by Jonathan Cape

A copy of this book's Cataloging-in-Publication Data
is on file with the Library of Congress.

ISBN 978–0–19–086739–3

1 3 5 7 9 8 6 4 2

Printed by Sheridan Books, Inc., United States of America

For Sara Willis
And for Julian Walton

Contents

Introduction

'Words are so misleading.' Noel Olivier

On 7 September 1962, in a lofty house on Kensington Park Road, a show-down took place between Christopher Hassall and Noel Olivier. Hassall was a hefty, good-looking and multi-talented man; an actor and poet in his youth, he had for many years collaborated with Ivor Novello as his lyricist. Together they had produced some of the most popular musical shows in British theatre of the 1930s and '40s: *Glamorous Night, Careless Rapture, The Dancing Years, King's Rhapsody*. In 1953, Hassall had published a well-received biography of his friend, the patron of the arts, Eddie Marsh. Now fifty years old, he was a popular man, comfortable in literary and theatrical circles, a man with a certain air of glamour; used to a friendly welcome. He counted Noel's cousin Laurence Olivier, 'Larry' to Hassall, as a friend. In September 1962, Hassall had all but finished work on the first truly authorised biography of a famed war poet whose romantic profile was familiar to every schoolchild in the country. Noel was supposed to complete the picture.

With her siblings, she had been a key character in the story Hassall was trying to recreate in his book. The Olivier sisters, of whom Noel was the youngest, were the beautiful, enigmatic daughters of an impor-tant socialist. They had gone through life intriguing and alarming people, fending off besotted admirers and insisting on surprisingly modern lives for themselves; lives that had sometimes tilted unapologetically towards disreputableness. In other words, Noel should have been a gift to a biographer.

But she had proved an elusive quarry. For more than two years, she had ignored and side-stepped Hassall, put him off and, in doing so, put back the publication of the biography, which was by now more than a year behind its schedule. 'She is still in a state of psychological resistance which she seems unlikely to overcome,' an old friend of Noel's warned Hassall. 'I hope that you will not wait indefinitely.'

A planned collection of the poet's letters had already been hampered by Noel's intransigence. Noel had been one of the earliest and most implacable opponents of publication. Not only had she refused to relinquish any of her own letters, she had also asked that no mention whatsoever be made of her in the volume, nor any photos featuring her appear.

Hassall complained that the omission of the Olivier correspondence had left the Letters 'gravely incomplete'. This, of course, was Noel's intention. What was told in those missives was not only part of the story of the poet's life but part of the story of hers and her sisters': lives that had reached far beyond their entanglement with this posthumously famous man. They had had plenty of opportunities to reconsider their position – the Oliviers had first been asked for their letters in 1915 – but none of the requests or arguments in the intervening years had changed Noel's mind nor had she ever felt much need to engage in the various debates that went on about publication, even to explain her own decision.

When, after some of her closest friends interceded, Noel agreed to meet Hassall, her suggested Friday (she offered him a single, two-hour slot) happened to be a particularly inconvenient evening for him. But Noel had laid down her conditions and so Hassall cancelled his appointments, put together an index of references to her in the biography, and asked his sister to host them in her London home.

On 7 September, the accommodating Joan Hassall put out dinner on a table laid with flowers and candles. Noel arrived punctually. Yet from the moment she appeared at the door, Noel was a disappointment to Hassall. Instead of the anticipated opponent, 'a minute, shrivelled, old woman, with no hat but a mass of very white hair, limped forward, dragging her right leg', he told a friend, 'everything about her seemed <u>afflicted</u>; her face, thin and drawn, made her nose seem too big and protruding'.

Wrong-footed by this first surprise, Hassall proceeded in confusion. 'What can I do to help?' Noel asked when she arrived and yet how could she not know? She was carrying only a small handbag, which meant she had not brought the letters he was counting on, and claimed not even to know where they were. 'I haven't rummaged,' she announced maddeningly. He asked if he could see the letters, if she did find them; she 'recoiled' and then hedged. Perhaps they could at least use the time to go through the index: he offered to read out passages from his book that mentioned

Noel, for vetting and even correction, but she declined and instead, after a dinner in which a bewildered Hassall left the conversation to his sister, departed the house with a small black briefcase (provided by Joan), stuffed full of the typescript pages to read at her own leisure. 'It will be very painful,' she said, taking the bag. 'Not a bit,' came the reply. 'It isn't the least bit boring; you might even be amused by some of it.' Hassall walked Noel through the dark to the tube station and watched her limp towards the escalator. He raised his hand to wave. She did not turn.

It was hard to imagine the beguiling teen who had once captivated Hassall's subject, Rupert Brooke. The real Noel, Hassall insisted, was repulsive, 'a poor little char', who yet smiled sweetly at him, 'with a soft, kindly look in her eyes'; she was a pathetic creature, so 'ravaged' as to rob him of a worthy opponent, who yet managed to frustrate all of his intentions for the meeting, remaining doggedly non-committal and non-compliant in the face of both charm and hectoring, someone who forced him to admit: 'I've never met such a difficult customer.' Noel, it seemed, had entirely confounded him.

Despite this unpromising start, as he reflected on the evening, Hassall was cautiously optimistic. Perhaps, reading the biography, Noel would be 'profoundly shocked', 'acutely embarrassed'; perhaps she would recognise 'that reticence is vain and fully co-operate'. Only then did he realise that Noel had managed to get away without leaving her address.

That Noel Olivier should humbly overcome one biographer, and resent the intrusions of various others, begs the question of why someone would dare to write a whole book about her and her sisters. Margery, Brynhild, Daphne and Noel never courted attention (which is not to say they didn't receive it). There is no reason to think they would have approved of such a thing. Charting the struggle between Noel and Christopher Hassall – seeing her challenge him over the interpretation of events he had no experience of, and she could have no academic distance from – illuminated, for me, the wrangle, the theft and the responsibility of biography.

I liked to think my motives were benign. From my first enticing glimpse of the Olivier sisters – so striking particularly because they always seemed to appear together – I had no doubt joined the ranks of people who had admired and romanticised them, both during their lifetimes and after-wards. I was intrigued by that collective term, 'the Olivier sisters', which cropped up alluringly in accounts of the Neo-Pagans: the hopeful young people who gathered around Rupert Brooke in Cambridge before the First World War. The more I learned about the sisters, the more they appealed. It wasn't hard to imagine the sheer visual impact they made on people, or why, in 1909, Jacques Raverat suspected his friend Rupert Brooke was in love with all four of them. The young Oliviers were very good-looking indeed. They grew up among socialists who hoped to make new kinds of lives possible for women, so they lacked the usual inhibitions, and had more than the usual ambitions, of Victorian girls; they split their time between England and Jamaica, so they had mysterious other lives; they were in their element in the natural world in a way that seemed to embody the ideals of the Neo-Pagans. The eldest, Margery, was precociously clever and politically outspoken. Brynhild's beauty surpassed almost anyone's and she had a knack for bringing people together, which came to the fore when drawing the Bloomsbury Group into Neo-Pagan camping trips (much to Lytton Strachey's alarm). Daphne, second youngest, was dreamy and idealistic; Noel physically uninhibited. I just wanted to indulge my curiosity, I told myself; I wanted to get close enough to see what they were like on their own terms.

There was so much to tell: born towards the end of the Victorian era, the Oliviers' lives spanned almost a century. From a bucolic childhood amongst progressives, when they performed plays for George Bernard Shaw, picnicked with Russian political exiles and were taught croquet by H. G. Wells, the sisters emerged into the Caribbean reaches of the British Empire, the frantic optimism of Edwardian Cambridge and onwards into lives of increasing independence from one another, through the bleakness of the First World War, the emergence of a host of philosophies for life, and the highs and lows of the women's movement, before contracting towards each other again to see out another world war.

They were of their time and yet extraordinary within it: suffrage campaigners, pioneers in medicine and education; D. H. Lawrence was disgusted by them, H. G. Wells enchanted. The writer David Garnett idolised them his entire life. Virginia Woolf tried, and failed, to work out what lay behind their mysterious 'glass eyes'.

Interesting women have secrets. They also ought to have sisters. If one is to have an interesting life, as each of the Oliviers undoubtedly did, one needs co-conspirators, people in one's corner. Yet any sister will tell you that being a sister is both a blessing and a curse. Being known as one of 'The Oliviers' must have been a trying merging of identity for women of strong-willed and independent natures. How to respond to a note from Maynard Keynes addressed to 'Miss Any Olivier'? Virginia Woolf once recorded seeing 'dim background figures [...] turning out to be Oliviers – varieties of Oliviers'. The sisters found their self-perception challenged by 'varieties of Oliviers' drawn by friends, lovers, poets, memoirists and biographers. I was about to add to these approximations.

The Oliviers were, from girlhood, unusual – distinguished. They seemed wild with freedom and daring, and somehow they managed to translate this quality into adulthood as well, where it became determination and an ability to know their own minds: less exotic attributes, perhaps, but singular and valuable nonetheless. They had a wide-ranging audience to contend with. They were assessed and commented on by those in their thrall or those just released from it, those they offended with their beauty, apparent hauteur, views or failure to reciprocate feelings. And as they were private types, these outside views were, for the most part, the ones that were recorded.

Someone who knew them for most of their lives described the Olivier girls both as 'savages' and as strikingly 'noble'. This seemed somehow to sum up the problem. A savage is surely an unknowable creature, perhaps dangerous, observed always from an uncomprehending distance. Nor is there any great generosity in attributing nobility to a 'savage'. Their observers may allow them wisdom, for instance, but they comfortingly insist on their simplicity, their primitiveness, at the same time. The Oliviers might have impressed onlookers but they were still girls, still women. So Rupert Brooke associated a teenaged Noel with the elements: sun, sea, earth and fire, and offered her the compliment of having a mind that was 'clean and clear like a man's'. Both adjectives – noble and savage – are words that betray a lack of intimacy with their subject. Which begs the question: how does it feel to be that subject?

We all grapple with the shifting incongruities of how we see ourselves and how we are seen; confronting the mismatch can be a sharp challenge to our sense of ourselves. For girls and young women, the gaze of others could be said to be a more threatening, or at least confusing, force in the establishment of who we are. A group of sisters like the Oliviers fascinated me: siblings are our earliest audiences and challengers, after all, and I wondered what growing up inside their sisterhood meant for how each of them later faced the world. A tight-knit group may be off-putting to outsiders but may also remove the need for them. It seemed to me that the Oliviers had been raised in such a way that might have left them untroubled by the gaze of those various others: surely a liberating way to exist.

As Virginia Woolf's biographer Hermione Lee wrote, 'Biography sets out to tell you that a life can be described, summed up, packaged and sold.' This book, even though it puts the Oliviers centre stage, would never have been able to describe or sum up complete lives. With some possible exceptions, the sisters did not live their lives publicly (in the sense of being public figures) and did not want to. Rather the opposite. Detailed records of their existence simply didn't exist. There were, of course, long periods in each of their lifetimes when nothing much happened beyond the absorbing business of everyday life. Very few people live at a pitch that can maintain narrative momentum. This book, I soon realised, could only visit the sisters for short periods. I decided to acknowledge the gaps, to leave blanks where I found them, to instead recreate seven eras of the Olivier sisters. These would be seven stages in four women's lives, following them as they gradually developed separate trajectories. Growing up, for them, was also a process of growing distinct from one another. Occupied in youth, as many people are, with questions of how to live (what to want and whether it would be possible to get it), they were also working out what kind of impact outsiders would have, or be allowed to have, on their bond, how to protect that bond and yet how to distinguish themselves from their sisters. By the era of middle age and the Second World War they had new centres of gravity, holding together families and homes that had become part of a new national 'front'.

I liked the idea that these visitations could be tailored specifically to the sisters and what was happening with them. History as it exists is not always a good fit for women. Traditional periodisation sometimes seems irrelevant: can one talk of a Renaissance when one's subjects are, in political, economic and sexual senses, facing a retraction rather than a blossoming, for example? Similarly, women's lives, I think, fall into slightly different eras from men's, and did so especially in previous centuries.

Working out how to write about people who did not live publicly, and rarely wrote about themselves, has been a particular challenge for those writing about women. Virginia Woolf herself once acknowledged that, 'Very little is known about women.' This is partly because women have been the supporting cast of history. Righting the balance has required a restoration, an identification of the people behind the omissions. It hasn't been easy. Women have often participated in their own effacing;

they have chosen not to give themselves away, and it is often women who need them to perform new roles who later draw them out. There lies the question of the author's motivation, for in seeking to reclaim something, one is inevitably claiming something for oneself.

Hassall was of course interested, first and foremost, in his subject: Rupert Brooke. Sometimes a biographer has to be terribly single-minded. But the further Hassall went with his project, the more he viewed Noel Olivier as nothing more than an accessory to his hero. Here was the problem behind their confrontations: Hassall couldn't understand why Noel didn't simply put her own point of view aside – in dealing both with Rupert Brooke and with his biographers – as he was so happy to do on her behalf when reconstructing Brooke's short life.

For someone writing in 2017 and 2018, the Oliviers' insistence on unknowability was intriguing and exotic. We were all pretty preoccupied with the self, with identity, and by who had the rights to tell which stories. Perhaps privacy had gone out of fashion and we no longer believed in the private individual. Other people were everywhere, and could be brought into the public discourse at the least notice; their thoughts and secrets, their everyday doings and their lies and fantasies about themselves were part of a collective platform; maybe turning real people into characters seemed benign because we were everywhere doing it to ourselves.

To me, the sisters' lack of cooperation with Eddie Marsh, Rupert's first biographer, and Noel's with Christopher Hassall, was an act of resistance, an indication of their pride, which assumed that no one else had the right or ability to comprehend what they themselves had experienced or witnessed. Noel's resistance was nevertheless twinned with a kind of humility (though inextricable, too, from her characteristic stubbornness). It was, I thought, a traditionally feminine means of resistance. It reserved something to herself, which is why it enraged the keepers of Rupert's flame, even as she insisted on withdrawing from the memorial battleground. She was supposed to sacrifice herself – for that is what giving up secrets, speaking frankly of buried memories, is – to the service of a Great Man and his legend. She refused, which was an unacceptable act of independence.

Despite all the personal display of current times, we might still accept that truly knowing another person is impossible. We like to think of ourselves as unique and mysterious, possessors of unplumbable depths. Finding out about other people is then a tantalising challenge.

All too often in the reading I began to do about the Oliviers, I felt that the love and awe, but also the judgement, that the sisters inspired had obscured what was truly remarkable about them. Between them they had been unusually well educated, at a time when education was still thought to be damaging to ovaries, and had embarked on interesting careers. All four sisters lived dramatic personal lives, complicated by their legendary beauty (particularly in Brynhild's case) and their refusal to be restricted by the expectations of others.

The Olivier sisters embodied the Neo-Pagan ideal and inspired its icon, Rupert Brooke, but they could not be contained within that unthreatening, nymph-like identity. Noel, the youngest and sometimes the wisest, was single-mindedly determined about her goal of joining the tiny minority of female doctors in Britain. Brynhild – quite possibly the most unreadable sister, blessed with poise and charm; charged at times with both a lack of intellect and a status-aware hauteur – established her own code of emotional and sexual integrity and stuck to it, insisting on what she wanted from life and paying the price. Margery battled to matter and to contribute – alarming claims from a woman – and she battled mental illness and the medical profession. In her youth she was inspired by politics, active, collaborative and also romantic, caught in the bind her society set up for women who might want to work but might also want love. Nor does Daphne ever seem to have chosen the path of least resistance. Though naturally retiring and prey to anxiety, she did not simply accept what was offered to her but sought something more, and held fast to ideals that gave her adult life meaning, eventually introducing Steiner education to Britain and leaving a legacy that survives today. They each came up against deeply entrenched beliefs about women's physical and mental deficiencies, and confronted prevailing ideas about what it is appropriate for a woman to have, to want and to do – ideas that have still not entirely left us. Again and again the Olivier sisters proved to be ahead of their time; emancipated when society still punished women for being so. They were educationally and socially privileged but how well did that really serve them, when the world had yet to catch up?

PART ONE

Devils, Not Girls
(Childhood)

Bunny would always remember searching for the Olivier sisters. His part of the woods had been invaded by a tribe known to the local children as the Reivilos ('Olivier' spelled backwards) and he and his father had known for some time that, somewhere amongst the bracken or in the branches, the elusive band was hiding. The two Garnett men spent weeks on the alert: ears pricked for young, female voices; ready at a moment's notice to jump out and intercept the sisters as they crossed past the Garnett house. Without clues they simply searched the woods on long walks together. It seemed strange that the Oliviers didn't want to be found, for Bunny and his father meant no harm; it was only that Bunny was curious. The Reivilos had been building and he wanted to see what they had made, but Margery, Brynhild, Daphne and Noel were determined to remain hidden.

Hut building was an obsession for the children of Limpsfield, a vital skill in their version of rural life. Bunny had erected his own oblong hut with Harold Hobson. They had stolen heather from the Common one night to thatch the roof and had fashioned walls out of old packing cases. The Pease children had gone underground: digging a hole in the bank of their garden and driving a chimney-shaft through the mud-roofed structure in order to have the luxury of a fireplace. Others built tree-houses with wooden planks stolen from the local quarry on Sundays.

In the end, it was winter that gave the Oliviers away. The leaves fell and the hut was exposed. It was only a matter of time, then, before the Garnetts stumbled upon it and Bunny could stand, amazed, in front of the sisters' masterpiece. He could see now why the Reivilo headquarters had been so hard to find: it was built in a part of the woods with plenty of undergrowth, cleverly nestled amongst the heather and bracken that grew beneath the birch trees. The looming branches of a Scots pine provided shelter; inside there were two separate rooms, with enough space for eight – perhaps even ten – people; plus a roof so sturdy that extra visitors would be able to lie atop it without disaster. High craftsmanship had been employed. The sides were woven wattle, insulated with dry undergrowth; the roof was made with heather, just like Bunny and Harold's, but the sisters had made theirs strong by stitching it together with string. They had even thought of a window, carefully camouflaged, from which to keep watch for outsiders. Though they had plenty of space for them, the sisters had no need of visitors.

The Oliviers were not happy that their hut had been found. They certainly knew that it was something special: Daphne and Noel posed for a photo beside it, pride and mischievousness pasted across their faces. A small Noel, in a draping, possibly velvet, dress, hair-band struggling against loose hair, clings to a thin tree and leans – proprietorially and precariously – against the side of the hut. Daphne hangs an arm along the window frame, as if to show how very obvious it had been all along.

But that was enough for them – they preferred privacy to accolades from the others. Besides, there was no special novelty for them in outdoing the boys. They could climb better and exceeded them in physical courage. They were so much in their element among the trees that they were practically Limpsfield's very own woodland sprites. Bunny – their first and most earnest admirer – was used to approaching the row of trees that ran between Limpsfield Common and the High Chart and seeing four girls

> in white jerseys and dark blue knickers, frocks or skirts discarded, high above one's head. One swarming sloth-like up a diagonal branch; another resting among the topmost twigs; a third, getting ready to spring across a wide chasm between two trees, would be rocking herself to and fro upon a thin branch like the bob on the upright pendulum of a metronome, while the fourth was watching and advising. Suddenly the oscillating figure would let go, springing from her perch to clasp a branch from which she would hang for minutes over the abyss.

They were hugely active children; robust, adventurous and blessed with parents who rarely interfered. They enjoyed riding and bicycling and in the winter they sledged in the snow. Brynhild liked clay modelling and had access to a carpentry workshop. Noel liked dissecting small animals.

From the beginning of their lives, the sisters stood out. They were the children of two admirable people. Their mother, Margaret, was a small, clever, neatly formed woman with luminous blue eyes, to whose charms most men (including, Bunny had noted, his own father) were far from oblivious. And then there was Sydney Olivier, her husband. He was tall, with dark features that told of his Huguenot heritage, and a commanding air that made lesser men uncomfortable. He was physically and psychologically tireless – totally impatient with people who didn't agree with him or couldn't keep up with him intellectually – a man with too much vigour ever to be manageable, and one who 'never dreamt of considering other people's feelings'. George Bernard Shaw, who had known him since his youth, felt him to be a man apart, 'an extraordinarily attractive figure [...] distinguished enough to be unclassable. He was handsome and strongly sexed, looking like a Spanish grandee in any sort of clothes'. With typically Shavian hyperbole, he predicted that Sydney 'could have carried a cottage piano upstairs; but it would have cracked in his grip'.

Those who came across his daughters in the woods would have found four conspicuously attractive girls. Margery and Daphne were the darkest; brown-haired and brown-eyed. Brynhild was the fairest of them all, with apple-red cheeks, a bone structure that could already send people into raptures, and captivating eyes that some said flashed and sparkled in firelight. Margery was tall and handsome in Sydney's way, with an already well-developed Olivier temperament. She could blow hot and cold in a moment, the way their father did. Daphne was the romantic, dreamy one, who sometimes glided about with flowers in her hair, or swamped in furs, reminding people of Shakespearean heroines. Noel might have been the one people noticed least. The baby in a gang of formidable siblings, she grew up quiet and self-effacing, a little like Margaret in this way, but tougher on the inside. When Bunny's father decreed of her 'Heart – hard. Hard as nails!' it stayed with her. She 'grinned with pride, and never forgot'. She never felt pretty, next to the others, and that stayed with her too. The girls were often dressed alike, though the older two got to wear white lace collars over their dark dresses, and even when Margery and Brynhild drew themselves in their 'One Penny Book of Pretty Story's and Pictures', they were identical: long brown hair, long blue skirts, sensible shoes. But in the story they also gave themselves red caps, and built a boat (which sank).

Sydney's pride and aristocratic bearing were identified in his daughters early on; observers described a nobility of 'looks and manners and in attitude of mind' quite impressive for children. Certainly the girls were serious, especially Margery but she had three younger siblings to keep track of. Often left to their own devices, the girls grew up to be independent and determined, unconcerned by the views and feelings of others. When you have three sisters, do you really need anyone else? This, perhaps, was the crux of a problem that seemed to accompany the praise: their air of disinterest made others uneasy. Somehow they were noble but also, on occasion, 'as unthinkingly cruel as savages. Sometimes they were savages.' Though they may not have known it, this set them apart from the beginning, because in the 1880s and '90s, when they were being born and growing up, there was still a decade or more of the Victorian age to go, and a good little Victorian girl was supposed to worry about pleasing others very much. Girls with brothers, particularly, were expected to use the opportunity to practise providing comfort to men, in preparation for fulfilling futures as 'angels of the home'. With no brother available for this purpose, the Olivier girls learned only to please themselves.

Before he was a father, Sydney Olivier was a student at Oxford, then a promising clerk in the Colonial Office and, at around the same time, a leading light in the Fabian Society. He joined the Society in the same month that he married Margaret Cox, in 1885. A newly-wed should probably not describe his wedding merely as 'an inoffensive service' but it was true to Sydney and Margaret's relationship that he did. She, in fact, had rejected organised religion long before he had. Sydney's father – an Anglican reverend of private means, father to eight, one of those Victorian patriarchs always described as 'stern and overbearing' – had warned his son that he regarded marrying Miss Cox as a 'wanton burning of [Sydney's] ships'. Sydney did not care. Sydney had turned his back on all of the things his father represented.

Margaret was the daughter of the impressively named Homersham Cox, a mathematician, writer and circuit judge. She was the oldest girl of his nine children, who formed a close-knit and radically minded brood. Margaret lost her faith when a younger sibling died in infancy, after weeks of desperate care had failed. Her brother Harold taught maths at a college in India and later became a Liberal MP. She was related to the radical, socialist, homosexual, environmentalist, poet philosopher Edward Carpenter by marriage. Sydney was an old school friend of Harold's, three years older than Margaret, and their engagement coincided with her sister Agatha's betrothal to the sculptor Hamo Thornycroft, so that, when Sydney and Hamo visited, the two couples provided genial chaperones for each other by setting off on long walks that somehow always split off into two private rambles.

Before he married, Sydney had lived in dingy rooms in Paddington with his brother, and packed his life with work, study and politics. He took on inspections for the Sanitary Aid Committee, which involved turning up uninvited in the slums of Whitechapel, waiting while prostitutes dispatched their clients, or artillerymen shaved at the windows, and asking them about their landlords' failings. At the Colonial Office he befriended an unprepossessing young clerk named Sidney Webb, whom he was the only person to have beaten in the Civil Service entrance examinations (they came first and second). Webb was formidably clever; he had a methodical mind and a head for figures. The pair were united in their outrage at London's poverty and squalor. One night, Sydney told Margaret, he 'sat up till one [...] talking on all manner of subjects with Webb and a man named Shaw, a very clever and amusing man, who defends the most atrocious paradoxes with much ability'. So began his friendship with George Bernard Shaw, who was at that time a struggling journalist and familiar figure in the radical milieu of London, who tramped around the city in alarming clothes, declaiming wherever people would listen on a broad range of subjects that included vegetarianism, socialism and the arts. The friends discovered a tiny conversation group calling itself the Fabian Society, which they took in hand and refashioned under their own leadership. Along with Graham Wallas, Sydney's friend from Oxford, Sydney and Webb became known as 'The Three Musketeers'; Shaw was their D'Artagnan.

Margaret and Sydney became parents within a year of their marriage but they had no intention of confining themselves to domestic bliss. Though the couple had evenings in together, when Sydney read to his wife from favourites like William Morris's *The Story of Sigurd the Volsung and the Fall of the Niblungs* (from which they would take the name Brynhild) or they discussed John Stuart Mill, Kant and Hegel, their life was electrified by politics; debates and gatherings dominated their evenings. London during the years that the couple lived there, between 1885 and 1891, was a maelstrom of meetings and speeches, of awakening political activism, of social unrest, simmering tensions, of new answers to old problems. This was the decade in which the term 'unemployment' first came into general use. Working men marched the streets, rioted. The police exceeded them in violence. The city was dark: poorly lit but also a place in which one in eight lives ended in the workhouse. Middle-class people concerned by all of this might once have turned to the Liberals but Gladstone's government of 1880 had failed to deliver on promises and, in 1886, the Tories returned for almost twenty years of dominance. Instead, those people took themselves to the Reading Room of the British Museum, to the lecture rooms, to meetings, to the streets.

Sydney and Margaret's generation – appalled by the self-satisfied negligence with which their parents had greeted the collateral damage of the Industrial Revolution, dismissive of their stuffy interiors and oppressive morality, and corrupted irretrievably by the knowledge Darwin had given them – were on the search for something new. A new way to live. They cast about for meaning, and for a means of action, and a range of minority movements sprung up to greet them.

If one was convinced by Marx, there was the Social Democratic Federation, established in 1881, waiting to receive you. The Federation ruptured three years later, creating the Socialist League, headed by William Morris, Eleanor Marx, Ernest Belfort Bax and Edward Aveling. Those more concerned with the 'cultivation of a perfect character in each and all' might be drawn to the Fellowship of the New Life, whereas those who put their faith in the disestablishment of the Church of England and republican government might find the National Secular Society more suited to their tastes. There were anarchists and vegetarians and anti-vivisectionists. Or one could try positivism (which attracted Sydney), theosophy, and the Society for Psychical Research, the Zetetical Society and the London Dialectical Society. It was a shifting, disparate mass, not easily organised into ideological categories. Its members cooperated and broke apart, raged at and reasoned with one another and the outside world. They scuffled and shouted, even with ladies present. Shaw and the Musketeers debated with one another so furiously that onlookers thought friendships would end. When May Morris reflected on the Socialist League, which her father financed and in which she played a crucial organising role, she felt that 'the wonder is, not so much that divergences became evident once more as time went on, but that we ever held together at all'.

Sunday evenings were spent at Morris's Kelmscott House, where Socialist League meetings and talks were held in the old coach house. Along with Shaw, Webb, Graham Wallas and a Fabian couple, the Blands (Hubert and Edith, who wrote children's fiction as E. Nesbit), Sydney and Margaret also frequented the Hampstead home of the anarchist Charlotte

Wilson, where meetings of the misleadingly named Hampstead Historic Society were held. The house was a genteel setting, better suited to the (relative) moderates of the Fabian Society, and there ideas were hashed out and slowly fashioned into the policies that would guide the Society. Margaret's memories were of meetings which combined an intoxicating experimentation of thought with middle-class comforts: 'Someone read a paper and this was followed by discussion, often very vigorous and exciting and lasting till Mrs Wilson interrupted it with sandwiches and drinks'.

To uneasy onlookers, as these years rolled on, it seemed that everything would be remade anew. Most troubling of all, the New Woman was on her way. Women were in evidence all over the socialist movement and they did their best to link feminist goals with the socialist agenda. The women's movement began not just with the suffragists but as part of a revolutionary moment. What was more revolutionary than rights for women, more usually classed with lunatics and children than as citizens?

Women such as Eleanor Marx (the Marx's youngest daughter), May Morris and Charlotte Wilson looked to socialism rather than suffrage (which was also denied to working men) to address the 'Woman Question'. They put their heads above the parapet of the domestic sphere and they lived with the consequences. In an age when women were not supposed to leave their homes unaccompanied, the chief Fabian activist Annie Besant (married, in a former life, to a clergyman) had the extraordinary courage to expose herself to ridicule and harassment as one of the few political women who was an enthusiastic public speaker. She lost her children when she was tried for disseminating advice on contraception. Eleanor Marx lived as the wife of the already-married Edward Aveling, with whom she co-wrote the seminal tract *The Woman Question: From a Socialist Point of View*. May Morris moved Bernard Shaw into her marital home before eventually divorcing her husband.

Despite their unending work for social and political causes, the women fell victim to a conflict between the importance of the 'Woman Question' for left-wing intellectuals and the need for those groups to appeal to the working class, where a commitment to conventional gender roles prevailed. Progressives who put their faith in electing socialists to Parliament pursued a strategy that excluded women and that engaged with the institutions that maintained their subordination. Comrades did not always look like comrades. Within the broad range of views encompassed by the radical movement, women such as Annie Besant and Eleanor Marx had thrown their lot in even with men who despised them. Belfort Bax resented the suggestion that socialist men should treat women as comrades or 'read into their relations with their wives and other female associates an intellectual companionship which is not there'. On a personal level, there were many such betrayals. Shaw married someone else before May Morris's divorce came through; Aveling drained Eleanor's finances before leaving her for a younger woman and finally, many believed, murdering her.

These women were well aware of the misogyny they had to contend with, even within their own ranks, and were capable of spirited takedowns. 'Let us pretend to be serious,' wrote Annie Besant in response to a Belfort Bax article, 'and see if we can find anything in Mr Bax's paper which may pass for argument.' But in that frequently applauded and supposedly feminine way, these women were self-sacrificing: they had devoted themselves to furthering a cause that often showed little interest in repaying them, because they believed in its rightness. They could see clearly that their only chance was to revolutionise the entire social system: as Charlotte Wilson put it, 'a woman who is not a Revolutionist is a fool'.

Safely married and fairly respectable, Margaret took none of the risks that some of the women she met in Charlotte Wilson's drawing room were taking. Neighbours remembered her 'nimbleness' in conversation but she was too self-effacing to stand out in the intellectual cut-and-thrust of Fabian gatherings. Nevertheless, it was important to Sydney that they share their ideas; 'I always feel defrauded if I think we miss speaking of the things in your mind,' he wrote, shortly before their wedding.

As the family was settling down and expanding – Margaret had three babies in three years – Sydney was dedicating himself more and more to the Fabian Society. The tension between women's rights and the working man's interests was less acute here, as the Fabians had little need to appeal directly to the working classes. It was a middle-class mission through and through, and it embraced female membership from the start. Charlotte Wilson was on the first executive committee; Shaw described Annie Besant as the 'expeditionary force' of the group. In 1894, Sydney would sit on a Fabian committee established to prepare a tract advocating civil and political rights for women, a document eventually drafted for them by a daughter of the American suffragist Elizabeth Cady Stanton.

Sydney was convinced that capitalism was behind society's ills and that socialism was the solution. But the Fabians were not convinced of the need for revolution. Instead they formulated a policy of working through existing institutions and by gentle persuasion, with the straight-forward dissemination of undeniable facts, to achieve socialism in Britain. 'If we prepare the way before it, and receive it gladly, it will come to us peaceably and as a welcome friend,' counselled Edward Pease, who succeeded Sydney as Secretary of the Fabian Society.

At first there were few outside the Society who believed in this measured approach. The leader of the Social Democratic Federation had taken to drilling and parading an 'army' of working men in the streets of London, preparing them for the impending upheaval. By the autumn of 1887, radicals had laid claim to Trafalgar Square as a place for speech-ifying and demonstrating; for weeks the station was blocked and the National Gallery was stranded in a rabble. The vicar of St Martin-in-the-Fields was kept busy providing hot coffee and sandwiches to the unfortunate police constables deployed to keep the peace. Six thousand people signed a petition calling for the square to be cleared. On 8 November, the Metropolitan Police Commissioner banned meetings there until further notice. This put the organisers of a gathering planned for the thirteenth in a difficult position.

Margaret Olivier could see the tensions building. What followed was, she wrote, 'an outcome of the general atmosphere', in which fear and distrust festered on both sides and the misery of the poor demonstrating in Trafalgar Square was met with foreboding by those whose daily lives were disrupted by it.

The meeting was confirmed and was soon understood as a demonstration for freedom of speech. Plans and people accumulated. The various radical contingents of London would march on the square from different sides and take possession from all of its entrances. The thirteenth was a Sunday and the Oliviers were at home when Sydney announced that he was going to see what was happening. Margaret insisted on accompanying him, leaving the eighteen-month-old Margery and six-month-old Brynhild with the nursemaid. They arrived to find that an enormous crowd had already gathered, with spectators continuing to pour in from all sides to see the marchers, and to see what would happen to them. Policemen stood guard around Nelson's Column and their mounted colleagues made periodic sallies into the crowd to force the people back. Around the Oliviers, pinned into place by a rowdy mass, a few people were knocked down. Sydney hated being immobilised – he wanted to see the fate of the processions in which his colleagues were marching – but there was nowhere for them to go. The agitation spread. Just as it seemed that the mood would darken, the crowd was distracted by the appearance of mounted soldiers in scarlet uniforms. The reaction was anticlimactic. 'Very slowly, on their beautiful horses, these brilliant figures proceeded to ride round,' Margaret remembered. 'People in the road made way for them. Presently I heard cheering. Obviously the crowd admired the uniforms. As the soldiers passed more and more people started to cheer.' Sydney and Margaret watched as the crowd dispersed. The couple had been standing in the wrong place: everything had happened before the demonstrators reached the Square.

At Seven Dials, the police had fallen on the procession led by Annie Besant, aiming their truncheons at people's heads. George Bernard Shaw had escaped as Annie Besant tried to persuade the scattering marchers to erect barricades, before admitting defeat and leaving too. Three people were killed, fifty arrested and an estimated three times as many injured, in what became that era's Bloody Sunday. If this was the great confrontation between the socialists and the state, it was clear who had won. The SDF's 'army' of underfed and unarmed workmen proved, unsurprisingly, to be no match for the country's police and military. 'Following on the scare caused by these disturbances a number of nice respectable young men got themselves enrolled as special constables,' Margaret noted drily, 'and on the following Sunday took up their positions in Hyde Park and elsewhere and waited for further trouble. But nothing happened.'

In the absence of a revolution, the Fabian approach gained in authority. In the year that Daphne was born, Sydney became something of a public figure when the Society published a collection of lectures by its members. Copies of the *Fabian Essays in Socialism* 'went off', in the words of its delighted editor, Shaw, 'like smoke'. The general public, shaken by the disturbances of recent years, turned out to be keen to know more about socialism. The first print run was gone within a month; a year later the book was still selling 400 copies a week and within two years the Society had sold 27,000. Before that Sydney helped to support the striking Match Girls, victims of Dickensian conditions in the Bryant & May factory, who had organised under Annie Besant's guidance and whose cause elicited great public sympathy (and much unwelcome scrutiny of the company's shareholders). This growing visibility attracted new members to the Society (a sixfold membership increase by 1892), among them Keir Hardie and the Pankhursts, and more income in the form of subscriptions. The Society was establishing itself as a reforming force and branched out with a number of provincial satellite societies in the north. But just as word spread, Sydney left the country.

'Your last mail was very important and welcome, bringing as it did the children's photos,' Sydney wrote to Margaret from Belize in February 1891. 'It is very jolly to see the babies' faces again, even on paper. You must tell them I have all their dear little heads on my table to say "good-morning" to me and "good-night".' Sydney's income depended on his job in the Colonial Office, a career doubly jeopardised by his political radicalism and his impatience with colleagues. Advancement required a foreign posting, so in 1890 he spent six months as Colonial Secretary in British Honduras. Margaret and the girls stayed in London. Separation was a fact of life for the families of colonial servants and long absences were compounded by slow methods of communication; bundles of letters that had to cross the world on ships. From now on, Sydney would periodically disappear from his daughters' childhood.

The photo would have shown him Margery, now approaching her fifth birthday, a three-year-old Brynhild and Daphne, a true baby at less than eighteen months. For a time, Margery's experience of her father was in little slips of paper, probably enclosed inside letters to her mother, in which Sydney wrote her messages like, 'My dear little girl MARGERY. I send you this instead of a kiss. Your loving FATHER.'

Margery had been born in a small flat in Maida Vale and, though the family had now moved to a house on the same road, Margaret felt that she was raising her girls in the wrong environment. 'It had a pleasant outlook over recreation grounds, also a good nursery,' she admitted, but there was also 'a sooty little garden where [Sydney] planted tulips and the babies got very dirty whenever they were allowed to play there'. By the time of Sydney's return in the spring of 1891 they were ready for a move.

Naturally, there was an ideological element to their departure for the countryside. In many ways, Sydney and Margaret's brand of socialism had more in common with the aesthetic movement headed by Morris than with the economic and technical interests of Sidney Webb. Sydney's politics were firmly rooted in the lives and spirits of living people, something that earned him Morris's praise in a generally hostile review of the *Fabian Essays*. Many socialists idealised country life in their rejection of the industrial society; for them the city symbolised the ugliness, degradation and moral conventions of Victorian society. One of Margaret's closest friends, Kate Joynes, had inspired her by moving to a small workman's cottage in Kent with her husband Henry Salt, where they established themselves in 'The Simple Life', doing their best to live off the land and manage without servants. The Oliviers were also friendly with Edward Carpenter, an icon of the Simple Life movement. It is possible, too, that the Oliviers were tired of the grime and disaffection in London, that they wanted something better than a sooty little garden for their girls.

Margaret Olivier

Sydney in Antigua, 1895

As their friend E. Nesbit once noted, 'London has none of those nice things that children may play with without hurting the things or themselves – such as trees and sand and woods and waters.' Limpsfield, at the foot of the North Downs, had these things in abundance. There was just a smattering of cottages in the village, which was set beside a common, with a large pond and an old windmill at the corner. Woodland stretched out for half a mile from the Chart village. For Margaret, 'it was an enchanting country. Besides the beauty of the Chart woods and the commons there was the scent of it all, the smell of fir trees and the mossy soil – and there was the view over the Weald.'

Until now, Limpsfield had been the Oliviers' summer village, where they had spent brief holidays before Daphne was born. Sydney and Margaret purchased a long lease on a small cottage within two miles of Oxted station, so that Sydney could still spend two or three nights a week in town after they moved, and commissioned the Fabian craftsman, W. L. Philips, to convert the building into a family home, which was christened 'The Champions'.

It was a long rectangular house. Most of the rooms ran off a gloomy corridor along one side of the building, so that their generous windows faced out across the Weald from a vantage point set above the sloping garden. No other dwellings were visible from the windows; the variegated fields and hedgerows stretched peaceably away for miles, uninterrupted. Used to their polluted garden in Maida Vale, five-year-old Margery and her little sisters, Brynhild, four, and the baby Daphne, had the prospect of all of this to explore. Behind their new home they had the Common, too, and dense woodland, populated with evergreens and crunchy bracken. It was a place for scrambling and climbing things and, very possibly, getting extremely muddy. For Christmas the next year they were presented with yet another sister, Noel, surely named for the holiday, whom we might be tempted to think of as Margaret and Sydney's reunion baby. Along with Bessie, their housekeeper, and a grey parrot named Polly (a gift from a friend in Africa), their household was complete.

Once they had found this haven, the family's friends began to find them, and so it was that they were not living in splendid isolation for long. First to arrive were Herbert Rix (of the Fellowship of the New Life) and his family, and the Peases, who moved into a converted oast house within walking distance of The Champions (they brought their eldest son, Michael, and Nicholas arrived a few years later). Then came the Garnetts, who wanted the Olivier girls as playmates for their only son, Bunny (still, at this point, known as David). Margaret and Sydney had known Constance Garnett and her sister, Clementina Black, early members of the Fabian Society, for years. Inspired by the Russian exiles she had come to know in London, Constance had learned Russian whilst pregnant and was now at the outset of a career as the pre-eminent translator of Russian literature, eventually introducing English readers to Tolstoy, Dostoevsky, Turgenev and Chekhov. Her husband, Edward, was forging a reputation as London's most important publishers' reader and had recently discovered a writer named Joseph Conrad. The Garnetts built a house, called The Cearne, on the other side of the woods, in a spot so secluded that friends took to calling them 'The Wood People'. The economist and social scientist J. A. Hobson and his American wife, Florence, also appeared, with Harold and Mabel in tow, and took a house nearby. The writer E. V. Lucas brought his writer wife and daughter Audrey to live a little further along Greensands Ridge, and, not far from them, lived Kate and Henry Salt.

Agatha and Hamo Thornycroft also moved with their children to Surrey when the Oliviers left London. The girls' grandparents lived in Tonbridge, in neighbouring Kent, and there they spent Christmases with their four Thornycroft cousins and another cousin, Ursula, rampaging under the eye of a maiden aunt named Dora, until their grandfather emerged from his study to hush them.

Before they knew it, the Oliviers were part of a community that they had more or less established themselves. Here were men and women who had broken (in some cases painfully) with their families, and forged new identities for themselves in the roiling melting pot of London. They had made themselves homeless and when they sought a kind of retreat, they knew they would have to establish it themselves. Their political ideals found expression in all aspects of life. Ford Madox Ford (then Hueffer), who himself lived in Limpsfield for a while when Margery was twelve, found them an odd and self-important bunch, who stuck out in their attempts to blend in with country life. 'Limpsfield was the extra-urban headquarters of the Fabian Society,' he recalled of the time. 'Its members then wore beards, queer, useful or homespun clothes and boots and talked Gas and Water Socialism. They were Advanced.' 'Advanced' was a term commonly applied to the Olivier parents and to their daughters when they grew up. Almost never deployed as a compliment, it nevertheless acknowledged the sense of forward motion such people carried with them, and the element of denigration – the sense of sniggering behind hands at a sincere man in 'Indian' sandals, like Edward Carpenter, or a young woman on a bicycle – spoke to distance emerging as people of Advanced Ideas surged onwards towards a different future, leaving others behind.

Though the Oliviers and their friends did try to adhere to their understanding of country mores, they were not greeted warmly by local personages. One late-comer family found that they had to buy property through an intermediary, such was the resistance to any expansion of what was eventually dubbed 'Dostoevsky Corner'. Sydney simply could not leave something alone if he thought it could be improved and quickly gained a reputation as the 'firebrand in the neighbourhood'. In the early 1890s, he led a slate of candidates to victory in the local parish council elections. One personal mission he set himself was fighting attempted enclosures of the land. 'I live in a country parish where the rights of cottagers and the privileges of the public in the commons are continually threatened by the powers of the Lord of the Manor,' he wrote, and he worked to preserve the common and public rights of way, defending people's access to public spaces that the landowners seemed determined to cut off. If, on family walks, the group came across a 'Notice to Trespassers' where a right of way was established, Sydney would tear the sign down himself and fling it into a ditch.

Meetings, of course, were common; visitors often found themselves lecturing in Fabian drawing rooms (a fate that befell the artist Walter Crane when he stayed nearby). Sydney added a long gallery to The Champions, where speeches and performances could be held, and charades played.

Between them, the Fabians of Limpsfield had a busy schedule of visitors, attracting many of the literary lights of the day. George Bernard Shaw, in flight from one woman or another, joined Sydney in day-long walks through the local country from The Champions, the journalist Henry Nevinson visited, John Galsworthy found himself fending off the Garnetts' mentally-disturbed cat at The Cearne, whilst Joseph Conrad was sometimes to be found playing at boats in the laundry basket with Bunny.

At home the Oliviers addressed the vexed question of domestic labour with a characteristic compromise between middle-class standards and forward-thinking: their servants sat to dinner with them. Sydney would call his family to the table himself (and was usually ignored by his busy daughters).

The radical, yet somehow restorative, atmosphere of Limpsfield also attracted Britain's impressive collection of foreign political exiles. As therapy for the trauma of his imprisonment-without-trial in St Petersburg, and entrapment in Siberia, the Jewish political exile David Soskice was given work in the gardens of The Cearne and Ford Madox Ford's cottage (he later married Ford's sister). The Armenian poet and revolutionary Avetis Nazarbek, along with his wife and band of bodyguards, was briefly offered sanctuary in Limpsfield. Prince Kropotkin, the Russian scientist and anarchist, by now a kindly old man with a fan-shaped beard and a heart problem, stayed nearby with his wife Sophie, and impressed Margaret by erecting a tripod over a small fire at an Olivier picnic to boil a kettle, taking the family outing to whole new levels of efficiency. Constance Garnett's mentor (and, it has been suggested, her lover) was the revolutionary Sergei Stepniak who, unbeknownst to his English friends, had assassinated the head of the secret police on the streets of St Petersburg; he was a favourite with the children until his untimely death at the end of 1895. Edward Garnett told a somewhat surprised Bunny that Stepniak's mother had been a princess and his father a bear. After serious thought, Bunny attested loyally that 'That bear that was Uncle Stepniak's dad was a *good* bear'. Fanny Stepniak taught the Olivier sisters, Bunny, the Pease boys and Harold Hobson the natural sciences, taking advantage of their surroundings to conduct rambling nature walks.

A cooperative atmosphere reigned; residents helped each other with the establishment of homes and homesteads and educated their children together. They built ugly, impractical Simple Life homes from local stone, and patiently waited for them to weather into something inconspicuous.

When the family first moved to Limpsfield, Margaret's help with the girls was Gertrude Dix, a red-haired and freckled young Fabian who in a few years would write some of the stand-out novels of New Woman literature. Gertrude saw her role as 'helping to rear beautiful children for the state' and revelled especially in the chance to help raise girls, optimistic about the gains the Fabians would make for them: 'I believe they are going to have a better time than has hitherto been possible for us,' she told friends. Gertrude took the girls on walks, told them stories 'without morals' and tried to apply 'principles of freedom' to their upbringing. This meant, for example, that if they tried to rush into one of the appealing local ponds with their boots on, she did not 'like the ordinary nursemaid cuff them and call them naughty'. Instead, she told the children to 'do what they desire' and showed 'them by precepts & example they should take their boots off first'. The little Oliviers proved a handful. From time to time, Gertrude wondered 'if all socialist infants are so exhausting'. 'If these are only socialists,' she asked herself, 'what must anarchists be?'

Four girls was perhaps always going to be a challenge. As a young child, Margery was restless and rarely demonstratively affectionate. The arrival of a sibling in Brynhild had introduced squabbling to the family: 'wants one thing directly she sees the baby with it', Margaret remarked in the conscientious notes she kept on her growing daughters. Daphne was easier, though also most inclined to cling to her mother. When Noel arrived she reminded Margaret of Brynhild's cheerful disposition at the same age. Noel was 'a very good child', who would lie unobtrusively 'for a long time in [her] perambulator or on a chair talking to herself'. She was Margaret's healthiest baby, something her mother put down to spending 'nearly all her time in the open air'.

As she grew older, Noel's interest in the natural world expanded. Her companion for scientific expeditions was the devoted Bunny, with whom she shared a fascination for animals and their anatomy, and a proprietary knowledge of the local woods. Bunny had first encountered Noel as 'a little girl nearly a year younger than myself, with a disproportionately large head and steady grey eyes'. He was besotted. Prey to their unending curiosity, Noel and Bunny (a nickname he had earned after adopting a rabbit skin cap as a small child) developed an ingenious method for ensuring that they could be awake and outside in the earliest morning, to catch the forest in its most undisturbed state. Each would go to bed the previous evening with a length of string looped around one foot, leaving the other end to dangle out of the window. Whoever managed to wake first would make their way to the other's house and tug on the string hanging outside. In this way, no one else was ever disturbed; need ever know, in fact, that Bunny and Noel were making their way 'through the mist at four o'clock in the morning'. They were rewarded by scenes of animal romance – 'two stoats making rushes at each other [. . .] hares almost tumbl[ing] over our feet in their love-making' – that seemed only too pertinent to Bunny's blossoming adoration.

Noel could gaze upon the most decomposed – or the freshest – corpse with clear-eyed scientific interest, unmoved by gore or mess. She took a practical interest, too; the pair collected small skeletons in the woods, skinned rabbits and moles, tanned the hides, and taught themselves, with varying degrees of success, to stuff birds. One of Noel's cousins knew her as 'a small thing with brown bare legs, in a holland frock with a piece of string tied round the waist and a large knife hanging from it'. On one of their early-morning foraging missions, Bunny and Noel stumbled across the keeper's larder on a small pheasant preserve and, unable to resist the wealth of possible exhibits for their collection, staged an audacious raid. They came away with a magnificent haul: 'stoats' skulls, mummified weasels [. . .] the tails from several rotting cats [. . .] the skull of one as well'. They fled all the way to The Champions, where they scaled the wall and laid their finds out for display in the summer-house. It was here, under the withering condemnation of Daphne, who appeared shortly afterwards, that reality – and a foul smell – set in. Daphne expressed her disgust in the crushing manner that older siblings muster best, and the two daring thieves sat chastened and disappointed. Even liberated young ladies, it seemed, have limits.

Daphne, Margery, Brynhild, Noel

At first the Hobsons, Garnetts and Oliviers made up their own tiny progressive schoolroom under the tuition of Carl Heath, the brother of Edward Garnett's long-term mistress, Nellie. Margaret, whom the girls nicknamed 'The Wala', also set aside mornings to teach her daughters herself. 'I have ordered the "Encyclopaedia Britannica" for you to read,' Sydney informed them, 'and have written to Dr Burton to ask him to teach you [...] he is such a learned person that you will be lucky if you induce him to become your tutor.' Burton was a lecturer in physics at UCL, who did indeed teach the girls. They also had a Swiss governess, engaged during a nine-month spell in Lausanne, whom they nicknamed 'the Switch'.

Sydney never spoke down to his daughters, rather expecting them to keep up with his own intellectual musings. He showed an interest in their interests, asking, when he was away, how dancing classes and clay-modelling and bicycling were coming along (restricting himself to suggesting only that bicycling was best done in the company of Mother), and engaging in discussions about the shortcomings of Shakespeare. In a letter to an eight-year-old Noel, he took the trouble to praise her capital letters.

Of their first ten years in Limpsfield, Sydney spent a total of more than three away from the girls, when either he or they were abroad (Margaret took them to Lausanne without him when Noel was six and Margery twelve, to ensure they spoke good French). During his travels, he cast about for things to describe to them, seeking always to engage their minds and imaginations, encouraging them to be as 'wideawake' (as his wife described him) as he was. His letters to them frequently return to the sugar-making process (one of the chief industries in the West Indies); one memorable missive described how canals work. He did not just want his daughters to imagine the world but to understand the mechanics of the lives and industries built upon it.

Always considered an aloof and disinterested figure, he could be hugely affectionate to his daughters when they were small. On one occasion, shortly after Noel's second birthday, when Margaret was away, he reassured his wife that, 'It is alive, and apparently well. I had it in my bed this morning and it made me sing. When I sang "kiss it in bed and cuddle its head", it corrected me "Gimme Bap" [...] Just now it is wielding the inevitable pencil and showing me "pretty men" it had drawn.'

In encouraging intellectual engagement, Sydney (who, as a student, had persuaded his parents to let his sister join him in Oxford) was making a conscious choice; a choice that many Victorian fathers would have regarded as an unacceptable risk. Provision for the education of women had been gradually improving since the 1870s but warnings about the perils of provoking female brains emerged from the medical establishment in tandem. Respected figures like Henry Maudsley, a fellow of the Royal College of Physicians and an eminent 'expert' on mental disorders, warned parents that intellectual competition with boys could have a disastrous effect on the minds of young women. Girls' 'nerve centres being in a state of greater instability, by reason of the development of their reproductive functions,' he explained, 'will be the more easily and the more seriously deranged.' In fact, the fate of the British race, it was often held, was under direct threat from the education of women.

Margery, Brynhild, Daphne and Noel were lucky, then, to be growing up in a place dominated by extraordinary women. For, though they may have been raised under the influence of a forceful, accomplished and inspiring man, they were also under the sway of a mother with strong opinions, a woman who had a personal background of unconventionality. Far away in London, when Noel was five, Millicent Garrett Fawcett established the National Union of Women's Suffrage Societies. Elsewhere, emancipation was already underway. Whichever Limpsfield household one peers into, the wives and mothers were women to be reckoned with, with their own work, interests and commitments, which were often entirely independent of their husbands' concerns, and political activism that predated their marriages. When Bunny was less than a year old, Constance

Garnett had set off to explore Russia by herself, armed with secret corre-
spondence between revolutionaries. Her sister had been the one to alert
Annie Besant to the Match Girls' plight. Elizabeth Lucas was a writer like
her husband, and collaborated with him on a number of books for children.
Marjorie Pease established a women's Liberal Party group for Oxted and
Limpsfield and was an indomitable local organiser; the 'terror' of Ford
Madox Ford, she was often seen 'dragging at the reins of a donkey in a
governess-cart', in which her squabbling sons were precariously piled, on
her 'ceaseless errand of getting people together'. Princess Kropotkin had
been a pioneer of women's education before her exile and David Soskice's
first wife left him not long after their arrival in Surrey, to continue her
medical education in Paris. The girls' nanny was published alongside
George Bernard Shaw in Keir Hardie's newspaper, gained modest celebrity
(and notoriety) through her novels, and eventually left for America to set
up home with a man who shared her radical ideas.

The women in Limpsfield had faced down huge psychological pressure
and social disapproval to be able to fulfil their intellectual capabilities,
and they were notable exceptions to the rule that educated women could
not marry or raise healthy families. Their education had been crucial to
their lives. Charlotte Wilson, who had attended Newnham College in
Cambridge (which opened in 1871 with only five students), told George
Bernard Shaw that it had been 'the porch through which I entered the
world'. Constance Garnett had escaped a limiting family home through
her scholarship to Newnham; Graham Wallas's wife Ada had also studied
there. Within this constellation of incredible women, the Olivier girls
had no reason to doubt their abilities.

In a posed photograph taken four or five years after the family moved to
Limpsfield, the sisters lean against each other as if physically bonded. A
fair-haired Noel takes centre stage, with a frank and friendly smile at her
photographer. She is starting to grow into a sturdy and stocky child.
Margery, darker-eyed and with a darker complexion, rests her temple gently
against her baby sister's head, her smile revealing large front teeth that
have not yet grown apart (though they will). She and Brynhild wear wide
collars of white lace. Daphne, still showing signs of babyhood in her round
face, looks a little as if she has recently been roused from her bed. Of the
sisters, she had the curliest hair. It was hair that could be teased into a
wild mane when she needed to pass as an outlaw.

One thing that the serious-minded, socially conscious Olivier family endlessly enjoyed was amateur dramatics. Sydney wrote several plays (he and Shaw were early readers of each other's work), some of which were performed in London, and composed songs for his girls to perform in their own. In this most literary of neighbourhoods, there was plenty of opportunity for collaboration; the adults, if anything, seemed to get more involved than the children. Bernard Shaw was summoned to Limpsfield on occasion for dramatic presentations, once even offering comments on a production of his own play, *The Admirable Bashville*, for which Bunny was particularly commended in his role of the Zulu king, Cetewayo. (Margery got to be the prize fighter, Cashel Byron.) The gallery room of The Champions was put to good use in productions that stretched the limits of what might be considered 'amateur'.

One memorable success was *The Usurping Baron*, which the Olivier sisters put on with Bunny, his cousin Speedwell and the Hobsons, when Noel was about eight and Margery fourteen or so. The play took the Robin Hood legend as its impeccably socialist subject matter. Bunny's father wrote it for them. He produced it, too, like a professional. He knew exactly how to get the best out of his cast: knew when to coax and when to rage, how to keep egos in check and avoid any diva antics. Rehearsals were highly-charged. The Oliviers made up the bulk of the cast and arguably took all of the best parts. Bunny's cousin got to be Robin Hood but the real hero was Margery, as the outlawed nobleman, Piers. She played him with her characteristic gravity; there was something noble in all the Oliviers but Margery had a silent intensity and the authority of age.

Daphne played the heroine, a precocious New Woman-type called Lucy, who appeared onstage with 'spear in hand, and bow and quiver on back'. She was Robin Hood's niece, raised in Sherwood Forest, and she had the misfortune to be out alone when the evil baron discovered one of his deer slain by outlaws. His henchman Swarthum (Brynhild in a fetching cap and drawn-on beard) was charged with hunting down anyone with 'bow in hand or quiver on their back'. When Lucy is uncovered crouching in the bracken, the two men are appalled by the evidence of her emancipation:

> What creature art thou, dressed in rabbit skins?
> Art thou a man, girl? Or art thou some New Woman;
> Who doth disgrace her sex by venturing forth
> Into the world where only men should strive
> Each against each, for bread to keep alive?

Swarthum is compelled to explain, in a knowing nod to the Olivier girls' status as a local phenomenon, that Lucy is one of four 'bold brown-eyed wenches' whom folks say 'be devils, not girls. They can climb trees like monkeys, and their father ha' been shipped overseas for a dangerous man.' Faced with this information, the baron decides that the safest thing is to have Lucy hanged 'lest she corrupt her sex'.

Lucy keeps her dignity bravely throughout; her pride prevents her from begging for her life. Fortunately, the handsome Piers arrives just in time to rescue her with some fine sword-play. The young couple take to each other at once and Piers vows to avenge himself on his dastardly uncle, the baron. Lucy is soon able to return the favour when Piers is himself captured by Swarthum. She takes her beloved to the outlaws' camp, deep in the forest, where they sing rousing outlaw songs, welcome Piers into their ranks, and plot an assault on the baron's castle. Maid Marion forms the vanguard with Robin, entering the castle in disguise and helping to overcome the enemy. The baron is rapidly dispatched, freeing the land from tyranny and oppression for ever (and bringing to mind, no doubt, Limpsfield's own Lord of the Manor). Piers and Lucy declare their love, and Robin Hood is granted a final address to the audience, in what might be read as a ringing defence of the Fabian colony in Limpsfield:

> So shall ye know
> What 'ere the Powers the world outside may sway
> Courage and Love, my friends, reign here to-day.

On the opening night at The Cearne, the stage was immaculately set. The leaves and bracken actually made rather a mess, with hindsight, but by whisking the pot that swung above the fire out of the way each time the curtain descended, the stagehands managed to avert disaster. Everything ran smoothly. The cast were well-drilled enough that the audience had no idea of the explosions backstage (Bunny and Harold launched themselves at each other in the green room, each incensed by the other's newly discovered love for Daphne. 'Did you know,' Mabel Hobson asked Brynhild, 'that you & Daphne are worshiped as goddesses by Bunn[y] & Harold?'). Lucy was the perfect role for someone of Daphne's romantic bent and she played it to perfection. There was something transcendent about her suffering; everyone seemed to fall for her. It was unusual for Bryn not to be the centre of attention but she never had Daphne's knack for drama. Bryn didn't mind being in the background.

The comedy was left to Noel, Gavrolio the Jester, and Bunny, playing a Friar-Tuck-type character named Father John. It had taken him some time to get to grips with the tubby clergyman – perhaps he felt himself more suited to a heroic role – but once he inhabited the little bald man, he got it just right. The two turned out to be naturals and their kinship of spirit made them the perfect foils for each other.

The cast of The Usurping Baron: *Daphne and Margery are next to each other on the left, Bunny frowns behind them and Brynhild is visible in her drawn-on beard behind. Noel is perched above the executioner and Edward Garnett looms behind the children*

The play was a great success, which was fortunate considering the eminence of the audience. The Oliviers, Hobsons and E. V. Lucas had packed The Cearne out with guests, and the Salts had brought Bernard Shaw along. It could have been a rather nerve-racking first night but the children were used to writers.

If any doubt did cross the children's minds when it came to their parents' reaction, it was thoroughly displaced by a second performance put on for the village. They had felt, in their hearts of hearts, that the intelligentsia of Limpsfield had been a little condescending. Did George Bernard Shaw, like a kindly uncle, tell all nine-year-old boys that they were born actors? Could E. V. Lucas and his guests be trusted to respond as if to equals? Though they roared through Noel and Bunny's comic turns, there was always a risk that these sophisticates were being just a little bit charitable.

The reception of the second performance, though, was undeniably spontaneous, the applause genuine. Their neighbours absorbed the pathos in the play. Where the children's parents had been charmed by the comedy, the villagers were appalled by the abuses inflicted on Daphne's heroine. She stole the show. The sight of her wandering the forest, enrobed in her snow leopard's skin, tormented by the dastardly baron and his henchmen, was almost too much for them; they took her to their hearts without reservation. Here, the cast felt they had triumphed. They were among friends. This friendship would soon prove an illusion.

Edward Garnett had ensured that there was plenty in *The Usurping Baron* to entertain the grown-ups of the first audience, with in-jokes at each other's expense, mockery of conservative confusion over the Fabian women's dress and independence, and politically charged references. The play closed with a pointed jab at the jingoistic fever that seemed to have taken a prolonged hold over Britain as the nineteenth century drew to a close. The evil baron, meditating on the (false) news of Piers' death, which he himself has ordered, laments his nephew's passing in a speech that seems distinctly worded to deride the moral hypocrisy of an altogether more contemporary Imperial government, recently embroiled in the Boer War:

> Sad it is that strange necessity
> Should force our unwilling hands to do these deeds
> Which in the abstract we do not approve of
> Which 'tis British destiny to do

'We only war that war may cease on earth,' the baron continues, diverging somewhat from his recent bereavement:

> Till all mankind with happy smile may cry
> England! Thou didst annex our lands! Oh blessed day
> That made us English under England's sway!

The entire speech could have been written for Sydney, who had stormed into the Garnetts' house only a few months previously, raging about an internal document he had seen that day in his office: a draft of the ultimatum that the Colonial Secretary Joseph Chamberlain had persuaded the government to issue to the Transvaal Republic. War, Sydney predicted, would be the result. He was right. Bunny remembered the day acutely: the grown-ups gathering, angry and strained, 'the sense of seething indignation in all members of the little group'. 'A new era had begun,' he wrote later. 'The last gift of the Victorian age to the new century was war.'

Sydney had worked for some time in the South African Department of the Colonial Office and it was there that his opposition to his employers began. He had been angered by the way in which colonial policy seemed to be dictated by the needs of the South African Chartered Company, which ensured that the economic exploitation of native populations was prioritised above all else. Sydney believed in a benign concept of Empire, in which imperial rule was only justified when it conveyed the best of European 'civilisation' to less-developed countries. Cecil Rhodes and Chamberlain's expansionist aims and aggression infuriated him. In a letter to Shaw that year he condemned 'the fundamental absurdity of asserting that the British have a right to the whole earth and a duty of annexing as much of it as they can lay hands on – in order that they [...] may hold up holy hands and talk about all the good we shall do with it. We shall not do good. When have we ever done it?'

The Fabian Holbrook Jackson observed that, after the trial of Oscar Wilde in 1895, the literary and journalistic vitality that had characterised the first years of the 1890s 'suffered a sudden collapse as if it had been no more than a gaily coloured balloon'. The rest of the decade belonged to the *Daily Mail*, established in 1896, which made its name in stoking 'the Jingo flame', already much fanned by the imperial ambitions of Chamberlain and Rhodes, and fed further in the hysterical Jubilee celebrations of 1897. By 1899, it was ready to explode into a furnace at the outbreak of the Boer War, a week before Daphne's tenth birthday. Liberals who called for a swift resolution to the conflict were met with an onslaught of pamphlets equating them with traitors.

The Limpsfield Fabians had never truly been accepted in their adopted home but the mood now turned poisonous, even among the ordinary people whose rights they had sought to defend. Their children met the same hostility. Harold and Mabel Hobson's father was another of the most vocal critics of the conflict; his book on the subject was published in 1900. Bunny and Harold were stoned by local boys; the Olivier sisters were followed by shouts of 'Krujer!' when they ventured into the village. Bunny's father volunteered for a small force who, armed with ash sticks, defended local 'pro Boer' meetings.

The Oliviers and their peers had grown up with a sense of difference and now understood what it meant to be persecuted for that difference. The local children had always taken their parents' cue and treated them with suspicion. Bunny only learned that his parents were atheists when the boy who cleaned knives for them told him they would go to Hell. Bunny had become a half-wild creature, timid around strangers. The Oliviers practised their own precautionary rejection of outsiders. Daphne and Margery especially loved to argue, and were keen to debate new concepts, but they held fast to their own ideas, which were inevitably influenced by their parents' politics. Sydney might have been prevented by his job from commenting too publically on the Boer War but his daughters made their own views clear when they burned an effigy of Joseph Chamberlain – identifiable by his eye glass – on the Common that Guy Fawkes Night. This conviction, only strengthened by the hostility of their neighbours, taught them contempt for the views of the majority. They learned that public opinion could not be counted on for moral guidance. (Before long, news would break of the horrendous conditions in the concentration camps established by the British clearing the veld, in which almost fifty thousand people – including over twenty thousand children – eventually died; yet support for the war remained high.) From now on the sisters looked to themselves to establish the best course in any given situation. Their pride and self-sufficiency was sometimes interpreted as touchiness, sometimes cruelty. Even Bunny could be treated as an outsider. When he offended Daphne as the group lay about in the grass one day, she punished him by rising, standing above him, and hurling a brick into his stomach. Her sisters signalled their allegiance in the contemptuous silence that met his howls.

Even amongst his oldest friends, Sydney found he could not count on support for his anti-war stance. He was incensed by the Fabian Society's failure to condemn the conflict, sticking instead to the Webb-ordained pragmatism. The situation was only diffused when Sydney was appointed Colonial Secretary to Jamaica towards the end of the year. Among his colleagues in Downing Street, there were grateful murmurs that the posting had been made for the sake of peace and quiet.

Sydney left in January and was gone for almost an entire year. As usual, he worked hard and he wrote letters home. He missed Margery's fourteenth birthday, Brynhild's thirteenth and Daphne's eleventh. In his letter for Margery's birthday, he was obliged to let her know that her pony had fallen and broken her knees. A new pony would have to be found. This must have been a hard blow to receive on a birthday, for the ponies were a matter of some importance. The sisters all rode at home and Sydney had promised his girls that they would have ponies of their own in Jamaica. He had agreed to accept the post for a minimum of three years and so, for the first time, his family were readying themselves to join him.

One day, a year after the Garnetts discovered their hideaway, the girls returned to find their hut destroyed. Someone had smashed up the lovingly constructed roof and vandalised the craftsmanship of its walls. The branches of the tree that supported it had been hacked away. The head keeper, employed by the landowner who had hunting rights in the woods, had found the hut and torn it down; something he had no right to do, because the land was, and always had been, open to the public.

On 1 January 1901 (in the fashion of those days, the 1890s were held to run between 1891 and 1900), *The Times* sententiously welcomed in a new era: 'The twentieth century has dawned upon us; and as we float past this great landmark on the shores of time feelings of awe and wonder naturally creep over us.' Always a few steps ahead, the Olivier women had already sailed away, leaving England and Limpsfield to the battle over the country's conscience, all five of them so seasick that Sydney had to brush and plait his daughters' hair himself, and carry them on to deck as they began to feel better. In the very last days of 1900, they arrived in Kingston. A double life had begun. Though Limpsfield would remain home, the sisters became used to coming and going from Jamaica. For the fellows they left behind in Surrey, their long absences and sudden reappearances would only add to the mysterious allure of the Olivier girls.

The Oliviers in Kingston, Jamaica

PART TWO

How to Live

(Or, Eight Years Later)

I

The Basel Pact

At Portishead, in Somerset, overlooking the Severn Estuary, a group of young and self-conscious people made a pact. It was September 1909. Margery and Bryn were on a clifftop with their friends Rupert Brooke, Dudley Ward and Bill Hubback. Overcome and energised by a uniquely youthful sense of joy, they began to wheel and run along the path, relishing the sun and wind and views that the scene had to offer them. Rupert recited a verse by the poet John Davidson, who had recently disappeared nearby. What if Davidson were not exactly missing, they asked themselves, what if he had simply absconded from a stifling middle age?

There are two types of people, Rupert explained later to Jacques Raverat, another friend: those who grow old in spirit naturally as they age and those who only do so because of the demands of society. Margery, Bryn, Rupert and a select group of their friends were of the second type. Only they weren't planning to grow old. They were living, as Rupert described, 'splendid lives – with Art and Friendship and the great blusterous beautiful world about us – now'. But they recognised the dangers ahead:

> We are twenty-something. In 1920 we shall be thirty something. In 1930 we shall be forty something. [...] Still going to the last play, reading the last book; passing through places we've been in for twenty years; talking to rather fat, rather prosperous, rather heavy, married, conservative, suspicious people who were once young with us; having tea with each other's wives; 'working' 10–5; taking a carefully organised holiday, twice a year [...] disapproving of rather wild young people ... [...] We *shall* become middle aged, tied with more and more ties, busier and busier, fussier and fussier; we *shall* become old, disinterested [...] the world will fade to us, fade, grow tasteless, habitual, dull; and at xy years, in a stuffy room, with

all our relatives, wife's relatives, friends, servants, and medical attendants, around, we shall swollenly stupidly and uninterestedly – *die!*'

So on the clifftop they had devised a plan. They would continue into adulthood to lead the worthy, important lives they were all expecting to lead. Then, on 1 May 1933, they would excuse themselves from their homes and families and meet for breakfast at Basel station, in Switzerland. From there, the plans were less clear. They would simply vanish 'from the knowledge of men' and 'make a new world together'. Once the pact was formed, they began to send 'damn serious and splendid' offers to their friends to join them. The rest of the Oliviers were initiated. Daphne felt that she would have to think it over but she and Noel signed up in the end. The pact became an ill-guarded secret that the friends nourished and which nourished their friendship in return, a symbol of their shared ideals and their exclusivity that they returned to to burnish and gloat over, like outlaws checking on buried treasure. It may have rained for three weeks in Surrey where Margery went next but, she wrote to Rupert, 'it will be fine on Basle platform in 1933'.

2

Margery Strikes Out

The young often disapprove of the world they inherit but these friends were going further than most in rejecting it entirely. All four of the Oliviers were in the midst of the defining years of their youth, not yet entirely established as individuals with separate lives, and busy – whether they knew it or not – with complex and crucial workings-out for the future: what to want from life, how to love, how to distinguish themselves from each other and how to allow for the arrival of significant others. Important questions that added up to just one: how to live?

The wholesale rejection of a disappointing world was more characteristic of Rupert's approach than Margery's. He was expecting them all to establish in 1933 'a Heaven of Laughter and Bodies and Flowers and Love and People and Sun and Wind'. This was a heaven, it seemed, that could only exist in isolation. It would perhaps resemble the scene in Grantchester, a village two miles or so from Cambridge, where Rupert had settled in 1909, taking rooms in a house called The Orchard. There he enticed his friends – Margery and her sisters; Cambridge students like Justin Brooke, a good-looking and good-natured actor who had been at school with Jacques at Bedales, where Noel was now studying; Ka Cox, Dudley Ward, Geoffrey Keynes, Eva Spielman and Bill Hubback; and Gwen Darwin (an aspiring artist) and her cousin Frances (a budding poet), who were not students but belonged to the Cambridge institution that was the Darwin family – and lazed on the lawn, or in a punt drifting on the river, writing poetry or reciting it to his guests, working patchily on a fellowship application, startling his landlady by going about barefoot.

Within the Cambridge bubble, Rupert was already something of a celebrity, popular among those drawn to boyish good looks but also admired for his conversation and intelligence (in September 1909 four of

his poems appeared in *The English Review*). Eminent men like Henry
James were impressed by him, and when the bohemian painter Augustus
John brought his (literal) caravan of wives and children to camp at
Grantchester that summer, Rupert fitted in easily with them as well.

Rupert Brooke in 1913

His friends enjoyed lively communal breakfasts, invigorated by a swim
in the river or in Byron's Pool nearby, and languid afternoons in the dim
dappled shade of the lawn. They argued with, read to and admired one
another. One of the Pye sisters, friends of the Oliviers from Limpsfield,
remembered Rupert hanging from a poplar tree to dry his hair, with
'the topmost leaves almost sweeping the long grass' as the branch bent
beneath him. Brynhild was introduced to Rupert at the end of 1907 on
a skiing trip and made a strong impression on him, as one of the few
people whose beauty was just as striking as his. Rupert, in Grantchester,
was their epicentre. Blond, precocious, funny and talented; he gave them
the sense that they were part of something special. Something Virginia
Stephen, an aspiring novelist who visited him there in 1911, was perhaps
trying to capture when she dubbed them, half-mockingly, the 'Neo-Pagans'.

There was no specific Neo-Pagan creed. It was more a way of life, or
rather a way of leisure time, influenced nevertheless by Fabianism and

the Arcadian philosophies of Edward Carpenter. It reflected a frame of mind that came across as carefree – an outlook that relished the outdoors, the elements, swimming naked and tramping over hills, sleeping out in the open air (activities personified by the Olivier sisters). Its membership had a socialistic, utopian streak, a kind of innocence and enthusiasm that matched the times.

They thought they had found a new way of living, a freer lifestyle that embraced the natural world around them, but their experience of these days, at a time when Victorian prudishness began to fade and young men and women mingled to a tantalising extent, was tinged by the fear that it couldn't last. Gwen Darwin, watching her friends, could hardly bear to

> think of all these young beautiful people getting old and tired and stiff in the joints [...] We are at our very best and livingest now [...] one suddenly stops and sees them all sitting round – Rupert and Geoffrey and Jacques and Bryn and Noel – all so young and strong and keen and full of thought and desire – and one knows it will all be gone in 20 years.

So they planned for the future in order to deny it. After a time, the Basel Pact came under negotiation. Some of the signatories suspected that they might be engaged in important work by 1933, work that they would not, in good conscience, be able to abandon. Margery advocated for allowing members to join for 'a term of years' only, something that Noel, chiming in from her school in Hampshire, warned could turn the whole thing into nothing more than a holiday. Dudley Ward and Eva Spielman, who once made a vow 'by all the powers that guard Basle station of 1933', began to doubt Margery's true commitment to the scheme. Was she one of those people who got an idea going without ever really believing in it?

Margery had every reason to expect to be doing important work one day. In London she was part of (and had perhaps helped to establish) an informal youth branch of the Fabian Society, known as the Fabian Nursery, and she was now one of the leaders of the Cambridge University branch, which had been founded shortly before she arrived by a Trinity student named Ben Keeling (the only one of the friends to decline the Basel invitation). Keeling was a flamboyant and committed socialist, described by H. G. Wells as 'a copious, rebellious, disorderly, generous, and sympathetic young man', who was well suited to the turbulent political scene at the university. He had once coated the stairs outside his room with margarine and looped electrified wire around his door to thwart an unfriendly visit from Tory opponents.

Margery, an economics student, was on the committee of the Society as Treasurer. Together the Cambridge Fabians arranged lectures from such sympathetic figures as Bernard Shaw, Hilaire Belloc, Edward Pease, Hubert Bland, J. A. Hobson and H. G. Wells; many of them people who had known Margery from childhood. When the Webbs published their Minority Report on the Poor Law, which recommended an entirely new system of national welfare, Margery was elected to the group that reported on it before the Cambridge Fabians began their campaigning in its support.

The Fabians were the first undergraduate society in Cambridge to welcome both male and female members. Margery was a student at Newnham College, one of only two colleges for women. Alongside her on the committee were familiar faces from the Nursery like Amber Reeves (another daughter of prominent Fabians) and Dorothy Ostmaston, who had grown up in Limpsfield. Margery took over as Treasurer from Ka Cox, who was also a Newnhamite and Fabian daughter, whose father, a stockbroker, had died suddenly when she was eighteen and left her orphaned and financially independent. Ka was a caring, undemanding figure, whom everybody seemed to like and many to rely on. Other Newnhamites admired the group from an awestruck distance. The handsome Amber was 'intellect personified', daring enough to proclaim the relativity of morals in a lecture to the college Philosophy Society; Ka Cox 'a miracle of poise, maturity and charm.' Margery had less of their self-confidence but matched them in seriousness of purpose, though she distinguished herself by her capacity for uninhibited high spirits. (The Fabian men in Cambridge, she told Bryn, were too sober for her taste. Ben Keeling in particular she longed to tease.) Rupert was on the committee too, with his old school friend Geoffrey Keynes, the sombre younger brother of the economist Maynard, and John's student Dudley Ward, another economics student and close friend of Rupert's. For sheltered young women like Eva Spielman, the daughter of wealthy Jewish parents who had taken some persuading to allow her to go to Newnham at all, the meetings of the Society, where young men and women debated everything from religion to poverty to sex as equals and without embarrassment, were a revelation.

A Fabian summer school in North Wales. James Strachey is immersed in a book on the left, Margery and Rupert are looking challengingly at each other by the fireplace a few faces to the right. George Rivers Blanco White, another Cambridge student, is leaning across someone to read, and Amber Reeves is on the far right.

Since coming to Cambridge, Margery had joined the small fleet of young ladies on bicycles who zoomed from lectures to debates to picnics to punts in a purposeful blur. Even her sisters had struggled to keep sight of her. She had a lot on her plate: economics studies, her Fabian committee duties, a busy social calendar. Serving as Treasurer had not been an easy job. ('I even succeeded in explaining to the Treasurer how it was that I had received £2 for Fabian Literature, and yet possessed only 11d.,' Rupert told a friend early in 1909. 'But oh! her conscience!') There was the pressure of having to report on the Society's finances and to speak at its meetings. When Brynhild and Daphne returned from Jamaica that year, Daphne felt Margery had grown distant and self-important. Brynhild, informed of 'how remote & immaterial' all her activities sounded, had given up writing to Margery altogether. Cambridge had proved a revelation to Margery. It gave her the chance to strike out as an individual, separated from the precocious younger sisters whom she loved but who, she was afraid, were proving more appealing than she was. In Cambridge Margery, now twenty-three, could distinguish herself, inspired and liberated by new influences but building on all that was no doubt comfortingly familiar from her Fabian background. She was perhaps truly busy and fulfilled for the first time in her life.

For all her work, though, Margery would receive no degree when she eventually took her Finals (sitting exactly the same exams that the men on the economics tripos took); her matriculation had gone unrecorded in the university archives; when Newnhamites were elected to the Presidency of the Cambridge Fabian Society, the college authorities prevented them from taking office. The first female students had arrived in Cambridge in 1869 but forty years later women had still not achieved full membership of the university. Everything was arranged to make it perfectly clear that, whilst women might have managed to find a way *in* to Cambridge, they would never be part of it. Newnhamites could attend lectures only when permitted by the lecturer, not by right, and could only access the university library on the same conditions as members of the general public. (Margery borrowed Rupert's library books instead, which she promptly left on a train: 'You are right,' she admitted, 'I am not to be trusted and ought to be slain.') The Newnham dons had no say in the setting or marking of exams, even of those taken by their own students. Whenever Cambridge women had attempted to claim rights of membership, they had been met with hysteria.

In 1897, when Margery was eleven, a vote on degrees for women was arranged at Cambridge's Senate House. Appalled, undergraduates had filled the road outside in protest, lowering an effigy of a female student on a bicycle over the street outside. Students at Caius College were said to have spent £50 on flour, rotten eggs and fireworks for their demonstrations and, when the women's request was denied, a mob of young men charged down to Newnham in riotous exultation, turned back only by the dignified presence of Newnham's 'lady dons' at the gates.

The legacy of this hostility still acted on Margery's life in the town. The senior staff at Cambridge's women's colleges were in a delicate and contradictory position. They had opened Cambridge to women by insisting, by being difficult, but that same visibility became a risk as soon as they had gained a foothold. There were influential dons in Cambridge who would expel women if they got the chance. Afraid of drawing attention to themselves, guarding anxiously against all the slurs they knew were being held ready against their students, the Newnham authorities enacted strict pre-emptive controls. The girls were forbidden to walk in the street with any man who was not their father or brother, visits from male undergraduates had to be chaperoned by an older woman, there was a college curfew of 11 p.m. (which meant they often missed the last act of performances by Justin Brooke's Marlowe Society) and a register was taken each evening at dinner; special permission was required even to be outside of the college after 6 p.m. Girls who questioned the rules were met with vague explanations of the risks of 'unpleasantness' arising. On top of this, without centuries to amass assets, the women's colleges were poor. Rooms were cold, the girls braved cockroaches in dark corridors at night, and the food was meagre.

By 1909, the early pioneering days when Newnham women had felt the full weight of history on their shoulders were beginning to fade. Newnham dons complained that their charges were more focused on their social lives and hobbies than they were on academic attainment, but the precariousness made the busyness crucial. The whirl of these full lives was in fact testament to how much the Newnham students valued everything Cambridge grudgingly offered them. Margery and her contemporaries gained not only a world-class education but independence and agency, new interests to take up, new types of people to meet. They strained at the college rules.

Nevertheless, Newnham dons knew what held women back and tried to provide a haven from those things. College life was crucially designed to free the students from domestic distractions and give them a space reserved for work. College maids kept Margery's rooms, bringing hot and cold water and making her bed. If her shoes needed cleaning, she simply left them outside her door and it was done. Each room had an open fire, laid each morning by a 'woman from outside' (of their college and outside of their privilege, too).

Margery's room was in the attic, regrettably too small for a piano, with an 'appalling' carpet but 'comparatively harmless' wallpaper decorated with yellow daisies. Newnham provided its students with a beautiful, well-stocked library, a gym and laboratories. There was, intentionally of course, almost no need ever to leave the grounds. Many of the bedrooms looked out over a sunken garden, hedged with roses, and beyond that stretched sports fields. The college buildings were red brick with generous white windows and proud Victorian chimneys, fanciful turrets and curved gables. Formed of these grand buildings, there was something elegant yet substantial about the college, at once ladylike and bold, mirroring the difficult balance sought by the women it housed, of being both unthreatening and assertive; a sanctuary for women that was determined to remain.

In the Fabian Society, too, the students were finding fault with their elders. The supremacy of George Bernard Shaw and the Webbs remained, and there was frustration with the slow rate of change they effected. In 1906, during a brief period when the Oliviers were in England, the Society had caught the attention of the novelist H. G. Wells, who launched a leadership challenge (which ultimately failed). Sydney supported Wells's campaign for change and the writer had become a close family friend.

Margery at Newnham

Wells had touched a nerve in identifying the blind spots of Fabian policy and he took a radical view on matters of sex and morality that electrified his acolytes in Cambridge. By the time Margery began her studies, almost a quarter of the Fabian membership was female, yet the Society had failed to take a formal stance on suffrage. (Beatrice Webb, Sidney's impressive wife, had only withdrawn her opposition to women's enfranchisement in the last few years.) Wells had marked women out as 'a huge available source for socialism' and set out to woo them, both politically and personally. In lectures he decried bourgeois marriage as a version of private ownership and insisted that women needed independence from men if they were to be liberated. Daphne thought him 'a wonderful man', though she was drawn more to his books than his person. This put her rather in the minority, for when the small and sprightly Wells preached free love, he meant it. In Limpsfield, Bunny was convinced he could detect sexual tension between Wells and the radiant Bryn (then in her late teens) but this they had managed to dispel with a violent game of rounders. The Blands' daughter Rosamund's flirtation with the novelist, on the other hand, was said only to have been ended by a paternal punch at Paddington station, when the couple tried to elope. In Cambridge, it was an open secret that Amber Reeves was having an affair with Wells. When she was supposedly revising for her Finals that year, she was in fact indulging in 'days of insatiable mutual appreciation' with him in Southend.

In Newnham, the question of women's political rights was the cause that united dons and students. The campaign for the vote had swelled into a well-organised and eye-catching movement, which marshalled women into mass acts of pageantry. Cambridge women marched under their own banner in a series of suffrage processions in London. The previous June, seven separate suffrage processions, made up of tens of thousands of women in the campaign colours of white, green and purple, bearing between them seven hundred banners and thousands of flags, converged in Hyde Park in what was, according to some sources, the largest physical gathering of people so far recorded. It was a sight to behold and a direct challenge to the Prime Minister's claim that the 'Woman Question' only interested radicals.

In March 1908 several senior Fabian women established their own group within the Society 'to strive for and to safeguard the freedom of women in the Socialist evolution now taking place'. The circular in which they announced themselves was distributed with the help of a Miss Cox and a Miss Olivier. In the June suffrage event, a Fabian contingent was present, marching under a banner that had been designed by May Morris and was carried by Marjorie Pease and Amber Reeves's mother.

For the Olivier women, suffrage was a family matter, and Margery marched in suffrage processions beside her mother, aunts and cousins. Margery (unlike Margaret) had grown up with the prospect of a university education flickering in her future like a beacon; she and her sisters had always expected to take their places in the world one day. They could only be frustrated with a society that offered them these opportunities like gifts without extending them rights; and with the 'Old Gang' of the founding Fabians, who considered themselves reformers but failed to openly support the suffrage campaign. Daphne was bored of reiterating the same old arguments over and over, knowing, somehow, that the resistance to extending suffrage went beyond rational argument. 'He said everything one expected,' she told Noel of one such encounter, 'all the old arguments in order against suffrage, etc., and when I demolished them one after another (yes, of course I did, it was easy) he said he couldn't argue but wasn't convinced.' She was demoralised by listening to men she regarded as 'certainly not qualified to vote' discuss politics, whilst a man on the voyage home to Britain told Brynhild off for misleading him about Daphne's age, because, not realising she was only nineteen, he had discussed the suffrage debate with her.

Their mother noted warily that Margery seemed preoccupied with 'sex questions'. She saw this as an extension of Margery's teenage interest in boys, perhaps related to the insecurities that sprung from being always accompanied by her popular and extraordinarily attractive younger sister Bryn. Though Margery was clever, impassioned and willing to hold her own in the energetic Cambridge debates, it was the 'gleaming silence' of Brynhild that seemed to attract men. But 'sex questions' were, in fact, much in the air at Cambridge. Daphne herself spent the summer, when she wasn't having bad dreams about her exam results, debating the 'eternal & awful marriage & sex problem', wondering whether women would 'miss much by not getting married'. As the suffrage campaign gathered ground, more and more women asked themselves what it meant for relations between men and women that the male establishment seemed so opposed to women's rights. Feminists considered, researched and publicised the myriad ways in which women were disadvantaged and oppressed. Some called it a 'sex war', in which men and women faced each other from opposing sides. The Oliviers' nanny had exhorted her fellow socialists to fight 'the damnable system which makes [married] women the slaves of contracts'. A generation later, young women were subjecting the system to scrutiny.

Meanwhile, Amber Reeves had fallen pregnant. She and Wells briefly eloped to Le Touquet before returning in defeat, partly because he had no intention of divorcing his wife. Instead, Amber married Rivers Blanco White, one of the young Fabians, who knew all about the affair and pregnancy. Daphne was astonished to hear about the wedding, little suspecting that it was Sydney, practically alone amongst Wells's friends in not condemning the couple outright, who had encouraged Amber to accept Blanco's proposal. Daphne had never liked Amber, who seemed of that condescending mould that Margery had grown into, and was pessimistic about Blanco's marriage: 'What a hell of a time she will give him!'

Sydney was of course on the wish list of Fabian speakers and during a brief visit home from Jamaica in 1908, he had agreed to address the Cambridge Society. Margaret seized the opportunity to visit Margery and brought Noel, soon to start school in England, and Daphne with her. In Jamaica, the Wala grumbled about Margery's 'Cambridge intellectual groove – in which Eva, Rupert & Co were the only people in the world'. At a dinner thrown by Ben Keeling in Sydney's honour, she got to see them for herself and guests were treated to the striking image of three of the Olivier sisters together. Margery: very slim, with a small, almost doll-like face and a noticeable gap between her two front teeth. Noel, at fifteen, still not fully formed into her adult self. She was more strongly built than her sister and had even features and startling grey eyes (an orange streak in one of them) with a gaze that Jacques likened to receiving an electric shock. Daphne's pretty face took on a mournful expression when at rest. Yet it was Bryn, not there that evening, whose rare beauty, cool and refined, was, to many, fascinating in its own right.

After dinner a group of twenty or so retired to the young don Francis Cornford's rooms to continue the discussion. Sydney was in his element, engaging with the students, but Margaret noticed that the Newnhamites seemed 'afraid of making themselves heard'. Noel, probably more overwhelmed than anybody, said almost nothing, but drew unwanted attention by smashing one of the cups. Rupert, seated beside Margery, leapt at the chance to reassure her.

3

Noel Watches Margery

Easter, 1909

'By the way why that out-burst of pity for me? Because I'm a girl? If so, I don't require it thanks.' Eva Spielman to Noel, November 1908

Over Easter, Margery's focus was on taking her Part II (the last set of exams before Finals loomed) in May. For the break she had decided on a reading holiday with Evelyn Radford, a fellow Newnhamite and Fabian committee member, and Eva Spielman. Eva was one of Margery's closest friends, a messy and endearingly earnest person. She had first met the Oliviers whilst visiting Dorothy Ostmaston at Limpsfield. Encountering the sisters in their element had had a lasting effect: she was ever after enthralled by their good looks and 'unconventional and care-free life', as Dorothy put it. Ben Keeling recommended a cottage at Bank, a hamlet in the New Forest. It seemed perfect. Not only was it secluded but the landlady's cooking was superb and left them entirely free to study to their hearts' content. Easter meant holidays for Noel, too, so she was added into the mix.

At Bank, Noel quickly discovered that the others were serious about studying. Left largely to her own devices, and perhaps a little lonely, she observed them with rueful amusement. Evelyn, she reported to her mother, 'read enormous books, on the coinage of ancient Greece & such like stodge, under a beach [sic] tree all day long', whilst Eva and Margery secreted themselves deep in the forest, or shut up in one of the bedrooms, where Eva coached Margery in economics. While Margery was testing herself with timed papers, Eva would join Noel in the garden to read under the trees.

In an outrageous act of condescension (in Noel's view), Eva insisted that Noel read *Lorna Doone*, thinking that it would help her to appreciate the landscape of Exmoor, which was to be the next stop in Margery and Noel's holiday. Noel was unimpressed – with the story and the instruction. She knew exactly why she had been designated her own reading: to keep her occupied and out of the way. She retreated to the shade of the trees, wrapped up in a rug, more often snoozing than reading.

What Noel failed to mention in the report to her mother was the one interruption of the scholarly peace: a four-day visit from Rupert and Dudley Ward. For whilst an unsuspecting Noel had been idling quietly and resentfully in the benign neglect of the other girls, Rupert had been engaged in a flurry of intrigue designed to track her down. Margery had let slip about the Bank retreat and issued a vague invitation for walking in the New Forest, little realising the frantic machinations this would trigger.

Noel's real induction into Margery's Cambridge set had been a play: *Comus*, which Rupert had agreed to stage to celebrate Milton's tercentenary in 1908, recruiting his friends to help. Things had quickly got out of hand: a venue change raised the nightly audience to 1,400, invitees to a pre-performance dinner included the Poet Laureate and Thomas Hardy, and the national press sent reviewers. On top of everything else she had to balance, Margery had found herself learning a processional court dance popular in the sixteenth century called the Pavane. Though their parents went back to Jamaica after the Cambridge supper, Noel had remained in England to start at Bedales in the autumn so Margery had responsibility for her. Noel was put to work painting scenery and helping Gwen Darwin sew costumes. Rupert had made matters harder for himself by taking one of the principal roles. '[A]n Actor-Manager's life is a dog's life,' he wrote to Frances. His only consolation was the sight of Noel among the paintbrushes.

From the skiing trip in December 1907 when he had first met Bryn, Rupert had written to his cousin, 'There is One! ... oh there is One, aged twenty, *very* beautiful & nice & everything'. By the time of the next skiing trip in December 1908, his interests had shifted. He summed up the holiday thus: 'Switzerland fair [...] Noel Olivier superb.'

In the months after the trip, Noel's name came up again and again in Rupert's letters to his friends, usually in terms of tracking her movements, laying plans to find her, and coy references to how wonderful she had been in one place or another. Though Rupert made his admiration for Noel clear to his most trusted friends, he said nothing to Margery and very little to Noel herself.

Now, harbouring his precious information and unsure of how to exploit it, wary of alerting Margery to his intentions (and their object), he enlisted the help of Dudley Ward, whom he knew she liked and trusted. Dudley was to gather the details of the stay in Bank and orchestrate a chance encounter that would allow the pair of them to join the party. Rupert urged Dudley to fish for information with the utmost discretion and reminded himself at the same time that he 'must think of other things; and be calm'. This was difficult for him to do; the prospect of seeing Noel was delicious. '*You must not breathe a word!*' he warned Dudley. Elaborate plans, involving charts, timetables and decoy holidays, ensued. The family of one of Rupert's school friends lived close to Bank. Rupert invited the friend on a trip so that he could make a reciprocal visit in April, shortly before he was meant to join his parents on their holiday in Sidmouth, without arousing suspicion. After a shamelessly brief stay, Rupert slipped away with Dudley to the Newnhamites' cottage. 'I turned, and turned, and covered my trail,' he boasted afterwards: everyone had been told something different about where he was, leaving him with four stolen days to spend with Noel.

Suddenly, someone appeared at Bank who could give Noel their full attention. With *Lorna Doone* surely abandoned beneath the beech trees, Rupert took Noel for long walks in the forest and rides on New Forest ponies. As a group they tramped and cycled and debated. (Or, as he described it, he spent the days 'singing to the birds, tumbling about in the flowers, bathing in the rivers'.) He came away ecstatic. Though they could only have spent snatched moments alone together during the preparations for *Comus*, Rupert had spent the time since then nurturing the idea of his love for Noel. At a Fabian summer school with Margery in 1908, he had been in a secret romantic frenzy over her youngest sister. By the autumn, invited to another Fabian dinner hosted by Ben Keeling, Rupert had established a clear hierarchy of Oliviers: he savoured the opportunity to see Daphne and 'the golden Bryn' but asked plaintively whether they couldn't kidnap Noel from her school in order to have her there too. Margery was a presence only to be tolerated: 'most noble of Ben to endure [her]'. Bank was his first opportunity to spend time alone with Noel. Margery had no idea.

Afterwards, Rupert wrote to Jacques that his Easter holiday had culminated when he 'came to a Woman who was more glorious than the Sun and stronger than the sea, and kinder than the earth, who is a flower made out of fire, a star that laughs all day, whose brain is clean and clear like a man's and her heart is full of courage and kindness; and whom I love'. He was deliriously happy and, in contrast to the conscientious

Margery, blithely facing the likelihood of failure in his own exams, having done no work for weeks.

Noel, Margery and Evelyn Radford at Bank

A photo of Margery during their stay at Bank shows her looking slightly agitated, as her friends pile atop her playfully. She holds a blanket tightly around her shoulders; the young women are perched on a wicker chair in a bare-looking garden. In another, she stands between Evelyn and Noel, an arm gripping Noel's shoulder protectively. It is hard to tell whether she was unsettled by Rupert and Dudley's arrival. Olivier holidays were usually open, fluctuating affairs. The group had grown so close that there was little reason to be surprised by Rupert's desire to spend time with her, to be wherever she was. Attention from young men was something she relished. It had not yet crossed her mind that one of her contemporaries could be infatuated with her little sister.

For Rupert, safely ensconced with his parents in Sidmouth, two poems came out of the time in Bank. One was his first mature work, a poem (which he eventually sent to Noel) that reflected lovingly on a girl's 'brown delightful head': 'Oh! Death will find me, long before I tire/ Of watching you'. It was a gentle, watchful love, very different from the bravado and romantic posturing to his friends or the feverish pursuit of Noel in which he had so far indulged. Very different, too, from the scenario recalled in the other poem, written for a competition in the *Westminster Gazette*, in which a patient lover awaits the object of his affection, only for her to ruin his besotted ruminations with her banalities:

> You came and quacked beside me in the wood.
> You said, 'The view from here is very good!'
> You said, 'It's nice to be alone a bit!'
> And, 'How the days are drawing out!' you said.
> You said, 'The sunset's pretty, isn't it?'
>
> By God! I wish – I wish that you were dead!

It won the competition.

Somewhere between the two imagined encounters perhaps lies the truth of Rupert's feelings for Noel: he loved the idea of her, of the inexperience that put her slightly beyond his reach, but he must have known, too, that in this kind of affair the reality would always bring disappointment.

Noel herself would almost certainly have identified more as the duck in the *Gazette* poem than as 'a Woman more glorious than the Sun'. She didn't even see herself as a Woman yet. When she wasn't at school she spent most of her time following in the wake of elegant and precocious young creatures like her sisters, just as she had tagged along at Bank. After the reading holiday, she, Margery and Eva went walking across Exmoor, travelling there via Dorchester. Caught in the rain on the way, and then refused entry to the church because of her lack of a hat, Noel drew a rueful image of herself to her far-away mother:

> I had on an extremely short gym tunic and a sweater, on account of the rain both of these were completely covered by that short mackintosh cape of mine, which only just reachs to my knees, below it emerged two stumpy legs in thick navy blue stockings, terminating in extremely old, stumpy brown shoes; and to crown all was my ridiculous head & disheveled hair – rain soaked & wind blown.

As if this description weren't evocative enough, she provided a doodle of an endearing if artless figure, with shapeless clothes, untamed hair and outsized, potato-shaped feet. She did not fail to draw a comparison with her eldest sister, in 'a brown coat & skirt, & an orange-brown hat with a red – scarlet – silk scarf on it & an orange silk scarf round her neck', looking 'very fine', in other words, 'especially in contrast to me'. It is hard to imagine Noel knowing what to do with the ardour of a beautiful, intense Cambridge poet. Perhaps, convinced of the self in the dumpy sketch, she did not even believe in it yet. Perhaps Rupert himself, so mysterious with everyone else, hadn't let her in on the secret. But it would be under the glare of Rupert's attentions that she would make the transition from girl to Woman.

After the Swiss skiing trip in 1908, Noel and Rupert's correspondence had got off to a slow start. At first, perhaps not quite sure of the meaning of Rupert's excitable letters, Noel took a slightly puzzled, slightly mocking tone; seeming more self-assured than she did in person, quite ready to put him in his place. 'Lay down your Swinburne and attend,' he commanded and she quickly upended his authority, thanking him tartly for his 'kind advice about literature [...] Perhaps you *thought* I hadn't heard of Shakespeare, but I have [...] We get quite a good education here, you see.'

When he asked permission to own a photograph of her, she at once gave and took. 'You were right in considering it almost unecessary to ask my permission,' she told him:

As far as I am concerned you may have as many photographs – of me (or others) as you like, as long as – this condition must be stuck to – you dont expect me in any way to facilitate the obtaining of them either by money or trouble.

Rupert described himself writing alone in his house, just out of a 'very long and very hot bath', a suggestiveness swiftly undercut by his asser- tion that Noel was anyway 'too young to be asked [about the photograph] or consulted about anything; it is purely a matter between Margery & myself'. This romantic interest and insistence on Noel's youth sat side by side uncomfortably. Noel was sixteen, only fifteen when the twenty- year-old first took an interest in her. Rupert hadn't quite decided how to address himself to Noel, as to a child or a love interest. But he was right that their relationship would be, at first, a wrangle between him and Margery.

In the summer, elated by their time in Bank and liberated by the last of his exams, Rupert redoubled his efforts to see Noel. He planned to visit Bedales with Jacques. 'Regard the situation from every side,' he prompted. 'Shall I just ... see you about? Or shall I definitely *see* you?' Noel's response was hardly encouraging. She offered a time when they might meet but, feeling either conflicted or playful, added a postscript in the third person. 'She wishes you weren't coming; but she dare'nt say so out right, for fear of offending your pride.' Rupert was 'cr-r-rushed'. When they did meet, in July, they were accompanied throughout by Jacques. ('Don't you let on I know I'm going to see Noel,' Rupert wrote to Dudley Ward at the time. 'It will be (if it is, at all, ever) purely accidental. So don't frighten the stupid, starched, stuffy, slick, Margery-the dear!') Jacques was French, volatile and the son of a rich man. He thought he was in love with Ka Cox, then found he loved Gwen Darwin as well. He was curious about Noel, having met her sisters recently in Grantchester and decided that Rupert was in love with all of them. Together Noel and Rupert were awkward and tongue-tied. 'I didn't say about a thousand things I meant to,' Rupert mourned afterwards.

Part of Noel's evasiveness may simply have been that she wanted to keep Bedales to herself. She was, to her mother's despair, wholly absorbed in life at school and a terrible correspondent (she had this in common with Bryn). Among her sisters, Noel was still very much the baby – 'Nodie' or 'Nodules' or even, sometimes, 'that Nodules child' – a situation exacerbated by the fact that, with Sydney and Margaret away, either Margery or Brynhild was always responsible for her. In a way it was an unusually privileged position to be included amongst their attractive and precocious friends. But the arrangement left Noel with very little control over her own life and her older sisters were often too preoccupied to give her much notice of what they intended for her movements. She went where her sisters went and spent her holidays with their friends. Term-time she cherished for the company of her peers. They had their own occupations and love affairs, their own world. Bedales gave her a community that was all her own, one which included the Pease brothers; Mary Newbery, daughter of Scottish artists; and Ferenc Békássy, a Hungarian aristocrat who wrote poetry in two languages and with whom she enjoyed intimate conversations in the hushed environs of the library. Ferenc adored Noel and while his admiration for her was only hinted at in English, it was given free rein in the Hungarian verses that none of his friends could read.

Bedalians were a pretty distinct group and they felt it. They took pride in the school's reputation as a pioneering establishment, which rejected almost entirely the methods of the traditional public school. Its founder, J. H. Badley (known affectionately as 'the Chief'), was deeply influenced by the Simple Life principles of Edward Carpenter, which had inspired Margaret and Sydney. He set up a school in which traditional authority, obedience and hierarchies were ignored; children were encouraged to take the initiative in their own educations and had a whole range of hands-on activities to choose from: bookbinding, photography, meteorology, orchestras, life-saving, riding, shooting, skating, boxing, dancing, fencing (this last was compulsory for older girls). His wife was a dedicated supporter of women's suffrage. The ethos was outdoorsy and free, which meant that Noel was primed to slip into the Neo-Pagan way of life. (She was no stranger to nude bathing when she met Rupert. Badley had given a lot of thought to mixed swimming among his students, and when and at what age bathing suits would be required. The matter was decided during one Bedalian camp when Noel dived naked from a high board in front of everyone. Bathing suits became compulsory.)

Perhaps the most unusual aspect of the Bedales approach was that it was co-educational. Popular opinion still held that educating adolescent girls alongside boys was rife with danger, because teenage girls' energies should be channelled into growing strong reproductive systems rather than trying to keep up with lively male brains.

Yet from her sisters' friends, Noel received word of great prospects for women. 'Just think of the contrast between what [a woman] can & does do now & what she did only a generation ago,' Eva wrote to her. The Newnhamites in Noel's life were sure of a new age approaching, one of which they were determined to take advantage, and were exhilarated by the challenge of forcing a slowly unsealing door open wider still. 'Thank goodness you & I just live in a time when the forward movement has taken root & yet when there is still a lot to be fought for,' Eva went on.

As much as romance, the interlude at Bank had put Noel's own academic future at the forefront of her mind. Rupert presumably intended the description of that mind as 'clean and clear like a man's' as a compliment but it was amongst the dedicated young women of Newnham that she began to worry at the question of what she would do after Bedales. The school's independence meant that the curriculum paid little heed to the requirements of external examinations. This, along with the evidence of Noel's horrendous spelling, worried Margaret, who used it as another reason for proposing that Noel leave the school and continue her studies elsewhere (preferably Jamaica).

Determined to stay, Noel began to work for university entrance exams, doggedly turning to German (at Daphne's recommendation) and Latin. Trying to convince her mother that she needed to remain at Bedales to prepare, she listed her occupations:

> I am quite pleased & happy & doing logarithms and learning lots of Latin and lots of german, things about passive moods & inverted sentences after prepositions & all sorts of lovely speeches by Socrates & Demosthenes and how to play cricket & how to do Swedish drill and how to draw – from life & from the 'antique' – and how to get on with people & young children – & in fact all the accomplishments that an Englishman's daughter could devise. The piano I will take up in my old age.

Noel as seen by Noel, 1909

4

Being the Olivier Sisters

'Loge is most flourishing. Margery pretends to think him ugly, but in unguarded moments she says "Loge! Beautiful dog".' Daphne to Noel

'Loge is hideous but splendid.' Margery to Brynhild

Sydney's job continued to cleave the family. The sisters were caught between life in England and keeping Margaret company in Jamaica. She was lonely there, often with only Noel's dog Loge (an enormous, and enormously loving, brindled Great Dane) for company, and she missed her daughters terribly.

The family had returned to England in 1904 with Sydney's posting complete, only for him to be suddenly recalled to the island in 1907, after a devastating earthquake led to his unexpected appointment as Governor of Jamaica. The earthquake was the worst disaster to hit the capital, Kingston, in over two hundred years. Chaos descended: most buildings in the town were completely destroyed; no one knew how many were dead, towers of dust seen rushing through the streets were in fact residents, coated in debris, searching for loved ones. Almost immediately a fire caught and raged, uncontrollable, for at least two days. 'Brigade hopeless from the start,' wrote an observer, 'no water; trains toppled over, poles crashed across roads; everyone felt sickening helplessness, people kneeling, crying "O God save us!" impossible to quiet them. Heartbreaking wailing.'

Looters rampaged through the smouldering town, from which the stench of fatalities had begun to rise. When the incumbent governor resigned, the Jamaicans requested Sydney's return, remembering his controversial but effective stint as colonial secretary. He had only a few weeks to pack up in England and set to work with his characteristic energy on arrival. By 1909 much of Kingston was restored and the new governor's residence, King's House – a large, white, crab-like edifice, built in ferro-concrete to withstand future earthquakes and fringed with buttresses that crouched along the ground and first floors – was finally completed as 1910 approached. Bryn and Noel had spent most of the year after their parents' arrival with them in Jamaica, though Noel returned to England in 1908 to start school at Bedales. Daphne switched with her then, and stayed the whole of the winter, until well into 1909.

Though Noel preferred to be in England, the older sisters found Jamaica beautiful, and recognised the romance of evenings outside in the warm, with mists 'rising and creeping all about us, [looking] like a great lake in the valley'. The island had an embarrassment of natural riches: the Rio Cobre, numerous waterfalls, the famous Blue Mountains to the east, lush flora, green hummingbirds that held themselves aloft with a frantic grace as they sipped from flowers. It could be a mysterious place, hard to know and quick to surprise. Downpours would arrive out of nowhere, hillsides reduce themselves to debris, or rivers appear where roads were meant to be; Daphne and Bryn's horses might get spooked; once the family car burst into flames in the King's House stables.

In many ways, the island was perfectly suited to the sisters' wild streak. Jamaica's natural splendour never failed to affect them. 'One thinks one c[oul]d satisfy one's soul with its beauty alone, there is so much of it,' Daphne wrote. She and Bryn explored the island in typically dramatic fashion, charging about on their horses even at night: 'Galloping astride under the tropical moon. Nothing can equal it.' When they went to investigate an abandoned house with friends on Valentine's Day, Bryn and their friend Mabel simply broke a window and climbed through the bars to take a look around.

In February they devised an excursion to the peak of the Blue Mountains. Brynhild and Daphne, with two others, rode up to Abbey Green, a coffee estate on the way, and peered all over Whitfield Hall, a long, low, green-roofed house sheltering among trees in high-altitude isolation. In the cavernous lounge, they sat around a fire while Bryn read a Sherlock Holmes story and then had to wait until their companion had checked thoroughly beneath her bed before any of them could sleep. The next morning they rode up to the peak, 7,402 feet above sea level, the temperature dropping with every foot climbed, two of them managing the whole ascent side-saddle. The sisters had carried a reckless physical courage with them from their Limpsfield childhood, which served them well on horseback climbs. Daphne revelled in the 'glorious tangle' of branches, bamboo and staghorn moss that reached across their way; all of it wet and clinging with mist. At the top, cloud obscured their view (on a clear day, it was said you could see to Cuba) and so, after a meal and a quick game of bridge, they made their way back down the mountain, peering over a cauldron of clouds 'seething and boiling' in the valley thousands of feet beneath them.

Sometimes, on a drive along the coast or sailing close to the wind as the sun dropped towards the horizon, Daphne would find a kind of 'madness' fall upon her, which was really just *joie de vivre*, hard to express within the limits of propriety. When Daphne could please herself and relax, the scent of lilies mixed with brine from the sea or the sight of an 'enchanted' coral reef in moonlight could intoxicate her, so that she would throw caution to the winds and try the gentlemen's cigarettes or tear off her shoes and stockings and leap into warm water and soft white sand, persuading her companions to build sandcastles and run races in the dark, confessing with half-hearted guilt to her diary later.

Yet life moved at a leisurely pace. 'Half the joy of life in Kingston consists in loitering,' the Jamaican journalist Herbert de Lisser wrote. The heat and dust were extreme; the Oliviers had taken a house in the hills west of Kingston, 'Fort George', to which Margaret and her daughters would retreat for respite.

At the beginning of 1909, Daphne began to feel stifled by the small society and the standards she was expected to maintain as a daughter of the Governor. After being trapped at one of an endless series of functions on 9 March, she confessed to her diary: 'I begin to hate dinner parties [...] it all seems so futile. There was a lovely moon and I wanted to rush madly about the garden and I had to sit there talking grown uppishly and behaving nicely.' She complained of the 'awful strain' of having to constantly think of things to say to people she encountered over and over: 'One's stock of commonplaces gives out!'

Before long, few people were safe from her increasingly frustrated judgements. 'What fools people are!' she cried silently from her seat at a dinner party. 'They seem quite proud of the fact that they have no brains!' She pitied the 'crowd of ultra respectable people' and subjected the local characters to merciless depictions in her diary. Miss Bryam 'struts like a proud hen, and cackles like a startled one'; Mrs Malaubre was vulgar ('her hair is nice, but her voice is awful & the one is not her fault, the other is'); Mother Barton 'a gorgon' and 'old grue', scheming to find her daughters husbands; Mr Stokes nothing more than an 'under-bred, overfed, [son] of a gun!' – 'very amusing but [...] such a little worm'; Mr Sharp, on the other hand, 'a brainless blighter'; Mr Litchfield possessed a pet mongoose, 'which exactly resembles him'; Mrs Maurescaux was either mad 'or else she drinks opium, I sh[oul]d think, or laudanum', and though the Misses Bryam were nice, it was 'a pity they have such loud voices'. Bryn had to tell her to be less critical of people but her keen social eye was one of the ways she kept her mind occupied, away from England and their friends.

Whatever her wise advice, within the close confines of the family home, Bryn was struggling to get along with the Wala and felt just as suffocated as Daphne did. They were often on the move but always within a limited circle in which everyone seemed to rotate together repetitively, swapping gossip (various weddings always anticipated for Bryn) and invitations. 'Here I am,' Bryn wrote once to Eva Spielman from Fort George, 'same old place – same old people.'

Despite this lack of intellectual stimulation, there is no particular sign that the sisters took an interest in, or were troubled by, the controversies of their father's incumbency. Sydney paid a level of attention to the health and education of Jamaicans that was pretty well unprecedented among governors, and had a special enthusiasm for public works. He was ahead of his time, insisting on the importance of the 'steadfast exclusion from public policy of all theory of race discrimination', and setting up a series of lectures on socialism at the Institute of Jamaica.

He also had an autocratic personality that sometimes made him unpopular. In 1909 the National Club was established with the goal of political reform and Jamaican self-government (membership was open to native-born Jamaicans only). Its leading light was 'Sandy' Cox who left his job at the Court for the Parish of St James after Sydney accused him of being absent from duty without leave. Cox launched a court case for libel against Sydney, which he lost, and was from then on involved in a political campaign against his governorship.

The sisters left no record of having considered these issues or to having been called upon for their opinions. This was part of their experience of Jamaica as a place of interludes: to them the interesting questions were the ones that occupied their friends in England. Daphne's contribution to local discourse was to circulate Cicely Hamilton's *Marriage as Trade*, an 'inquiry into the circumstances under which the wife and mother plies her trade'; and whilst both sisters engaged in the 'good works' expected of them on the island, larger political questions affecting the country did not seem to occupy them. Perhaps the family politics assured them they were on the right side of history. Yet Brynhild's frustration with local Jamaicans as poor models for her paintings seems somehow to sum up the disconnect that enabled young women with a genuine concern for social justice and welfare to look at the people whose island they lived on without seeing much more than scenery.

The sisters were living a life of colonial luxury, one that involved plenty of games: charades, dumb crambo, bridge, hide-and-seek. Every day was polo or every day was tennis. On 28 January, Daphne recorded 'a most strenuous day' of polo *and* tennis. Daphne loved the exertion of games, of doing battle with the immobilising heat of Kingston. Casting an eye over her exhausted male teammates after one hockey match she reflected sagely, 'it's good for them to run and play with girls'. The sisters were accomplished horsewomen, able to impress in the athletic shows and contests of Kingston. Brynhild even managed to carry off the prize for the 1908 Ladies' Potato Race at the gymkhana, a feat which involved liberating a potato from a pole and dropping it into a bucket whilst on horseback.

Alongside the games and excursions were the obligations that came with being the Governor's daughters. They were called upon to make visits and appear at public functions, to be present at openings and sit through endless speeches; they helped their parents inspect the produce and give prizes at local competitions and cattle shows. On progress around the country, they were halted every time local people took the opportunity to present petitions to Sydney. They were well aware of being watched in public and they took these duties seriously, keeping their fearsome personal commentaries private. In a close community, there was little separation between public and private and the sisters had to be on their guard with all but a very small number of acquaintances. 'At home' could mean a reception or a tennis tournament or a dance at King's House as much as it could mean charades and reading at Fort George. Margaret, both retiring and aloof, often left the sisters to step in as hostesses. This was stressful but it didn't entirely go against Bryn's capabilities; she could, with only a little complaint to Noel later on, receive guests, dispense tea and entertain people who refused to play tennis at a tennis party single-handedly. She had an eye for the domestic (table settings, light gardening, dress-making) and was adept at arranging the house.

Daphne would help the servants hang Chinese lanterns in the King's House garden or sew her own costumes for fancy dress balls at

Kingston's grand hotels. She had inherited her mother's love of music and on rare occasions could be prevailed upon to perform. Other than that, she found the duties of a hostess a drain, too prone to questioning and analysing herself to feel entirely at ease when interacting with others. In a crowd there was the risk of boredom; she knew she could turn small talk on 'like a tap' but found the talking of it wearying. She had been known to sit totally immersed in a book beside affronted guests, much to Bryn's disapproval. Bryn, almost two and a half years older, had far more poise, or perhaps under the gaze of so many admirers she had simply been trained to hold herself perfectly still.

Island society did, at least, provide them with a number of young men for entertainment, not least the officers of the West India Regiment. Daphne and Bryn enjoyed their attentions but often chafed at the expectations they arrived with. All too often they casually attempted to 'improve' or 'guide' Daphne, never needing an invitation to offer advice. Yet these directives were met with annoyance and derision; she was firmly resistant to direction but confused by the bickering that followed her rejection of it. Of Charlie Pringle, a friend and constant feature in her Jamaica diary, she wrote: 'We always seem to quarrel somehow, at least to spar, it's rather a strain. He seems to have a fixed idea about certain characteristics of mine, and he wants to alter them or something.' Charlie attempted to improve the sisters' minds by making them read aloud from Bacon's essays, which only perplexed them, and wrote Daphne letters that were, she noted, 'by way of being poetical'. She struggled hard to take him seriously, all the while berating herself for not being nicer, but the fact was that she knew her worth and it was not easy to be instructed by a self-important young man. An officer named Sidgwick, whose 'gentle patronising manner' grated on Daphne, was privately reprimanded for commenting on her personality: 'What does *he* know about it? He had much better open his eyes, and see for himself, instead of following vague rumours in his judgement of characters.' Growing up had somehow not made the Olivier sisters more susceptible to others' opinions and they despised those who were swayed by them. Their main concern was only that people should presume to know them at all: 'I don't like to be seen through + labeled,' Daphne mused. With so little time, space or agency of their own, they preferred to keep their true selves for themselves.

Sidgwick had called Daphne 'intolerant' and 'proud' and she knew that he wasn't the only one to think so. She and her sisters were all independent and the more they participated in society the more they came up against these condemnations – or misunderstandings – of their nature. In 1909, men expected women to take instruction. Some of them made the mistake of telling one sister what they thought of another, somehow failing to realise that the sisters' loyalty was to each other, expecting sympathy where they met none.

Daphne made a guilty note when Margery and Noel went back to their respective studies in England, conscious that work was the casualty of her Jamaican lifestyle. She was determined to prepare for university entrance exams – 'I think of all the advantages of Newnham and how jolly it must be there,' she wrote to Margery, 'and Plato and Virgil don't seem to be any obstacle' – but all she really wanted to do, aside from the fun and games, was play her violin. She was reading – and loving – Wells's newly published *Tono-Bungay*, alongside articles and papers on Fabian affairs, and the sisters would pore over the *Saturday Review* and allow what they read to infuriate them. 'I think it is good to rage from time to time,' Daphne admitted.

Brynhild and Sydney with guests

Daphne with a polo team

Back in England at the beginning of July 1909, Daphne was woken by Margery and Bryn storming into her room waving a piece of paper: she'd passed her Cambridge entrance exams. Characteristically, Daphne had felt welcomed by the landscape of Limpsfield that spring when she'd returned to take the exams: 'Pink apple blossom against a blue sky and sunshine – It is still "home" then.' She and Bryn settled themselves into the hammock in the garden at The Champions, to read and receive visitors. Bunny, now a chunky, inarticulate teen, and Harold Hobson and the Pye siblings and the Radfords (offspring of the poet Dollie Radford, who was a friend of Sydney and Margaret's) were gratifyingly pleased to see them. Margery, also basking in good exam results, was home for the holidays.

A new face was added that summer. Maitland Radford and Bunny were both good friends with Godwin Baynes, a medical student and Cambridge rowing blue who had been at the December skiing party. This huge, handsome and playful character enlivened the Limpsfield picnics with comic acrobatics, jousting matches with Bunny (heads protected with baskets) and soulful harmonising with Daphne in the evenings. Daphne was a little overcome. 'He is too glorious,' she told her diary.

Daphne accompanied Bunny and Harold on forays into the surrounding countryside, spending the night in accommodating farmers' barns when they stayed out late (though Daphne had to be snuck out of the barn in the early hours, since few farmers were accommodating enough to approve of young men and women sleeping side by side on their property). Towards the end of the month, Bunny arranged a camp on the River Eden, close to Penshurst in Kent. Over the summer the Neo-Pagan friendship group shifted to accommodate people like Bunny, whose Limpsfield upbringing made him a Neo-Pagan at heart and whose closeness to Noel made him a person of interest for Rupert. Penshurst was a classic Neo-Pagan setting. Here they set up their tents in quiet water meadows that ran to the riverbank. An old bridge stretched across the river and beyond that was a pool ornamented with yellow water lilies, perfect for bathing. Maitland, Harold, Godwin, Dorothy Ostmaston and a young lecturer at Cambridge, Walter Layton, had agreed to come. Margery was away for a Fabian Summer School in Wales but Bryn departed The Champions to help set up while Daphne waited for Noel to get home from school, before the two of them joined a couple of days later.

On the way they got lost, circling the camp on their bicycles before finally sighting someone running around in a hayfield in a bathing gown: a sure sign that they were in the right place. Cautious at first, the two younger sisters refused to stay the night, despite Godwin's urging, and on their return the next morning they were met by the news that Rupert, who had now graduated from Cambridge with a poor Second, and Dudley Ward had appeared unexpectedly after the others had gone to bed. Indulging in his usual intrigue, Rupert had established the Oliviers' plans in advance and decided to surprise them. Now he was there, though, finding himself on Olivier turf, he sat silently until they managed to break the ice with bathing in the river. Noel was perhaps most at ease with Bunny (one of her few contemporaries at such gatherings). They shared an instinctive, unselfconscious paganism that the Cambridge crowd (mostly recipients of far stricter upbringings) could only attempt to emulate. Bunny's friendship with the Oliviers was untroubled by sexual longings. For him, to 'fall asleep within a yard or two of a lovely girl without a thought of trying to make love to her was natural [...] It was simply part of the social climate [...] and had nothing to do with innocence or its reverse, not a matter of morality but of manners.'

Bunny thought the sisters were shameless. When the locals arrived to claim their river on Sunday, he admired the calm way in which a naked Daphne and Noel asked a group of local boys to make way for them on the bridge, so that they could dive. In reality, the older sisters were not quite so unconcerned as Noel. Daphne felt 'bashful' to see the 'yokels' standing observing them and Bryn was horrified by the mixed swimming in public. They preferred lying in a field reading Yeats with Godwin. Rupert eventually disappeared on a long walk with Noel, and Daphne and Dudley had to pick them up in a boat and ferry them back to camp, nearly sinking the vessel in the process. After dark they were all able to bathe in more privacy, in the light of a bicycle lamp they had propped up in the long grass, which lit the way as the friends took running dives into the water. Late at night, they lay about in tents talking and singing. Bunny had not known Rupert for long and, watching him over the fire as they ate dinner, he began to fear that Rupert's 'friendliness might be a mask'.

The Oliviers' own camp took place the following month in the Ashdown Forest. Once again, Bryn, taking Noel with her this time, went ahead to gather supplies with Rivers Blanco White and another friend, before Daphne and Margery followed. The sisters had been worrying about Blanco. By this point, the news of Amber's pregnancy and the shaky three-way arrangement between her, Blanco and Wells was out and disapprobation had hit them hard. Horrified, Beatrice Webb wrote to Sydney to warn him to keep his handsome daughters away from the predator Wells, only to discover that Sydney had known about the affair for months. H.G. had installed Amber in a cottage in Surrey to await the arrival of their baby and continued to visit her there, with Blanco graciously allowed entry on the weekends. Meanwhile, Amber's parents and the Webbs howled outrage from London and tried to put an end to Wells's visits, and the Olivier sisters did their best to keep Blanco occupied.

A fresh scandal hit the couple later in the year when Wells published *Ann Veronica*, a novel which – for those in the know – was clearly drawn from his affair with Amber. Ann Veronica was a young woman determined to defy her father, live independently, and find emotional and sexual fulfilment. When the novel was attacked in the *Spectator* in November the scandal reached its full proportions. Libraries across the country banned the novel, one library committee member declaring that he would rather send his daughter into 'a house infected with diphtheria or typhoid fever than put [the] book into her hands'. (Margery had read it aloud to Brynhild, Daphne and the Wala.)

Society closed ranks against Wells and his wife, and friends refused to be seen with either of them. Sydney was in a difficult position. He had supported his friend throughout the affair but for his daughters to continue to be seen socially with Wells (Margery and Bryn sometimes stayed at the Wells family home) risked compromising their reputations. Whether or not they discussed it explicitly, Sydney and Wells came to the conclusion that Wells should keep his distance.

In agreeing this, however, they had reckoned without the sisters' own views. At the height of the scandal, Brynhild caught a glimpse of Wells hiding behind a stand of paintings at an exhibition she was viewing with Bunny on Bond Street. Bryn called out to her old friend and an awkward pursuit followed, as Wells honourably attempted to flee. The pair eventually cornered him, at which point a flushed and righteous Brynhild declared: 'I won't let you cut me, Mr Wells, so don't ever dare try to do so again.' It was an exceptional expression of loyalty and Bunny felt sure that Wells was as pleased as he was embarrassed. After a few moments of polite conversation, Brynhild relinquished the novelist, having made her point.

The beginning of the camp at Ashdown was dampened by incessant rain. The sisters were reduced to sitting about in their tent, singing through all of the songs they could think of and darting out every now and then, squelching barefoot through the mud, to try to keep the fire going.

Rupert was holidaying in altogether more genteel surroundings at a spacious vicarage that his parents had rented at Clevedon on the Severn Estuary. He had wangled an invitation for Margery and Brynhild, so they departed early, leaving Daphne and Noel alone with Blanco, who tried their patience by interfering with how they ran their camp.

'[H]e will give advice about lighting fires [...],' Daphne complained to Bryn, 'putting a large handful of very wet sticks on one's carefully guarded flame. It is very difficult to protest, one murmurs under one's breath "Am I lighting this fire, or are you?"'

*

'I told my Mother that the chief end of Life was Pleasure, and she burst into tears.' Rupert Brooke

Mrs Brooke had a number of reservations about the Olivier sisters. She had heard troubling things about them – 'they'd do *anything*, those girls,' a friend who had known them in Jamaica told her – and she was afraid that her son had fallen in love with the notoriously beautiful Brynhild.

Rupert's mother doted on him and had been one of the primary forces in his life; she was a formidable woman, dubbed 'the Ranee' by her son, who was a little afraid of her. Under her supervision, Rupert had had a very different upbringing from the Oliviers. For him, being unconventional was a new discovery.

When the plan to rent the vicarage for the summer was mooted, the Ranee allowed Rupert to invite friends, probably knowing that he would want at least some of the Olivier sisters to join him. She might not have expected all of the many guests, Rupert's friends from Cambridge, she received in addition: among them Dudley Ward, the economist Gerald Shove, Hugh Dalton, Eva Spielman, Gwen Darwin and the long-suffering James Strachey, who had been a companion of Rupert's at King's. (James had arranged Rupert's election to the Apostles, a secret university society of which James's older brother, the critic Lytton Strachey, was already a member. Pale, with round glasses, clever but usually in despair, he was prey to Rupert's provocations, miserably unable to abandon the hope that Rupert might one day come to bed with him.)

Perhaps unsurprisingly, the holiday was not a success. Despite hosting this great mass of young people, Mrs Brooke and her husband found themselves entirely neglected. The casual attitude of the guests horrified them: they did exactly as they pleased during the day and failed, even, to dress for dinner or to spend a little time entertaining their hosts after the meal. Brynhild and her sister made a particularly bad impression, appearing late and resplendent in white dresses for breakfast each morning, quite oblivious to any wrongdoing. Eventually, Rupert had to beg his friends to pay his mother some attention and they contritely set about plotting to make amends, with such concentration that they delayed dinner all over again. Still Mrs Brooke reserved her harshest criticism for Margery and Brynhild, choosing Gwen, a squarish, quietly determined and respectable young woman, as her confidante. 'I can't understand what you all see in these Oliviers,' she grumbled, 'they are pretty, I suppose, but not at all clever; they're shocking flirts and their manners are disgraceful.' By the end of the summer, the Ranee was submitting Rupert to what he described as 'nightly anti-Olivier lectures'.

He was disappointed that the usually enchanting Bryn had failed to convert his mother. The problem was, he realised, that Bryn wasn't interested in winning over Mrs Brooke. She did as she pleased and that did not include sitting in the drawing room with a judgemental matriarch. Instead, she was quite happy by herself or lazing with the others in the garden or 'plung[ing] up mountains all day' (and making the Basel Pact whilst up there).

Bryn had developed a hard-headedness when it came to carving a space for herself. This was in evidence in the weeks after Penshurst, when Godwin Baynes proposed to her. Though Rupert had been besotted with Noel all summer, he was still able to take envious note of Godwin's attentions to the older Olivier at camp. Godwin had a physical strength and boundless vitality that was reminiscent of the sisters' father but, as Daphne had found, he could make people feel wonderful about themselves and had the knack of focusing on a person as if entirely absorbed in them. After camp he had written to Brynhild, 'I think romance reaches its fairest heights in these nights of wide, starry solitude.'

Brynhild, however, was unmoved. She had begun work in the studio of the Arts & Crafts architect turned artist, goldsmith and jewellery designer Henry Wilson, in a small village in Kent. Wilson was an associate of William Morris and Walter Crane and Brynhild had joined his studio as an apprentice in jewellery design, though Wilson flatteringly described her as 'a fellow worker, a sort of companion student'. Of the sisters, Brynhild had the most in common with the artists of the Neo-Pagans, like Jacques and Gwen, though her studies at the Royal College of Art had been cut short when the family returned to Jamaica. Though she wasn't overtly political like Margery and Daphne, her art existed in conversation with the socialist mission. With Hermann Rosse, a Dutch student at the RCA, who was now studying at Stanford, she discussed their work as a contribution to an improved world. 'I want to make this place fit for a better <u>future</u> generation,' he told her. 'I think socialism will clean this world.' The beautiful things that Bryn would design were going to form part of this optimistic alternative to the dirt and misery of poverty. Bryn told Daphne that talking to Godwin was a waste of time; that it drew on energies she wanted to preserve for her creative endeavours.

This wasn't the kind of response Godwin was used to. Underneath his energy and friendliness (Bunny compared him to a St Bernard), was a need for affirmation and he was accordingly liberal with his affections. He had already been engaged to at least one young woman at Cambridge and, as Brynhild was no doubt aware, her cousin Rosalind Thornycroft was currently rapturously happy in the belief that *she* was going to marry Godwin.

Godwin tried to explain it to Bryn:

> I am not disturbed when I think of Rosalind and then of you, I see you both so clearly and know I can be faithful to both. One cannot put a padlock to one's heart and give it to one woman. Love comes to one like light from the stars. No single star can blind one to the glory and wonder of the firmament.

Bryn failed to be overcome by such sentiments. Whatever Godwin's hopes, there would be no engagement.

5

Negotiating Outsiders

'You must not do this – don't you see? – you must not tell or let her in any way know what you feel now, are you not strong enough to see her without? If not you must do as you said – run away; and come back – later.' Despite Bryn's poor showing as a houseguest in Somerset, it was Margery who had really disappointed Rupert. For it was at Clevedon that he confessed his love for Noel and Margery had responded in the worst way possible. She was categorical. Noel was too young for love. Just as some members of the medical community saw education as a threat to women's proper development, so Margery saw love – a 'great terrifying all absorbing thing' – and marriage as the death of a woman's individual mental development. Marriage was a risk, not to be taken until a woman was '25 or 26'. 'Juliet,' she announced, 'would if she had lived have been miserable by the time she was 22 or 3.' Margery could not allow Noel's work and ambitions to be disrupted.

The force with which she wrote shocked Rupert and he was offended that she failed to see things in the romantic light in which he viewed them. He wrote back, seeking to impress her with his logic and some quotations from Shakespeare. This unleashed a fierceness that made him briefly wish for siblings himself, if only to be loved so strongly. 'Are you sure this is final?' Rupert told Dudley she had written: 'If it were not, and you went on now so that she came to love you, have you thought how it would be with her? (I think I would find a way to kill you.)'

Not only did Margery disapprove but she had clearly warned the Wala, too, because their mother declined permission for Rupert to take Noel to see *King Lear* in London, as he had requested at Clevedon. From now on Margery did her best to keep Rupert at bay, not unreasonably concerned about his sincerity and begging him to understand that Noel wasn't ready for romantic entanglements. Evading and tricking Margery became a kind of game for Rupert. To Bryn he would complain that she was 'one of these sanctimonious people with consciences'. Margery's tone could be sanctimonious; she often spoke as a big sister, telling Rupert that he was not yet mature enough to understand the potential impact of his love on Noel, who seemed a baby to her. She rubbished his self-important protestations, whilst attempting a kind of lofty, kindly, scolding tone that wounded his pride and secured his enmity. 'What can I have written to you that you should send this shower of platitudinous remarks [...] you silly silly,' she wrote. Worst of all, she implied that Noel was far from head over heels in love; in fact, she had not even understood the meaning of Rupert's poems, which Margery had taken straight home after Clevedon and presented.

As the oldest, with their parents so often absent, Margery felt a strong burden of responsibility towards Noel and she sought now to safeguard her prospects. She must also have been shocked. Rupert was only a year younger than Margery; six years older than Noel. An(other) infatuation with Brynhild she might have expected. ('It's such a responsibility taking Bryn about,' she had once told Rupert. 'People always fall in love with her.') But choosing the youngest was out of the natural order of things.

Margery didn't try to prevent Rupert from seeing Noel completely. She only asked him to wait for Noel, who wasn't yet ready for a great romance. ('If you were older & wiser or a woman you'd see,' she assured him.) He was welcome to visit The Champions, where he could spend time with Noel under the eye of her family in the old-fashioned way.

Nevertheless the situation took a toll on an already overloaded Margery. When Bryn and Daphne had got home from Jamaica earlier in the year, Margery had seemed ill and overexcited and in Cambridge friends had remarked on how exhausted she was. When Margery returned for the autumn term, the Newnham don Jane Harrison soon tried to persuade her to take some time out, concerned that she was close to collapse. Newnham was particularly sensitive to such cases, keen to avoid any implication that university life put young women's health at risk. Though Eva Spielman tried to persuade her otherwise, Margery gave in and agreed to accompany Margaret to Jamaica, taking a year out from her studies. Daphne, who turned twenty in October, decided to join her. She had found the autumn dull without Noel and may not have wanted to start at Cambridge without Margery's reassuring presence.

The sisters spent Christmas apart. Brynhild and Noel, on the cusp of another long separation from their mother, stayed with her, whilst

Daphne and Margery joined friends – Rupert, Jacques, Godwin, Ethel Pye (now inducted into the Basel Pact), the artist Olive Hockin, Eva Spielman, Dudley Ward and others – in Switzerland. Hugh Popham, another Cambridge student, who had recently been toying with the idea of proposing to Margery, had been horrified to learn in the autumn that she would miss the next academic year and joined the trip as his last chance to see her. In England, Amber Reeves gave birth to a baby girl. Eva had seen her before they left and reported that the Blanco White marriage might have a chance. Margery ended the year as she had started it, sweeping downhill on a toboggan at midnight. Daphne recorded the moment in her diary: 'we went onto the toboggan run and went down [...] "We" means "Us" which are special people.'

A skiing party in 1908. Rupert stands on the far left; Eva Spielman, Noel and Margery are seated on the right.

*

Before they left for Jamaica, Daphne and Margery stood outside in the freezing cold, the Newnhamite Dorothy Ostmaston beside them, clutching their petitions. It was January 1910 and the country was going to the polls for the general election. Suffragists had seized the moment, determined that this should be the last election in which women were denied a say, and had organised suffrage petitions at the polling stations. Well-versed in meetings and debates, the sisters had decided to take their convictions to the streets. It wasn't in Daphne's nature to draw attention to herself – nice girls did not stand about in the street accosting strangers, after all – and it took her a while to build up courage. She watched, impressed, as Dorothy followed men who tried to ignore her and engaged them in argument without letting her good-naturedness slip. Daphne forced herself outwards and in a rush of pride found herself growing 'bolder & bolder' until she was quite 'brazen & persistent'. Yes, some of the men were 'hopeless duffers' but that was to be expected. A little crowd of onlookers gathered around them, offering cheerful support. Before long, she realised she was enjoying herself. The women stamped their feet and clapped their hands to keep warm, and when a snowstorm started they remained resolutely in place as flakes fell on to their sheets and bled the ink of the signatures. Towards the end of the day, as darkness fell, Margery and Dorothy stayed outside, to the delight of their loyal audience. 'You stick to him, miss. Don't give up,' the lingerers called out, erupting with laughter as respectable men tried to evade the women. Whenever a long debate ended in a signature, the young campaigners were rewarded with cheers. On a day like that, suffrage didn't feel too far away.

The sisters had a crucial role to play in making a spectacle of themselves. This visibility was key not only to secure a hearing for the Cause but also in asserting a claim to the public realm. Women joined the national discourse, physically and metaphorically gaining themselves a place on the platform. Where once women like Annie Besant had been lone voices, it was now common to hear a woman's tones raised in public speech and protest, and young women like Daphne could pester men outside polling stations in an act that, though daring and unusual, was no longer unthinkable for a 'respectable' woman.

*

> 'You unnatural child, you unnatural sister! Why haven't you written to us to cheer our aching hearts?' Margery to Brynhild, 1910

Word arrived that Godwin and Rosalind Thornycroft were officially engaged. Brynhild and Daphne were pleased (and perhaps a little relieved) to hear the news. Daphne hoped charitably that Godwin would 'pull himself together & not let his affections stray off again'. In England, their grandmother was delighted and only noted sadly that none of

Margaret's 'pretty girls' had yet accomplished the same thing. 'It is such a mistake to think they will find perfection by delay,' she warned.

In fact, marriage was in the air in Jamaica. Margaret depressed Daphne by raising the subject when Margery celebrated her twenty-fourth birthday that April, after weeks in which Daphne and her mother had been spectators to a fraught love affair unfurling between Margery and Sydney's personal secretary, Christopher Robinson.

Daphne wasn't exactly sure what depressed her about the idea of Margery's marrying. Sydney had appointed Captain Robinson, an Irishman, the previous year and he was in almost daily contact with the family. She had tried hard to get to know him and her feelings about him fluctuated. She found that they fundamentally disagreed about everything, from the public school system to class distinctions (he approved of both). He seemed an odd match for the sister who earnestly discussed socialism with naval officers on moonlit sails while Daphne went into ecstasies over the mysterious beauty of the night. The Wala had a better impression of him. 'Robinson is I suppose a typical Irishman,' she told Bryn. 'He talks tremendously & is generally amusing. [...] He deals with the servants in a cheery masterful manner which answers every purpose.'

It didn't help that Margaret mentioned Rupert and Noel in the same breath as this new couple. Perhaps that was the crux of the problem. Rupert's love for Noel had captured Daphne's imagination and Robinson was a very different prospect; he was a military man with none of Rupert's intellectual precociousness. Though Margery had noted the appeal of Robinson's 'beautiful red uniform with a white helmet, with red plumes!' in a letter home to Bryn, he was otherwise a tall, thin man: 'lank' was Daphne's first impression. Margery's relationship seemed both too pedestrian and too troubled; it couldn't compare.

Daphne had a ringside seat for the affair, the couple's captive audience as they alternately bickered and whispered conspiratorially with each other. They needed company, so Daphne was almost always with them, but she had quickly realised that they were only interested in each other and was hurt by their inattention. She grew tired of trying to walk or ride beside two people who were always trying to fall behind and be alone.

Daphne had never felt so dispensable. Margery was mostly silent and moody, only coming to life when Robinson was nearby. Daphne, in full younger sibling mode, was disgusted by how 'silly' Margery became in his company. She resented their private exchanges of 'inanities' and was afraid of being replaced, of finding that her own sister would 'probably never "have any use" for [her] again'. Though it was clear to Daphne and her mother what was unfolding, the unspoken nature of the relationship generated an odd mood of tension and uncertainty. Perhaps feeling that things were going too far, Margery's parents began to express disapproval and Margery responded with tempers and explosive confrontations. Daphne found herself doubly excluded: left out of Margery's war with their parents and out of her romance. Daphne was appalled when Margery sided with Robinson over them and found it shameful that Margery would apologise to him for Sydney's behaviour. Being in love seemed to involve the casting aside of dignity that Daphne was not ready to allow for.

For Margery, her confrontation with Rupert had exposed the limits of her absorption in Neo-Pagan life. Much as she admired the cleverness of her Cambridge friends, she knew that none of them (herself included) had much experience of real life. Their purposelessness had made her impatient. She described Rupert's life as 'dreamlike'. As an economist, passionate about political causes, Neo-Pagan vagueness didn't interest her. She had grown up in the company of Limpsfield's eccentric reformers; a beautiful boy in an open-necked shirt and bare feet was unlikely to impress her for long, however much he might shock his landlady. Moreover, the romances of the group had begun to exclude her. Margery would have had good reason to feel ill used by Rupert, and no doubt Robinson's interest was a salve to her pride. The prospect of marriage brought a crucial contradiction to the fore: Margery's desire for self-determination (and the necessary independence) was difficult to reconcile with her deep-seated need for love and recognition (a need sometimes thwarted by reticence).

As tensions at Fort George rose, Margery finally confessed her own unease to Daphne, sensing that the situation was running out of her control. Daphne warned her not to make things worse but the couple continued to huddle in corners, trying to pretend as if the others weren't there. Margery knew she was being watched but she refused to put anyone out of their misery, probably because she didn't know how to.

Hurricane season arrived, bringing tremendous storms that trapped them all inside or out on the terrace together. Daphne recorded them as menacing onslaughts:

the rain comes down with a roar, like pebbles thrown at the roof continuously out of the great gravel carts that God keeps up above there. But

the sounds become welded into one sound, one roar, as it comes faster
and heavier. Little white fountains leap & die and are replaced.

In this unpredictable atmosphere, they moved around one another with
taut nerves. King's House was full of workmen putting the finishing
touches to the new residence, so that in Kingston the family was feeling
invaded and displaced, surrounded by incessant noise. At the end of
July, the girls' cousin, Ursula, joined them for a visit from Russia, where
she was teaching, and brought some relief, but Margaret was often the
victim of Margery's rages, particularly if she made any kind of plans
without consulting her daughter first. It mattered to Margery to be
acknowledged.

The Wala felt for Robinson and her daughter, watching them experience the pangs of young love, but she found herself wanting everything
settled. She could sense an 'undercurrent of [...] desires' that troubled
her and found Margery difficult to talk to and impossible to read. Daphne
was somehow easier for her to reach, though in their closeness they
sometimes stimulated each other's anxiety. Margaret had long been wary
of Margery's intellectualism, which seemed to leave her out, and was
impatient with her reservations about marriage. They couldn't seem to
understand each other, the ordinary generational divide between mother
and daughter exacerbated by the huge changes in middle-class girls' lives
between Margaret's youth and Margery's. Even Sydney and the Wala
sometimes found themselves astonished by their daughters' freedoms
and felt that they failed to appreciate them.

For Margaret, who hadn't gone to university because she was needed
at home, and had instead been coached via letter by her brothers in
Cambridge (who assured her that their fellow students couldn't do better),
her daughters had incredible advantages. She had spent her life identifying
as someone with radical views, so when Margery and Ursula debated
marriage laws, arguing over whether people shouldn't be allowed to
marry and divorce as they pleased, Margaret just found it 'curious to
hear the old familiar jargon of 30 years ago given out again with such
confidence & as if it were something new & not early Victorian or early
Edward the Confessor for that matter'. Such things had begun to bore
her. 'At all events I don't want to go over it all again.' It didn't seem to
matter that, despite the progress that had been made on their behalf,
her daughters were still grappling with the same questions, or that in a
generation none of those questions had been answered.

Yet from the beginning of Margery's life, her mother's feelings towards her had been coloured by unease. Margaret had met motherhood with an anxiety that perhaps shielded ambivalence; unable to shake a cold in the weeks before Margery's birth, she had harboured 'impressions [that] the child would not live'. After that, aspects of her daughter's behaviour, which might charitably have been dismissed as a toddler's ordinary outbursts (especially when faced, as Margery soon was, with a new and usurping sibling), were instead condemned as 'tyrannical', 'selfish', 'fretful & worrying'. There was a lack of reciprocity in Margery's childhood encounters with others that disturbed her mother and in 1910 there was still incomprehension between them.

In the heat, Ursula succumbed to a fever. One night, rather than lie awake listening to her cousin toss and turn in her sleep, Daphne undressed and combed her hair out on the balcony, watching the sea. Only when she eventually rose to go to bed did she catch sight of Robinson sitting on the steps beneath her, head in hands. Margaret asked herself what it was exactly 'that seem[ed] suspended, hanging over us? [...] we cannot help or hinder, we dare not move'.

Both sisters were committed to being in Cambridge for the beginning of the academic year in October, setting a departure date that threatened to bring everything to a head before Margery was ready. As they began to pack for their return, still no one knew how things would be resolved. Margery was mulishly hard to fathom. Even Daphne wasn't privy to her sister's real feelings. Margery mentioned nothing in her letters home to Bryn, and Daphne found it hard to fill in gaps she had little intelligence on. 'Really,' she told Bryn, 'I shall have to write a novel.'

When the couple did finally reach an understanding at the beginning of September, it was Robinson who told Daphne of the engagement. Relieved that things were finally settled, she tried to be delighted for them but when she raised the news with her sister, Margery pretended not to understand what she was talking about. Daphne harboured a sense that her sister was making a mistake and, unable to discuss it with Margery, wallowed in despondency. '[W]ill it be tragedy?' she asked herself. 'Or perhaps something not dramatic enough to be called tragedy, a straining and straining and a widening of a rift, which is temporarily bridged by the emotions, until ...?' Unsettled by the strange atmosphere, Daphne looked forward to being able to talk things over with Brynhild, who had a knack for soothing her.

Daphne wasn't the only one who was worried; the day before they left she had to spend the evening reassuring Robinson, who didn't seem at all sure of Margery's commitment. Still Margery said nothing. Perhaps, Daphne thought, this was normal behaviour for a young woman about to be parted from her fiancé. Margery had insisted on completing her final year at Newnham before the wedding, so they had an eight-month separation ahead of them while Robinson remained at his post in Jamaica. Finally, after weeks of agitation, the sisters reached the peaceful limbo of the boat home. They lay on deckchairs watching the sun set behind mauve, pink and green clouds as the coast receded and Daphne was grateful for Margery's sudden, uncanny tranquillity.

Margery, probably in King's House

6

The Sisters' Picnic

When they arrived home from Kingston in October 1910, Bryn shooed Ursula and Daphne off to bed and stayed up late talking with Margery. Determined to get the whole Robinson story, she even carried off Daphne's diary. Bryn had been prevailed upon to join the Wala in Jamaica. But before she left, the sisters enjoyed a brief and welcome interlude when they were all in the same country. It had been eight months since they had all seen each other. The Oliviers' generation was the first in which young women of their class were really let loose from the home. They had an unprecedented freedom of movement, which, coupled with their frequent separation and the absence of their parents, could be disorienting. All of the sisters felt an unsettling sense of homelessness and feared losing common ground with one another. How far could their bonds be stretched before they began to fray? Even when she was in England, Daphne couldn't shake the habit of thinking of Noel 'as being five weeks away' and Brynhild, checking in on The Champions during her parents' absence, was 'overwhelmed with melancholy at the sight of the house' standing empty.

Soon after Daphne and Margery's return, the sisters took Ursula to visit Noel at Bedales. They emerged from the station to find Noel running towards them, waving her red handkerchief in their direction. She flung herself into Bryn's arms before embracing the others. The visitors had brought a picnic and they made their way towards the Downs, along dusty lanes and through hop fields, until they found a warm spot in which to spread out their lunch. They were happy and a little in awe of one another. The two youngest were busy taking in the changes they saw in each other, little sensing the same alterations in themselves. For Daphne and Brynhild, being middle siblings meant that they got to observe the processes of growing up in advance and in retrospect in their sisters.

Margery, it seemed to Noel, had grown thin and sallow-skinned. They discussed her engagement and Noel's ambitions. Noel couldn't help being intimidated by Daphne, poised on the verge of university life. 'Daphne seems to be getting more & more terrifying,' she confessed to their mother, 'she is so independent & critical & if she makes a single foolish remark, one always feels that it is an effort on her part to humour one. I'm sure she considered me a failure & will probably send the most deadly accounts to you if she sends any.'

Daphne wrote proudly: 'Mammy dear, she is a very beautiful child'. 'Her eyes are perfectly glorious – very big – and blue-grey and serious. And she looked well – brown & rosy with a smooth skin. Splendid creature.' She even slipped in her own plea on Noel's behalf for her to be allowed to stay at Bedales, where she was clearly happy.

Noel and Bryn's closeness was palpable. They seemed to have much to say to each other and agreed on everything; they even declared Jamaica ugly. Bryn, perhaps seeking to assert herself as an artist amongst her intellectual sisters (particularly now the youngest two were heading for academic life as well), claimed to have progressed beyond the need for scenery, valuing only the beauty of art. For Daphne, still half enveloped in the scented airs and dramatic views of the island, yet afraid she would soon forget it, this was odd and isolating to hear. Daphne was closest in age to Brynhild; finding Noel so matured – finding, even, that she enjoyed her company as a person and not just a sibling – was a little startling. Noel, she reported to their mother, 'struck me as much more human than she used to be'.

As it grew dark, the older girls walked Noel back towards the school. She wanted them to see its lit windows. To Bryn, the day had felt 'quite historical somehow'.

The sisters with Sydney at a picnic

'I have treated you badly keeping you in the dark about plans like this –
but (as you seem to have dimly suspected) I have been having a riotous
time.' Brynhild to Noel, July 1910

Brynhild and Noel had had an eventful summer of their own. The two
were well suited and not only because of Brynhild's laissez-faire approach
to older-sistering. The pairings that summer replicated a natural sympathy
between the sisters. Margery and Daphne were the ideologues, more
open to agitation of various kinds. Brynhild and Noel disliked drama,
declarations or strong emotions; they understood each other. Keeping
Noel under surveillance would have been too much effort for Bryn, who
didn't deem it necessary. 'I dont think you need worry,' Brynhild cheerfully assured the Wala that year. 'After all she is old enough now to be
responsible for herself. I should feel it rather absurd to be "looking after
her".' (This ability to disengage and reserve her energies for herself,
paradoxically enough, was what often gave Bryn's admirers hope. Nobody
could quite lay claim to Bryn and so they could all believe that she might
be theirs.)

Following in Bryn's wake was fun. She was shamelessly interested in
nice clothes and was by far the most competent at organising people.
Bryn merrily plundered Noel's wardrobe, and carried choice items away,
dispensing fashion advice as she went. She wasn't afraid to be seen as
frivolous, knowing perfectly well that Margery and Daphne would
condemn her for it. Even when it came to idiosyncratic spelling, Bryn
and Noel were a pair.

In England, too, the Oliviers had reached a point where they had to
explore how their relationships might be renegotiated to accommodate
outsiders. Love and jealousy are bound in complex ways for sisters and
the one never precludes the other. Jealousy tends to be related to fierce
pride; love with protectiveness and derision. It isn't always easy to take
the people one knows the best seriously, especially when they've been
seen climbing trees, throwing tantrums and running about in woods;
but everything that happens to them also *matters* more. Daphne watched
mutinously as Captain Robinson fussed about keeping her sister out
of the rain in Jamaica, tempted to exclaim at the miracle of her sister's
survival during 'all [the] years when she hadn't had him to protect and
shield her from the perils and discomforts which the world provides';
yet the idea of their union moved her to tears. Margery's dreams for
herself she held just as strongly for Noel but, unlike Bryn, she couldn't

imagine Noel grown up. When it came to Bryn, Margery had a special sensitivity. It was an extreme version of that common characteristic of sorority – that some of the strongest, most elemental love is reserved for the person or people best equipped to hurt one, people who can, at times, feel like an existential threat. Margery loved her sisters at the same time as feeling that, by outshining her, they prevented her flourishing.

Bryn had had her own flirtation with Rupert. Yet she looked benignly on the relationship between him and Noel, seeing its elements of sweetness, touched by the shyness between the two of them when they came face to face. Bryn was far more relaxed about giving them space to spend time together. She also had a kind of careless generosity that Margery lacked, passing on the compliments that Godwin had paid Daphne in the warm nights of the previous summer, even when he was far more interested in Brynhild herself. She did not have Margery's ability to fixate on one thing and her sense of duty was less well developed (she was only the second oldest, after all). For her part, Daphne was unselfishly excited for Noel and only mournful to be separated from her just as things with Rupert were blossoming. If anything, this new sign of maturity in her sister made Daphne, second youngest, a little afraid of her.

Rupert's year had started badly, when his father died in January. He took over housemaster duties at Rugby for a term, spending a miserable winter brooding over Margery's opposition to his desires. 'I hate and despise her more each day,' he told friends. A plan to see Noel momentarily at Birmingham station as her train passed through on the way to Wales for an Easter holiday had failed. Noel, ever the pragmatist, warned him that it wouldn't work and it didn't. He caught sight of the back of her train as it departed.

Noel admired Rupert and ordered the *Westminster Gazette* to Bedales in order to be able to read his poems. Slowly, and now with an inkling of Rupert's feelings, she began to ease into the back and forth of their correspondence. In March, she told him of the strain of having to sit at the headmaster's table at supper. 'He always give[s] such brief answers and looks so absorbed in his own thoughts and sausages,' she wrote. It wasn't the elevated dialogue Rupert might have wanted but she was, at least, warming up. She was beginning to invest in their correspondence, too. Still unused to Rupert's bantering style, she could unbalance them in sudden flashes of guileless sincerity and vulnerability. 'If you ever wrote again dont be scathing,' she warned after he complained about her vagueness over the Birmingham station scheme, 'such letters are a dissapointment after the excitement of seeing them in the letter-rack, and not many letters come for one.'

Noel seems to have absorbed some of Margery's warnings against emotional intensity too early in life. Her most trusted sister, Bryn, also had a personal motto about 'keeping a-hold of nurse', probably inspired by Hilaire Belloc's comic poem 'Jim, who ran away from his Nurse and was eaten by a Lion', but which spoke to her belief in maintaining a safe distance from anything that could devour you. An Edwardian childhood was long-lasting (puberty also arrived later) and that suited Noel. She wrote to Bunny that term that she enjoyed childhood because she didn't have to be serious; there was nothing in it that was 'dangerous & vitally affecting'. Noel saw youth as a pre 'grown up stage' between the ages of fifteen and twenty, a time to enjoy a prevailing 'feeling of impermanence'. It was an era she was experiencing with interest and she had settled on a philosophical approach to the extreme and transitory influences of adolescence. Part of the charm of life now, she admitted, was that 'every incident & emotion in it absorbs one at the time, yet one knows in the intervals that because of the youth in it all it is not so serious as to make it dangerous'. Expressing an attitude that could only stand her in good stead for her friendship with Rupert, she wrote that 'the goodness of an influence depends not on its length of effect, but on itself & what it was whilest it lasted'. The Oliviers never wanted to commit them-selves, Bunny scolded her in return, and would miss out on life's emotional adventures.

If Rupert conceived and developed the closest thing to a Neo-Pagan ideology with his ideas, personality and poetry, the Oliviers were the driving force behind the outdoor gatherings for which the group became known. Bryn chose the location of the next Neo-Pagan camp – Buckler's Hard, on the Beaulieu River – on a scouting mission with Dudley Ward and recommended it on the basis of its 'splendid landing stage to dive from & hay fields'. Tents were raised in July in a remote clearing where the friends were shielded by woods from the gaze of day-trippers in boats. The sisters were joined by such a crowd of people, coming and going, that there were times when Noel felt overwhelmed. Almost everyone there was older than her: Jacques, Ka Cox, Hugh Popham, Eva Spielman and Bill Hubback, Godwin, Harold Hobson and the Pye siblings. Only Bryn's catering and management skills could rise to the task.

They had hired their own boat for the holiday and spent every day out on (or in) the river in the sunshine. The communal life of camp re-wrought relations between men and women, who could exist in far closer proximity at camp than they could anywhere else, in a setting where the distribution of labour – the sharing of the cooking, for example – had its own political implications.

The camp at Buckler's Hard was the beginning of an ecstatic summer, a few weeks when life seemed to open up and display the riches it had to offer. The girls tied scarves in their hair, rolled up their shirtsleeves or took their clothes off altogether and plunged into the river. Everyone was always running around in some game or sprawled on rugs on the grass, talking and watching the fire. Ethel Pye couldn't help memorialising the scene later in a letter to Bryn, even though they had both been there:

> tents & camp-fire, people cooking & bringing bread & wood & water – the boat arriving up a golden river in the distance, while one lets down the sails, Hugh struggling with the anchor, people washing in the oyster ponds, fir trees on the distant bank, gold sky, blue distance [...] Oh yes, and someone bringing the blankets off the gorse bushes [...] Oh! Bryn the mossy wood-walk to the spring. And the wood smoke smells, & frying bacon, & the stars, & nice woolly blankets. You couldn't forget them if you tried.

When Rupert and Noel were dispatched to collect fire-wood, he seized the chance to express his feelings. Whatever she said, Noel's response was clearly encouraging. Ever cautious, she asked him not to say anything to their friends back at camp but Rupert's glee was so obvious that the others soon believed the pair was engaged. After a fitful and confusing start, they were recognisably a couple.

Brynhild and Noel stayed at Buckler's Hard into August and had only a day's pause at The Champions before they headed to the next event in the Neo-Pagan calendar. The Marlowe Society had agreed to reprise a performance of Doctor Faustus for a group of German visitors to Cambridge in August. Brynhild was the obvious choice for Helen, the face that launched a thousand ships. Justin Brooke had been persuaded to return and direct, and Rupert played the Chorus. Rupert had arranged

for Bryn and Noel to stay with the Pye sisters at the Vicarage in
Grantchester, where they remained for ten days, giving Noel and Rupert
the space and time to revel in their newfound intimacy. Rupert read
Paradise Lost to Sybil and Noel as the three of them perched high in a
chestnut tree. In the evenings he punted them home in the dark, able
to identify their landing spot at the Vicarage by the rustle of the poplar
in the garden.

Brynhild as Helen of Troy

Noel was a lowly understudy to Envy, so her main duties were the
sewing of costumes with Sybil and running into town for last-minute
supplies like gold card. She reprised her scenery-painting role, working
side by side with Rupert. Jacques Raverat observed them coolly,
intrigued by their relationship. To him, the seventeen-year-old Noel
lacked the grace and artistic sensibility that would make her Rupert's
match. He watched Rupert tap Noel on the nose with a paintbrush

and considered the joke more suited to Noel's temperament than his friend's poetry.

The performance was on 17 August. Noel sat in the audience beside the Germans, unaware that she was being observed by another competitor for Rupert's heart: James Strachey. Grudgingly, he reported to his brother that Noel 'certainly look[ed] intelligent as well as beautiful'. Afterwards the cast, still in costume, went on to a housewarming party at the new home of Frances Darwin, who had married the classicist Francis Cornford; they processed by torchlight through the dark streets with Bryn at their head, before collapsing for four days of relaxation in Grantchester.

Noel stayed shy and reserved throughout it all but she was enjoying herself immensely. Whilst everyone laughed and chatted over dinner, she and Rupert secretly tangled their feet beneath the table, hugging their new understanding to their chests. It was a relaxed and cheerful period, unusually lacking in tension. A number of love affairs had been satisfactorily settled: besides the Cornfords, Eva and Bill, and now Jacques and Gwen, were engaged. Peace reigned.

When they all parted, Bryn had to return to work with Wilson in Kent, so Noel stayed first with the Pyes in Limpsfield and then with Mary Newbery's family in Suffolk. From there, she wrote to Rupert, full of secret joy: 'what happened at Camp & at Cambridge [...] just makes me gloat & dance'. Aware of the new dawn in their relationship, Rupert had taken up his pen to write to her on the same day, declaring his elated note to be 'the first letter I have ever written to you'. Brynhild meanwhile assured the Wala that Noel had had early nights at camp. Noel felt sure that Bryn could see the change in her without being told. '[O]ther people dont notice,' she told Rupert, 'except Bryn, who was always a sympathetic person.'

'I don't think I've ever spent such a mad summer,' Noel told her fretful mother after a final holiday at Jacques's family chateau in Prunoy, and she wasn't the only one to remember it as something special. Meditating on her new diary at the end of the year, Ethel Pye wrote to Noel, 'I have been gazing at June, July, and August, wondering if I shall be able to put down something really epoch-making like [...] this year.'

Noel at Buckler's Hard, with Ethel Pye in the background

7

Daphne Mediates

'Apparently there are objections to Newnham students riding on Sunday. I've been trying hard to find out what they are. All I can elicit is that some mysterious "people" will point the finger and say: "Ah we told you this higher education of women came to no good – you see they are disreputable Sabbath breakers" and this sort of thing is bad for the college they tell me. It's all very interesting, isn't it?' Daphne to Maynard Keynes

In October 1910, Daphne's first term at Newnham was slightly overshadowed by her sisters' romantic affairs. She turned twenty-one soon after arriving at Cambridge. This was the usual age for students starting at Newnham and Girton: not only did it often take longer for women to reach the entrance requirements (thanks to the deficiencies of most schooling available to girls) but it also tended to take longer for families to consider their daughters old enough to leave home. Daphne was only now approaching real maturity and, in a sign of this, her sometimes schoolgirlish diary fell into abeyance as she plunged into Newnham life.

'Daphne is doing more things at college than you can imagine,' Ka told Noel. She had planned to study economics, like Margery, and had spent time at Fort George wading through Marshall's *Economics* – a heavy tome – trying to understand the law of supply and demand, until one day dawned so lovely that she slammed it shut and stared at the sea instead. She then began to read in preparation for a history degree – Gibbon's *Decline and Fall*, Seeley's *Expansion of England* – but Eva mentioned modern languages (she knew somebody who enjoyed it) and Daphne took herself to the Jamaica Institute and borrowed a book on German literature. When she got to Newnham, she was asked, not unreasonably, to clarify what it was she had decided to study. 'French and English,' she told them.

Rupert quickly resumed his plots to see Noel at school. He seemed to enjoy the intrigue as much as he did the reunions but she preferred to dignify their relationship by proceeding without deceit. 'If we cant meet without schemes I would rather, by far, not see you for half a year,' she told him. Now that there was nothing to hold him back, Rupert lavished her with his love. 'I adore you. You are Noel. You are supreme.' This was necessary as Noel, victim to her low self-esteem, seemed unsure of his affections from the beginning. There had been shaky moments in Prunoy when only Bryn had brought comfort –'I dont think I can rely on anyone as I can on her' – and the renewed distance between the two of them led to misunderstandings that made Rupert frantic. He decided they would spend the Christmas holidays together on a reading trip with Ka and Jacques in Wales. But Margery and Daphne were going to Switzerland for Christmas, and Noel was going with them.

'Margery is a damned fool. I am <u>very</u> angry,' Rupert warned Noel when he discovered this, trying to assure her that he was furious on her behalf: 'The foolishness, and the damned impudence, of her thinking she can interfere with you – with You. I feel furious. Ka, too, quite agrees with me.'

When Noel was under pressure, she abdicated responsibility. 'I want to come,' she replied, 'but Margery knows best.' Rupert nevertheless counselled that Margery would have to concede if Noel stood up for herself. Her sister was 'idiotic and wicked', and if she thought she could prevent Noel from falling in love until she was twenty-five or twenty-six, 'as we know, she's plaintively shutting the stable-door, after the horse has escaped'. He tried a direct appeal: 'Noel, I must see you. I love you.'

It became a struggle over who had the most influence over Noel: her sisters or the new group of grown-up friends who had taken an interest in her on Rupert's behalf. Jacques stepped in to add pressure. He and Rupert had adopted a style of world-weary authority, which they embellished with casual anti-Semitism and anti-feminism. 'I shall see Margery & Daphne [in Grantchester]', he told her, 'they are entirely contemptible women, those sisters of yours: You've heard of their folly, how they are bent on flying over to Switzerland at Xmas with a hord [sic] of barbarians, jews, pigs & other creatures of God, instead of coming with us to Wales, and philosophy and peace.'

Noel's sisters were surprised and hurt at the idea that Noel might prefer to spend the holidays with other people, particularly those she had seen so recently. Margery may also have been alarmed to discover just how close Noel had grown to this new group (including Rupert) in her absence. 'Margery & I are really very nice,' Daphne wrote, trying to smooth things over. 'You might go further & fare worse.' Whilst Rupert and his camp made negative comparisons between Bryn and Margery, and egged Noel on to resent her sisters' 'interference', Daphne and Margery continued to see them on a friendly basis all term. Perhaps even more susceptible than Noel, Daphne was intimidated by the older Ka's poise, though she could see her manner of talking 'in a very grave quiet voice about trivial things [...] almost imposes on one to think they are important'. ('I wonder if you find many people at home just a trifle affected & snobbish in their intellectual attitude?' the Wala asked innocently from Jamaica.)

Whilst Bryn was keeping Margery's fiancé occupied in Jamaica, Daphne was also fending off Hugh Popham, who had fallen in love with Brynhild over the Easter holidays but was now reduced to appealing to Daphne for news of her. All four of the sisters were under pressure to fulfil duties in Jamaica. It wasn't just that the Wala needed company but that the sisters drew people to King's House in a way that improved Sydney's popularity on the island; they had a political role as hostesses and attractions. Unlike the others, Brynhild had no academic excuses for remaining in England.

Brynhild wanted the space and opportunity to work at her designs but, though she dreamed of a jewellery workshop of her own, she wasn't ambitious for her career. Daphne had to warn her that the non-appearance of commissioned items was ruining Bryn's 'reputation as a bussiness woman'. (Bryn did, however, design Eva Spielman's engagement ring: a cupid set on a square of red enamel, which Eva's friends and family found 'extremely original and unconventional'.) Her work in Wilson's studio, which she described as making 'hinges, of gold, about one sixteenth of an inch long while the other pupil hammer[s] copper very loudly', was damaging her eyesight and she had to keep abandoning the work.

Because she was beautiful and capable, Brynhild seemed to have two distinct but not especially appealing roles at Neo-Pagan gatherings: organisational and decorative. Having to return to Jamaica, where she was expected to provide very similar services, was equally depressing.

Brynhild found that she wanted a place and a purpose of her own. Just before she left for Jamaica, Hugh Popham had tried to offer her these things. Forgetting his earlier interest in Margery (who had spent the previous summer labouring over how to respond to the poetry he sent her), he had decided, before Brynhild left, that it was time to state his case. Hugh was a cousin of the Radfords and a familiar face in the Hampstead gatherings of Radfords, Thornycrofts and Oliviers at the opera, ballet or out on the Heath. As well as a close friend of Margery's, he was a fellow Kingsman of Rupert's and a regular feature at Neo-Pagan gatherings. Brynhild had grown close to him and had told him of her reluctance to leave England. In this confidence he saw an invitation, or at least a chance, and he wrote afterwards asking her to marry him.

Brynhild liked Hugh. He was clever and active, a Cambridge diving champion (something sure to impress her younger sisters), self-depre-cating, shy, hard-working and wryly humorous. But he was still an undergraduate and this may partly have prevented Bryn from considering his proposal seriously. She was also still in touch with Hermann Rosse, whose letters she preserved carefully. (If she was concerned about Hugh's friendship with Margery, the news of Robinson must have put her mind at rest.) She was nevertheless pained by Hugh's declaration, fearing it would only cause Hugh suffering and irreparably alter the footing of their friendship.

Brynhild was the most attentive of the sisters, perceptive and thoughtful when it came to others, less shy and skilled at defusing tension. Newcomers gravitated towards her. 'Bryn was infinitely the nicest, of course,' James Strachey reported after one gruelling camp. 'Really a most sympathetic character.' But as Hugh found, she was not an easy person to read and he had tormented himself with the thought that she was 'without heart' and had known of his adoration and enjoyed ignoring it. Her 'extraordinary faculty for being friends' meant that the young men who hovered hopefully around her also eyed one another suspiciously, wondering who had the best chance. (It also apparently cost her the sympathy of the more Victorian-minded women in their group. Gwen preferred Noel, she once told Frances Cornford, because she wasn't 'shallow or minx like like Bryn'.) Bryn knew that her cool composure was not always enough to fend off the admiration of her male friends. She had found that it was never a question of 'encouraging' their hopes but rather that she would have to be 'actively objectionable' to discourage them. '[D]on't think I mean anything I dont say,' she warned Hugh.

In this maelstrom of male desires, Brynhild's own point of view was easily eclipsed. 'Perhaps you did not know I could mind things,' she chastised Hugh when she turned him down, feeling that everything in her life was 'almost unbearably difficult'. She was wary of making any firm decisions when she felt so at sea but also miserable to have marriage on her mind, with no appealing proposals to match it.

Brynhild's first act on arriving in Kingston was nevertheless to persuade their mother to let Noel stay in England. 'I've done my best for your career,' she informed her sister. 'We were quite right I'm <u>sure</u>. Wala will get over being grieved.' It was an act of selflessness. Brynhild was quite aware of what she was giving up by being in Jamaica. 'I dislike not being able to work at anything – because work is one of the things that makes Life worth living,' she tried to explain to Noel. '[N]o one will ever persuade me that I am doing any good by accompanying Mother to [...] distribute prizes to-morrow or that I made the very slightest difference to anybody or anything.'

Margaret reported confidently that Bryn was 'accepting the climate & the life here with her usual placidity', but she admitted that this placidity extended to doing very little and lying long in bed in the mornings. Bryn's stillness masked an internal panic, in which, she wrote later, she felt 'caged & frantic'. She was just as constrained as Daphne by the demands of life as the Governor's daughter (all the more acute for her as Sydney relied on her charm at gubernatorial functions) but, paradoxically, only marriage seemed to offer her a release from familial obligations, a life that would be her own.

Though Rupert was convinced that Margery was intent on destroying his relationship with Noel, it seems far more likely that she was preoccupied with the decisions she was facing in her own life. Throughout September and October, the Wala unleashed a barrage of letters about Margery and Robinson, debating with herself whether the separation could be allowed to go on, writing relentlessly to Margery's sisters, trying to sound out her intentions whilst listing his numerous virtues. Robinson was impatient to marry. Would Margery risk losing him?

It wasn't that the Wala didn't take her daughters' education seriously but that she couldn't conceive of it as the main thing in life. Yes, Margery should certainly finish her degree, or Noel be allowed to go to school, but she didn't see the sense in prioritising these things over securing the man who loved you or being with your family. In defending Robinson, Margaret took the opportunity to air her grievances about the way her daughters treated her and take aim at their Cambridge friends. 'The girl who has his love has something worth more than all the "friendships" with "intellectual" people [Margery] has ever made,' she wrote.

> [...] his mind too is extraordinarily clear. He never mixes up issues – in the disconcerting way some even quite clever people do [...] Margery herself often tires me & makes me stop talking because she seems to be fighting the point at issue (if there is an issue) without any sympathetic attempt to see the other side & also without reason on her own.

Nobody seemed sure of Margery and yet only she knew how complicated the situation really was. In November, Margery wrote to Robinson admitting to doubts about her feelings for him. Since returning to Cambridge, she had decided she preferred another man who loved her. Hugh Popham was confused by Margery's opacity on the subject of Bryn that winter, until he realised that Margery had no inkling of the feelings he had developed for her sister in her absence. On the contrary, during one particularly intense conversation on the subject of love, which he found 'very puzzling and rather distressing', it perhaps dawned on him that they were talking at cross-purposes.

In March (earlier than originally planned) Margaret and Robinson began the journey back to England. Margery cabled to say she wouldn't see her fiancé. She was on holiday with Daphne, Bill and Eva in Wales, expecting Hugh Popham to join them, whilst he was writing to Bryn hoping she would be back in time for the May Balls in Cambridge.

On the crossing, Robinson complained to Margaret about the 'unkind' way Daphne and Margery treated their 'defenceless' male friends. Love was perhaps the only thing that stripped men's defences away. (These defences included massive social, political, educational and economic advantages, a monopoly over democratic representation and most professions, and the legal upper hand in most cases.) Marriage was something they were all expected to enter into, yet they had little opportunity to assess potential partners properly, so that friendships could intensify quickly and alarmingly. The various courtships that went on around the Oliviers were often fraught, partly because they resulted in almost irrevocable conditions, but perhaps because they represented a brief period in which the usual power dynamics between men and women were subverted and women held the cards: they could say no, or change their minds. When the advantages passed back to the man on marriage, it was hardly surprising that some women put off the decision. The Wala found little support amongst her daughters in her campaign to salvage the betrothal. Daphne pitied the domesticity of her friends who had married and, after the sisters' picnic, Noel had told Rupert brusquely that 'all that business – children' seemed 'a poor thing to wait for & look forward to'. Robinson's trip was to no avail. Though Margery did meet him, the engagement was abandoned.

For once, Brynhild was sympathetic to Margery, uniquely able to empathise with her position. She and Sydney made their own way across the Atlantic in April, in time for Sydney to attend the coronation of George V in London that summer. Bryn spent the voyage playing with children on board and meditating on what a good mother she would make, feeling she ought to marry soon. She, too, was returning to uncertainty at home. 'One cant go on living the life of the idle rich for ever,' she wrote doubtfully.

One of the few people who encouraged her in her craft was Hermann Rosse. In February, he wrote to Brynhild in Jamaica, making it clear that his thoughts had also turned to home-making. 'From the first time I saw you [...] all I did, or thought or made has been more or less interwoven with some vague notion of you,' he wrote. 'I very much want to know from you, if you ever would think of marrying me if I could offer some prospect say in the next 3 or 4 years?'

Whether this prospect would have appealed or not he never knew because instead of leaving time for the letter to reach Brynhild, and for her to reply, he accepted an eighteen-month position in The Hague, and promised to set up a firm with a friend in California after that. Jamaica had once again put Bryn at a remove from her life. 'Had you been anywhere within reach,' he wrote after confessing his decisions, 'it would have been easy to talk things over and it certainly would have been nicer.' Bryn still apparently did not altogether discount the possibility of an engagement, suggesting to Hermann that they should get to know each other better and inviting him to visit her in England.

They saw each other in May. Hermann, opting himself to focus on his career, showed a particular sensitivity to Brynhild's challenges:

> If a father does not keep [a woman] [he wrote], a husband does or the family helps them but neither the father nor the husband nor the family nor anybody else really expects them to do anything that is excellent on a professional level.

He felt her craft to be important nonetheless: 'You must get to work, and do things, make something very beautiful, I think you could!'

The great question of Noel's Christmas holidays had not been resolved until 22 December. For weeks over Daphne's first term at Cambridge, all the implicated parties sent messages to one another, trying to work out who was making the final decisions. To add to the chaos, the Bedales term was suddenly cut short by an outbreak of scarlet fever, leaving the stoical Noel in an emptying and panic-stricken school as anxious parents arrived to evacuate their children and Margery tried to arrange a way for her to get home.

The lure of spending Christmas with her sisters was strong and Rupert's attacks on them had backfired. Noel wrote to him only at the last moment, from the taxi on the way to the station, seeking to put a safe distance between them as she defended Margery against his accusations. 'For goodness sake dont abuse her anymore,' she warned him.

8

How to Love

In their Swiss hotel at Christmas, Margery and Daphne had put it about that they were celebrating Noel's sixteenth birthday, rather than her eighteenth, so that she was freed from being treated like a young lady. '[S]o much simpler than the "Miss Olivier"ing business,' she explained to the Wala.

Margaret and Sydney knew perfectly well that their daughters did things that other parents wouldn't allow, like reading *Ann Veronica* and sleeping outside in the woods with male friends, and it didn't seem to alarm them at all. Sydney only noted, to an old Fabian colleague, his amazement at 'the astonishingly good time this generation has'. Perhaps the palpable innocence of the Neo-Pagan lifestyle helped put their minds at ease. For all the Oliviers and friends swam naked together, slept side by side and wrote poetry about each other, things rarely went further. This did involve a degree of suppression – James Strachey miserably battled an erection whilst bathing with Rupert – but if anything can be considered a philosophy of the Neo-Pagans (or rather of Rupert's) it was cleanliness, from which beauty followed. His imagined women were woodland nymphs or water sprites, not suffrage campaigners or sexual beings.

This insistence on chastity marked the Neo-Pagans out in a generation and social milieu that was seeking freedom in all its forms. Godwin and Rosalind consummated their relationship once they considered themselves engaged and, to Beatrice Webb's alarm, Ben Keeling's new wife gave birth after only six months of marriage. Amongst the Neo-Pagans, cracks had begun to show in the adherence to Rupert's ideology. Their friends were all pairing off, whilst he was infatuated with a schoolgirl who didn't even seem particularly keen to see him. Faced with Noel's diffidence, Rupert had to supply all of the romantic momentum himself. 'You have almost only ever written about arrangements, or about misunderstandings. Write – once – for the letter's sake!' he begged. 'Write yourself.'

Her relationship with this demanding poet was damaging Noel's confidence, always a delicate thing given her embarrassment of impressive sisters, and she was shamed by Rupert's articulateness and the way he had to encourage her to meditate on 'serious' things. She dutifully read the books that he and Jacques recommended to her and she made an effort to engage with Rupert's needs. Referring to him in the third person, in a protective distancing move, she wrote of when she had fallen in love with him (she, like Rupert, dated this from their first meeting): 'I got excited when people talked of him & spent every day waiting & expecting to see him & felt wondrous proud when he talked to me or took any notice'.

Rupert spent the Christmas break with Ka and Jacques, licking his wounds. Ka was also in a bad way, facing up to the fact that she had now definitely lost Jacques to Gwen Darwin. Usually Ka gave the impression of calm waters. She asked little of her friends, and offered them much. Young men brought their problems to her and she was always willing to listen. In her vulnerability, a moody Rupert somehow managed to hurt her feelings and the depth of his remorse when he realised what he had done made him take a second look at his feelings for her.

So it was, then, that Rupert made his way to Limpsfield in January feeling conscience-stricken. He planned to spend the spring in Munich, with some travel in Europe, and was determined to tell Noel what had transpired between him and Ka before he left, wanting their relationship to be as open as possible. Noel took the opportunity to gently lay out the limits of what she could offer him, with striking maturity. Since she had got to know him properly, she told him, he had become 'a person whom I loved better than anyone else but from whom I neither needed nor expected more than to see him at times & talk to him'. She made no claims on him and his ardour had put her into retreat. 'I get worried & sorry when you look devoted & I dont mind about Ka [...] at all, & I never feel jealous; only affraid of your loving me too much.' She loved him almost as one loves an idol one never expected to come down to earth. She wanted him to understand that she was 'affectionate, reverent' but could not be 'a lover'.

Writing from Munich, Rupert seemed to accept Noel's hesitancy as sexual and promised he wasn't 'wanting anything more'. Any other implications of her letter he ignored, cheerfully describing them as 'lovers' anyway. 'Sometimes [...] I love you so much that I feel frightened at our very names.'

This reconfiguration may have suited them both. Noel was then in her final year at school, channelling her energies into establishing a university career. She had decided to become a medical student and wanted to try for a London degree, which offered practical training. Bunny, himself a student of botany and zoology in London, had been sending Noel enthusiastic career advice, noting the 'shining examples' of Marie Curie (who that year won her second Nobel Prize) and Hertha Ayrton (a former Girton student who delivered a second paper to the Royal Society that year). Rather than wait for her, Rupert had shown worrying signs of seeking comfort elsewhere. She, too, had other friendships that were almost as important to her, including her bond with Ferenc Békássy who had recently left Bedales and was due to take up a place at King's in Cambridge in the autumn. While Rupert had to wait to see Noel, Ferenc had been a regular companion. The two shared many interests and Feri, as his friends called him, bore a similar mix of shyness and sophistication, coming from a literary and cosmopolitan family. He made the most of his opportunities to observe Noel, as his letters would one day attest. '[W]hen you're not looking at me, and not talking;' he wrote once of her profile: 'a head-on-one-side business that makes me want to – I don't know! Do everything and nothing – makes me hold my breath.'

Rupert, on the other hand, was drawing closer to Ka. At Limpsfield he had been frustrated to find Noel within the protective bosom of her family. Though he realised that he owed Margery an apology for his accusations, he insisted on seeing Noel's sisters as a barrier to their love. The Oliviers' dynamic confounded him and persistently left him as the outsider. Ka came with neither of these restrictions: she was an orphan and lived the true New Woman lifestyle thanks to the wealth her father had left her (her own sister, with whom she now lived in London, was much less of a hindrance). In both physical and emotional terms, Ka was far more available to Rupert.

Before Beatrice Webb had known about the affair between Amber Reeves and H. G. Wells, she had marked out their friendship as something to disapprove of. The young Amber was, she wrote, 'a terrible little pagan'. Though the Oliviers did not belong to any tribe that had labelled itself (not since the days of the Reivilos anyway), they might have been comfortable with the term pagan: for Rupert et al., a pagan would have been a creature untainted by organised religion, who retained an innate goodness and innocence. Rupert saw this in Noel, insisting on identifying an inner wisdom in her, despite her extreme youth. Her love of the woods and river, when expressed to Rupert in 1908 and 1909, inspired him to consider life's transitory nature. 'We have inherited the world,' he wrote after a conversation one night as he escorted her home from Grantchester. 'Why should we go crying beyond it? The present is amazingly ours.' Something about their disdain for convention that so alarmed Mrs Webb was equally as fascinating and alluring to Virginia Stephen, who used the same terminology in 1911 to name Rupert and his friends.

There was admiration beneath the mockery. This was a group of young people (Noel was a decade younger than Virginia) who swam in rivers, slept outdoors, relished nature and idealised a perfect, chaste kind of love with a naïve sincerity. Virginia, used to a more cynical and interior atmosphere, where most of the men seemed to be in love with each other, rather than with her, was intrigued. Eager to try new things, the aspiring novelist even bathed naked with Rupert in Grantchester and was disappointed when her friends and family failed to be shocked.

In 1911, Virginia's orphanhood was seven years old. She was at work on her first novel and had survived at least one serious breakdown, possibly two. She was a woman with full knowledge of the complex and sustaining bond possible between sisters. Though she lived on Fitzroy Square in London with her morose younger brother, Adrian, her emotional centre of gravity was her sister Vanessa, who lived nearby with her husband, the critic Clive Bell, on Gordon Square. Between the two women was strung Bloomsbury, a group originating with the Cambridge friends of their now deceased brother Thoby: Lytton Strachey, Clive Bell, Saxon Sydney-Turner. In 1910, Virginia had achieved brief notoriety with the Dreadnought Hoax but had also had to leave London for a prolonged rest cure on doctor's orders. She had found herself sidelined in Vanessa's life by her marriage and her absorption in her sons, born in 1908 and 1910.

Virginia was friendly with Ka Cox, Gwen Darwin and Jacques Raverat (not to mention intrigued by their complicated romantic history) and got to know Rupert in 1909. James Strachey's infatuation with Rupert and the beautiful people who gathered around him had long since caught the interest of his older brother, Lytton, who was at that time making a sketchy living as a critic. When Virginia did meet Noel that summer she was, perhaps inevitably, disappointed. The girl with Rupert was 'only a pretty chit', she reported to her sister Vanessa; perhaps she hadn't been an Olivier at all.

They may not have got to know Bloomsbury until 1911 but the Oliviers were already alive to the stirrings of modernity, or modernism, with which the Bloomsbury Group was inextricably associated. Daphne had been to the post-impressionist exhibition in London, possibly the most controversial display of paintings in British history, in December. She had also, in 1910, been charged by Noel with securing her sister a copy of Ezra Pound's latest book, something that proved a challenge at the bookshop: 'the dear man didn't seem ever to have heard of the renowned poet'.

James had finally met Noel at the end of July but he and Lytton were treated to the full Olivier effect later that summer when their quiet holiday evening was gatecrashed by the three younger sisters, with Rupert and Justin Brooke, visiting from their camp nearby.

'How incredible they seemed, the five of them,' James told Ka:

> how dazzlingly beautiful, and how even kind! Lytton himself couldn't help feeling a glow. Ah! it's not often, is it? that the three Miss Oliviers and the two Mr Brookes look in on one. So they sat and talked and laughed and ate and drank – and then they got up and went back again into the darkness.

It was at this camp that Bloomsbury and the Neo-Pagans came together under canvas. The Neo-Pagans had arranged to take over a Bedalian camp that Noel and Justin were attending at Clifford Bridge, on the edge of Dartmoor, in August. Bryn again had a crucial organising role, taking charge of the cooking and finances of the camp. After the Old Bedalians departed, leaving their tents and bearing the Chief, who had injured his leg playing 'tip and run', away on a luggage cart, his arms full of the ladies' hats, Bryn and Daphne arrived with Hugh Popham, Rupert, Justin Brooke, Geoffrey Keynes and Maitland Radford (who used the opportunity of the camp to fall in love with Bryn). They had the River Teign to bathe in, Justin and Rupert performed play readings for them and the whole group staged a 'man hunt', with Bryn as the quarry, who successfully (and characteristically) managed to evade them all.

The Bloomsbury contingent viewed the venture with some trepidation. Virginia arrived one night with Ka, her enthusiasm already dented by the eight-mile walk from the station, to discover that the camp had emptied out on a jaunt, leaving the pair without welcome or food, apart from a mouldy summer pudding that Justin had forgotten to throw away, which they unsuspectingly tucked into in the dark. They were followed by James, who was toying with the idea of falling in love with Daphne that summer. Fuelled by his enchantment after their visit, he had ill-advisedly accepted the sisters' invitation to join them. Valiantly trying to get into the spirit of things, he decided, on arrival, to spend the night outside in order to see sunrise over the camp. Ka and Justin discovered his frozen form under a gorse bush when they emerged to put the porridge on at 5.30 a.m. Thereafter he retreated back to Lytton, who had refused point blank to sleep on the ground. Gerald Shove, another Apostle, who spent the day lounging in his suit and trilby hat, also only lasted a single night (long enough, Ka noted, for him to fall for Bryn as well). Maynard Keynes fared rather better and earned Bryn's admiration. Virginia also eased into it, even adopting the gypsy scarves the Oliviers sported. They went on long tramps on the moor, pushing themselves to the point that, on one occasion, Brynhild and Noel concealed themselves around a bend in the river while their friends stopped for tea; stripped, and soothed their aching bodies in the cold water. 'We just tingled & shivered in a sort of ecstacy,' Bryn remembered, 'cold & heat – pleasure & pain – Oh so wonderful – I have never been happier.'

Clifford Bridge: Noel, Maitland Radford, Virginia Woolf and Rupert (left); Daphne with Geoffrey Keynes (top right); Ka Cox beside Rupert (bottom right)

The Oliviers' collective love of these punishing walks went beyond their love of the outdoors. They seemed, too, to take pleasure in pushing themselves, to be intrigued by the limits to which their bodies could go. The craze of their generation of women being to prove themselves, Noel and Brynhild seemed to appreciate the endurance trials of long walks, climbs, athletic games, and to enjoy their own physical fitness and the challenges to which they put it. Nor did their feats go unremarked. James Strachey was charmed by one young man's admiration for Noel during a weekend in Limpsfield:

> 'Noel', he enthusiastically exclaimed to Bunny and me, 'oh! she's simply marvellous. Stronger than me, she is; and fights like a bull-dog. And see her climbing! My word! I shouldn't care to try that traverse she made yesterday. And so on.

It was a long camp; more than three weeks for Justin and Noel, and towards the end tempers began to fray. The Oliviers had seen plenty of Rupert over the summer, shuttling between Limpsfield, Cambridge/ Grantchester, Oxford (where the Oliviers had briefly settled) and London, but the relationship between Noel and Rupert was on uncertain ground. After an interrogation by Jacques, Rupert had reflected (to Noel) on how their relationship was 'so very peculiar: so very much our own'. Noel certainly did not want what Jacques and Gwen had. 'I dont want their emotions,' she responded. 'I know quite well what they are like, they destroy all one's judgement & turn one into an ape. I refuse to be blinded to anything about you, good or bad.'

As the camp drew to an end, a conversation with Noel caused Rupert to lose his temper, storm off and cry himself to sleep on a hill nearby. They were probably arguing about Noel's contact with Ferenc Békássy. A letter from Feri had arrived at the camp with a declaration. 'Wherever I am and whatever I do, from writing poetry to flirting on various occasions,' he wrote, 'I always suddenly begin thinking about you. And really, there is no one else I care to be with so much – or say talk with – there is no one else I can talk with!' Noel showed it to Rupert.

They were still practising their policy of openness with one another, and Noel was also well aware of how much time Ka and Rupert were spending together. Perhaps yearning for the simpler times of his stolen days at the Bank reading party in 1909, Rupert had suggested that he and Noel fit in a private camp for the two of them before Bloomsbury arrived at Clifford Bridge but Noel had dismissed the idea, remarking pointedly that he would have to wait until she was twenty-one. She was conscious of the obvious terms of comparison between her and Ka, appreciating how Rupert must love 'the exquisite though comfortable isolation of Ka, living with her sister in a flat'. 'Perhaps you will explain more about your conversations with her?' she had challenged him in July. 'Oh, it would have been so much better, if you had married her ages ago!'

Ka had diplomatically tried to keep her distance from Rupert since he had returned from Germany but – intent on comforting her after Jacques and Gwen's wedding – he had badgered her to come and stay with him in Grantchester, which she did, briefly, in July. After that, it was impossible to deny any longer that he loved her. In Ka, he found someone with the kindness and patience to buoy him. Rupert compared her to 'a Cushion, or a Floor'. It was intended as a compliment. 'I think you're really a most lovely and splendid and superb and loved* person [*by me]', he told her. Despite this, he had no intention of giving up Noel.

Brynhild and Margery climbing

In the autumn of 1911, Noel began her studies in medicine at University College London. Her relationship with Rupert had weathered a number of disappointments: the difficulty of keeping him happy, the loss of faith engendered by his feelings for Ka, the realisation about his previous infatuation with Bryn. Her feelings were far removed from the first flushes of excitement and adoration, part of the memorable summers when Neo-Paganism was at its best. She had been hurt and wrong-footed but she had also genuinely eschewed any opportunities for possessiveness even, at times, to Rupert's disappointment. No doubt this was inseparable from her determination to be a doctor, which, especially for women, demanded a fearsome single-mindedness. Surrounded by her mother and two eldest sisters in London, and wary of giving up her time, Noel now established her family as a buffer to keep Rupert at bay.

In September, Noel made one of her periodic attempts to explain herself to Rupert. She did so by illustrating the psyche of 'The Olivier', a creature that foreswore the formation of close bonds and lived, for the most part, in isolation, only making use of companions that came its way before losing interest in them (or being disappointed by them):

> things like 'The Olivier' can bear with all kinds of folk at first, [she wrote] extracting from them what is good until they are, as it were, boiled dry; whereupon we at last look at them critically, & seeing at one time all the objectionable qualities, which we had at first been blind to, conceive for them a bitter contempt & ennui. Thus it is, that such as us have many delightful acquaintances, it may be, but few good friends.

The thing about being an Olivier, of course, was that there were four of them, so they could afford to discard outsiders, knowing that isolation would never be absolute.

Nevertheless, given Noel's new independence, the autumn and winter of 1911 was also the great chance for their relationship. Noel and Rupert took tea together, went for walks, attended concerts. After more than three years, they were finally having the courtship of an ordinary couple.

Yet Rupert was himself working desperately on his delayed thesis, and preparing for the publication of his first volume of poetry, and Noel also laboured to balance the demands on her time. They drove each other to distraction. Rupert struggled to reach Noel because she was always on her guard, a position she was forced into as he couldn't help haranguing her for it. She could never muster his passion or eloquence, so constantly felt at a disadvantage. As she warned him, she began to fear his moods and recriminations, the knowledge of which sapped the warmth from his moments of sweetness and adoration.

By mid December they had reached crisis point. Rupert's first collection, *Poems*, was published that month but without the dedication he had offered Noel. His poetry had already begun to earn him attention beyond Cambridge (his allowance from the Ranee supplemented by poetry and essay prizes), and though the rebelliously visceral imagery of the book proved difficult for many reviewers to swallow, he was finding himself and his audience as a poet. But though she was the muse for the second section of the collection, Noel had refused his public acknowledgement.

They both, in their own different ways, believed in the sanctity of what had passed between them, perhaps because it belonged to a time of innocence and hope – to the era of the Basel Pact (already two years old) and everything that meant – and this made it difficult to surrender. They were also coming to see that neither of them could fulfil the other's needs. Noel had, almost unconsciously, counted on Rupert's love over the most important years of her adolescence; she felt in some way that he was 'essential' to her life but she also couldn't find a way to fit him into it.

Rupert warned Noel that he couldn't continue unless she could make some kind of commitment to him. She made a last-minute defence of their relationship before Christmas but Rupert couldn't help but lay out his grievances, demolishing the possibility of a reunion. He seemed to feel betrayed by the fact that the Oliviers had every appearance of being liberated and independent yet remained inextricably tied to their family. He sneered at Noel's sensitivity towards her mother, insisting it was only deference to respectability, and made grandiose claims for an alternative life in which Noel made herself entirely available to him: 'the heights you might be on'.

Noel saw the real problem as 'the awful difference between our loves – mine the poor, stolid, best-that-I-can-do and yours – oh heights – would grow & weigh us down again – beat us down'. Rupert had promised her that he could accept her as she was and she had worshipped him for it but he had never stuck to his promise. His need for a grand, all-encompassing Love would crush her. They had discussed the possibility of Noel and one of her sisters joining Rupert at a reading party in Lulworth at the end of the year with Justin, James and Ka. She refused to come, suggesting that they resolve things in writing instead.

With his relationship with Noel in this desperate, almost final, state, and struggling with insomnia after his final push for his Fellowship application, Rupert headed to Lulworth hoping for rest, a chance to recover and, no doubt, for the endless sympathy of Ka. But on arrival he not only found his rival for Noel – Ferenc – in residence but also that Ka had invited two extra Stracheys and asked Lytton to bring the painter Henry Lamb, a man known for his sexual conquests, and with whom Ka had recently become involved. Rupert took in the situation, received Noel's letter and retired to his bed.

Noel didn't hear from him again until 6 January 1912. When Henry Lamb had arrived at Lulworth, the extent of Ka's feelings for the painter had become clear. She told Rupert she was in love – with the wrong man – and he flew into a panic. Turning from Noel, he had expected to find Ka ready to receive him; now he demanded that Ka marry him. She refused but, as he worked himself into a frenzy, took fright and agreed to travel to Munich with him instead. Telling Noel only of a 'horrible business between me & Ka', Rupert explained that he was ill and needed to go away. 'Please forget me entirely till I'm decent & well again if ever I am.'

Noel must have regarded this as the end of their relationship. It was probably later, as news arrived from friends, that she understood that Rupert was in the grips of a breakdown. Before he could go to Germany, Jacques and Gwen had taken him to the eminent specialist in 'nervous diseases', Dr Maurice Craig, in London. Craig diagnosed the breakdown and recommended immediate rest. Rupert went to Cannes with his mother, from where he launched a stream of letters to Ka, leaving Noel in silence.

9

Brynhild Chooses

Ka did not spend long with Rupert in Munich before she decided to bring him home, unable to cope with him alone. Though he wasn't sure he was ready to see her, and was already planning a return to the continent, Rupert reached out instinctively to Noel, with his own version of an apology, after he got back in March. 'I've treated you badly,' he wrote. 'Illness pain madness & the horrors must excuse me.'

In his absence, Noel had gone back to enjoying her life in London, taking up dancing and making friends with James Strachey. She wasn't sure how to respond to Rupert's illness. She had no way of establishing his state for herself, bar the ominous feeling she had had about his state of mind over the autumn. Margery had written to Ka for news and she had reassured them. Throughout his breakdown, which dragged on, on and off, for most of the year, Rupert withdrew from Noel when he was at his very sickest. This may have been because he knew perfectly well that others were better equipped and more inclined to take care of him, but it is also possible that Rupert wanted to reserve his best self for Noel, wanted her to continue to believe in the 'golden-haired Apollo' Frances Cornford had described when Noel had first known him. She participated in the distance, no doubt partly as a defensive measure and because she was put off by his intimacy with Ka. (In Germany Rupert and Ka slept together for the first time, though Noel was probably unaware of this.) Perhaps she also wanted to preserve something of the young man she had fallen in love with.

The Oliviers' reserve, their dignity and most of all their lack of obvious emotional response to him continued to grate on Rupert in 1912. 'You seem to expect *me* to expect the whole family to be in mourning, tears, and insomnia,' he declared to Ka when she reported on a visit to them in March. 'No. It's not done, or thought of, in those circles.' Jacques Raverat, whose own well-being was far from robust during these years, blamed the Oliviers' upbringing 'according to the most modern and advanced principles, in almost complete liberty' for a serious lack he identified in Noel: 'little sensitivity, no tenderness, no imagination'. Tenderness and sensitivity, particularly towards their men (men who may well have covetously resented what Jacques described as Noel's 'excessively perfect health'), was a chief feminine attribute, something that such 'emancipated and determined' women cast aside, Jacques seemed to think, to the peril of those around them. But Ka also failed Rupert in London by refusing to cut Henry Lamb out of her life and his interest in the sisters was quickly rekindled.

Noel was wary of Rupert but the Raverats, firmly in his camp, urged her to be 'very very kind' to him. Brynhild wanted to see how he was for herself and agreed to join him in the New Forest in April. Her impressions on her return can't have been reassuring, for she and Margery both began to encourage Rupert to stay in England, rather than to return to the continent, not realising that he wanted to return with Ka, whom Bryn for one regarded as a poor alternative to her sister. Though his feelings for Ka were waning, Rupert was convinced that leaving was his best chance for recovery.

In April 1912, as Brynhild was making her way back from the New Forest with Rupert, news broke that the *Titanic* was in distress. The ship had embarked on her maiden voyage on the day Bryn arrived to check on him and as they returned to London, stopping off for tea with Virginia, who marvelled at Bryn's unyielding visage ('she has a glass eye,' she wrote afterwards to Ka, 'one can imagine her wiping it bright in the morning with a duster'), the papers fretted over a series of conflicting reports. A crowd gathered at the White Star office near Tottenham Court Road, which stayed open all night. The telegraph company was besieged with people wishing to send messages to passengers on board. Within forty-eight hours it was clear that the early, hopeful reports had been mistaken. Instead, *The Times* admitted, the *Titanic* 'was entirely alone in her agony, just as much isolated by the suddenness of her ruin as if wireless telegraphy had not existed'. With tentative foreboding, the paper wondered if there had been enough lifeboats on board. To the reporter, the disaster was an answer to Edwardian hubris. After all the startling progress of the last years, the *Titanic's* icy descent was a reminder that 'man may still be the plaything and victim of the natural forces which he conceives himself to have mastered'.

The extended Neo-Pagan summer, now only a memory, had coincided with the long afternoon of Edwardian optimism, a flourishing of hope in the face of uncertainty, which now showed signs of decline. As the news of the *Titanic* grew worse, people comforted themselves with stories of heroism on board the sinking ship; of steely nerved first-class passengers ushering women and children into lifeboats. Not only were these examples of courage and self-sacrifice uplifting, but they also affirmed a beleaguered worldview, threatened by post-impressionism and Wellsian morals, in which innately superior upper-class men protected the frail members of the weaker sex.

In Britain, a growing number of women was battling to overcome this concept of womanhood, further tearing at the seams of Edwardian society. The triumphant pageantry of the early suffrage movement was now irreparably wounded by violence. When Sydney returned for the new king's coronation the previous year, he would also have witnessed the corresponding suffrage march, an estimated seven miles long, which included a contingent of six hundred women who had been imprisoned over the course of the campaign, or their proxies, carrying silver-tipped arrows. In April, public imagination was caught between the *Titanic's* tragedy and outrage over force-feeding, then being imposed on hunger-striking suffragettes, which was depicted that month in an artist's impression in the *Illustrated London News*. For many women of the Oliviers' generation (though especially working-class women from the textile industries of the North) the militant suffrage campaign gave them a cause that demanded of them all the energy and sacrifice they had in reserve. Though someone like Bryn contented herself with doing her Christmas shopping at a suffragette bazaar, others went further. The sisters' friend Olive Hockin would be arrested the following year for her part in a suffragette arson attack. Police found wire cutters, a hammer, a gallon of paraffin, a bag of stones, a false car licence plate and a bottle of corrosive liquid in her flat. The terms of the conflict had changed.

The coronation suffrage procession, 1911

The concept of woman as the frailer sex was one to which Rupert whole-heartedly subscribed. His own version of freedom was closer to indecisiveness and when it came to sexual matters, he was profoundly uncomfortable with the idea of an equivalent freedom for women. In fact, Noel's reticence in this respect suited Rupert, who did not approve of the sexual precocity of the New Woman. In a poem inspired by Noel, he expressed gratitude that his 'wild sick blasphemous prayer' was never granted. Instead (and in contrast to Ka), Noel could be the untouchably wise muse.

Rupert's prospects in England were bleak: he had damaged all his relationships, settled nothing, and had heard that the Fellowship he had hoped
for had gone to someone else. 'Friend of my laughing careless youth,' he
declaimed to Hugh Dalton that Easter, 'where are those golden hours
now?' He returned to Germany to await Ka. Noel still didn't know what
to think. '[T]he future seems a jungle,' she wrote to Rupert before he left.

In 1911, Margery's Cambridge career had ended in the severe disappointment of a Third. Bryn was tactless, referring to the scholarly Margery
as 'an old fraud'. It had always been a struggle for Margery to have her
studies taken seriously. Her graduation had been delayed by well-
meaning interventions over her health and her mother's ongoing pleas
for company in Jamaica. Sydney – who had most opportunity to observe
his daughters in Jamaica, where there were so many distractions, and
who no doubt compared what he saw of his daughters' youth with the
relentless work and achievements of his own – had branded all of his
daughters 'frivolous'.

Graduation deposited Margery on the shore without providing a realistic vocation. When Daphne had considered studying economics, she
had meditated on the few doors the subject would, in reality, open for
a woman, and could only think of lives that didn't appeal: 'I don't want
to teach in a school, I don't want to be secretary to some Social
Organisation. I don't feel I sh[oul]d be able to go about lecturing – all
these things are the openings one gets from taking the economics tripos'.
Margery now found to her cost that access to education provided her
with little to cash in on in reality when there were not yet the career
opportunities to make use of them (this was another factor, some
suspected, in the diminishing determination of Newnham students). The
sight of her mother's (and Bryn's) purposelessness and apathy in Jamaica
must have been a frightening warning and she had only recently declined
the option of marriage to Robinson. After the stimulation and activism
of her student days, what next?

Her academic failure was followed by further disappointment. When
Brynhild returned from Jamaica she had decided that the best course of
action with Hugh Popham would be to keep him at arm's length. Margery
had perhaps confided her hopes about him, as Brynhild refused to see
him when she visited her sister in Cambridge in June. (She was, however,
also considering the possibility of a European trip with Hermann Rosse

at around the same time.) Avoidance proved easier to decide than to put into practice, however, as Bryn and Hugh moved within the same small circles, and when Hugh graduated he also had more confidence in his chances. Once Margery realised that her feelings for Hugh, which seem partly to have emerged in tandem with her doubts about Robinson, were no longer reciprocated (if they ever truly had been) she collapsed. The Oliviers were used to her fluctuating moods but in October 1911 Noel reported wearily that the latest 'crisis' was 'more terrible than any there has been'. Perhaps Noel's discomfort with Rupert's illness was connected to an unease about Margery's volatility. Margery's suffering was intense and palpable but no one quite knew how to help because, as usual, no one seemed quite sure what had happened.

As the Neo-Pagans went their separate ways, they glanced back with the beginnings of nostalgia. Dudley Ward, preparing for his own wedding, wrote to Margery as if the days of the Basel Pact belonged firmly to the past: 'I wonder, Margery, whether you four people ever realise what you have meant to us all. I'm glad I knew you.' Dudley married in May 1912; Jacques and Gwen had done so in 1911, Virginia Stephen finally accepted a proposal from Leonard Woolf; Brynhild and Hugh grew closer. Noel moved in with Eva Spielman (now Hubback) and her new husband and prepared for exams that summer, so that she could continue on to the London School of Medicine for Women. Daphne was absorbed in Newnham life. Margery struggled. By May 1912, she seemed to Noel still 'terribly mad'.

The same month, after a year of silence, Hermann Rosse wrote to Brynhild to say that he was planning to marry a woman he did not love, if she could offer him no hope of marriage. There is no sign that she replied. Perhaps, at around this time, Brynhild had made her feelings for Hugh known.

The Wala was still in England and that summer, as the sisters gathered at The Champions, antipathy between the two oldest, only a year apart in age – at once too close and too far apart – flared up again. Margery and Bryn could never understand one another and, to make matters worse, they were sharing a bathroom. For all her tact and friendliness with other people, perhaps even because of it, Brynhild got on Margery's nerves, whilst Bryn was impatient with Margery's demands, her attitudes, her need for attention. Margery had all the responsibility of the oldest but seemed to command little of the respect. Noel complained of her lack of efficiency, the others rebelled against her hard-cast ideas. She didn't have Bryn's quiet charm or legions of admirers. She didn't have Robinson and she didn't have Hugh Popham, who was presumably at the root of the latest bad blood between her and Bryn. She may have once thought that it was dangerous to marry before twenty-six, her age in the summer of 1912, but others were wondering if it was dangerous *not* to have married by then. 'I think all this reluctant virginity is horrible,' Jacques wrote sympathetically to Noel, who had told Gwen of Margery's plight. To Margery herself he wrote of all the things they had to look forward to: 'You have got to marry & bring forth a lot of children; and I've got a great deal of work to do.'

Margery

Noel, who had always had an affinity with Brynhild, now worried for Margery. She was 'pale as tallow and her eyes [looked] suspicious & desperate & affraid'. Her quarrels with Bryn shocked the family and she argued incessantly with the Wala. And it wasn't just family: Margery had developed a habit of impulsively taking against other people. The younger sisters were exasperated – shouldn't the eldest sister be the most reasonable? Wasn't childishness the preserve of the youngest? Margery's behaviour was making life difficult for everyone; worst of all, it was leaving her isolated within a family that always hung together.

Yet to outsiders, there was little sign of Margery's torments, or the way she tormented her family. She was pleasant and interesting and attractive in her own right (though she needed the reassurance that this was so). For many Neo-Pagans, and in Bloomsbury, she was a cherished friend. She had even managed to charm the exacting Stephen sisters, who liked her best of all the Oliviers. When Noel and Margery visited the Raverats in August, Noel was reminded of how well she used to get on with her sister. Away from home, Margery seemed cheerful. '[T]here is nothing to be jealous of here,' Noel noted, 'and she is happy.' Some simply assumed that Margery's eccentricity was part of an artistic nature. After her visit, apologising for not having written, she asked the Raverats beguilingly, 'what the good of pleading that one drifts and dreams'?

One day in July, Margery unexpectedly announced that Hugh Popham should marry Brynhild. She insisted implacably that he visit the house without delay, and so, despite resistance from the Wala, and distinct reluctance among her sisters, he was summoned.

Bryn's motto of keeping a-hold of nurse also spoke to the wisdom of appreciating what you have in hand; she had told Hermann Rosse, too, that 'in judging men the safest criterion to use was what they did and not what they "talked"'. Hugh had loyally been waiting for his moment and had secured a long-hoped-for job at the British Museum. 'I think it is almost impossibly much to ask you to marry me,' he wrote to Brynhild after visiting. 'I don't think you are a person of very strong passions [...] I don't think I am either.'

Hugh, who had good prospects, had loved Bryn from a patient and respectful distance, and was part of the network of families she knew best, must have seemed a safe option. She was ready to promise not to 'slip away forever while you're not looking'. But she had also finally got a professional workshop of her own for her jewellery, complete with a deafening gas engine. Hugh realised that Bryn didn't want to be rushed but he couldn't help himself. 'It is quite simple for me', he wrote, 'marriage, marriage, marriage!'

In July, Bryn, Noel and Daphne went to stay with Maynard Keynes at a small hotel he had booked out at Everleigh, in Wiltshire. The painter (and James Strachey's cousin) Duncan Grant, Gerald Shove, Justin and Geoffrey Keynes were also there. It wasn't quite a camp (Bryn was amused by the luxury of the 'suite of apartments' Maynard had arranged for them) but the sisters were in high spirits, perhaps grateful to get away from The Champions. They went riding over Salisbury Plain, Daphne and Bryn revelling in the chance to gallop recklessly again, Noel accidentally colliding with the back of her horse's head and emerging with a swollen lip. In need of more sedate entertainment, they also played croquet on the lawn and went for walks in the mesmerising countryside. They stumbled across an aeroplaning station and watched soldiers practise taking off in new Avro planes, thinking that they all 'looked like doomed men'.

Then Rupert arrived. James had escorted him back to England from his latest stay in Europe but he was not better: his weeks with Ka had only confirmed his sense that he no longer felt anything for her, and, in Germany, he had brooded on the thought of Noel enjoying herself in London, falling under the influence of Bloomsbury, whose members he blamed for Ka's entanglement with Henry Lamb. When Noel went to stay with Virginia for a weekend, he asked Jacques anxiously if he was 'keep[ing] on her the eye of responsibility'.

Rupert's new antipathy towards Lytton had put his friendship with James under strain. But James had provoked an additional outburst by admitting to quite unforeseeable feelings for Noel. In false tones of jovial male comradeship, Rupert responded viciously. It would be mad of him, he assured James, to sacrifice their friendship 'for an off chance at a cunt'. Instead, he offered James advice for how to survive the heartless Noel. '[S]he's just a female,' he warned, 'so she may let you down at any moment.' But he predicted worse for Noel, who would have to fall in love one day, 'when she'll suddenly feel a sort of collapse & sliding in her womb, & incomprehensible longings. It's when the ova suddenly begin popping out like peas.' When that happened she would be at risk for once:

> ripe for anybody [...] Some rather small & very shiny man, probably syphilitic, & certainly a Jew. She'll crawl up to him, will Noel [...] and ask him to have her. And no doubt he will. I need hardly ask you to visualise it.

James's closeness with Rupert could not last much longer. Amongst the ugly tangle of the disbanded Neo-Pagans, it was Noel's 'decency' that he had fallen for. 'I'd simply forgotten the possibility,' he told his brother.

Bryn's arrival to tend to him in the New Forest at the crucial moment in the spring had also reignited Rupert's interest in Noel's sister. From Germany he thought longingly of their time there. 'I feel so full of gratitude & love towards you,' he wrote. '(You don't like things being put directly. Never mind. Poor Bryn. You must lump it.)' Brynhild was not encouraging. 'Do you know,' she marvelled to Hugh instead, 'that I wake up every morning very suddenly & wonder what it was – whether I was cold or wanted a biscuit or what & suddenly I remember – why! I love Hugh.' At Everleigh, Maynard grumbled to Duncan about having to watch Rupert 'making love' to Brynhild through the windows of the house, little knowing that she was only trying to fend him off. She and Rupert spent hours arguing over plans for a sailing trip later in the summer, at which Bryn had hoped Rupert would chaperone her and Hugh, until, exasperated and forced to explain herself, Bryn found herself making, as she later reported to Hugh, 'a comprehensive state-ment about my feelings and intentions such as would have amazed you to hear!'

Hugh diving

Rupert took Bryn's announcement about Hugh badly. He seemed most of all to fear losing people. He was, after all, the kind of person who had invented an ideal future in which his friends would all abandon their lives and keep him company in a second, carefree youth. It was only when a woman he admired seemed about to slip into someone else's arms that he would reach for her most decisively. Even in the early days, surrounded by attractive women who idolised him, he had set his sights on a schoolgirl who was almost always beyond his grasp, choosing a person he could not yet get to know and on whom he could therefore project whatever he desired. Rupert persisted in believing that women were innocents who risked a fall and whose weakness meant they couldn't be trusted. Marriage was the solution, though it came at the cost of their radiant girlishness. In Rupert's mind, despite his cruel, derisive and inconstant treatment of the women around him, his love had an incredible elevating power, which could make things clean and innocent and good. Bryn remarked wryly to her sisters after her ordeal with Rupert that his views had become 'dreadfully conventional'.

The sisters moved on: Daphne and Noel to Switzerland with Ursula and the Wala, Brynhild to Wales with Hugh. Rupert, left behind, wrote to Noel in despair. They were bound together by the history of their love, he told her, and he couldn't live without her. He planned to break things off definitively with Ka. Then he sent an appeal to Bryn, explaining that he had to see her again, as if it were his last chance. Then he spoke to Ka, who loved him (and whose fling with Henry Lamb proved short-lived), ending their affair and leaving her, nerves utterly shattered, in devastation.

'I think if you hadn't been as you are, I might have been sad last year & I wasn't,' Ka had written to Noel in the spring of 1912. She and Noel were never especially close but in some gossamer way they were united, if not against Rupert then certainly by him and in spite of him. Noel was always ready to defend Ka, disliking, in her straightforward way, Rupert's unjust accusations, and the two women sustained a cautious friendship. Their decency towards one another mitigated the pain of the group's apprenticeships in love. 'I think this is a sort of clumsy affection I'm trying to express,' Ka continued.

Noel responded to Rupert with a forthright rejection. She couldn't stand his fixation on their love – a thing wrenched out of shape by the pain they had caused each other – as the solution to his problems. She had already weathered the sadness of their relationship ending and he would simply have to face it too. She no longer loved him, if she ever had, and she certainly couldn't marry him. Though over the months of his recurring illness Noel had frequently worried that Rupert would harm himself, she refused to allow herself to be blackmailed.

Earlier that month, Adrian Stephen had proposed to Noel. She was increasingly friendly with his older sister and Virginia was hopeful that Noel could break Adrian out of his lethargy. Noel, however, had no interest in Adrian and viewed this latest infatuation with something approaching despair. It obliged her to turn him down, which was awkward and painful, and pushed her into 'silly *sorryness* & absurd *pity*'. Noel's rejection sent Adrian into a long depression, which Virginia continued to hope might be alleviated by a change of heart in Noel. On one occasion, Noel was furious to find herself ambushed at Virginia's country house when Adrian was invited without her knowledge. No doubt she was tired of the assumption that, if a man fell in love with her, she somehow became responsible for his happiness. All the men who loved Noel had slowly worn away at her confidence. She was nineteen years old; the responsibility seemed immense. 'I am too disgusting to go about at all, to be capable of hurting good people,' she wrote.

After a childhood that had seemed to deny them nothing, Noel's adolescence and her sisters' youths had been an induction into a reality that would require accommodations and compromises, a revelation that people came with expectations, that love could be painful and threatening. Noel was learning what mattered most to her and what she was willing to sacrifice for it. In Switzerland, she tried to distract herself by climbing glaciers with Daphne, the two sisters roped together for safety, and Rupert continued to write.

Once Brynhild's engagement became official, she felt in a strange mood. 'Time fairly rushes past,' she told James, '& people are flung out left & right. It seems very unlikely one will ever find them again.' There were also worries about what might happen after the wedding. Bryn had warned Hugh, she told Rupert, against expecting 'perfect conjugal harmony'. 'In these times when women make larger demands on life – larger perhaps than in the nature of things can be fully satisfied –' a colleague of Hugh's warned her, 'matrimonial voyages require increased skill.'

A constant flow of letters rushed back and forth between Bryn and her fiancé, strategising over the obstacles posed by the Wala, who objected to the speed of proceedings, which meant that she and Sydney were likely to miss the wedding. Bryn tried to reassure Hugh. 'You must'nt take Mother seriously,' she told him. 'Its never done'. In the end, Sydney, delighted with the news, saved the day by sending congratulations from Jamaica and urging Margaret to stay on an extra month so that she could attend the ceremony.

Rupert sank further. To Noel, he sent threats: 'I feel it very probable that I shall smash up altogether this autumn. I think a great deal & very eagerly of killing myself, if my present state goes on.' She suggested that they meet in the safe environs of Limpsfield and he agreed, though he bitterly rejected an invitation to The Champions, envisaging a conspiracy of heartless women waiting in the house to laugh at him.

Noel was back from Switzerland in mid September. For her, her relationship with Rupert had ended the previous year. Over the following months – over more than a year, in fact – whilst Rupert had swung high and low, from woman to woman, Noel's life had continued, her feelings had changed, her resolve had slowly hardened. He had left her for Ka, openly pursued her sister, ferociously insulted her family and bombarded her with threats and pleas. She met Rupert and confirmed her need for a separation.

Finally accepting that he couldn't change her mind, Rupert made plans to return to Germany. He declined an invitation to Bryn's wedding but wrote regretting the chances he thought they had missed, admitting his envy for Hugh, 'for marrying you, living with, & copulating with you, & having your beauty & fineness'. Brynhild's decision to take a firm step towards the future had only unmoored him further. He realised that her marriage was the end of something.

Rupert had a dream of Grantchester, a memory turned to mirage by nostalgia during his sickly days in Berlin in 1912. He dwelt in its cool breezes, beside its shaded river, within its careless optimism, polishing Neo-Paganism up for public consumption in his poem 'The Old Vicarage, Grantchester' (which he originally titled 'The Sentimental Exile'). The Oliviers had embodied the guilelessness of Neo-Paganism; healthy, forthright and yet mysterious, they inherited and revelled in the simple life of long summers at camp and on the river. Rupert's Neo-Paganism, increasingly defined (as much as it ever was) by opposition to the realities of a modern world that harried him, had a different, darker core. His ideal was designed to exclude and to limit, to reserve the best of England's hidden pockets of peace and beauty to those with the childish cleanliness to deserve it; people with 'straight eyes'. Ultimately his Neo-Pagan women were dumb creatures, sidelined from the intellectual exercise the men could manage, denied the right to contribute to the group-definition he undertook in letters and poems. Once the Neo-Pagans shed this untouched quality, they could only be cast out of their Eden, a prospect not worth living for. The Oliviers had moved far beyond this rotten creed, slipping into a mixed and welcoming London, forming friendships with people who were entirely alien to Rupert's ideals, maintaining for themselves only the aspects of Neo-Paganism that had always been theirs. The Neo-Pagans had, undoubtedly, had something precious, but the more Rupert tried to preserve it, the more he spoiled the memory.

Noel at camp

'I had a characteristic scrawl from Dorothy, saying that if our married life were as happy as theirs, we were to be congratulated. I don't want to be nasty but it is the most depressing thing I have heard yet.' Hugh to Bryn, August 1912

On 3 October, Brynhild and Hugh had a small wedding, though Noel and Bunny had planned 'feasts & riots'. It was in time for the Wala to attend but Sydney remained in Jamaica and so it was far from lavish, slightly subdued. Bryn had wanted to marry in a church but Hugh insisted on a register office. Ka was there, and James Strachey and Bunny, and Hugh's sister acted as witness. The bride, twenty-five years old to her groom's twenty-three, wore a rust-coloured tweed dress and looked as beautiful as ever. After the wedding, Bryn stood on the pavement and said goodbye to Margaret, wanting to express her affection for her 'dear, wee Wala' before she left for Jamaica, but holding back. Then the sisters separated into their independent lives. Margery to The Champions to rest in the peace and quiet of Limpsfield; Daphne to Cambridge to start her final year at Newnham; Noel into lodgings with Ethel Pye to begin her studies at the London School of Medicine for Women.

All day, Bryn had drawn strength from her sisters. After weeks of trouble over her wedding she had felt vulnerable, oddly emotional. Setting off on her honeymoon, Brynhild boarded the train, sat down, and looked at her new husband with a sinking feeling.

PART THREE

The Wretched Remains

(Or, Two Years Later)

I

New Year, 1915

On the first day of 1915 something made Daphne return to her diary. In the year she would turn twenty-six, she reread the entries she had written at twenty and twenty-one. Here and there she went over fading pencil in ink and even added tiny commentaries on her younger self's efforts. Parts of the diary seemed dull and uninteresting now and she marked them out, making it easier for some future reader to skip to the good bits. All of which begged the question, who was the diary for? Why did it suddenly require attention? Only a few years on, Daphne was treating her old journal as a historical document. Six months into a war that was supposed, according to received wisdom, to have ended the week before but had persisted with unnerving momentum, it was clear to Daphne that in reading those disappearing pencil entries, she was looking back on a lost time. At the very beginning of 1915, Daphne had realised that nothing was ever going to be the same again. The world of 1909 and 1910 had been irrevocably put aside.

In exchange, Daphne was conscious of a mysterious maturity in herself that promised an age of self-discovery, now that all the crowded rush of growing up seemed to be over. 'I have lately, I fancy, begun to see the shape, dimly, of the vast bulk of knowledge in this world,' she wrote. 'I have had inklings of the joy which is to be got from linking details to form a whole, and perceiving the interrelations of separate wholes.' Most of all, she was turning back to music, which had always inspired her 'with awe and an excited longing'. It wasn't easy to justify her absorption in it, and having two medical students (Noel and now Margery, too) in the house didn't help. Daphne had made her own tentative enquiries about 'making herself useful' in France but they had come to nothing. 'I'm not the least ashamed to be learning harmony instead of fainting in an operating room,' she wrote defensively to friends. Instead, she offered her services as a singer or violinist to the officers she knew who might be looking for entertainment for their troops, well aware of where her strengths lay. Noel poked fun at her dreamy sister's comparative, or perceived, lack of drive. She wrote to Rupert from a philosophy lecture in which the speaker had lost Daphne's attention, reporting that 'she only rouses herself for the phrase: "the point at which the body & spirit meet is *Action*". And shakes her head, because she can't bear action & is affraid that he will soon say: "The object of Life is Action". To which sentiment she is strongly opposed. Contemplation is preferable (& not to be classed as action).'

Daphne was writing her diary from the top of the family home on Marlborough Road in St John's Wood in London. 'We three aunts live there in at[t]ics, & work,' Noel told people. It wasn't King's House but it was capacious enough to hold the three sisters, their parents, Selma (the housekeeper) and her helpers, a young Barbadian man who had brought Loge over from Jamaica for them and decided to stay, eliciting much curiosity from the neighbours; another dog and a cat called Jeremy Joshua, beloved by all but Sydney and Loge. To Noel, it was a 'Paradise'. 'Living in the bosom of the family is after all the most reliable method,' she felt. They had a garden overcome with apple trees and grapes, and mulberries hung over the wall within picking distance. When Brynhild and Hugh brought Tony to visit the atmosphere was decidedly homely. Bryn's sisters doted on their nephew; Noel even found Sydney and Margaret's delight in their grandson touching. The baby made her 'dotty with pleasure & amusement' and Margery, who had been there when he was born, and had given him his first bath, updated people on his weight gains with unashamed pride. Almost from the first night of his life, Margery's nephew had seemed to her to be 'quite unique'. With her sisters to do the boasting for her, Brynhild, her beauty only enhanced by recent motherhood, maintained her usual cool silence, though she was rumoured to be heard talking aloud to the baby (and herself) when she thought no one was listening. She had horrified Vanessa Bell by deciding to do without a nurse to care for her son. '[T]hese neo-pagan mothers evidently mean to do the thing thoroughly,' Vanessa told her sister in dismay.

Daphne and Noel had spent Christmas at Lytton Strachey's picture-postcard thatched cottage in Wiltshire where he was working on his magnum opus, *Eminent Victorians*. Lytton had invited the sisters for James's sake, knowing him to be hopelessly in love with Noel. He was personally far more attracted by the company of Bunny and his friend

Frankie Birrell, his other guests, who were staying nearby. (All that could be said in Noel and Daphne's favour was that they had refrained from bringing Loge with them. Lytton had greeted his presence on a Scottish holiday with Noel, James and the Pophams in 1913 with horror. 'A DOG! – One of those dreadful vast ones, standing higher than a table – ugh [...] imagine my anguish,' he told Henry Lamb.)

The thin, bespectacled, thirty-four-year-old Lytton had once admired Noel for being 'incredibly firm of flesh, agreeably bouncing and cheerful', but in his own home the high spirits had proved something of a handful. The Oliviers could hardly claim to have been on their best behaviour. Though Lytton kept things suitably highbrow by reading aloud from his own work during their stay, by the time Christmas Day dawned, Daphne, admiring the great box hedge that guarded the house, suddenly found herself leaping from the road on to the welcoming mattress of springy branches. The others joined in, pelting themselves into the hedge and sliding down into the garden until a despairing Lytton emerged to tell them off. On top of the exhausting Olivier vitality ('You must have seen how happy we were,' Daphne wrote apologetically afterwards), Daphne had a tendency to hold forth in what Bunny described as 'tones of indignant emotional idealism', which was no doubt somewhat trying to someone used to sparring with Virginia Woolf.

How different this New Year was from the previous one in 1914, Bunny reflected later on the same day that Daphne unearthed her diary. Then, they had drunk spiced burgundy and rum by the fire in the woods and Tony had been nothing more than 'a thing to be thought about'. Now, 'Hugh is billeted at Roehampton & thousands of men are awake to ward off bombs from T[ony]'s unconscious head.' Noel had her own moments of contemplation. Putting together a photograph album in the autumn had left her in tears. 'We walk about so bitter,' she wrote ruefully to James Strachey, '& then creep home & moan over our diaries, our correspondence & our photographs.'

In that unforgiving January, when snow fell but the sky stayed black, and walking the pavements meant wading through wet mud, and the city was busy with Belgian refugees, Bryn's home provided a welcome haven. It was on Caroline Place, an offshoot of Mecklenburgh Square, conjoined to Brunswick Square, territory of Bells and Stephens, which linked to Hunter Street, where the hospital in which Noel and Margery were studying stood, red brick and vast, only a short walk from the palatial British Museum and its Prints and Drawings Department where Hugh worked. In other words, the couple had moved into the patchwork of not particularly respectable squares of Bloomsbury, which led into each other as if according to that unspoken internal logic that seemed somehow to govern the affairs of its inhabitants. Bryn's house was built on the estate belonging to Coram's Foundling Hospital. The buildings were substantial and from the outside appeared uniform, but within they divided and divided again, usually amongst friends.

The sisters' weeks were given shape by the Tuesday-evening meetings of the Caroline Club, so named for Bryn's address, at which Bunny, Frankie Birrell (a small, excitable and incorrigible gossip), Justin Brooke, James Strachey and Arthur Waley, a colleague of Hugh's, gathered to read Restoration dramas (or what Noel referred to as 'plays by lots of [...] English gentlemen (all dead) whose names I cant bring to mind'). For Bunny and the sisters it must have harked back to the energetic performances of their childhood, though it was Frankie, with his genius for casting, who ensured its success.

These were the homely equivalents to Adrian Stephen's poker parties around the corner at Brunswick Square, which Bunny, and sometimes Noel, frequented with enthusiasm; or to the parties held by Maynard Keynes on Gower Street, at the house where he let rooms to Gerald Shove and his new wife Fredegond, the artist Dora Carrington, and Katherine Mansfield and her lover John Middleton Murry; and where the Old Bedalian Paul Montague once stripped down and performed war dances he claimed to have learned on an anthropological expedition to New Caledonia.

Whilst the city's theatres were filled to bursting every night with men in uniform and the people to whom they were saying goodbye, the Caroline Club provided comfortable evenings of privacy, companionship and bawdy drama, where the cast and audience were nourished with cocoa, cake and the sweets invariably contributed by James. Tuesday evening had become a kind of open house at Caroline Place, as friends and neighbours such as Clive and Vanessa Bell, Maynard Keynes, Lytton Strachey and Gerald Shove dropped by to serve as audience. Some of Brynhild's talents found their best expression at 5 Caroline Place, where she had the budding family of her own that she had wanted. If Hugh's patient and beseeching love ever wore thin, the lively home kept her occupied and distracted.

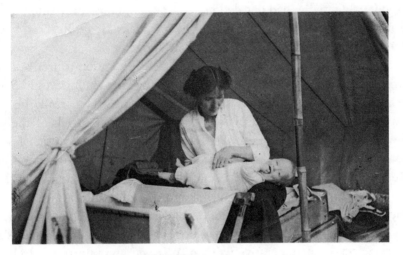

Brynhild and Tony at camp, 1914

2

Noel

In March 1915, Bryn broke the news to Noel that Rupert's brigade had left for the Dardanelles. Noel had asked him to write if he expected to go but evidently he had decided not to. He had, however, written to Ka from the ship on the day he sailed. 'Isn't it luck?' he wrote. 'I've never been so happy. 80 or 100 thousand of us altogether.'

Rupert had told Noel that war would be the solution to most of the world's problems ('perhaps [...] lock jaw or typhoid ending would make it all very complete & clear,' she retorted privately), but really he was expecting the war to end his own. After the emotional trials of the last few years, he was looking forward to the brutal simplification of war. Rupert had absorbed more of the militarism championed at schools like Rugby than his friends may previously have realised. Men like him had been conscripted before they were born, taught to dream of proving themselves on some thrilling battlefield one day. He looked forward to an experience of male fellowship uncomplicated by homosexual approaches or uncooperative women. War was an opportunity to blow away all the uncertainties and painful experiments they had waded through, to revert to old stories about what men were and what they did.

War opened up new fault lines in the Oliviers' friendship groups. Hugh and Bunny had clashed immediately, with Hugh welcoming the declaration in 1914 (which came while they camped in Cornwall) and Bunny attacking him for it. Hugh had enlisted in the Artists' Rifles, one of the volunteer battalions gathered under the London Regiment after the formation of the Territorial Force, and was stationed at Roehampton (before his division moved to the Tower of London). Rupert used his contacts to secure a commission in the Royal Naval Volunteer Reserve, Geoffrey Keynes joined the Royal Army Medical Corps (RAMC) and was soon sending Noel accounts of the atrocious conditions he found on the continent, Maitland Radford also enlisted in the medical service, and Ben

Keeling joined up. Within weeks, Godwin Baynes reported to Maitland that 'the whole country is trying to induce everybody else to enlist'. But within Bloomsbury, many greeted the war with horror. When Noel brought Rupert along to a Caroline Club meeting in late 1914 the tensions were awkwardly clear. The changes in Rupert were marked: instead of the open-shirted, sensitive poet of Grantchester they were confronted with a young man in uniform, his blond hair cropped short, recently returned from an abortive expedition to Antwerp, where he had witnessed long trains of refugees. As always it was Bryn who tried to ease the atmosphere, encouraging him to tell them about the expedition, but his hostility to the pacifists James and Frankie Birrell spoiled the evening.

Noel and Rupert had maintained a fitful correspondence since their relationship ended, working towards a tone of affection and kindness. When Rupert left for a tour of America (which he extended into the islands of the South Pacific) in 1913, they had a tender exchange in which their feelings for each other were clear again and finally sufficient as they were. Noel's response to pain was curiosity; now that she and Rupert were back on speaking terms she hoped that they could be honest with each other and analyse what it was that had happened between them. As usual she was quite prepared to put herself at fault and her experiences of love had made her pessimistic about finding an accommodation with the ways of the world. 'I'm even sorry about a few things,' she had told him. 'Sorry you got injured. Sorry I wasn't nicer. But chiefly sorry that the world's too difficult to fit in to.'

Yet Rupert was ready to admit that he had mistreated Noel and it pained him to know that she was berating herself. He had other women in his life, part of the alien circles in which he now moved as a sought-after poet-socialite: they were actresses, daughters of the Prime Minister, aristocrats; but he was still capable of caring for Noel. Her sense that the world had no place for her alarmed him. 'My dear, what's up?' he wrote. 'Have you a pain anywhere?'

Noel and Daphne spent Easter 1915 at The Champions. Noel was so immersed in Virginia Woolf's new novel, her debut, *The Voyage Out*, that Daphne seized it up in curiosity as soon as she had finished it. Tentative (and premature) news of Virginia's recovery from the breakdown that preceded publication was finally reaching them and Noel couldn't help but view the Stephen siblings with 'envious admiration'. She relinquished the novel happily, glad to have someone to talk it over with, while the last chapter 'soak[ed] in'.

In London, on Easter Sunday, the Dean of St Paul's gave a sermon that was presumably intended to give solace to the bereaved, and to strengthen the resolve of a nation at war, but was first interrupted by a man protesting the conflict who had to be escorted from the cathedral before the Dean could continue. When he did, he read a poem by Rupert. It began:

> If I should die, think only this of me:
> That there's some corner of a foreign field
> That is forever England.

The poem came from a series of sonnets that Rupert, by then part of the short-lived Georgian movement, had published in *New Numbers*, a poetry journal established shortly before the war. For the Dean, it spoke of a 'pure and elevated patriotism', which had 'never found a nobler expression'. In his verse, Rupert articulated an eerie kind of optimism in facing death and prepared for combat as a cleansing, perhaps simplifying, experience. The Dean's sermon was reported in *The Times* and Rupert became a nationally known figure, whose words encapsulated the enthusiasm that had sent Hugh and thousands of others away from home. For one student at Newnham, he expressed 'the mood and atmosphere [...] The strange exaltation, the burning patriotism, the enormous upsurge of the early days.' For the Oliviers, Rupert could hardly have seemed further away.

When Rupert had set sail, some of his men were worried that they wouldn't make it in time to see action. Rupert never did. In Egypt he was struck down with what seemed to be sunstroke and, though he insisted on remaining with his men when they were deployed towards Gallipoli, he was eventually persuaded to transfer to a French hospital ship on 22 April, less than two months after he left England. By then he had been diagnosed with acute blood poisoning, contracted from a mosquito bite. Word reached Eddie Marsh, Winston Churchill's secretary and the man who had secured Rupert's commission, of the severity of his illness. He cabled to Rugby. The Ranee's reply was swift, brief and desperate: 'If message of love can be sent send it please at once.' Later that day, Rupert died.

On 25 April, Eva Hubback was bracing herself to call on the sisters at Marlborough Road. But in the morning she heard that James had already told them the news. All she could do was ask Margery to give Noel her love.

The people who had known Rupert at his worst grieved for him. Dudley Ward, to whom Rupert had entrusted his last instructions, made a round of calls to let everyone know. James was shattered. Lytton regretted, particularly, that Rupert had not had the time to repair old friendships. Maynard Keynes, who had lost patience with him some time ago, found himself crying over the loss. In Cambridge, Jacques listened to the birds and realised that Rupert would never hear them again. Before his death Rupert had written a kind letter to Ka, which soothed her in the early days of her grief. Margery bore up bravely, tasked with supporting her two youngest sisters.

Noel cried for two days. Her friends and sisters did what they could to help, but Eva, knowing the sisters as she did, knew that they 'would want to be quiet & let alone'. Mary Newbery, Noel's close friend from Bedales, drew comfort from the fact that Noel 'had made up [her] mind not to have Rupert'. But this was little comfort for Noel. Though she had decided to let Rupert go, his death was, she felt, the final confirmation that she had lost the love of her life.

Rupert was buried in an olive grove on the island of Skyros. In England he was richly rewarded for dying: for dying unblemished by shells or trench mud, in a spot imbued with classical mythology, and just before the bad news began to arrive from Gallipoli, where his fellow officers went after they buried him. He was rewarded for dying before anyone was hardened to the news of young men's deaths, for dying so willingly and for writing, before he left, the kind of poems that could be read out in a cathedral on the day of the Resurrection. Rupert became a symbol of the great sacrifice Britain was going to have to make to win the war. His death turned him into a hero.

As shock reverberated around Rupert's friendship group, others recovered quickly enough to put the news to use. On 26 April, *The Times* published an obituary under the initials of Winston Churchill, First Lord of the Admiralty, who commended Rupert for his patriotic sacrifice, for stepping away from life with manly composure, and reminded others that nothing less was expected of them too:

> He expected to die: he was willing to die for the dear England whose beauty and majesty he knew: and he advanced towards the brink in perfect serenity, with absolute conviction of the rightness of his country's cause and a heart devoid of hate for fellow-men. [...] he was all that one would wish England's noblest sons to be in the days when no sacrifice but the most precious is acceptable, and the most precious is that which is most freely proffered.

The process of losing Rupert, which had begun for Noel and her sisters four years earlier, came to completion as the flawed man of whom they had unfiltered experience was transformed into a mythological hero before their eyes. Even their father, who had been impressed by Rupert, commiserated with his daughters in these terms. 'I think when he came into the Aegean sea', he wrote, 'the older gods were jealous of him and Artemis slew him.'

The issue of *New Numbers* in which Rupert's sonnets had appeared sold out almost immediately. In the press, Rupert was eulogised in ways that made him unrecognisable to Noel and her sisters. His friends quickly began to realise that the man they had known might be entirely obliterated by all the myth-making. Gwen Raverat protested that all of the tributes she had seen 'might have been written about King David, or Lord Byron [...] or any other young man that wrote verse and was good-looking [...] they never got the faintest feeling of his being a human being at all'. They complained that his memory had been hijacked for propaganda. The message of it all was: 'He did his duty. Will You do yours?'

Eddie Marsh, Rupert's literary executor and a man few of them knew well, took it upon himself to write a memoir of the poet. The text became an unsatisfying compromise between him and the Ranee, which only whitewashed Rupert and did nothing to challenge or humanise the glittering image of the soldier poet. Sybil Pye received a copy during a period when Noel (whose robust health soon seemed a thing of the past) was confined to bed. She wrote asking whether Noel was 'still too weak to hear a shock'. 'It's strange,' she said of the experience of reading the memoir, 'because familiar people & things seem rather far away, & there are new ones of course.' Sybil advised Noel to choose a 'strong moment to read it in; it's apt to pursue one into the next day & through the night in rather a domineering way'. Noel had not had too many strong moments at her disposal just then, and chose to put the moment off. Most hurtful when she did read it, Sybil suspected, was going to be the entire omission of Noel herself from the narrative. Marsh had grown close to Rupert only in the last years of his life and it seemed clear that Rupert had never confided in him about Noel. She might read the memoir and find that she was deemed of no importance whatsoever.

Sybil also sent Noel some recollections she had written herself, a text full of memories that belonged to all of them: long evenings in the garden at Grantchester, Rupert reciting poetry on the river. Reading it, Noel was confronted with someone else's impressions of some of the defining moments of her youth. Though she could not resist suggesting additions to Sybil's memoir, it must have been oddly disempowering to watch as these narratives were constructed. Throughout July 1915, plans for a memorial for Rupert were under debate. The Ranee had always disliked the Oliviers and left them out of everything, preferring to rely on Geoffrey Keynes, Eddie Marsh, Frances Cornford and Dudley Ward. Daphne and Margery were also anxious to read Marsh's manuscript but when they did the sisters were unimpressed. Encouraged by their diplomatic response, he asked to see their letters from Rupert, hoping to find something to include in the memoir. They sent nothing.

It was clear that in the story that was going to be told, for now, about Rupert there was no space for the Olivier sisters. The only way that they could regain any control was to keep their own version to themselves, preserving some of the truth about Rupert within their unshaking claim to privacy. Daphne had urged her sister to face up to the question of the memoir but she, too, was inclined to withdraw. 'Personally,' she wrote, 'I think the slighter and more obviously deficient as regards the "whole truth" Eddie's memoir is left the better.'

Rupert had always feared Noel's exposure to the corrupting influence of a society he identified with Bloomsbury. But he little understood that the Oliviers' wildness existed in spite of their familiarity with social mores, not because of protection from them, and that they combined it with a dignified adherence to their own principles, a set of tribal standards that paid little heed to prevailing ideas. So all four sisters stood by their friends whether they fought or not, and then revolted against the falsehoods central to the memorialising of Rupert, a man they had nevertheless esteemed and loved.

In the early days of the war, the person Noel had perhaps feared for most was Ferenc Békássy. Unlike his English friends, Feri had no choice but to present himself to his regiment in Hungary at the outbreak of war. Writing to Noel as he prepared to go to the Front, he had taken the opportunity to reflect on the years he had spent loving her and to mourn for the affair they had never had. Shying from his hopes before the war, Noel had tried to suggest a break from seeing each other, an idea Feri had persuasively dismissed as absurd, given their long friendship. The fact that she had held back no longer mattered: 'I can't tell you [...] all the feelings and impulses and ideas which you will always stand for (in that private world of mine which belongs to nobody else) but the best part of myself was made up of them for these three or four years.'

When Rupert heard the news of Feri's deployment from Noel, he was sobered by the idea of one day facing Feri, a fellow poet, Kingsman and friend, in battle. 'Dreadful if you lost all your lovers at once,' he replied. 'Ah, but you won't lose *all*.'

But the month after Rupert's death, Noel received Feri's last letter, forwarded by his sister. It was dated May 1915, five days before he left for the Front. After that, Eva Békássy wrote, 'he was always in the worst place and took part in the most terrible battles'. Ferenc had ridden to war on a horse bedecked with three red roses, a reference to the roses in the Békássy family crest, and had fallen in the Bukovina. Like Noel, he was twenty-two.

Noel could draw comfort from the fact that she had replied to his letters from the army, even though they contained declarations of love that she found hard to face, because the fact that she had done so had meant so much. In one letter, full of love and questions, she had written silent answers to his appeals in the margins and in the spaces between the lines:

> I wonder did you sometimes think it would be much more convenient if we had nothing to do with each other? *NO.* Or did you think it was really pleasant to think I was in love with you, *NO.* [...] There are such a lot of people who love/admire/adore (etc.) you, do you wish there were none, *NO.*

Noel and Maynard Keynes (who had befriended Feri at King's), perhaps the people in England who cared for him most, exchanged polite notes about the news, hardly different in tone from their usual correspondence. As mourning and commemoration became a national project, individual grief retreated into a very private affair. Comfort was in details, in absorbing as much as it was possible to know about somebody and their end. Letters, photos and mementos became precious. Noel had the treasured copy of John Donne's poetry which Rupert had given her and packets of letters from both men. She offered Maynard, who hadn't heard from Ferenc in some time, the chance to read the letter forwarded by Eva Békássy, a final scrap from him now that no more letters would arrive. But Noel wasn't prepared to take any risks with the talisman and instead copied the letter out by hand.

Days before leaving for the Front in May 1915, Ferenc had been thinking of her, thankful for the dreamlike lives they had been given before the war. 'I still thought a lot about how sad it was,' he wrote:

> that everything among you is changing, though I had felt it would never change, and how sad it is that I suppose things will never be quite the same again, and that the last four years were so splendid [...] I wonder whether everything that happened before the war will seem quite far-away afterwards?

Almost all of the most meaningful relationships of his life had been built in England: 'I long to see you, and all of you again. I often think of you. And we shall meet, Noel, shan't we, some day?'

Ferenc Békássy

As James explained to the tribunal he had to attend in March 1916, he was possessed of a 'deep conviction that war to-day involves evils that are far too terrible to counterbalance any good that could conceivably result from it'. With the passing of the Military Service Act in January 1916, conscription locked every man into a war career and each had to decide what course theirs would take. James and Lytton, as well as Bunny, Gerald Shove, Adrian Stephen and Vanessa Bell's lover, the painter Duncan Grant, decided to apply for an exemption from military service on the basis of a conscientious objection to the war. The government had made allowance for just such an objection – Britain was the only one of the major belligerents at that time to do so – but they had not gone so far as to clearly define what constituted an acceptable objection of conscience. Instead, they left local tribunals of respectable citizens to judge the 'character' and 'genuineness' of applicants for exemption on a case-by-case basis. By the time James's turn arrived, these tribunals had a reputation for fractious encounters, hostility to 'conchies' and harsh decisions.

The pressure on people like Bunny and James, who was fired from his job at *The Spectator* by his own cousin for his pacifism, blasted some friendships apart for ever. Clive Bell's 1915 pamphlet 'Peace at Once' was publicly burned by order of the Lord Mayor of London. 'I spew you out of my mouth,' a furious Godwin Baynes, who had joined the RAMC, wrote to Bunny. For the sisters, the atmosphere must have had echoes of the jingoistic days of the Boer War when their family had been on the wrong side of public opinion. This time, however, they were not able to present a united front. Margery and Daphne were committed pacifists and Noel, too, viewed the war with misery and disgust, remaining utterly loyal to the many friends who refused to enlist (yet remaining in touch, too, with old friends who had gone to the Front). Daphne had been one of the few people willing to challenge Rupert on his new-found militarism: 'I don't doubt that your patriotism is based on sincere feeling,' she wrote to him in 1914, 'but I suspect that you insist upon it largely in order to distinguish yourself from your philo-sophically minded friends.' (She was well aware that Rupert would consider women singularly unqualified to comment on military matters: 'silly woman,' she imagined Rupert thinking to himself, 'she'd much better put down her pen & take up knitting needles. What do girls want trying to express themselves? WE'll do that for them. Now suppose you knit me a Balaklava helmet.')

Brynhild, on the other hand, was more ambivalent. Her husband felt that it was imperative that he 'do his duty' and was prepared to risk his life in the endeavour. She, too, described herself now as 'a patriot and an anti-[G]erman'. '[B]eing simple minded,' she wrote, 'I can believe that there are things worth dying for and which one could never get in any other way.'

James made things difficult by applying for total exemption from service, feeling that it would be dishonourable for him to undertake non-combatant service (which involved duties like trench-digging), which would free another man up for action he refused to take. Total exemption was almost never granted. James was assigned non-combatant service and immediately appealed.

Noel couldn't face James's tribunal, yet (or because) she needed him. He had become one of the most important people in her life; sometimes he was all that kept her going. James, by now a twenty-eight-year-old with flattened-down hair, spectacles and a beard, possessor of a convalescent, sometimes almost masochistic, air, was the youngest of ten children in a precocious family, seven years younger than Lytton, whom he revered, and born when his father was seventy years old. The Strachey precocity sometimes manifested itself as severity and inflexibility; James could be catty and over-sensitive. For women who rejoiced in physical fitness and the 'simple' pleasures in life, the Oliviers were surprisingly impressed by Lytton and James's demonstrative cleverness. Young men like Bunny who had failed to elicit Olivier sympathies were amazed and affronted to find these 'ruthless Valkyries', as Bunny knew them, submitting to Strachey dictates and catering to their frailties (Bunny would never get over the sight of Noel, Daphne and Margery preparing Ovaltine for James). The Oliviers also admired the Strachey sisters, one of whom had taught Daphne at Newnham. Perhaps the Oliviers recognised and respected something in the Strachey siblings' unbending collective attitudes, which made little allowance for outsiders. At Lytton's cottage in Wiltshire, or at the family house in Belsize Park Gardens, the Oliviers fell in with the Stracheys' scholarly regime (with occasional rebellions as Christmas 1914 showed), just as James was dragooned into manhunts when on Olivier turf in Limpsfield. (Noel spent Christmas 1915 with James at the Woolfs' country home, Asheham, in Sussex. Virginia offered her 'unlimited fresh air – a bed in the orchard under the stars if you like'. Noel requested a bed inside, however, and further disappointed

Virginia's illusions by reading *War and Peace* while she was there.) But it was James's capacity for devotion, so clear in his long relationship with Noel, that must have gained the sisters' trust.

Bunny, Hugh (in a hat) and Frankie Birrell with
three Oliviers at camp in 1914

From the Oliviers' house on Marlborough Road, Noel watched raids over London. 'You must write & tell me at once, if you're alive,' she wrote frantically to James on one occasion. 'Otherwise I shall know they killed you.' In 1915 Zeppelins had opened up yet another front in the war, putting British civilians at risk for the first time. Bombers aimed for the interchange stations at Euston, King's Cross and St Pancras, so that incendiaries rained down on Bloomsbury, where Brynhild was, leaving her housekeeper 'almost dead with terror'. At Marlborough Road, as Selma fled to the kitchen and burst into tears during one raid in October, Noel, Daphne and Margery all craned out of windows and tried to keep their eyes on the tiny shape in the dark sky.

In Noel's hospital wounded men arrived, damaged and disfigured versions of the young bodies she had seen on the banks of sun-blessed rivers in her short youth before the war, and the women who worked there were expected, wherever possible, to patch them up and send them back out to fight again. She dreamed of ghosts, of infant corpses, of Rupert. The war would not end. In some parts of the city, the guns from France could be heard through the night. A distant clatter-clatter, windows trembling, and then silence, somehow worse than the noise. 'Is the lull when *they* go over the top?' a nurse in Woolwich asked herself. The war was at once far away, happening in another place, to which friends disappeared and sometimes re-emerged from, and close enough to dog all aspects of life in England.

The Battle of the Somme, begun in July 1916, and battering on for imperceptible gains, sent the number of losses to unimaginable heights. Casualty lists ran to pages and pages, they arrived in the newspaper at breakfast. The government cast about for more soldiers and settled on those previously deemed medically unfit. By the end of the year the rejection rate had dropped from 28.9 per cent to 6.5 per cent. Young officers, expected to lead their men in battle, were falling in droves. In every Cambridge college bar one, the level of losses exceeded the national average. At King's, Rupert and Feri's college, it was double. Ben Keeling, Margery's old Fabian comrade, was killed at the Somme, leaving behind a young family; Ferenc's brother was interned as an enemy alien on the Isle of Man; one of the Pease brothers was conversely interned near Berlin, trapped in Germany at the outbreak of war. Policemen arrived at James's door, looking for Lytton, and Bunny and Duncan were watched by plain-clothes officers while they worked at their non-combatant service. The physical labour was making Duncan ill; the uncertainty and hostility acting psychologically on Bunny, turning him angry and explosive.

At work, Noel could slip into the bustle and rush and general urgency of hospital life, grateful to have recourse to employment that truly occupied her, mentally and physically, for long hours at a time. At the Royal Free, the close, almost closed, community of the hospital had echoes of the Bedalian (and Olivier) clannishness. Not only was she learning in the hospital – one of the students who accompanied each doctor like satellites on their rounds, observing and assisting in surgery, attending lectures and the pathology lab – she was also responsible for her own group of patients, so that she was always answerable for the pressing needs of others. Many women who entered hospital work during the war found a kind of surrogate comfort in tending to soldiers when their own loved ones were out of reach and in danger, or lost already. Ethel Pye nursed on the Marne, Evelyn Radford and Ka Cox in Corsica. Noel was greatly touched by some of her patients: a woman who lost her baby during a traumatic childbirth, an emaciated patient with a 'huge & grey & dark red & hairy' husband whose adoration for her was palpable and heartbreaking, later a soldier whose wife she befriended but who she couldn't save. In feeling for their pain, she may also have found some small allowance for her own grief and mounting misery as the war went on. In the hospital, too, the self-possession Noel relied on in her personal life became a vital asset.

The Royal Free Hospital's medical school, where Noel was a student, was expanding, and a new building was dedicated to the treatment of army officers as soon as it opened. In 1914, the school authorities had tried to close the wards housing soldiers to students but there had been such an outcry that they had had to relent. For the great majority of people, war was a hugely disempowering experience. During her shifts, Noel was at least *doing something*, and she was doing it in a setting that allowed her to express her natural compassion for others without the unwanted consequences that had dogged some of her friendships.

The Royal Free was the only teaching hospital to have an all-female medical school and its doctors were acutely aware of the opportunity the war presented. Though women had been eligible to study and prac-tise medicine for longer than any of the Olivier sisters had been alive, the system was still set up to restrict the ambitions of female doctors, barring them from posts in most general hospitals, limiting them (until the war) to the treatment of women and young children. The staff and student body of the Royal Free was bursting with suffrage campaigners. In offering their services to treat injured servicemen, they were also intending to prove themselves capable of treating men and serving their country.

As early as September 1914, two graduates of the Royal Free, Louisa Garrett Anderson and Flora Murray, had taken a surgical unit of five doctors to France (the desperate French authorities had proved more receptive to help than the British). There they set up a small operating theatre in the improbable environs of the Ladies' Lavatory at the Hôtel Claridge in Paris. Elizabeth Garrett Anderson, the first female doctor ever to qualify in England, saw her uniformed daughter off. 'Twenty years younger,' she told the gathered well-wishers, 'I would have taken them myself.'

Other units followed and these medics provided the women at Noel's school with their own war heroes. The student magazine kept its readers closely up to date on the units, wishing them 'all every success in their splendid work and envy[ing] them with all our hearts!'

When her first full year of training at the hospital began in 1915, Noel had hoped desperately to join them, setting her heart on a forthcoming mission to Serbia. The Serbs had just repulsed an Austro-Hungarian invasion, leaving them with a typhus epidemic, nearly seventy thousand prisoners and huge numbers of wounded. Dr Dickinson Berry was an anaesthetist and her husband, Sir James Berry, a surgeon. They had raised funds for a self-sufficient unit with X-ray apparatus and beds for seventy-two patients, and were planning to set off in January. Though they liked Noel when they met her, her youth and apparent frailty raised concerns. (Noel may not have helped her case by assuring them that her physical weakness was only down to a Twelfth Night party thrown by Vanessa Bell the evening before.) Nevertheless, she was preparing for her departure when, to her intense disappointment, they ultimately decided that they couldn't risk taking any staff under the age of thirty, leaving the then twenty-two-year old Noel behind.

The student magazine comforted students like her, unable to join the adventure abroad, that

> the old prejudice against the appointment of medical women is breaking down in the face of necessity, and many appointments are now open, either to women or men. We are sure that medical women will realise that by filling these posts they will be giving valuable help to their country and releasing men for service at the front.

War is all about men. Yet war also leaves the world to women. The magazine at the Royal Free had a practice of listing any medical appointments advertised in the country that were open to women, so rare were employment opportunities for its graduates. In the summer of 1915, when a quarter of the medical profession had joined up, this practice was abandoned. 'It is quite impossible to keep the list up to date', the editors wrote, as 'at present practically every appointment is open.' Men like Godwin Baynes had been chomping at the bit to go: 'I feel I cannot stand out of this bloody business any longer,' he had told Maitland Radford before he went, 'I feel dirty.' Women like Noel could now fill their places at home.

On Endell Street, in London, a military hospital opened which was staffed entirely, from surgeons to stretcher-bearers, by women, some of whom had treated suffragettes recovering from force-feeding. Like the Royal Free, it was close to big interchange stations, well placed to receive men newly arriving from the trenches. They came caked in mud and requiring urgent attention, having received only hurried and superficial treatment on the way. The Endell Street doctors saved lives, welcomed the press, published research papers in *The Lancet*; drew attention to their abilities by doing their best work.

Noel was driving herself to breaking point at her hospital, but that was just how she wanted it. Her health repeatedly broke down over these years but she forged onwards with a new recklessness, at work and at play, with James as her reliable companion for the latter. In the winter of 1916, life was on hold, and had been for over two years, and would be for a period nobody was able to confirm. The cumulative toll of this suspended existence was showing. In the autumn, Noel's depression deepened. 'Everything seems to be more & more miserable,' she wrote, wondering how she had managed to keep going for so long. Her grief seemed to be catching up with her; memories had become more painful than comforting and she was afraid to enjoy herself or do anything that didn't keep her feelings safely suspended. Sydney wrote directly to James – who after his tribunal found work with the Quakers in the Emergency Committee for the Assistance of Germans, Austrians and Hungarians in Distress – to protest the late nights, reminding him that his daughter 'has to get up early and work hard' and seeking to implement a bedtime for her, but it was often James who stepped in and took Noel away when she most needed a break.

The relationship with James was perhaps Noel's first adult affair. To Bunny the two looked 'more like man & wife than any pair I know'. But though she depended on him emotionally, Noel could not love James as he did her. She hated that she could only offer what she described as a 'deadly slight affection' in return for his devotion and was well aware how much she asked of James by relying on him without ever committing to a relationship. 'You are more patient than the Moon,' she once told him. Yet whatever she said, Noel and James were widely understood to be a couple, and within their relationship, the witty and introverted James had found an outlet for his kindness. Noel, too, allowed herself to fuss over James's health, to admit that he was 'adorable and all beardy'. If Sydney ever lost track of his daughter, he assumed she was with James. Though in the past she had honourably tried to cast James off, he had now become an integral part of Noel's life.

Unfortunately another woman also noticed James's qualities. The severe and androgynous Alix Sargant-Florence was a friend of the Oliviers; a former Bedalian (the only girl to make the boys' First XI cricket team, no less) and Newnhamite, who was now living in Bloomsbury. Noel had admired her at school (partly for being 'overpoweringly sensible'), but when Alix set her sights on James, her admiration may have waned (as did Alix's impressive equanimity). Although James and Noel had done just that, Noel jealously told James in October 1915 that for him and Alix to stay alone together on holiday would be 'improper'. Yet she seemed unable or unwilling to put a stop to their relationship by claiming James solely for herself.

Noel had achieved some much needed distance from her family by moving into student accommodation in Mecklenburgh Square, moments from Bryn's house on Caroline Place. In London, her relations with her parents were under strain. The Wala disapproved of Noel's friendship with James; Sydney, preoccupied with the family's finances, was liable to bursts of irritability. The couple had left Jamaica in 1913, their last months marred by rioting in which Sydney – wading into a mob to assist some trapped policemen – had sustained a head injury that Bernard Shaw thought had affected his personality. He had since been Permanent Secretary to the Board of Agriculture but the President of the Board, Lord Selborne, had resigned in protest at Lloyd George's handling of the Home Rule negotiations in June and Sydney was expecting to lose his job. Noel had found herself subjected to scolding when she returned home at the wrong moment and was drawn into the quarrels between her parents.

Nor could Noel now escape Alix, who lived in the same housing on Mecklenburgh Square and was tenaciously pursuing James, despite his well-known love for Noel. James was drawn to both women (at first almost involuntarily by Alix's persistence) but over 1916 Alix grew alarmingly emaciated as James vacillated. Living together was awkward, as Noel duly reported to James:

> [Alix] appeared in the bath room this morning as I was taking a cold sponge & I braced myself for a conversation, but she was very smiling and quickly said only – could she come to tea with me tomorrow, and I said 'do'. Then she handed me a note which she had been going to leave if I'd been out, & when she'd gone I tore it open full of expectation: and it said simply might she come to tea with me tomorrow. So she's coming to tea with me tomorrow.

Noel felt that Alix was trapped in a vicious circle: the uncertainty over James's feelings making her ill and her illness making the uncertainty affect her more severely than it did Noel. Daphne was outraged in 1916 when she learned James had again taken Alix on holiday with him. She was afraid that Noel was being honourable and letting Alix gain the upper hand, letting someone go, as she had done with Rupert, because her pride didn't allow her to articulate her feelings.

Noel did her best to sound disinterested to James – 'it isnt very jolly being a spectator' – but the fact was that Noel was more invested than she admitted. When James and Alix were together, she felt vicious. Of course she would have to address her letters to James to Alix's house, where he was staying, she had written that summer, 'or will it spoil her week-end to see my writing at the breakfast table?' Noel had spent months looking after everybody but herself, able to take refuge only in short bursts of illness. Though James insisted he still loved her, the prospect of losing him made her lash out.

Daphne came to visit Noel in London. She could feel it when they had gone too long without seeing each other, and the two drew back together like homing pigeons. In a way, it was easier for Noel to confide in Daphne than in James because Daphne didn't panic or overreact to hear of her misery, whereas when she told James how bad she was feeling, his reaction ('Please not be wretched [sic] or I shall come back and talk to you,' he telegraphed from his holiday with Alix) then plunged her into guilt for worrying him. From long training and old jealousies, siblings will never offer an excess of anything, particularly sympathy: whole lives have been spent monitoring the even distribution of everything from gifts to attention. The sisters could see through one another, and that could lead to callousness, but it also led to insight and the ability to confide in one another safely.

In November the two of them went to stay in a cottage Ka had leased in Aldbourne, near Marlborough. It was freezing cold but the house was equipped with blankets and hot-water bottles and space for Noel to invite James. He took his time in coming and Noel seemed to slip further into despair. She sent him reckless messages, trying to imagine a life that she could enjoy living. As she approached her twenty-fourth birthday, the world already seemed 'definitely & quite obviously spoilt' – 'and what is the point of putting up with the wretched remains?'

'Its very difficult to decide whether or not to die,' she told him, trying to imagine a way to live in the world:

It would be pretty easy & quite pleasant to sink into a steady despair – you know – & drop any attempt at interest in what happened. Or 1 night go about collecting all the relics that could be found & pass the time sniveling & mooning over them. And another way of not living would be to chuck even all that & simply keep the Nose to the Grindstone. Probably what I'd like best would be if you came too & we both – possibly at the end of some pilgrimage – committed suicide; I'll never have the energy to do it alone I see.

3

Daphne

Despite everything, it was not Noel who broke down at Rupert's death in April 1915. It was Daphne, unable to bear her younger sister's suffering, grieving for Noel's grief as much as for their collective loss, who collapsed. Reacting, perhaps, to her disempowered position as a witness to grief, unable to offer any immediate comfort, Daphne's inner resources failed her. She stopped eating and sleeping and yet was possessed with restlessness. As these deprivations took their toll she seemed to lose touch with her surroundings, becoming frighteningly manic and feverish, until she finally lapsed into incoherence. To her father she seemed 'out of her wits'.

Daphne's delirium was so severe that she needed constant attention. On the advice of doctors, her family committed her in May to the care of Hayes Park, a nursing home for the clients of Maurice Craig, one of the pre-eminent psychiatrists in the country, who had treated Rupert in 1912. There she was dosed with a sedative, probably the foul-smelling paraldehyde, and went to sleep. She would be lulled at Hayes Park for an entire summer.

In the weeks before her collapse, Sydney had worried about Daphne's absorption in her music, which seemed to negatively affect her mood and behaviour towards the family. But Daphne had also suffered from disappointments of which her father was probably unaware. At the beginning of 1915, aged twenty-five, Daphne suspected that, rather late in life, in her opinion, she was finally discovering love. Bunny Garnett had found his own way into Bloomsbury and it had changed him. Though he had not entirely shed the markings of his wild and isolated childhood – Lytton remarked on his heavy, pause-riddled speech with exasperation – he had a knack for friendship, a skill no doubt forced upon him as an only child surrounded by close-knit groups of siblings, and was developing a reputation as an eager lothario. At Christmas in 1914, Lytton had managed to subdue his guests by reading aloud from his own work beside a roaring fire, leaving Daphne and Noel in suitably impressed awe of their host. This private reading of Lytton's unpublishable *Ermyntrude and Esmeralda*, a sexual satire in which two teenage girls exchange any information they are able to glean about how babies are made, inspired Bunny, through its implicit critique of social hypocrisy, to a life of sexual emancipation and experimentation.

As the Olivier sisters observed his new attractiveness to both sexes with surprise, Daphne began to consider their old tree-climbing companion in a new light. At Lytton's house at Christmas Bunny was half sure that he was in love with Daphne. By January he realised his better self loved her; by February, on a weekend away with Gerald Shove and Bryn, he spent much of the time in Daphne's bed, kissing her and admiring her body. The freedoms of their old friendships had translated easily to the sexual frisson of London society. Keeping Daphne and Noel company while they bathed together one evening, Bunny felt 'jolly sitting with them naked & unashamed'.

War brings out the sex in people. At least, in wartime Britain there were certainly suspicions. The declaration in August 1914 was said to have triggered a wave of hysteria amongst women and they were held to be similarly agitated by the sight of men in uniform. This put gallant young soldiers at risk. The papers periodically condemned the women who spread venereal disease through the ranks (for who else could be to blame?) and special patrols took to the London parks in the evenings to disentangle couples. But amongst the inhabitants of Bloomsbury there had long been an element of sexual frankness unthinkable at Grantchester. This served Noel well at the hospital, where questions of 'delicacy' could still stand in the way of thorough training for women. She irreverently dubbed her gynaecology department the 'Cuntology post' and was amused to find her classmates reluctant to make a matching male model for the 'wool & pink flannel' female genitals she and a friend had fashioned for their class's demonstrations. When, in James's rooms, condoms fell from Noel's bag in front of Bunny and Frankie Birrell, she merely laughed, blushing slightly.

But it was still a rarefied state of liberation and outsiders were quick to judge women like Noel and Daphne. When D. H. Lawrence – one of Bunny's father's mentees – took it upon himself to warn Bunny against the 'unclean' people he was associating with it was not just people like Frankie Birrell, Duncan Grant and Maynard Keynes (i.e. homosexuals) that he considered a threat but Daphne and her sisters too. 'The Oliviers and such girls are wrong,' he told him. Daphne was two and a half years older than Bunny but he was, in fact, easily the more experienced of the two. It seems clear that Bunny's attentions raised her hopes for something more substantial between them: for her first proper love affair. But for Bunny there were just too many beautiful and interesting people in the world. After the sight of Daphne's body, he told his diary that he 'never want[ed] to see a man again [or] speak to one' but he was already poised at the beginning of a love affair with the drowsily beautiful Duncan Grant, as well as spending weekends with Godwin Baynes's sister and experimenting with a prostitute. Duncan became one of several people trying to work out where they stood. Bunny's 'kindness', his ability to pay sincere attention to people, to love them, was, Duncan warned him, 'very dangerous for poor people like me'. Daphne joined the ranks of the people he disappointed and hurt.

Bunny and Daphne in 1914

Hayes Park was a country mansion not far from London, with a porticoed entrance and gardens stretching over 60 acres. Maurice Craig may have been recommended to the family by Vanessa Bell, who had been treated by him during her own breakdown and had already recommended him for the care of her sister, whom Craig had been treating since Virginia's suicide attempt in 1913, and who exhibited similar symptoms to Daphne.

Earlier in his career, Craig had worked at Bethlem Royal Hospital (popularly known as Bedlam) and now ran a large and lucrative Harley Street practice, which catered to a number of Bloomsbury residents. He was also the author of the standard textbook of the time, *Psychological Medicine*. In other words, he was a true establishment figure. He also had the conservative social views of one.

It was relatively new for specialists in mental disorder to command such respect. But the neglect and horror of the Victorian asylum was fading, at least for the wealthy, and a professionalised elite was extending its influence. The male medical profession's view of women's mental health was inseparable from, and dictated by, their ideas about women's limited capabilities and inherent instability. In the last decades of the nineteenth century, a generation of psychiatrists came to prominence, headed by the incredibly influential Henry Maudsley, who issued terrifying warnings against the over-education of girls. Like Sydney Olivier and the friends of his youth, they had been inspired by Darwin's theories, but in their hands these theories were put to quite different uses. They believed that women were, biologically speaking, the weaker sex and their frailty made them more susceptible to madness. In the years that the Wala's generation attempted to clamber across the gender divides that stood between them and work and travel and education, the expansion of the psychiatric profession seemed perfectly timed to meet them, as doctors found themselves able to confirm not only that these same gender divisions of labour and opportunity were rooted in biological fact but that they were also, in most cases, medically necessary.

It became the case, then, that all women, whether mentally ill or not, ultimately came under the authority of men such as Henry Maudsley and later Maurice Craig. The medical establishment widened its sphere of influence until it conceived and patrolled what was normal behaviour, and what was to be allowed to, and from, women. Men decided how a sane woman looked, sounded and behaved. Noel was in an unusual position, at once of and subject to the medical profession. It was slowly becoming possible for women to be treated by women, but female doctors' need to be accepted into the profession also, to some extent, secured their complicity. Like the women running Newnham College, female doctors hoped to revolutionise the status quo but found that they first had to insinuate themselves into it, and tread extremely carefully to gain the foothold from which further change might be possible. When her sister fell sick, the respected experts Noel and her family turned to were all men.

These doctors believed that everyone had a finite supply of nervous energy – much easier to expend than to replenish – that should be carefully guarded; in women's cases the bulk of it should be diverted to the growth, maintenance and exercise of the reproductive organs. Female internal energy thus directed, there was far less available for mental processes. Since the 1880s, English doctors had relied on the 'rest cure' developed by the American doctor Silas Weir Mitchell to treat nervous or hysterical women. (Though anyone's mental energy could become dangerously depleted: Rupert had been submitted to a very similar regime during his breakdown.) The cure was based on a few simple principles: rest, distance from familiar surroundings or people, and the consumption of vast amounts of food. Good health was associated with quiet and weight gain. Based on the assumption that over-stimulation had caused the collapse in the first place, a rest cure was essentially designed to sedate and immobilise the patient. If her psyche wouldn't allow her to rest, a team of doctors and nurses would force her to.

Complete rest meant the removal of anything that usually stimulated or intellectually sustained the patient: writing in Virginia's case and music in Daphne's. Over the course of Craig's treatment for her latest breakdown, Virginia Woolf had put on three stone. The average was about three and a half. Leonard Woolf, recently married and desperately concerned for his seriously ill wife, consulted five of the most eminent British doctors, including Craig, over her breakdown. They universally disappointed him. Their insight and knowledge, he felt, 'amounted to practically nothing'.

Daphne would certainly have agreed. By the end of her first month at Hayes Park, she began to take notice of her surroundings and make coherent remarks. After her delirium passed, she suffered through her time there with a strong sense of grievance and asked Margery to help arrange her release. She didn't want to eat to excess – she complained of being force-fed – or to be parted from her friends or her music.

Daphne had always had a sensitive and in some ways conflicted nature, which she acknowledged and embraced. She was peculiarly susceptible to impressions and sensations; entranced by the multi-sensory experience of Jamaica, absorbed in the romantic aspect of Neo-Paganism. All this no doubt fuelled the creativity expressed in her music and the letters admired by her friends. Daphne was a deeply self-reflective person, always questioning, and familiar with a sense of having disordered thoughts and feelings. 'One's mind seems to be in layers each layer a mood, and each inconsistent and incompatible with the other,' she once elaborated to Margery. In the spring of 1915, she had simply reached a point, in generally emotional circumstances, when everything meant too much to her to be bearable.

Trusting in the expertise of the doctors, Sydney explained to his daughter that the misery and strain of the weeks around Rupert's death had 'supersaturat[ed] your inner sensibilities with feeling' and that her nervous system had 'to be recuperated by sleep and nourishment, which can only do their work when the brain is not stimulated by outside irritants such as conversation and attention to "business"'.

Beneath the obsession with music, the bereavement and her retreat into mania, one further thing had given Daphne's family cause for concern. Increasingly, she had been seeking something beyond the material world. Music, and the transcendental way she experienced it, went some way to filling that need. In the aftermath of Rupert's death, however, Daphne had come to believe that she had been in contact with the spirit world.

Daphne was very far from alone in refusing to believe that the dead had passed entirely beyond reach. The war saw a huge surge of interest in mediums, séances and various other means of contacting the spiritual world. Stories of supernatural phenomena in the trenches, where men were surrounded by death, helped to legitimise those generated at home. Several high-profile figures, most famously Arthur Conan Doyle but also the physicist Oliver Lodge, whose sons had been to Bedales, threw their considerable reputations behind the burgeoning field.

Daphne's own spiritualist experiences were connected with her friend Helen Verrall. Helen was several years older than Daphne and had got to know her and Margery at Newnham, where Helen's mother was a lecturer. During her college years, Daphne had put on tea parties for Helen in her rooms and the two had skied together in Switzerland. Helen was, like her mother, a medium.

Almost thirty years before Daphne lived there, Cambridge had been the birthplace of the Society for Psychical Research, a body that was founded to investigate paranormal phenomena in a rigorously scientific manner. It had a close connection with Newnham. The college's founder, Henry Sidgwick, was its first president and his wife Eleanor, also involved in the Society, was a Principal of Newnham. Helen and her mother could achieve certain states in which they received messages from spirits, who communicated through them while they wrote without conscious thought; a process known as automatic writing. In 1915 Helen was an assistant researcher for the Society and reported on possible sightings of an angel at Mons, which was said to have intervened to protect British soldiers.

As an area of enquiry, the spiritual world was by no means excluded from the mainstream. For many intellectuals, psychical research simply represented the next frontier in scientific discovery and for many ordinary bereaved people, the prospect of reaching out, past casualty lists and trenches and death itself, into invisible worlds in which their loved ones waited for them in safety was irresistible. For his part, Sydney was prepared to meet his daughter someway along the same line of thought. Though he had rejected organised religion early on, he had his own sense of the spiritual, and allowed that 'innumerable people who did not *perceive* these [phenomena] before, do under the stress of the losses of this war, perceive them'.

Daphne's thinking was undoubtedly confused and distressed, yet she rejected any attempts to dissuade her of her spiritual experiences. Instead, she cast about for people with the 'intuition' to help her understand them. During her stay at Hayes Park she was convinced that Margery, Noel and James were the only ones she could trust with her new-found knowledge. 'I have lived with whispers so long,' she told her oldest sister, in a letter she asked her to keep from their father, '& I have a strong sense that secrets of the spheres have been confided to me in trust not to be flung wantonly at the heads of people who stare stony eyed & say "But as a matter of fact". That's what "lunacy" amounts to my dear!'

Margery visited and was the recipient of her sister's bitterest complaints about her treatment. She mediated between her sister and her parents, able, from her position in the family, to identify with both camps. Daphne believed she had been unjustly incarcerated; punished because her ideas did not properly align with sanity as it was generally understood. Noel was grateful to have Margery to share the burden of care and worry. 'Mudie is magnificent,' she told James, 'she always is when everyone else has given up.'

By mid August the Wala was allowed by the staff to take tea with Daphne and walk about in the Hayes Park gardens with her, though she still prevaricated about sending her magazines, presumably warned not to allow her anything so interesting. She told Noel with relief that there had been 'nothing curious in anything [Daphne] said'. In September, Daphne was released.

The family had been carefully instructed on how to manage Daphne's re-entry to society. The isolation at Hayes Park was just the beginning of a long process of keeping her nerves in check. Sydney explained that Daphne must expect to live 'a quiet and <u>regular</u> life' for the time being. He wanted her to have a seaside holiday, where, he believed, 'The sun and the air and the sea [would be] a direct source of spiritual invigoration which can contribute to building up again the tissue of your nervous equilibrium.'

The doctor at Hayes Park had specifically warned against the company of 'too many discussive and exciting people', which seemed to put Noel and Brynhild's camp on the canal in Wiltshire with Tony, Paul Montague, Justin Brooke and others out of the question. Daphne was, however, allowed to join her sisters and nephew when they went on to holiday in Lyme Regis.

The world that Daphne rejoined was hardly a restful place. British people were under attack from the sky, poison gas had arrived on the Front and a German submarine had purposefully targeted the *Lusitania* that spring, causing the deaths of 1,191 passengers. There were rumours of an invasion and pressure was mounting on those who had so far failed to enlist. All the feelings that Daphne was certainly supposed to avoid were running high across the country.

Adulthood had altered the sisters' relationships of care and responsibility. Bryn had her son, first and foremost. For the others, the natural order of things seemed to have been upturned. Noel's professional vocation gave her a forward motion and a new authority in the family, as a point of contact with the severe edifice of the medical profession. Noel and Daphne had come to fall on opposite sides of the medical establishment. Only a few years before, Daphne's apparently sudden emergence into the grown-up world had unnerved and humbled Noel. But now Daphne seemed to be treading water, kept in limbo by the doctors with whom Noel had a special access and understanding.

Forbidden any stimulation, Daphne foresaw a period of aimless wandering for herself. Over the summer she was 'shrinking from the inevitable prospect of [...] "taking one's bag & walking" all the Autumn', but, as she suspected, that was exactly how she spent the months after her release. The stay in Hayes Park knocked her confidence badly. She was afraid that she had lost the powers of normal social interaction and was convinced that she had 'unlearned' the art of letter-writing, on which she would have to rely to reach out to her friends. To Ethel Pye she wrote letters that were both 'spooky' and 'uncharitable to the medical profession' (as Ethel reported to Noel) but her friends, like Sydney, were not overly alarmed by her interest in spiritualism, rather with the manner and context in which she expressed them. 'She'll learn to put the right amount of brake on her interest in the Spook World [...] which is of course quite a legitimate subject but this world <u>will</u> have to have its due,' Ethel wrote, not to Daphne but to Noel, who seemed generally to be regarded as the most reasonable sister to appeal to.

Brynhild and Tony in Lyme Regis

In the autumn of 1915, Daphne found a short refuge at Garsington Manor, Ottoline Morrell's country house near Oxford. Ottoline was a society hostess with an artistic bent; a tall lean woman with masses of red hair and an equally distinctive nose and chin. She had a genius for introducing people (though she had once perplexed James by thrusting Noel straight into the arms of Ramsay MacDonald at a party, perhaps falling back on the Olivier family's political reputation) and a tantalising mix of Bloomsbury artists, Cambridge academics and influential politicians regularly gathered at the soirées she held at her London house on Bedford Square.

Garsington was an Elizabethan manor house, which Ottoline had transformed with a colour scheme of bright red, sea-green and grey paint on the dark oak panelling and an excess of soft furnishings, incense and pot-pourri. Over the vibrant walls hung a collection of paintings by her friends, lovers and acquaintances, among them Duncan Grant, Augustus John and Henry Lamb. The house was set in 200 acres of gardens and farmland; a great ilex tree presided over the lawn. Ottoline and her family had moved there in May (her husband, Philip, was an MP who had sacrificed his career to protest Britain's entrance to the war) and quickly established the house as a retreat for friends needing a respite from London. First among them was D. H. Lawrence, who enjoyed it until Bloomsbury began to arrive.

Daphne visited with Alix and though one of the other guests that weekend was Bunny, there were plenty of other visitors to distract her: Duncan Grant was there, Bertrand Russell (who seemed to be living above the stables) and the usual household of Ottoline's family, staff and wards, plus an elderly peacock and a flock of pug dogs (chief of whom was named Socrates). Alix and Daphne arrived on Sunday afternoon and Daphne was immediately conscripted into a vigorous game of football. For those brave enough, there was a rectangular fishpond for swimming in, as well as the seemingly endless grounds to explore. The company was erudite and interesting but Daphne, who had turned twenty-six just before her visit, found herself getting very sleepy, she told Noel, 'unaccustomed as I am to conversation – but its nice'.

As the tribunals got underway in 1916, many of the Bloomsbury pacifists, directed to find 'work of national importance', sought agricultural employment. The Garsington farm was thereafter manned by artists, writers and academics who adapted to manual labour with varying degrees of failure. Meanwhile, Vanessa Bell (who absorbed Bunny rather than risk losing Duncan) rented a farmhouse called Charleston in Sussex, not far from Asheham, for her ménage à trois, finding Bunny and Duncan work with a local farmer.

Daphne wanted to be occupied. In the summer of 1916 she stayed with Eva Hubback and her children (two inquisitive daughters and a baby son), admiring Eva's decision to return to Cambridge to teach economics. 'I feel it's a splendid thing for the Cause,' Daphne told Noel, 'as well as for Eva, if she can be Teacher of Economics with three children.' For herself, though, she was worried. She regretted her growing distance from intellectual endeavour and feared that a kind of inertia, which would be hard to shake off, had settled over her mind. Casting about for work that she would be allowed, and work that would be useful, she settled on seeking out her own manual labour. She had to do something. Attending a meeting on 'The Land' out of interest, she found herself accosted by 'a couple of "patriotic" females who asked if I were "doing my bit". They are devils.'

With very little good news to report from the Front in the summer that the slaughter reached a height on the Somme, the papers spent 1916 expressing pleased surprise at all the things women had turned out to be able to do. Women were slowly drafted in to fill empty roles as, amongst other things, messengers, munitions workers, telegraph girls, tram conductors, taxi drivers and lamplighters. Attitudes, it seemed, would have little choice but to reform themselves. 'It is enough to make any feminist dance with rage,' Rebecca West wrote in the *Daily Chronicle*, 'to hear the continual exclamations of surprise at the fact that women can do practically everything.' (Yet, 'Are women capable of driving at night?' the *Daily Telegraph* pondered in 1917.)

Sydney recommended that Daphne undertake some training in 'gardening and minor agriculture'. Half of all food consumed in Britain in 1914 was imported and the German policy of unrestricted submarine warfare meant that the country now had to rely on what it could produce at home, and produce at a time of reduced manpower. With Lord Selborne, Sydney had been promoting the deployment of women to fill gaps in agriculture and trying to persuade the government and farmers – two bodies equally alarmed by the prospect – to accept the necessity of doing so. In the interim, the two men were forced to work through the numerous local volunteer bodies that had sprung up in response to the obvious shortages in agricultural manpower. Personal contacts also proved fruitful: Sydney's niece, Edith Olivier, was a member of the Wiltshire County Agricultural Committee who, aided by Sydney, was influential in setting up the Women's Land Army.

For a while, Vanessa Bell took in Amber Blanco White's two daughters whilst Amber worked in the Ministry of Munitions. Vanessa struggled to educate the girls alongside her own sons, and in January 1917, Virginia, assuming, perhaps, that unmarried women were sexually inactive and generally unoccupied, recommended bringing in 'one of our enlightened virgins, an Olivier say, (Daphne might do) [...] and mak[ing] her teach everything'. But Daphne (possibly aided by Edith Olivier) had by then found work on a dairy farm in Pewsey in Wiltshire, helping to manage a houseful of Land Girls.

The Wala rose to the task with a long letter of housekeeping advice ('Most girls like suet puddings, made with figs – or dates or ginger – or plain to eat with treacle or Jam') and sent Daphne a hot-water bottle to cope with the cold. Dairy work was hard, dirty labour, involving painfully early mornings and long days in freezing weather. There was a cheerful, communal feel to the dairy farm and perhaps, for Daphne, the novelty of a lifestyle completely alien to a governor's daughter. She enjoyed herself. The 'girls' were high-spirited and their clowning and enthusiasm lifted Daphne too, so much so that she urged Noel to visit and recuperate with her. Daphne enjoyed listening to her charges' romantic intrigues with something approaching a maternal air. 'They started by taking a great interest in the men labourers,' she told Noel:

> and I got quite bewildered trying to distinguish between Morris and Walter and Arthur and Isaac and "Shaver" who'd said or done this, that or the other. But most of them seem to have proposed to Alice – or said they would do so if they weren't married.

4

Margery

In February 1917, news arrived that Eva Hubback's husband Bill, one of the originators of the Basel Pact, had been killed on the Somme. Eva had been close to all four of the Olivier sisters for a decade; Brynhild had designed her engagement ring. Margaret asked Margery to make haste to Cambridge to be with her. It was, perhaps, yet more evidence of the Wala's state of denial when it came to her eldest child.

As Daphne edged towards wellness, Margery began to slip into agitation and fantasy. Even as Daphne had improved in Lyme Regis in 1915, Noel had noted with foreboding that Margery grew 'queerer & queerer'. She was restless and wanted to get back to London and 'exercise'. While Noel was forging ahead in the wards, Margery was back to lecture halls and exams. Having decided quite suddenly on medicine in 1914, Margery was, for the first time in her life, following where her youngest sister led. From being the bright academic of the family, she now struggled with her subjects and needed coaching from Noel in Noel's limited spare time. When she did return to London in 1915, she arrived to the news that she had failed her physics and biology exams. For a time she talked about dropping out of the university altogether and finding somewhere else to study.

Margery had a busy life in London and, as usual, plenty of friends. She spent weekends away with Ka Cox, Maynard Keynes, Bunny, Vanessa Bell and James's own eccentric sister Marjorie; she dined at Ottoline Morrell's house and the Woolfs'. She got on with her fellow students, who got used to her peculiarities and identified in her a romantic nature and the big-hearted selflessness of a good friend. She vacillated towards and away from people, ready with affection but all too often unsure of her welcome. Her genuine desire to be useful, so important to the New Woman, had driven her to campaign for Fabianism and suffrage, to work as an assistant to a doctor researching tuberculosis and now to study medicine; but she also had a far less practical side, given to make-believe. 'All the incidents of her life are probably surrounded with a halo of romance,' one of her friends observed.

For Bunny, ever inclined to romanticising, there was an elemental untamedness to Margery. None of the sisters, nor Bunny, had outgrown the tree-climbing of their childhood and when all of them were in Limpsfield together they continued to take to a line of beech trees to clamber from one to the other; the sisters shedding skirts to test old skills and demonstrate long-held prowess. It was in observing Margery's particular recklessness in this pursuit – something he must have identi-fied as subtly distinct from the sisters' general physical courage – that Bunny felt he witnessed 'the real Margery, a creature akin to the gentle and yet untamed satyrs and fauns, which people the woods in seventeenth-century pastorals'.

Margery's eccentricity was a well-established fact, as inherent to the Oliviers' knowledge of her as the gap between her two front teeth, and its familiarity obscured the slow changes in its make-up. While Sydney, Margaret and their daughters focused on the obvious disturbance of Daphne's sudden breakdown, amongst Margery's friends, others began to notice a new level of strangeness.

Margery's friends worried about her single status. She was now facing her thirtieth birthday and had so far failed to secure any of the trappings (husband and children) considered the most fulfilling (if not justifying) for women. Even the usually enlightened James had met Margery's decision to study medicine with something akin to outrage. 'I do feel very strongly that the real business of you (and for that matter of your family) is, in the sentimental old phrase, to _live_. By which I mean, among other things, to fall in love with people, to go to bed with them, and, damn it all, to have children,' he had counselled at the time, in a letter that he ultimately submitted to Brynhild, suddenly baulking at the thought of Margery's possible reaction. For in the letter he committed the cardinal sin of comparing Margery's success (or lack thereof) to Brynhild's: 'If you want to do something useful, to do the world a service, why have you let Bryn get ahead of you with T[ony]?' The Oliviers' nobility fitted them for one form of service: the production of fine children for the nation. 'There's genius in all the Oliviers and they should be recreating.'

At the beginning of 1916, Brynhild was entering her second trimester of a second pregnancy and Margery's mental equilibrium seemed to be shuddering. She went through periodic cycles of hope and despair in love, which demonstrated the extent to which she had internalised these assumptions about womanhood. Her disappointments often seemed inextricable from her sisters' love lives. Beside Hugh, she had been convinced that Adrian Stephen – once Noel's suitor – had been in love with her, and resented him and Vanessa ever after for disabusing her of this notion. Despite her passionate belief in women's rights, her need to be desired – or simply to be loved, to be validated by a proposal of marriage – destroyed her happiness. It was really Noel who had benefited most from the Newnhamite spirit, the vision that saw a life beyond marriage as possible, and who felt liberated to consider choices that her eldest sister did not seem willing to face.

In the early part of 1916, Margery began to talk about an engagement that was certainly imaginary. Less than a month before her birthday, she elaborated on this fantasy at a dinner in Bloomsbury, a conversation that Virginia Woolf described gleefully to Ka Cox afterwards:

> Margery Olivier had not been in the room a minute before she said 'I've just refused a proposal of marriage!' Nobody knew what to say. For some reason we all felt very awkward. She told us that the man is unknown to us, has £2,000 a year, and is employed in munition work: aged 32. Who can he be? Leonard inclines to think that she suffers from a disease of advanced virginity in which one imagines proposals at every tea party. Certainly, she's in a very odd state of mind.

A week later, Virginia, who had her own tendency to embroider stories, repeated the anecdote to Duncan Grant with self-aware irony: 'People don't seem to trust me now, except poor old zanies like Margery Olivier, who ran into the room the other night crying "I've just had a proposal! I've just had a proposal!"'

In Margery's friendship groups, everyone was well-versed in nervous conditions and artistic temperaments. Virginia, perhaps finding Margery's instability too close to home, was alone in being spiteful (though others had enjoyed shocking single women like Margery and Ka Cox with bawdy conversation and sexually explicit jokes). By contrast, Vanessa specifically identified (and commended) a special sensitivity in Margery, perhaps derived from her departures from reason, that set her apart from her sisters. Margery, she reflected, seemed 'to have had more experience of feeling and more imagination' than the younger Oliviers.

As the year went on, the Wala and Sydney seemed increasingly at a loss to understand Margery's restlessness but they continued to behave as if everything was all right. It fell to Noel to worry. In September 1916, she wrote to James to warn him that Margery was planning to visit him and Alix on their holiday: 'I feel more & more sure that she's off on another acute attack of her delusional insanity,' she wrote. 'Do call a doctor if she isn't completely recovered.'

The suitor Margery had chosen was Harry Norton, a talented mathematician and close friend of Lytton Strachey. Prone to nervous giggling after he spoke and currently in love with Bunny, he was not an obvious choice for an infatuation. Margery was well aware of this aspect of the sexual life of many of their friends – it was she who explained homosexuality to Bryn in 1912 – but the nature of her interest in Norton did not require any realistic hope. His own position is mysterious. He had certainly written to James expressing admiring curiosity about Margery when they first met but there is no evidence that they ever became particularly close. He never proposed to Margery but she had been intermittently obsessed with him for at least four years. In 1917 obsession had worked up into mania. Margery was distracted and overwrought, feverishly writing him letters that assumed their engagement and seeking out the gatherings at which she thought he might be found.

When she went to Eva in February 1917 she stayed only a single night before she insisted on returning to London to attend a party at the Omega workshops (run by Vanessa Bell, Duncan Grant and Roger Fry), despite her newly bereaved friend's attempts to detain her. She swore she would return but when she suggested staying with Eva for several days, Eva realised Margery was hoping to join her on a visit she had planned to see Norton, who also had an academic post in Cambridge. With Margery's parents apparently at a loss, Eva wrote directly to Noel. She told her that she would visit Norton as planned and ask him outright if there was any truth in what Margery had been telling people about their relationship. Then she suggested taking the risky step of asking Norton to make clear to Margery that her passion was hopeless. Eva felt drastic solutions were required. 'Everyone notices her,' she warned Noel.

Norton confirmed that he did not love Margery and had never encouraged her in her belief. The following day, Margery reappeared in Cambridge. When phone calls to Eva went unanswered, she phoned

Norton from the station, claiming to have no money to get home. Norton called Eva and the two of them took a taxi to the station, where they persuaded Margery to get on a train back to London. Noel had coached Eva over the phone on how to deal with Margery; she and Norton spoke about 'ordinary things' on the platform and were careful not to question anything she said. Eva did try to persuade Margery to see a doctor, however, and warned Noel that she shouldn't be left alone when she arrived.

In London the family was in an unsettled state. Sydney had lost his job, as he had feared, and was now preoccupied with persuading the War Office and Lloyd George, who had managed to manoeuvre himself into becoming Prime Minister, to appoint him to another position. Noel was trying to prepare for her qualifying exams. A nurse was hired to help keep Margery calm, or at least under control, but tending to her sister was now taking up whole swathes of Noel's emotional and physical energy and others were being drawn in too: their cousin Ursula, also supposed to be revising, was roped in to help; Alix Sargant-Florence stepped in too.

When Margery got back to London she was adamant that she had a tea date set with Norton in Cambridge and that she had to return there on the weekend. On Friday everyone at Marlborough Road was engaged in trying to dissuade her. The family consulted Dr Bernard Hart, a physician in psychological medicine at University College Hospital and author of the influential *The Psychology of Insanity*, who examined Margery and broke the news that he suspected she had a form of dementia: in other words, an incurable type of madness. 'It seems the cruellest disaster that could happen to anyone,' Alix wrote to her mother. 'Her family, I think, have hardly taken it in yet.' It seemed vital to keep Margery away from Norton, in order to starve the obsession of oxygen, but there was almost nothing they could do to prevent Margery from going, short of physically restraining her. The doctor warned them that to do that, he would have to formally certify her as insane. Somehow, they managed to keep her at home.

A few days later, Noel went away. She and James had been invited to stay at Vanessa Bell's farmhouse in Sussex, where Vanessa, Duncan and Bunny were living with Vanessa's sons by Clive Bell. Charleston was a slightly ramshackle house, set beside a large and picturesque pond and energetically decorated by the new residents. Noel needed peace and quiet to prepare for her final assessments but she couldn't quite disengage from home. Her parents sent her regular updates, each putting their own characteristic spin on events as they unfolded at Marlborough Road. The Wala tried to reassure her. They had a new nurse in the house to help them and had now alighted on Eva's plan for themselves. Sydney had written to Norton to ask him to send a final letter to Margery, which, with the doctor's consent, they proposed to show her. They realised they needed to force the situation to its crisis. Margery was technically confined to her bed but it was proving extremely difficult to keep her there. She would decide that someone had come to visit her, invariably bringing Norton with them, or that he was trying to reach her, and she would rise and prowl about the house; or she would feel a need to telephone him and a long argument would ensue as they tried to stop her. Often she could not be persuaded back into her room until late at night.

Margery had placed herself firmly at the centre of her own romantic melodrama, in which she was separated by force from the man she loved and who loved her in return, and as her behaviour grew progressively odder and then violent, she forced her family to take her seriously and to pay her the attention due to a romantic heroine. When she was this ill, she managed even to overshadow the radiant Brynhild, who had given birth to a daughter the previous summer.

Norton wrote as asked but if the letter reached Margery, it made little difference. Her psyche dismissed any attempts to puncture her delusion and so with each rejection, new theories arose to explain the couple's strange separation. In the absence of any direct access to him, Margery began to believe that Norton was sending her veiled messages in the words her family and friends spoke.

Sydney wrote to Noel with rather more frankness than Margaret, more inclined to rest the burden of the full truth on his daughter. The Wala was managing both Margery and the household alone, and they were about to fire one of their servants, who had been stealing food bought especially for Margery. Even if Margery was distracted with writing letters for Norton she kept at it until late at night and then woke her mother to take them to the post. It did not seem to occur to Sydney to protect Noel from bad news or to let her exams take priority. As a daughter of the family, he expected her to be there to support the Wala and help manage the household.

Dr Hart continued to warn them that unless she could be kept at home, Margery would have to be institutionalised but Sydney was plagued by the memory of Daphne's incarceration. He didn't see how he could justify that kind of intervention again: Margery was delusional but she did not put anyone at risk nor was she completely delirious as Daphne had been. Sydney was afraid that in a hospital Margery would be drugged to 'keep her quiet' and that as she recovered, she would come to resent him as his other daughter did. 'I would rather do anything else that is at all possible,' he told Noel. He could see that she was 'a bit crazy and is tiresome to the subjects of her illusions' but she was also vulnerable and he felt that incarcerating her would be an act of cruelty that would cause her terrific distress. There was something pitiful about Margery's state; she exhausted herself and cried constantly, convinced that everyone was inexplicably against her. Sydney wasn't prepared to give up on his daughter and let her become 'a life-long lunatic' just because of what he saw as the 'liabilities of her sex'.

Hugh and Brynhild visited regularly. On one evening Margery insisted on clambering in and out of her bath, believing that Bryn was calling her downstairs because Norton had arrived. After dinner she managed to dodge her nurse and fled down into the drawing room in her night-dress, expecting to surprise him. The next morning, she was worse. As well as what Sydney had taken to calling her 'Nortonania', she was now generally confused, frail and incoherent. She wandered round and round her room, begging her father to 'help' her. When he tried to leave the house, Margery hung from the window calling for him as he passed the garden.

The entire household was exhausted and finally coming face to face with the fact that some of the most distinctive things about Margery's personality could, in fact, have been signs of illness all along. Noel came back to London and arranged to stay with the Stracheys.

On the last day of March, a Saturday, Margery managed to break out of the house. The weather was still cold and, though she was intending to go to Gordon Square and find Norton (he kept rooms in Maynard's house), she in fact wandered aimlessly about the snow-covered streets for an hour and a half, dressed only in her nightgown. A neighbour found her and was able to persuade her back towards the Oliviers' house. But as they approached the door, Margery seemed to realise where she was and dashed away again, hitting the man as he tried to stop her. The neighbour alerted Sydney, who called on a local doctor for help. He eventually lured her back home. All through Sunday, Margery made continual attempts to escape. That night she was given a sleeping draught and Ursula stayed in her room. In the morning, still dressed only in her nightie, Margery tried to climb out of her second-floor window.

The following day, just over a week before her thirty-first birthday, Margery was admitted to the Chiswick House asylum under an 'urgency order'. Sydney wrote immediately to Daphne, seeking to justify the decision. He assured her that Chiswick House seemed 'well conducted' (though he also griped at the prices) and that Margery was only there as a short-term solution to get them through the 'present emergency'. Nevertheless, he knew what Daphne's assessment was likely to be: 'I am afraid you will think us very feeble.'

In truth, Margery was beyond their care. Brynhild and Noel, in supporting their parents' approach, found themselves in a heartbreaking position of collusion with all of the forces Margery was at war with. Brynhild had been given the task of tricking Margery into the taxi to the asylum, betraying her in the hopes of helping her; it was a horrendous corruption of the sisterly bonds of care and trust, as Margery went with Bryn only because she thought she could rely on her. Letters soon arrived for Noel, in which Margery turned to her as an ally in the one drama in which her little sister could not act as co-conspirator. 'Please Will you help me to be let free?' she begged.

The Chiswick House doctors who assessed Margery on arrival described her as 'anxious', 'suspicious' and suffering from delusions. Though she seemed 'acute & sharp' in reply to their questions, they nevertheless deemed her to be of a 'very weak mentality'. She made one half-hearted attempt to rush out of the building once she realised where she was but otherwise seemed relatively calm. She was under the impression that she had been brought to the house to meet Norton and simply plagued Bryn with questions about where he was or when he was coming. If Norton wanted her to stay there, she would wait for him. Once Bryn left, Margery behaved childishly with the nurses, insisting that they feed her the tea and toast she was given, but otherwise seemed cooperative. She went quietly to bed and was locked in with a nurse.

From then on, the doctors kept a careful record of how quiet – or otherwise – Margery was being. They noted how she slept and ate, noted her menstruation, delusions and sometimes the expression on her face.

The focus, as it had been at home, appeared to be on restraining her, in case she injured herself or fuelled her obsession, and no mention was made of any attempts at treatment.

Chiswick House had housed an asylum run by the Tuke family since 1892. Their practice, which dated from 1837, was known for being one of the first to attempt more humane treatment for inmates. In 1917 it was still run by a Tuke and there was little demonstrable change in management. But Noel was aware that, within her generation particularly, new ideas were circulating about the treatment of mental disorders. Freud had reached them. By the war, at least four of Freud's books had been translated into English and signs of his influence were observed with some alarm by the medical establishment, the *British Medical Journal* complaining of an 'excessive sexual probing which is so conspicuous in the methods of the present day' in 1914. Unable to ignore the drama at home, Noel had reached out to the friends and doctors she admired from Charleston, anxiously seeking other opinions.

Sydney and Margaret had turned to the best and most expensive doctors for their first-born, doctors who had little truck with Freudian ideas, who insisted that mental illness had a physical basis. Maurice Craig, who had treated Daphne, was doubtful about Freudian therapy and suspected that the topics it drew on would only distress vulnerable patients further. It seemed outrageous to many doctors that women, in particular, should be encouraged to discuss sexual matters openly with their doctors.

But in Bloomsbury, and amongst young, ambitious medics like Maitland Radford and Godwin Baynes, Freud's ideas had been taken up with much greater openness. Noel and her sisters belonged to a milieu that was thirsty for new ideas and already interested in the processes of the inner life. Leonard Woolf reviewed Freud's books as early as 1914. 'Freud slip' jokes had entered the group's vocabulary. Noel mentioned 'a most terrible Freud slip of the tongue' to James and wondered if her dreams about dead babies arose from the detached and emotionless way she sometimes had to face them at work. Before the war, Godwin had attempted to treat the depressed poet Edward Thomas with a version of a 'talking cure', despite the fact that most experts had greeted the idea of indulging neurotics in this way with derision. He and Maitland both sent advice to Noel from military hospitals in France. It seemed clear to Godwin that Margery's illness was down to the repression of sexual urges. 'If such a potent complex as sex gets no direct expression in action it either becomes repressed or distorted,' he explained, 'and you get these dissociation phenomena turning up.' He hoped for a revolution in mental healthcare:

> The majority of cases of definite insanity are due to conflict in the personality with the sex complex and I believe the amazing advance in our knowledge of the pathology of abnormal mental states will give us in the next few years effective means of prevention if these results are reflected in a sensible educational system.

Only a tiny minority of doctors was experimenting with these approaches, however, and they tended to be the young doctors who were now away at the Front. Even as some practitioners in England came round to exploratory treatments, these efforts were in response to the disturbing appearance of shell shock. Faced with the thousands of men – deemed perfectly normal and masculine when they left – returning from the Front in the grips of hysteria, some doctors were prepared to take another look at the treatments currently available. For both Daphne and Margery, Noel had consulted with Henry Head, an intelligent and pioneering neuropsychologist who had been, Adrian Stephen told her, 'a much more competent & careful sort of man' than the other doctors who had treated Virginia. During the war, however, he was preoccupied with treating officers. At Craiglockhart, a hospital for shell-shocked officers in Scotland, Siegfried Sassoon would be granted a subconscious and offered a 'talking cure'. Hysterical spinsters, however, were simply not the priority. At Chiswick House, new theories seem to have been ignored. Maitland urged Noel not to leave Margery there 'a minute longer than is absolutely necessary'.

Margery's sisters came to visit but could not hold her attention; she spent the time speaking persistently about Norton. Though there were quiet days, there were also times when she was 'hysterical & rather emotional' and began to make trouble at night; trying to force the window or attacking the nurse who held the key to her room. If anything, after a brief improvement, she deteriorated and took to calling noisily for Norton. When encouraged to walk in the garden, she wanted to know if Norton was there but soon began to suspect that invitations to the garden meant he was in fact in the house. Her mind worked doggedly on him and on escape, and though her reason wavered, these twin desires never did.

Margery expressed dismay at the obstacles that were placed between her and Norton, the mendacity and lack of understanding from those she had trusted, and seemed to fear that the separation – for which she was not at fault – might make him doubt her. 'Darling,' she scribbled to him in a letter she entrusted to Noel:

> They are stifling me and will not let me see you because I think they think I do not want you really and love you. Will you tell them I do? and try and see me face to face: Every time you come they take great <u>trouble</u> to tell me but incomprehensibly I never see you this door is kept slammed between and I plead + plead to every body to let you in or me out and I have struggled rediculously to get to where I thought you were + sometimes to try to prove I wanted you + sometimes in belief that on the issue hung whether or not they'd let us meet about sometimes: such things as whether my clothes should be taken off but also because I cannot lump being told what to do + where to do it and being in a prison + not seeing the streets makes me ache + ache + wanting my medical work + Noel + Alix + my people + Ka + Eva + all the others + you + [deletion] + streets + busses

Another missive to him went no further than the pages of the Chiswick House casebook.

To her father Margery wrote confused and rambling letters, scattered with deletions, adding to the back of the envelope: 'Please will you help me'. She also turned to Noel, using the old nickname 'Nodie', to let her know that she knew, now, that Brynhild had lied to her. In a crumpled and wandering letter, which Margery kept hidden under her pillow, she wrote to her youngest sister as the last one who might help her. She made valiant and illogical plans for the future: she would write a thesis and asked for her textbooks, as well as copies of Rupert's poetry. Most of all she was homesick, and wanted Eva, and Noel and Daphne. Then, after forty-two days at Chiswick House, Margery went into the garden, dodged the nurses, climbed over the wall and escaped.

5

Brynhild

During the bleak autumn of 1916, Noel was lonely and given to fears at night-time. Sometimes she decamped to Bryn's house on Caroline Place, seeking comfort. Bryn's new daughter, named Anne, had arrived that June and was widely reported to have the good fortune of taking after her mother. In the month of her birth, conscription was extended to married men and Hugh wrote to his father-in-law to tell him that he had given Sydney's address to the authorities, rather than Bryn's. Should anything happen to him, he wanted Sydney to be the one to tell her.

Hugh turned up unexpectedly on a short leave during one of Noel's visits. He was in good spirits, looking forward to a few days at home. But as Bryn began to list her engagements, Noel watched his expression fall. Brynhild had volunteer work and shopping to do; when the children's nurse, Marie, had her night off she would have to put the children to bed, she had to have 'Mrs So & So to tea'. The 'awful disappointment of domesticity seemed to depress him a little,' Noel told James, '& it was rather painful to see him resign himself.' Since her marriage, Brynhild had filled her life with all the bustle that domesticity had to offer. War threw the different worlds of men and women into sharp relief: whilst it represented a sacred haven from the rages of wartime, home was more distant than ever for men in the army and the reality of it could disappoint.

Brynhild's life was anyhow about to be uprooted. Hugh had been commissioned into the Royal Naval Air Service (a precursor to the RAF) and was then stationed in Killingholme, on the Humber. Noel predicted that it would be difficult to disentangle her sister from life in London but Brynhild went, letting part of her house to Gerald Shove and his wife Fredegond, and taking her children up to Lincolnshire. She left her housekeeper at Caroline Place and brought only Marie with her. The two women quickly found life in Killingholme almost unbearably dull, and Brynhild lived in fear that Marie would leave. The home Hugh found them was isolated and if London had seemed bleak and dark, their new home – near Grimsby – was worse. Even leaving the house was 'an absolute penance', thanks to the endless mud, and Brynhild experienced life there as 'horrible drudgery'. Once or twice Hugh was able to take her out to the picture palace at Grimsby but it was poor distraction. The officers, their wives and their attempts to entertain themselves bored her. She told the Wala she couldn't help feeling 'snobbish' about the 'feeble little farce' they proposed she take part in. Her run as Helen can hardly have seemed further away.

She stayed only because Hugh was nearby and by moving she had managed to cling on to a semblance of family life. On holiday at Everleigh in 1912, Bryn, Noel and Maynard Keynes had watched the planes at the nearby army and navy school. 'You've never known what a real thrill is if you've not seen one of those things just as it leaves the ground,' she told Hugh at the time. Now she could take Tony to visit his father at the aerodrome, and see her son beside himself with delight at the sight of the aeroplanes. Anne, known as Andy, was growing 'very rampageous', the Wala was told, '& kicks & shouts with glee'.

One winter night, as a raid was made over the Humber, Brynhild watched some far-off shelling and then retired to bed, surprised by the terror that kept her neighbours up all night. It was only the next morning that she learned Hugh had been sent out in pursuit of the enemy aircraft. He had run out of petrol five miles from land and faced the prospect of crashing in the ocean, until he sighted a Torpedo destroyer that was able to pick him up.

Despite this close shave, Hugh was generally just as unsatisfied as Brynhild. It was frustrating to be stationed on board an airship carrier, anchored in the Humber, when his family was so close by, and from day to day very little was required from him. The idea was for the pilots to fight off Zeppelins, intercepting them from the carrier, a plan about which Hugh was scathing. 'We occasionally go out to look for the German fleet,' he told Noel, 'but it has not yet been found. I doubt if we should recognise it if we saw it. I personally should never dare to drop bombs on it for fear that it was really Admiral Jellicoe. [...] Most of the time, while there is flying weather, we spend passing over & over an imitation submarine in a field dropping bomb after bomb.'

Hugh

Finally, Hugh was deployed. He left in May 1917, passing out of sight and into the war zone. Brynhild had kept her family together for as long as was possible. On the day he went, Margery appeared at Brynhild's house in London, making straight for Bloomsbury from Chiswick House. Brynhild found herself assuming responsibility for her sister, as if the moment her identity as a wife fell into abeyance, she was drawn back into the orbit of the Olivier family, with all the obligations that that entailed.

Margery refused to return home or to the asylum so Brynhild was left with the relentless task of keeping track of her: her movements, sleep and consumption had to be carefully monitored and argued over, and endless monologues about Norton endured. Brynhild struggled to find sympathy for Margery: her obsession with Norton was also a kind of self-obsession, which Brynhild found at best monotonous. Nor did she see any reason to excuse Margery's behaviour, which spoke to her of an 'almost continuous disregard of the feelings of other people'.

Brynhild's attitude was no doubt affected by Margery's attitude towards her. Since they were teenagers, their relationship had been shot through with resentment and jealousy, and Brynhild was tired of being painted by Margery as a tormentor, especially now she was a grown woman with an independent life. That month, Brynhild would turn thirty but Margery was still talking about old betrayals. When she was lucid enough to appreciate that she was ill, Margery put her violent jealousies down to Brynhild's youthful tendency to 'cut her out'. Bryn didn't attempt to deny the element of truth in this but of course she didn't view it in quite the same way either.

In the days after Hugh's departure, Margery averaged 'about three crises a day', with an inevitable flare-up at around 9.30 p.m., which would last until midnight. They were impossible days for Brynhild, who had little support and was already unsettled by her husband's deployment. Over and over, Margery would decide to call on 46 Gordon Square. Brynhild established a policy for dealing with these attempts: if after forty-five minutes she had not managed to persuade her sister to stay at home, she gave up and Margery set off on the short walk to Maynard's house. Brynhild could hardly descend into a physical tussle with her sister 'twenty times a day' and she was afraid that if Margery came to see her as the enemy, she would never be able to help her. A certain level of comradeship persisted between the sisters and she was counting on that to make a difference.

At 46 Gordon Square they were used to the sight of Margery hurrying up the steps, perhaps wearing that slightly plagued look she often bore, her lips parted in more of a grimace than a smile. The disappointment of not seeing Norton left her emotionally wrecked, and her manner, a little disordered in her appearance and responses, may somehow have anticipated this disappointment, showing tell-tale signs of a soul in disarray. Or perhaps with each visit she arrived with a renewed and incandescent hope, glowing with an obsessive love that never seemed to burn out. Either way, the housekeeper there knew how to handle her, and did it kindly. On occasion, Maynard accompanied a disappointed Margery home himself, in an act of kindness that only nurtured Brynhild's fondness and admiration for him. (It is hard to imagine Norton, a talented but nervy man, knowing what to do with Margery's frenzied attentions, yet he too remained respectful and considerate towards her family despite the embarrassments she must have caused him, and sought to comfort Noel with the example of Virginia Woolf's recovery from her own breakdown.)

Brynhild's relationship with her sister came under the most intense strain of their lives. It was a situation that threw the complexities of sisterhood into sharp relief. In this tightrope balance of cruelty and care, of resentment, reliance and pride, all the conflicts of siblinghood were acted out in extremes. Margery was the sick one, and Brynhild was all that stood between her and another spell in an asylum, yet Margery seemed to have the upper hand, forcing Brynhild to humble herself and plead with her, to tolerate Margery's attacks even while her life became devoted to her.

Brynhild was convinced that Margery's outings to Gordon Square were preventing her recovery and agreed with her parents that Margery needed to leave the city. After a fortnight that had 'been enough to add ten years to one's life', Brynhild moved to the countryside with her sister, back to the landscape of their youth, to a village on the North Downs called Tatsfield, which looked over Limpsfield and was only four miles from The Champions. It was Brynhild's thirtieth birthday.

At Tatsfield the Oliviers knew an Irish doctor who farmed 400 acres with the aid of what Brynhild described to Hugh as 'various lunatics – officers & men suffering from shell shock and other nervous results of war & peace'. Dr Sherrard was not an entirely conventional figure – after his wife's death he had married, and had fathered children with, his step-daughter – but locally he had a good reputation for helping mental invalids to cure themselves through work.

On the appointed day, Brynhild managed to get her sister as far as the closest station to Tatsfield, where the plan was for the doctor, whom Margery knew, to meet them, then drive down into the village where they would join him on foot before taking up residence on his property. When he arrived, however, he had another man with him and Margery smelled a rat. She fled. As Margery hared off across the fields, her sister had no choice but to follow her. 'Nothing on earth, she swore, would ever induce her to go near his place,' Brynhild later reported, and 'there followed the most preposterous scene', which was not only emotionally gruelling but embarrassing and ridiculous, abhorrent to Brynhild's reserve: 'me begging, explaining, arguing, almost weeping and both of us running for almost two miles'.

Finally, exhausted and beginning to see the absurdity of the situation, Brynhild suggested that they go home to London. It was days before she managed to persuade Margery to return. When she did, Brynhild, Margery, Andy and Tony were installed in a cottage on the Sherrard farm together. It was a spacious house, with a cold bath and a lady provided to cook for them. They were surrounded with fields 'white with big daisies' and a dishevelled garden with fruit trees in the hedge. On lazy afternoons they crawled through the hedge to lie in the shade of the hayfields on the other side, and during their half days of work, three-year-old Tony accompanied his aunt and mother to hoe their plots or plant celery. Country life suited the children, who grew brown in the three weeks of glorious weather that greeted them. Brynhild didn't have to worry so much about where Margery got to in the middle of nowhere, and there were times when her sister was even nice to her. In these circumstances she began to feel more optimistic. Brynhild's life was temporarily on hold – she had almost no income and had not yet let Caroline Place – but she was tentatively hopeful for the future. Sydney had found a new job, which he was already bored by but at least paid the same as the last, and Brynhild hoped that 'when the cheap & obvious methods have done as much as they can' Margery might be treated with psychoanalysis. Brynhild did not seem to doubt that Margery would recover. She could see her sister's present illness within a continuum of her whole life, which was scattered with what Margery's sisters referred to as her 'crises', ranging in severity; Brynhild's engagement had been blighted by one of the worst in 1912. Five years later they were dealing with something much more alarming but there had also been years of (sporadic) calm. Brynhild saw no reason not to hope for a return to normality – if only Margery's version of normality. They could stay in Tatsfield until the end of July and then, by the end of the year, she thought, she could be back at home and Margery back to studying medicine.

Brynhild had been writing the same letter to her husband for a month and she didn't want to send it away. It was impossible to imagine that he had gone so far and had been gone for so long, when so much had happened in his absence. Brynhild was waiting anxiously for news of him: 'Shall I ever hear from you again?' she asked plaintively, separated from her husband, her home and all the trappings of her former life. 'I cling on to this letter [...] when I send it off I shall feel so as if I'd broken a link.'

In Port Said in Egypt, Hugh alternated between boredom and terror. He was stationed close to the war zone and could be called out to fly at any moment, a prospect that made him realise how desperately he wanted to live. 'It is dreadful being so frightened,' he admitted to his sister-in-law, and yet he was well aware that he was not meant to admit his fear. Long intervals between the periods of danger only seemed to offer more time to dwell on the odds of surviving. Under these conditions, it was almost too awful to think of Brynhild.

The two of them struggled to maintain a meaningful connection. News arrived only sporadically from home; the letters came by ships that often fell foul of German mines and patrols. By mid August, Hugh hadn't heard from his family in weeks and few of his letters had reached England. When they did arrive they came in a confusing order, so that Brynhild was never really certain where he was. Correspondence was subject to censorship; generally soldiers were unable to tell their loved ones precisely where they were, what they were doing or pass on information about the whereabouts of other friends or family (Hugh asked several times about Paul Montague, who was possibly stationed nearby, hoping to come across his familiar face out in the desert). A particular style of letter-writing emerged, written around the edges of the biggest thing in their lives: the war that necessitated the letters. Couples communicated in empty phrases and euphemisms, made meaningful only by the contact they attempted. Wives tried to write letters that didn't threaten morale, filled with domestic detail that could only emphasise their distance from the war zone; people who longed for each other found themselves engaged in parallel chains of missives, which rarely intersected because of the delays and losses. In the face of these challenges, Brynhild felt apathetic about writing to Hugh, though she hoped always for word from him. Revisiting all the drama – and tedium – of her days was trying and, she imagined, dull for him to read. Writing felt insufficient and even seemed, sometimes, to widen the gap between them. 'I wish to God you were here,' she told him. 'I cant get at you at all by writing – in fact it makes you seem even more remote to have to mount on this absurd scaffolding of letters. I want you yourself here this moment.'

Brynhild had experienced a harsh shock in returning from Lincolnshire to find her sister so ill at Marlborough Road in March, and she seemed to draw comfort from taking over responsibility for her, however difficult it was. She truly believed that the therapeutic establishment at Tatsfield might be Margery's one chance for recovery, and she guarded it carefully. Much as she felt that Margery needed a more sophisticated therapy, in the immediate term achieving that magical balance of calm and occupation did really seem to have its benefits.

Sydney and Margaret were on hand to help with the children but Brynhild kept them strictly away from Tatsfield and warned them not to interfere. Daphne came home to Limpsfield for the summer and she and Noel both visited to help ease the burden on Brynhild. Noel was alarmed by how much weight Bryn had lost – if anything Margery, who was fatter and browner and had a new short haircut, looked better – but Brynhild put a cheerful face on things for her younger sisters. Noel was inclined to see the absurdity in the situation, needing to find some accommodation with the inescapable, traumatic fact of it. 'The dear old Mud' had been perfectly nice to her when she visited, she told James, and 'only attacked me four times & only once actually <u>fell</u> upon me with her claws'. With respect to Dr Sherrard, Noel allowed herself some professional superiority. He was, she felt, 'completely superstitious', yet she had to concede that he had succeeded in asserting some influence over Margery.

Sybil Pye and Eva visited and both proclaimed Margery to be much better. But only Brynhild lived with the reality. She saw that Margery could sometimes seem deceptively well and was worried that if her sister got access to her friends in London, they wouldn't appreciate the risk and would inadvertently wind Margery up to fever pitch again. She could tell that Margery was itching to get back into the fold. Gallingly for Bryn, it was clear that Margery found her companionship dull. Even worse, when Daphne visited, Margery announced that she could bear working the land at Tatsfield if *Daphne* was there to keep her company.

Eventually, Brynhild grew so dispirited by her sister's company that she wrote to Alix Sargant-Florence asking her to visit. Alix, subjected to hourly interrogations about her relations with Norton (and here Margery was not far off the mark, as Alix and Harry Norton had indeed had an affair), teased Margery good-naturedly about her preoccupation with him. Bryn had hoped that Alix could act as a 'decoy' but instead the visit backfired drastically.

On the day that Alix left them, a Friday, Margery insisted on returning to the city with her. She promised Brynhild faithfully that she would stay one night in Caroline Place and then come back, and that she would wire for her sister if she needed her. When no word came over the weekend, Brynhild began to panic. Dr Sherrard shared her concern and on Sunday he suggested that Brynhild leave her children and go and look for her sister. At Caroline Place, Brynhild found Margery's things but no other sign of her. She called at Gordon Square, where the inhabitants of no. 46 had had a welcome respite over the summer. They confirmed that Margery had already visited twice that weekend. Norton had refused to see her and Maynard and Clive Bell, though friendly and pleased to see Brynhild, had no information to offer about her sister's whereabouts.

When Brynhild got back to Caroline Place, Margery's things had disappeared. Brynhild spent a sleepless night mired in foreboding before Margery finally reappeared the next day. She had apparently simply spent the weekend wandering the streets, lost to any sense of time, fixated on finding Norton. Then she had stayed the night with a friend, who had in fact left a note for Brynhild at Caroline Place. But by this point Margery had worked herself into such a state of paranoia that she had secretly returned and destroyed the note, afraid that it would lead the police – or some other nameless pursuer – to her.

Brynhild now had the challenge of persuading Margery back to the safety of Tatsfield. Each time they began the trip to the station, Margery would identify omens that meant they should turn back at once, so that they inched towards it and then shied away again, over and over. Once they got out of London, Margery refused to let them get the bus that would take them the rest of the way, instead forcing Brynhild to walk for two and a half miles in the pouring rain, stopping every ten minutes to insist that they return to the city. When Brynhild finally lured her on to a bus, they had to sit on the (uncovered) top deck, and when they were dropped off Margery doubled the length of the walk by refusing to keep to the road, preferring to drag Brynhild across the fields, presumably to avoid detection. They got home at night and Brynhild, exhausted and achy, had to spend the next day and a half in bed.

At times like this, Brynhild despaired of meaningful progress and yet was still not prepared to entrust the job of caring for Margery to anyone else. By September she had resigned herself to the likelihood of staying in Tatsfield until at least the end of the year. She hoped that the unsettling experience of her days alone in London would have made Margery appreciate her dependence, but instead Margery still seemed to hold all the power. In the strange psychological tussle between the sisters, it was Brynhild who was afraid of their co-imprisonment being broken.

*

Things began to improve again when the sisters persuaded Dr Sherrard to let them renovate one of the cottages on his land for themselves. They threw themselves into the work. Unaware of an Olivier family passion for home decoration, Dr Sherrard was inclined to think that the sisters' desire to 'get thoroughly tired out & dirty in doing these things can, in two young ladies, only be ascribed to mental aberration', Bryn told Hugh, but she persuaded him to let them carry on.

Their community at Tatsfield began to expand. The sisters hosted poker parties for Dr Sherrard's secretary, a Mr Rowe, and his nephew, Raymond Sherrard, a raffish and charming young second lieutenant in the Essex Regiment who had crashed his motorbike whilst on leave and was now conveniently exempted from returning to the Front for the foreseeable future. Aside from them, the ragtag society the sisters assembled was peopled largely by children – including Dr Sherrard's three young sons – and other patients. As in their Jamaica days, though with quite different company, the Oliviers formed a little hub for local society. They established cricket teams and instituted afternoons of hide-and-seek and obstacle races through the barns. They entertained the young men to quiet evenings in their cottage.

All too soon, the inevitable complication arose. Raymond Sherrard took it upon himself to keep the appealing Olivier sisters entertained during their stay and became a regular visitor on the weekends. He enlivened life at Tatsfield, organising bridge parties and outings to drink ginger beer in the village.

Brynhild saw the danger early. She tried to warn the doctor and then Raymond himself but went unheeded. Margery's new fixation took root. At first Brynhild was more or less resigned to this development and enjoyed Margery's rare cheer. Raymond's presence close by was also useful for keeping Margery in Tatsfield. But the corollary to Margery's interest in Raymond was an almost immediate conviction that Brynhild would exert her 'evil fascinations', as Brynhild derisively described them, 'to lure him away from her'.

Soon Brynhild had to sit through Raymond's visits in frustrated silence, for fear of Margery's recriminations when he left. To her own regret, as the young man was welcome company for her too, Brynhild finally decided to ask Raymond to stay away.

After a brief flourishing, life in Tatsfield thus seemed to contract again as autumn arrived. Noel and Daphne were both leaving for new occupations and there seemed little hope of Hugh returning in the near future, or anyone suitable presenting themselves to relieve Brynhild of Margery's care. Like almost everyone else, Brynhild was afraid of the future because the war (and, she must have felt, her own particular circumstances) looked like it could go on and on, soaking up all of their youth and energy, making them strangers to the people who loved them the most. 'I am overwhelmed with gloom sometimes,' she told Hugh, 'at the thought of you stuck in that beastly hole doing nothing and the years going on and me being quite aged when you return.'

Margery and Brynhild in Tatsfield

6

Christmas, 1917

'There was a party at Bryn's on Wednesday [...] Margery was there; exquisitely beautiful with short hair, and no more mad than the rest of us.' James to Lytton

'Dear, dear! – I don't like this intermingling of lunatics. "No more mad than the rest of us" – yes, quite so, that's just what's so intolerable. Very soon every landmark will be obliterated, and all the world an asylum.' Lytton to James

After qualifying, Noel got the job she wanted and was appointed House Physician at the Great Northern Hospital. 'Its as bad as getting married, to pass an exam,' she told James in the summer, as gifts and congratulations flooded in, but she had reached the goal that had kept her moving through the worst years of her life; the culmination of six years of gruelling determination.

Noel had had the good fortune – though it did not, of course, present itself in this way – of training for medicine at the moment when the prospects for female doctors made great strides. This was the cruel bargain of the war: the opportunity for recognition came at a cost that few women would willingly tolerate. The year that Noel graduated, the Germans began to sink hospital ships as part of their policy of unrestricted submarine warfare and in response to this 'unforeseen and hitherto unimaginable development', the War Office decided to treat the wounded initially in France, meaning that more doctors had to cross the Channel. Before long the British Medical Association was protesting that the country had run out of doctors. While the military had over 12,000 for five million soldiers, at home there were just under 15,000 doctors trying to tend to 34.5 million people. Aware of this shortfall, seven of the eleven London hospitals opened their doors to female students. But the Royal Free, the only London hospital that would contemplate training women before the war, was forging ahead. When its new building was opened by Queen Mary in October 1916, newspapers used the opportunity to remark on the good work women doctors were doing. Noel had studied there – and qualified – during its years of vindication.

She had decided to specialise in the treatment of babies and children. At the Royal Free, Noel's hero was Dr Florence Barrett, a senior staff member who led a well-timed fund-raising drive to provide maternity, paediatric and infant welfare facilities for the hospital. Dr Barrett was among the first to appreciate the significance of antenatal nutrition for infant health and had organised voluntary centres providing food for undernourished women and children in the city. When the student body arranged a gift for Dr Barrett, it was Noel who solicited donations.

As the war rattled on, and it became clear just how quickly modern warfare could drain the country's manpower, high infant mortality rates in Britain finally provoked the outcry the Fabians had long sought to elicit. To the press, church and government, it seemed more productive to delay the loss of life until those citizens were old enough to fight for their country. '[I]n the ultimate issue of things babies are of greater import than battalions,' the editors of the *British Medical Journal* wrote, 'and they are the true dreadnoughts of a nation.' These new national priorities meant that there were new resources available in the area of medicine Noel had chosen. 'Darling, there have been two babies since I stopped [writing],' Noel once drily informed James from her ward, 'more soldiers for England . . .'

The summer she graduated should have been full of rewards for Noel but it was bittersweet. She had agreed to join the Old Bedalians meeting in Petersfield but could muster no enthusiasm for a camp that would gape with absences. Missing friends plagued her and she often dreamed of Rupert. Brynhild, too, was unsettled by reminders of the past. She had been astonished to learn that Mrs Brooke was visiting The Champions earlier in the year. Rupert's mother was visiting the Wards, who were renting the house from the Oliviers, but the news reminded Brynhild of old slights. '[P]erhaps she may even not know whose house it is,' she wrote to Hugh, '(oh but she does.) [. . .] she will have bad nights there I should think.'

At the end of August, James had taken Noel on holiday with Lytton and Dora Carrington, the crop-haired art student known to all by her surname, who was sharing rooms with Alix and was friendly with the Oliviers; she and Lytton were, somewhat to Lytton's surprise, at the outset of a long-lasting relationship. Afterwards Noel and James had made slow progress back towards London. The city was under attack and their train could only inch towards it, stopping for three hours at Wimbledon where they walked up and down the platform to keep occupied and then curled up in rugs on board to rest. From the windows of the train they had seen shrapnel shattering above them, 'tiny white sparks (like stars) twinkling in the sky'. When they arrived at Noel's lodgings there was no one awake to admit them, so the pair found a hotel room for the night. Then James went on to find Alix.

Nevertheless, rumours circulated that James and Noel were going to be married. In reality, Noel was shy of commitment, still grieving for others, and Alix, who was said to be 'smoking & "black coffeeing" herself to a ruined heart' but was in fact probably suffering from anorexia, continued to pursue James with a mad pragmatism, or what Virginia Woolf described as an 'air of level-headed desperation'.

The rumours were plausible enough for Hugh to write to Noel with a qualified blessing. Like Rupert and the Raverats, Hugh seemed to have reservations about the Stracheys. He was suspicious of James's influence and told Noel he had, at times, blamed James for 'spoiling' her. Bloomsbury must have seemed like a closed world that offended many of the sacred tenets of Edwardian masculinity: heterosexuality, physical fitness and now combatant status. When Hugh admitted to Noel that though she might be 'strong enough & self-reliant enough not to mind what people think', he did mind, he may have been referring to the general condemnation with which conscientious objectors like James had to contend. Military service mattered to Hugh and he had put his life on hold to serve his country. In the same letter to Noel he expressed his amazement at the news that his daughter was walking; he hadn't seen Andy in over four months.

Hugh felt, he said, that after 'what [she] had suffered', Noel had been bound to change. It is hard to know what change, exactly, people like Hugh identified in Noel at this time. Certainly she was no longer the primitive teenager who had entranced Rupert. Those Neo-Pagan days had turned out to be a fortunate coming of age; she had since spent her early twenties in times that made few allowances to youth. She was a rare creature still: a woman of authority, both within her family and now in her work. She was learning to survive bereavement, personal traumas and depression. She knew how to save lives, how to treat male bodies, she knew her own sexuality, she was coming to know her strength.

★

There were signs that 'Bloomsbury' was reforming, in slightly altered shape, in London. In October, Leonard Woolf established the 1917 Club, named for the February Revolution in Russia, on Gerrard Street ('the rather melancholy haunt of prostitutes daily from 2.30 p.m. onwards') in Soho. It was intended as a meeting place for like-minded people, people interested in peace and democratic principles, and became a hub for radicals and intellectuals; the kind of place where Virginia or the Olivier sisters could turn up and be sure of finding friends taking tea by the fire. Noel and Alix became fixtures, and Bryn and Daphne were sometimes seen there (Virginia once arrived and found 'someone I took to be Bryn, but she answered to the name of Daphne'). The Club was a swift success and over one hundred people attended a celebratory dinner after its first general meeting in December, including Daphne, who was up from Cambridge.

Daphne had celebrated her twenty-eighth birthday in Cambridge that October. Eva had leased an 'absolutely hideous but comfortable' house there, in which she rented rooms to Daphne and to Charles Ogden, the publisher of *The Cambridge Magazine*. Daphne had returned to Cambridge to work for him.

Once merely the editor of an undergraduate rag, during the war Ogden had become a determined defender of civil liberties and his magazine had gained a reputation for publishing pacifist articles. Clive Bell was one of the contributors and Siegfried Sassoon's protest against the war first appeared in its pages. In 1917 the magazine was consequently under siege in the national press and in Parliament. On at least one occasion, patriotic students smashed up its offices.

As well as a gallery, which sold artwork by members of the Bloomsbury Group, Ogden ran two bookshops in Cambridge. Daphne was brought on board to help manage them. There was a relaxed discipline to working life there, she told Margery:

> Some mornings I stay reading a book in the garden in the sun – others I walk through Kings & get to the office about 10.0 & make lists of old books & price stacks of poetry. At other times I go along the backs to Magdalen where we have a warehouse and we fumble about in semi-obscurity and clouds of dust heaving huge volumes.

But she soon also became involved in the magazine and, given her background in languages, it is probable that she was drawn into the

'Notes from the Foreign Press' section, which was made possible by a dedicated group of translators. It was this section that had gained the magazine a reputation, influence and circulation that reached far beyond Cambridge. The 'Notes' were intended as a way to get around wartime censorship by translating and publishing extracts from newspapers in the neutral and belligerent countries, thereby offering readers an alternative view of the international and military situation without publishing opinion pieces that would have drawn scrutiny. The reports revealed the presence of pacifists and internationalists in other countries, offered clues as to enemy tactics and showed what other nations were saying about Britain (and the possibilities for peace). The team of translators made it possible for the magazine to cover publications ranging across the political spectrum from France, Germany, Austria, Italy, Hungary, Poland, Russia, the Balkans, Sweden, Switzerland, Denmark and the Netherlands, as well as from the US. In doing so, it championed the provision of a varied and balanced coverage, something increasingly rare during the war years.

Margery was busy stripping The Champions and the Marlborough Road house with her requests for furniture for her new cottage. Brynhild had little in her own room there besides a dressing table from Jamaica and a framed photo of Hugh. He had been involved in the fall of Gaza and had come through unscathed; meanwhile, Paul Montague's plane had disappeared over the desert. Brynhild missed her husband and could only draw solace from a little space on Tony's neck, behind his ears, which reminded her of Hugh.

In December the cottage was freezing and Brynhild gathered the children by the fireplace in Tony's bedroom. Fortunately they were all spending Christmas at The Champions, with Daphne, the Wala and Sydney. Only Noel was kept in London by work but James had decided to stay too to keep her company and Daphne had no intention of letting her remain in London for the whole holiday. Despite Hugh's concerns about the strain she had been under, Brynhild was, in her way, settling in at Tatsfield, where her little family was thriving. That winter she received two delayed letters in one go from Hugh and sat down promptly on a frozen tree trunk near the post office to reply. 'The two babies are roving round among dead leaves,' she told him,

Andy in white gaiters coat & cap with a bright blue pinafore dangling below her coat. Tony in his same old scarlet wool [...] Their faces are absurd. Andy bright crimson, rather like a little barmaid, with fluffy hair. There is the usual drone of aeroplanes.

'It's too late to wish you a Happy Xmas,' she wrote later. 'All the same I hope you will be cheerful & one can have Devout hopes for a better new year. It could'nt anyway be much worse. Thats a comforting thought.'

Sydney, who had once worried that his daughter would end up a poet's wife rather than a doctor, could hardly contain his pride at Noel's new job. 'It is very satisfactory that she should have wound up and started her career so cleverly,' he wrote to Daphne. In 1913, only four years before, Noel had wondered if she and Rupert would ever be able to see each other without pain again. 'I agree that it would be nice to stroll along peacefully,' she told him, 'if it could be done. When I'm twenty-five & you thirty perhaps we shall be calmer, more restrained people, & will be able to.' The following year, preparing to start her training at the hospital, she had enjoyed the feeling of having her future mapped out for her: 'I shall be settled [in training], till I'm twenty-five, after that, I shall go from Hospital to Hospital earning little salaries [...] It makes me very pleased, that fate is clear in the main.'

Noel and Rupert had never reached their time of peace and reconciliation; his death preserved him as a question for her heart. But she was, now, stepping into a future of her own choosing. On 4 December, weeks before her twenty-fifth birthday, she signed off a card to James as 'Dr Olivier'. Brynhild, canny and perceptive always when it came to her youngest sister, had plotted out a new future for her. 'Bryn says that the best line for me in marriage would be a rather successful doctor,' Noel told James. 'She's quite right; I must see what I can contrive. It's obvious I'm never going to marry for love now, so I may as well be reasonable & vorsichtig about it. A medical man – full-blooded & energetic – will probably be the most suitable.'

PART FOUR

New Ways to Live

(Or, Five Years Later)

I

Ventimiglia, Italy, January 1923

In January 1923, a baby, newly named Philip, made his way through France in the luggage rack of a train. His mother and grandmother had lashed his cot in place with lengths of string tied across the swaying carriage, which, fortunately, they had to themselves. His six-year-old sister was restless but she and their three-year-old brother were well-behaved and the journey went smoothly. They were headed for La Mortola Inferiore, the first Italian village across the border from France, where Philip's great-uncle, Herbert Olivier, a portrait painter, had a villa by the sea.

Both Margaret and Sydney were taking the opportunity for a holiday but Sydney had gone on ahead, making his own assessments about Italian politics as he went. 'Mussolini,' he wrote to H. G. Wells, 'is getting a bit perplexed about his position. He is finding [...] that his supporters are embarrassing task-masters.' The family had missed Mussolini's march on Rome by only a few weeks but it didn't sound as though they had missed much. 'There were not many conflicts and the revolution was carried through almost without bloodshed,' *The Spectator* had reported approvingly.

For a shrewd man, Sydney was unusually oblivious to the reasons for Brynhild's departure. He seemed unwell when they arrived and Margaret resolved to keep the reality of the situation – what she termed 'all these tragic difficulties' – from him. Though Hugh was registered as his father, Philip was Raymond Sherrard's son. It's possible that Hugh hadn't even met him yet. In an outcome Brynhild surprisingly failed to foresee, her pregnancy had, she judged, made 'everything [in her marriage] ten times worse'. Brynhild had asked Hugh for a divorce and then escaped to Italy.

Hugh with the children in Draycott Fitzpayne, 1919

After the war she and Hugh had seemed to do what everyone else was seeming to do: settling back down to normality, picking up lives that had satisfied them in 1914, privately finding this more difficult than anyone admitted. Less than a year after Hugh was demobbed in 1918, they had another son, whom they named Tristram. But Margery's instincts about Raymond Sherrard and her sister – suspicions that had put relations between Brynhild and Margery under the old, familiar strain at Tatsfield – had proved right. Though she had told Hugh that she would ask Raymond to stay away to avoid another one of Margery's infatuations, he hadn't done so for long and, before the end of the war, he and Brynhild had begun an affair.

By the time of Hugh's return, Raymond had gone up to St John's College, Cambridge, to study Natural Sciences, one of many thousands of ex-servicemen belatedly arriving at university. He was twenty-six. As family life resumed, though she spent her time poring over maps to find ways and places for them to meet, Brynhild tried to conceal her feelings for Raymond. She was by nature a frank person but openness was in this case, she felt at first, a 'luxury one should not indulge in at someone else's expense'. She still loved her husband – 'I love him enough to want to make him as happy as I can,' she told Raymond without hesitation – but she no longer believed that there was a way she could make her marriage satisfying. 'It has taken me six years,' she reflected, 'to admit that I could not by changeing my own ways or by patience or a new house or something, achieve this state of being in love with complete understanding & being understood.' She and Hugh could still enjoy a night of dancing in London together but the love she felt for Raymond exposed the nature of her feelings for Hugh as fondness and loyalty only.

As ever, Brynhild followed a set of internal principles that allowed her to demand a certain standard of behaviour from herself whilst proceeding on her own terms. 'Its <u>my own opinion</u> of my conduct that matters to me,' she told Raymond. An illicit liaison held no particular thrill for her: she loved Raymond and wanted to dignify their relationship through honesty; she also hated lying. But when she admitted the affair to Hugh, Brynhild had found to her disappointment that her version of decency was not rewarded and that telling him simply ruined married life. Hugh was desperate. Brynhild's concern for him and her own desire for privacy meant that she did refuse Raymond's invitations to dances in Cambridge, knowing that her presence there with another man would set old friends who had settled in the town 'buzzing'. 'You don't know the sharpness [...] of people like the Cornfords, Raverats, Keynes,' she schooled Raymond, 'who would be bound to hear of my being up there & wont take 2 minutes in jumping at the truth – which is what I don't want. Not that they will think it very <u>odd</u>; but I cant bear them to know that I don't love him.'

Yet Raymond was determined that their relationship should receive acknowledgement, so that Bryn found herself caught between the demands of two men, neither of whom would tolerate mention of the other's feelings. Raymond was an opinionated, unconventional man. He liked to enjoy life – he could be excellent company and with his dashing motorbike he had charmed Bryn's young children – but he was also uncompromising. His (deliberate, she suspected) lack of discretion infuriated her. She resented being put 'in the position of being publicly possessed' and was no doubt beginning to sense that she had lost control of the situation.

For a while there was a lull. Bryn had tired of London and spent as much time as she could in Wiltshire, at a house she and Hugh had taken in Draycott Fitzpayne. It was not an isolated life. Desmond and Molly MacCarthy had a house nearby (providing, with their son Dermod, a companion for Tony) as did the Waterlows. Both couples would have been acquaintances from Bloomsbury. Sydney Waterlow had once proposed to Virginia Woolf. The MacCarthys were close to the core of the Bloomsbury Group; both writers, they grappled constantly with pecuniary problems and Desmond's failure to complete a novel.

Wiltshire gave Bryn more of the space and lifestyle that she wanted. It also gave her the Downs, the beauty of which she found 'simply enough to bowl one over'. Her lifestyle became distinctly rural-domestic, consisting chiefly in 'digging potatoes & feeding ducks & children'. She also spent time sewing with, or for, neighbours, negotiating the demands of the girls she employed as domestic help, catering to the needs of visitors and children; dealing with matters that, she noted, 'mean nothing to men who consider all womens "difficulties" products of the imagination'.

Hugh stayed in London during the week, working at the British Museum again, where he specialised in Dutch and Flemish Old Masters. Bryn's contact with Raymond remained, for a while, epistolary. On Saturdays the Pophams took evening walks on the Downs, having difficult conversations about the persistent young man in Cambridge, but on Sundays, she told Raymond, they became 'most energetic & controlled': gardening and raising their children together. His years of loving Brynhild had given Hugh an advantage over his rival: he knew how to give her the space she needed. 'It is because Hugh seems to leave me so free that I enjoy being with him,' she wrote warningly. 'I feel I can <u>breathe</u> because he has not such expectations from me & goes his own way quietly.'

Around the time Raymond graduated with a Third, Brynhild and Hugh were preparing to transfer their family home to Ramsden, the village in Oxfordshire to which Sydney and the Wala had retired, settling into an Elizabethan house once used by Charles I as a hunting lodge. The Pophams had bought a row of cottages close by and were having them converted into a family home. Restoration work was overseen by Sydney, who was sometimes visible on the roof with the builders. Brynhild seems to have been content for the children to run as wild in Draycott Fitzpayne as she had done in Limpsfield, perhaps distracted by her relationship with Raymond. But Sydney and Margaret also played a large part in their grand-children's lives: five-year-old Andy adored her grandfather, who smelled of tobacco and sang her old Jamaican songs. Margaret, rechristened Arnie by the next generation, schooled her grandchildren in table manners but also left a biscuit by Tony and Andy's beds, in case of hunger in the night.

Raymond soon moved close to Oxford. Tensions thrived: he pining for visits, Brynhild balancing her many obligations and loves. 'I do not feel free to sacrifice myself for any one person,' she told him. Brynhild was well aware of the six-year age difference between them, of Raymond's comparative freedom, of the admirers he had attracted in Cambridge. Their relationship fell into its own rhythms, with its own stresses and validations, like a marriage, and apparently feeling just as permanent. Raymond wanted them to have a child together. Brynhild resisted at first but his desire only grew, until it became, in her words, a 'mountainous eruption thrusting this way & that, spoiling everything'. Deep down, she admitted, she thought that pregnancy may relieve some of the pressure: 'he will be different to me as other peoples husbands are,' she had assumed, she told him in a fit of disillusionment in June 1922, 'he will suddenly become considerate.' By that point, she was pregnant.

Raymond Sherrard

Despite her new grandson, the Wala still hoped Bryn's marriage was salvageable and wrote to Noel asking her to pass on the message that 'whatever happens, for the next few months at any rate, Hugh [should] do <u>nothing</u>'. But the situation had become further complicated – perhaps beyond the Wala's appreciation – by Hugh's affair with Brynhild's cousin, Joan Thornycroft, who was married to the theatre critic Bertie Farjeon.

The family arrived in a beautiful place, lush with bright bougainvillea, fiery poinsettia and feathery clumps of bamboo. The houses of La Mortola stood staggered upon a hill, buildings crowded together, gardens studded with palm trees. The closest village was Latte, a poor and dusty place, once sustained by flower cultivation, an industry disrupted by political turmoil and hit by the loss of German buyers. Bryn watched the local women weaving baskets from bamboo to carry flowers they could no longer sell. She and the Wala set about getting in supplies and familiarising themselves with the language and currency. Italian lessons were arranged with local nuns for Andy. Various relations began to descend on the family: Hugh's aunt, then Brynhild's aunt and uncle, Noel's doctor friend Marie Moralt came and stayed at the bottom of the garden.

The retreat didn't bring respite. 'This place is lovely & brilliant,' Bryn told Raymond, 'but I am too hopelessly depressed on the whole.' A bad flu epidemic was sweeping Italy and, as Bryn put it, swept straight into her family. First Tristram, who had wandered off in the cold weather whilst the women were busy unpacking, then Andy and finally Bryn and the baby fell ill. Brynhild was confined to the villa they had taken with the worry of three small, sick children (Tony was at school in England). 'Poor little Philip is extremely brave,' she told his father, '& smiles though he can hardly open his eyes & is shaken by the most tremendous coughs.' Nevertheless, the baby had begun to reject Bryn's milk, and under stress and illness she soon stopped producing any. To make matters worse, Brynhild discovered that the children's nurse was violent with them and decided they could no longer be left alone with her.

She was already intensely regretting her separation from Raymond. A letter from Hugh had followed her from England, informing her that he would not agree to a divorce and that she would have to accept this; the sooner she did, he wrote, the sooner she might feel better. Bryn did not take this advice. 'I am no longer willing to sacrifice you,' she assured Raymond.

During the day, the brilliant light of La Mortola – a bright but somehow unobtrusive, uncombative light that drew artists and encouraged the nurturing of fantastic, exotic gardens – could warm even the winter days. That, though, was illusory. Once the sun descended, or sheltered behind clouds, the cold was sudden and biting. Night fell swiftly and with it, loneliness hit. 'I think it is a waste of life to go on like this,' Bryn lamented, 'I feel as I suppose a widow woman feels.'

Her misery was compounded by Hugh's affair, more from a sense of injury than of grief. She seemed affronted by the situation. Whilst the Wala worried that her daughter might have cut off contact with him, Brynhild in fact wrote to Hugh demanding that he break things off with Joan, at which he fell silent. Used to getting her own way, Brynhild now found herself trapped.

Raymond wrote helplessly from Oxford, afraid that she would give in to Hugh, resenting that she didn't tolerate criticisms of her husband, despite his obstructions. Bryn herself, granted space from both of the men in her life, seemed to be prevaricating, trying to work out what principles to apply to their situation.

'Happiness for everybody seems to me to be the only principle on which to base our actions,' Raymond wrote desperately.

> Therefore it is our duty to society, to the world, to be together at once & always; for until we are neither you, nor I nor Hugh can be happy in a real & permanent sense; & neither can we do our best for anybody. We are wasting life, we are losing our self-respect, & running the risk of injuring our minds for life.

Brynhild took comfort in her new baby. Presumably apprised of his paternity, the Wala claimed to dislike Philip and threatened to fling the child out of the window while Bryn was out, yet secretly she could not resist doting on him any more than Bryn could. (Unable to resent his son, the Wala had to settle for her enmity of Raymond.) Though everyone's health remained precarious, the little group of Oliviers set off on expeditions, making the most of the 'paradise' they had landed in. There was a steep climb down to the sea, past terraces of carnations planted in rows, along a coast fringed with firs and junipers. The drop down to the Mediterranean was dramatic and at the bottom glass-like waves frothed and then dissolved over pebble flagstones. While the children collected seawater in buckets, Bryn and the Wala rested in the sun. The famous Hanbury Gardens, the legacy of a nineteenth-century English businessman, which spread out over the land above them, opened to the public twice a week and was as nectar to dedicated horticulturists like Margaret and Brynhild. Orange and lemon trees, cypresses, bamboos, roses, succulents, fountains, statues and surprising vistas were all presided over by a peach-coloured palazzo, which gazed romantically out over the sea from its den of greenery.

As the stay went on, Brynhild formulated a plan. Her proposal was addressed to Hugh but the first person she shared it with was Raymond. It required his cooperation, for in it she offered to live with Hugh as his wife for nine months, not seeing Raymond but continuing to write to him, after which time, having given their marriage this chance, she hoped that he would grant her a divorce if she asked again.

'I do not think there is anything impossible to human nature in it – or anything dishonourable,' Bryn wrote. She had agonised over the plan but in reality she was clutching at straws. She did not think it was possible to force Hugh's hand and yet she could not tolerate, she said, being 'held to him by law'. She asked Raymond to forward the note, asking him, too, to bear the separation.

Raymond took it badly but he did as she asked, realising that his influence was limited. He found Bryn's reasoning, her attempts to behave well, absurd – 'though I see it appears noble, & justifies a pat on the back!' – all drawn from moral standards that were no longer relevant: 'tear away the angel's wings & underneath you find gathered up a few ideas which your parents put there when you were ten, ideas [...] which have been passed on from your forefathers'. Most of all, he did not want to lose Brynhild or see his son raised by another man.

When it reached Noel in London, the plan was again condemned. Noel had long despaired of all of them – Hugh, Brynhild and Raymond. Ever the voice of reason, she could not understand how the three of them (four if one included Joan, which she now did) had worked themselves into their overwrought state. Noel was worried about her sister making decisions in her current condition, concerned that Bryn seemed unable to articulate what she wanted or needed. Noel understood exactly how Hugh and Brynhild upset and goaded one another and she agreed with one aspect of Bryn's proposal: that what they needed was time: 'a chance to pull themselves together & settle the thing quietly'.

In this matter, though, Brynhild did not even consider Noel an ally. Bryn was single-minded about obtaining a divorce and she knew that Noel, in her fondness for Hugh and the Popham home at Caroline Place, could not whole-heartedly support that decision. '[S]he is preju-diced in favour of what she calls my present marriage,' she told Raymond.

The vocabulary of war, or rather its settlement, seeped into Noel's assessment of the situation. What she wanted really was for Raymond to stay out of the way. 'I hope,' she told him, 'that you will not oppose an armistice of some kind.' It was not only language that had gained new currency in England after the war, but also language, first adopted by Edwardian feminists, that seemed more apposite than ever when it came to relations between men and women. After one argument Bryn rushed to reassure Raymond that she had revised her position, 'lest you should be preparing a counterblast with all the heavy guns being massed to destroy the already-evacuated-positions'.

Bryn and Hugh's marriage had descended into a battle, where two people who had always got on well found themselves in implacable positions of painful reproach. Hugh didn't think much of Brynhild's plan either but was encouraged by the fact that she appeared willing to make concessions. As spring approached, he decided to visit La Mortola, arriving during a spell of appalling weather. He stayed in the villa with his wife, played with the children on the coast, showing off his old diving prowess to an admiring Andy, and picnicked on the beach with his family. Everyone kept falling ill. Relations between Bryn and Hugh veered between peaceful companionship and furious rows that reduced Bryn to what he described as 'states'.

To Raymond, Brynhild insisted that an amicable separation was of paramount importance. She knew full well that the law was not on her side and her greatest fear was that an injured Hugh would take the children from her: 'You know I am slightly fanatical about the children,' she reminded him. Under the law, Hugh could divorce Brynhild for adultery but she would have to prove another offence beyond adultery, such as incest, bigamy or desertion (none of which he was guilty of), on his part to free herself. She was facing the fact that the progressive politics she and her husband had taken for granted in their youth had suddenly become irrelevant. 'It is excessively irritating,' she reflected, 'as when one married a modern young man – formerly a member of the Fabian nursery – it did not occur to one that he would ever in any circumstances attempt to take advantage of such an anti feminist law.' She couldn't decide whether to return to England with him or not. 'At times there seems no possibility of our ever disagreeing for a moment – this is really our normal condition,' Hugh confided to Noel, 'at others there seems no possibility of our coming to an understanding. I think probably that is the true position.'

Andy at La Mortola Inferiore

Noel had learned a lot about relations between men and women: in love and at war. Her own marriage had had fiery beginnings. Dr Arthur Richards was a dark-haired and good-looking Welshman. Like Noel, he had been a medical student during the war; they had worked together at Charing Cross Hospital. Their marriage had provoked pleased and slightly mystified responses from the sisters' friends. Who was this Arthur Richards (or Jones, as Virginia insisted on calling him)? He was not of Bloomsbury, nor was he a survivor of the Neo-Pagans or their outer reaches; he wasn't even a Cambridge man. He was entirely Noel's. Of all the literary, romantic men Noel could have married, the stocky, sporty Arthur Richards, not known to paint or pine or compose, was something unexpected. For some, the idea was a disappointment. 'Why didn't you marry any of those romantic young men? Why? Why?' Virginia asked and Noel would give an evasive reply, making no special claims for her husband. For a person who valued privacy, he was a good choice.

Arthur was an energetic and quick-tempered, some might say full-blooded, young man who shared many of her interests: medicine, sleeping out, long walks. He was a keen sportsman and had been an excellent student. But he was also a noticeable departure: younger (born three years after Noel) and the son of a sea captain who piloted the ships coming into Llanelli Harbour. Noel was drawn to his down-to-earth nature, his lack of artifice. She loved what she did not see in herself: his ease with others, his ability to speak to anyone. He might even have seemed uncomplicated. In August 1920, Noel announced her engagement to the Wala in a typically understated way. 'So we thought it w[oul]d be nice to be married,' she wrote.

At the time of her engagement, Noel was a Resident Medical Officer at the Victoria Hospital for Children. She liked to walk in a loop, along the Chelsea Embankment until she reached the bridge near Victoria, then through Battersea Park to the further bridge, which would lead her back towards the hospital on Tite Street. RMO's stayed at Gough House, the hospital's eighteenth-century building a few doors down from the houses where Oscar Wilde and Whistler had once lived. The hospital itself, close to the river, was prone to damp and on wet days dew formed on the walls, where finger-drawn graffiti would appear along the staircase. As it was a hospital for infants, Noel could count on the companionship of other female doctors. 'We 3 lady doctors lead a fairly idle and relaxing life among the babies close to the river,' she told James Strachey.

Without independent means, young doctors could struggle to establish themselves in a profession that paid badly at the outset. Training depended on clinical experience, which depended on either securing a resident post in a hospital or working as an assistant to an established practitioner: both options poorly remunerated. Early on, Noel and Arthur's courtship was interrupted when he accepted an assistant position at a colliery practice near Cardiff, hoping eventually to save enough money to be able to continue his training with the goal of becoming a surgeon. For months, Noel's relationship played out in almost daily letters between two young doctors submerged in work. But this was another of the things Noel found she had in common with the young Welshman: they were both utterly and endlessly enthralled with medicine.

Medicine was the stalwart partner in their relationship. Arthur does not seem to have felt sure of Noel. His explosive temperament meant that grievances flared up rapidly and unexpectedly. He was jealous of her friendships and particularly of her history with James. Noel was in her late twenties when they first met and had survived, she told him, 'the most awful things [...] that could ever happen'; she was independent and sustained by friends and interests of her own. Arthur struggled to gain her full attention. He was resentful, too, of the people she admired, people who did not conform to contemporary standards of moral and physical health; some of whom, he raged, 'I look upon as being definitely diseased in outlook & in action.' He wanted to be assured that his devotion was reciprocated, that her love was exclusive, that he was not alone in the vulnerability of adoration. 'You are beautiful, kind and wise,' he told her before he left for the colliery practice, 'but somewhat elusive and too independent [...] Darling, I am yours but are you mine?'

Arthur's relatives did not approve of the match. His family was large and poor; his career hard-won and still precarious. Their relationship crossed class lines; they met instead in a professional identity (an identity that also distinguished Noel from the women she admired in the Bloomsbury Group), and the common ground they shared had to be supplemented by Noel's tutoring: how to cope with the housekeeper at Caroline Place, who to read (Joseph Conrad and Henry James). He took dance lessons to please her but spoiled the effect by sporting a black eye sustained playing rugby. After her affairs with Rupert and James, to not feel at an intellectual disadvantage must have been refreshing and bolstering but Noel had to tread carefully. Arthur was alert to any hints of superiority (social or academic): furious and proud when she made careless jokes about his native Wales, offended when she asked if he was aware of the 'commotion' Einstein's work was causing.

Noel's love for Rupert had taught her hard lessons. 'Please, I can't allow it,' she warned Arthur after one outburst, 'you must be more careful & conscientious about loving me & not let there be these little interludes of hate. They're a great mistake.' Falling in love again after she had given up hope was a revelation for Noel. '[Y]ou're as a matter of fact the only thing thats real at all,' she once told him and she was, she admitted, a 'slave to your smile'.

Arthur Richards (third from left) with colleagues

Noel had about as much enthusiasm for the trappings of a wedding as her father had had thirty-five years earlier. Yet she was married in the capacious St Martin-in-the-Fields church on Trafalgar Square, where her parents had once stood impatiently in the crowds on Bloody Sunday, five years before she was born. The Wala couldn't resist some playful surprise when she heard about the venue. 'Does this entail a white satin dress & orange blossom??' she wrote to the bride. 'And a party?' It did not. Noel's MD exams that year took precedence; she didn't even pick an outfit until less than two weeks before the wedding. On a Tuesday morning in December 1920, Noel, dressed in a grey suit, took to the aisle with her father and was married. Some of the couple's friends from Charing Cross had insisted on attending as well-wishers but otherwise Arthur and Noel came as close to their ideal – to meet somewhere alone, 'sign a book' and have done with it – as they could.

For both her own brother and for James Strachey, Virginia Woolf noted, Noel remained 'the unattainable romance'. James had married

Alix earlier in the year, supposedly to make travel to Vienna easier. They had left for Freud's consulting room, for both analysis and training. When the two of them met to say goodbye, Noel had disappointed James in her lack of sadness at parting. He had been her companion during the years of her deepest depression; the years, she had told Arthur, during which she felt 'only half alive', but the power of the Strachey influence had left her, she felt, at risk of losing her own identity. Others in Bloomsbury were less philosophical than Noel in seeing Alix emerge triumphant, finding one of its longest-running sagas draw to a pedestrian close. 'I find no excitement in this [outcome],' a petulant Virginia recorded. Even Alix began to find James's incipient devotion disconcerting: 'I do so like running after you, you see,' she warned him later, 'like the awful perverted woman I am.'

Though unattainable, Noel was still close by. Visiting Leonard's 1917 Club, Virginia would find 'varieties of Oliviers' in repose by the fire; Noel eased an anxious Carrington through the experience of an operation at a London hospital and continued to attend Vanessa Bell's parties. When Vanessa's youngest child, Angelica, fell seriously ill just after the war, Noel dispatched her friend Dr Marie Moralt to Charleston, who saved the baby's life. Noel was the only person bold or blasé enough to ask Mrs Bell outright who Angelica's father was. 'I suppose I must admit – though I know it's very dull – that my husband is the father of my child!' Vanessa had lied.

Noel got her books from Bunny and Frankie Birrell's new bookshop on Taviton Street, off Gordon Square, and read *Anna Karenina* alongside Arthur. He found the heroine uninteresting, 'too exacting & hysterical & unhappy', whilst Noel, perhaps enviously, admired her beauty and passion. The pair studied Einstein, whose ideas were shaking the foundations of accepted knowledge for their generation as Darwin's had for her parents': Noel and Daphne, with their cousin Ursula and their uncle, formed an 'Einstein Relativity Study Circle' to come to terms with him, intending to make the 1917 Club their regular venue.

Noel was no longer enmeshed in the Bloomsbury sexual labyrinth; on the whole the matter of her marriage was treated lightly. Maynard Keynes, Duncan Grant and Clive Bell sent 'most affectionate wishes for your success in your proposed legal proceedings', along with hotel recommendations for her honeymoon in Paris. Vanessa and Duncan sent paintings as wedding gifts. 'Where would you like me to send you

the Belle Bell which Grant grants?' Maynard, entrusted with practi-
calities, asked.

When it came to work, Arthur never criticised Noel's dedication, even
when it cost him her attention. 'I can't see that there's any excuse for
going in for this profession at all if one isn't going to do it as well as
possible,' she had told him early on and in this they were in agreement.
Establishing a career in medicine when you were without private means,
or, worse, a woman was not for the faint-hearted. But Arthur was
enraged when Noel mentioned discussing the 'possibilities for women
in medicine' with another female doctor. His pride extended, now, to
Noel. 'I hated the idea of you and that old hen discussing the "possibilities",' he told her. 'It seemed such a confession of weakness or even
failure. Darling, please take the position for granted and don't discuss
the "<u>possibilities</u>".'

But the reality was that no woman in medicine could afford to take
her position for granted. Noel was fortunate in the support of Herbert
Waterhouse, a well-regarded surgeon at the Victoria Hospital who had
enthusiastically offered himself as a mentor. On the face of it, women
had come a long way in medicine. In the year before Noel's birth,
there were only twenty-five qualified women on the medical register;
by 1921 there were 2,100: almost double the figure just before the war.
The war had been perverse in its fostering of optimism. However
much people wanted the conflict to end, they confidently predicted
that the changes it brought would last. 'There never has been a "going
backward" where the woman worker is concerned,' the author of *How
to Become a Woman Doctor* crowed in 1918. She was wrong. The 1920s
would prove it.

As the London medical schools filled up with new and returning
students, who glared from female colleagues to national unemployment levels and back again, it seemed that the medical profession
had become overcrowded. The London schools soon responded by
reverting as far as possible to the prewar status quo. In 1919, St George's
Hospital stopped admitting women as clinical students; others
followed suit. The following year, the University College Hospital
medical school's committee was urged by its students to reverse its
wartime decision to admit women. The most desirable recruits,
'Public School and Oxford and Cambridge men', were put off by the

presence of women, they were warned: a generation of men who had weathered the trenches could hardly now be expected to submit to the indignity of female superiors once these women graduated ahead of them. 'We need hardly point out, gentlemen,' the protesting students pointed out, 'the intolerable position of an ex-Service man who has, perhaps, as his House Surgeon over him, a girl of twenty-two.' In this case, the committee compromised by offering a strictly limited number of places to women (King's settled on a similar solution) but within a year the London Hospital Medical College stopped admitting women entirely. St Mary's, Charing Cross (where Noel had worked) and Westminster hospitals all followed in closing their medical schools to women. A Newnham student who had switched to medicine during the war and afterwards qualified at UCL felt herself and the other female trainees to be 'hated like poison' by the hospital staff – including the nurses. For qualified female doctors, openings were closing fast. When the London Hospital appointed a woman to a house position in 1922, the male residents threatened to resign.

In other words, apparently secure concessions to women were being wheeled back out of reach. In medicine, the authorities fell back on old excuses: that the discipline necessarily covered topics inappropriate for women, that women inevitably married and wasted their educations, that exposure to indelicate topics ruined women and made them unmarriageable.

In qualifying before the end of the war, Noel had been able to acquire experience that was crucial for her career and that women qualifying in the early 1920s, women who had been lured by promises of a welcome during the war, were now everywhere struggling to find. The welcome had vanished. At the Victoria Hospital, Noel had as her House Surgeon an ex-serviceman from New Zealand, a man who struck her as sulky, defensive and not particularly gifted as a surgeon. 'I suspect he has a mas[s] of buried complexes,' she confided to Arthur. Nevertheless, she liked him for being 'kind to me in not making me feel uncomfortable at being his bos[s] although he's been a Major in the war'. No doubt she was well aware of the reception that her contemporaries met elsewhere. Generally she relied on a great deal of diplomacy to get by, negotiating with the Secretary, Matron and other staff, which, she acknowledged, usually meant that she gave in at the first sign of a dispute.

Noel (standing) with colleagues

It was rare for women doctors to be married, rarer still for them to have children and practise. The London County Council soon stopped hiring married (female) doctors altogether. At work, Noel kept the news of her engagement quiet. It wasn't until shortly before the wedding that she confided in one of the (male) physicians who seemed friendly, and who offered Noel advice about how she might arrange to stay on at the hospital afterwards.

Nevertheless, there was, she told Arthur, 'nothing but nightmares living without you', and that meant that there was no way around marriage. When they planned for Arthur to visit her in London they had to arrange furtively to borrow James's flat from Carrington's lover Ralph Partridge – who spent his weekends with Lytton and Carrington in the countryside – and when Noel visited Arthur in Wales she fretted that the servants at the doctor's house would object to her presence. The idea of living together without marrying seemed impossible. 'I still wish we didn't actually have to <u>be</u> married,' Noel wrote to the Wala when she became engaged. 'It's a rotten plan & a menace to the success of any lives. We are driven like hens into a pen.'

*

Arthur Richards had learned early on that marrying Noel would mean becoming part of her sisters' lives too. Brynhild's entanglements put pressure on their relationship as early as the autumn of 1920, when Noel wrote to Arthur (who was in Wales) asking for assistance in a matter relating to Brynhild. It seems likely that her sister had fallen pregnant, and that she and Hugh had turned to Noel for help.

Abortion was illegal. In fact, as the only medical procedure that was officially outlawed, it was often referred to as the 'illegal operation'. Noel seemed aware in writing to Arthur that she was asking a lot and was careful not to apply pressure: 'You're not to oblige if you object at all.' Doctors could be prosecuted for performing abortions. In reality juries were reluctant to convict, and anyway were usually presented with untrained 'midwives', rather than doctors, usually when an abortion had gone wrong, but more worrying for Noel and Arthur than life imprisonment, the maximum penalty, would have been the fact that prosecution alone would mean being struck off the medical register. When Alix Strachey thought she was pregnant in 1918, Noel had refused to help.

Abortion was, perversely, one of the most accessible methods of birth control open to women (though particularly for working-class couples). It commonly involved the insertion of a sharp object, something like a pencil, into the cervix, or packing the vagina to dilate the mouth of the uterus. Alternatives like douching or the consumption of irritants like quinine were common; perhaps most popular were the pills advertised in women's magazines, thinly disguised as medicines to 'restore regularity' or 'remove obstructions'. These, at least, were generally relatively harmless (to both mother and foetus). Finding a doctor to perform the abortion of course reduced the risks. Though they presumably lacked practical experience, standard medical texts for students did contain discussions of abortions, so Noel and Arthur would have known how to cause a miscarriage.

Despite agreeing to help, Arthur was uneasy. The same textbooks also warned doctors against involving themselves in such 'unsavoury cases'. He worried about the implications for Brynhild and about supervision for her after they departed. Doctors were trained to consider such interventions (like much medical practice related to women's bodies) as beneath their dignity. Arthur asked high-handedly that Noel not 'engage' him for any more cases: 'I am not frightfully anxious for such work. It all arose out of your absurd confidences, which implicated me, and how could I refuse after y[ou]'d asked me? [...] I have other objections but it is necessary to see you & <u>tell</u> you.'

Nor was Noel comfortable with the task facing them. She admitted that the days leading up to their appointment with Brynhild were 'harrowing'. But this was partly due to a crisis that erupted in Ramsden at the same time that Noel and the Pophams were making plans. 'We are a terrible family & in a terrible state,' she told Arthur, 'nearly always, it seems to me. Is there no peace in the world?'

Even after years of dealing with Margery's illness, only Noel seemed to have given up hope of a complete cure, and she still believed that, if found, the right treatment could have transformative effects. The problem was finding a treatment to fit the disorder. Their hopes largely rested with psychoanalysis, which was catching on. Margery herself had latched on to the idea and was keen to be analysed. 'It is all experimental though I suppose!' the Wala conceded to Noel.

Their best contact was Godwin Baynes who, having separated from their cousin Rosalind (she fled to Italy with D. H. Lawrence), was in Zurich, training under the psychiatrist and psychoanalyst Carl Jung, a former protégé of Freud's. That winter, Margery's mania was trained on her father. She was these days capable of serious violence and he had to retreat to the National Liberal Club in London. Sydney consulted Jung in Switzerland, and plans were made to transport Margery there, but ultimately Jung felt unable to make the commitment. (His friend, Dr Nichol, saw Margery in London instead.) It was still far from clear that such an approach could help Margery – psychoanalysts largely concerned themselves with neuroses and successful treatment depended on a cooperative patient; Margery could be both volatile and incoherent – but the practice was still in its infancy and full of possibility. People like James and Alix Strachey were coming to analysis like disciples: there was no reason to think that it could not have wider benefits than had yet been identified.

Noel and Sydney were generally suspicious of the (affordable) options in England. There was no obligation for psychoanalysts to undergo any formal medical training; people who were interested in it were undergoing analysis, like James and Adrian Stephen, and 'putting up a plate' as analysts; others simply added elements of psychoanalysis to their therapeutic repertoire, or claimed to. Even the woman whom the Oliviers had hired as a nurse/companion for Margery offered to try her hand at psychoanalysing her, for a reasonable fee. There was also the risk that analysis could do more harm than good. The process could be taxing on the patient's emotional and psychological energy. In Vienna, James admitted to sometimes finding his sessions 'absolutely shattering'. Virginia Woolf noted darkly that her brother was being 'altogether broken up by psycho analysis'.

One thing that pushed the Oliviers towards exploring psychoanalysis and the 'quacks' disdained by their doctor daughter was the stark choice presented by the other options. Since Dr Sherrard's death early in 1920, they had struggled to find a place with a curative emphasis, one that allowed patients a degree of freedom as well as occupation. Asylums were often holding pens, with restraint at their centre. The Wala despaired that: 'Nearly everything [sic] other home for Lunatics means restraint, coercion <u>and nothing else.</u>' The novelist Antonia White, who spent many months in Bethlem after a breakdown in the early twenties, wrote of being force-fed, straitjacketed, drugged and tied down to her bed. Virginia Woolf, too, would write vividly about the memory of mental illness: 'You can't think what a raging furnace it is still to me – madness and doctors and being forced.' It was little wonder that Margery reacted so badly to any suggestion of 'control' and that the family found it hard to countenance returning her to a hospital.

It is difficult to imagine anything more frightening than what Margery, suffering from paranoid, persecutory delusions, must have experienced: believing herself to be in immediate peril – sometimes from those she had most loved and trusted – yet finding that instead of receiving help from the outside world, she was instead punished for her violent attempts to protect herself. The authorities lined up in allegiance with her tormentors: her liberty, in other words her only means of escape, was repeatedly threatened. There was no safe place for Margery and no one willing or able to be inside her reality with her.

After Noel and Arthur's visit in November, Hugh took some time off work to stay with his wife and promised to send them updates on her condition. A few days later, Noel forwarded a note from Bryn that hasn't survived. Though Noel and Arthur knew in theory how things should proceed, in practice they seemed a little unsure of themselves. 'I don't think the thing can have occurred,' Noel wrote on the basis of Bryn's report, 'do you?' Marie Moralt visited Brynhild and confirmed Noel's suspicion; she offered Bryn some 'advice', which Noel hoped would 'lead to good results'. It soon seemed that another intervention would be necessary, however, and the Pophams arranged to visit Noel in London. But events with Margery overtook them. In Ramsden she attacked Sydney, injuring him in the eye and leg, prompting a desperate telegram from the Wala (who presumably knew nothing of Brynhild's predicament) asking for assistance. Bryn arrived and bore Margery to London, bringing forward the transfer of both sisters unexpectedly. Whilst Margery had a hastily arranged afternoon psychoanalysis session, Moralt and Noel performed what Noel described to Arthur as 'certain services' for Bryn, before 'join[ing] in silent prayer that they might be of lasting value'. It was just under two weeks until Noel's MD exam.

Arthur returned to London that December, so any further exchanges they had about Brynhild were in person. There is also a gap in Brynhild's letters to Raymond from the week before Noel and Arthur's visit to Draycott Fitzpayne until after Noel and Moralt's intervention in London. They had all been careful not to commit anything specific to paper. In 1920, Bryn was still committed to her marriage: perhaps another pregnancy, if it did occur, would have been unwelcome. Whatever she asked, or didn't ask, of her sister, there was no new baby until Brynhild gave into Raymond a year later and Philip arrived in 1923. 'I have been in a more or less severe nightmare,' Brynhild wrote to Raymond in 1920, asking him to take her away somewhere to recuperate. 'I suppose you are not writing to me on purpose. I don't mind as I'm not in a state to appreciate anything.'

2

Stuttgart, Germany, January 1923

Before the Wala and her charges set off for Italy, Daphne had already embarked on her own European trip. She went to Germany, heading into a country, the Oliviers had been told, that was teetering on the brink of civil war. Margaret was still in touch with their old house-keeper, Selma, who now lived in Frankfurt. Along with fearful predictions she sent them reports of dire conditions, to which the Wala could respond only with packages and money from England. By the time Daphne visited, there had been almost four hundred political assassinations in the new democracy; the attempted right-wing coup of 1920 was a recent memory. In Stuttgart, in January 1923, she might have seen the everyday realities of an economy just caught in the tearing trajectory of hyperinflation. That year people used their almost worthless bank notes as notepaper and transported their wages home in wheelbarrows. If there was going to be more war, it wasn't even necessarily going to remain within German borders. While Daphne was there, the government refused to continue reparations payments and the French occupied the Ruhr region. It was a nervy and uncomfortable time; a time for journalists, perhaps, but not for tourists. Daphne was there because of a man she had encountered at a teaching conference in Oxford.

She had only attended the conference the previous year after coming across an advertisement by chance. It was billed as an investigation into spiritual values in education and was held under the presidency of the Minister for Education, H.A.L. Fisher. Though fate did not hang in the balance as openly as it did in Germany, in Britain people still had an anxious eye on the future. Hundreds of teachers descended on Oxford, keen to forge a new direction for teaching. 'It is extraordinary,' the *Cambridge Daily News* reported, 'how eager English teachers are to assimilate new ideas.'

Daphne sat in the audience of a lecture by Rudolf Steiner, a man introduced to them as 'a great teacher, a great philosopher, and a great writer'. This pale, dark-haired and dark-eyed figure was the founder of the Anthroposophical Society, and had been invited to speak about a school in Stuttgart, which was run according to his philosophy. Daphne was captivated. Steiner had a power over his listeners that some found difficult to comprehend. The socialist Rosa Mayreder wrote that his speeches could 'be classified in three categories: witty aphorisms taken from his wide reading, empty talk based on stock phrases, and incomprehensible hints at extra-sensory capabilities'. Yet for others his physical performance overcame even language barriers. One British attendee of a lecture he gave in Vienna came away convinced that she could feel 'the future of the Earth [...] hanging in the balance' as he spoke, despite being able to understand little of the German speech. With that first encounter in Oxford, Daphne embarked on a journey in which she became, in the words of a fellow follower, 'Steiner's devoted pupil'.

Anthroposophy was a break-away from the Theosophy movement, which Daphne may well have been familiar with in her youth. Founded by the mysterious Madame Blavatsky, Theosophy had gained followers in London and had attracted the attention of George Bernard Shaw. (Annie Besant became the society's President in 1907.) Theosophy's central basis was that the earthly realm was directed invisibly by a spirit world, with which Madame Blavatsky was conveniently able to communicate. Influenced by India and the occult, Blavatsky offered her followers letters from the spirit world, written in gold ink on green paper, delivered by the medium herself.

From the German branch of Theosophy Steiner established a related but independent movement that adopted a more sober and scholarly image. Anthroposophy was understood as a 'spiritual science' in which the spiritual world was made appreciable through the careful development of an individual's organs of perception. Steiner claimed to have had contact with the spirit world himself and taught that the purpose of life could never be truly understood without knowledge of this other realm.

In Oxford, Daphne was confronted with a man able to hold others in his thrall, to inspire intense loyalty and dramatic life choices; an indefatigable figure, who travelled constantly, wrote more than six thousand lectures and dozens of books, founded schools, developed new theories of agriculture, economic thought, architecture, dance and sculpture. In echoes of Freud's relationship with his followers, anthroposophists called their leader 'the Doctor'. His endless energy seemed testament to a kind of super-human ability.

By the time of his visit to Oxford, Steiner's ideas had already gained currency in Europe and had gained a foothold in England. In contrast to the ritual-laden Theosophy, his brand of thought was able to attract a number of intellectuals who, like Daphne, were unsatisfied with their knowledge of the sensible world. For them, the world as it was had been found wanting. A rising Labour movement or the enfranchisement of women may only have been superficial improvements to a plane that did not hold a monopoly on relevance to Daphne's life. 'You may, of course, deny the immortal element in man,' ran an article on Steiner in *The Nation*. 'Call him dreamer, occultist, clairvoyant, even crank, but do not doubt his consistency and ability. You know how worried you have been lately about the state of Europe. If you cannot go to Oxford or to [Steiner's headquarters in] Dornach in Switzerland, you might perhaps call at the Board of Education or any other government office, and ask what provision they are making for the souls of the people.' Daphne did better. After the encounter in Oxford, she signed up for a trip to visit Rudolf Steiner's school in Stuttgart.

Rudolf Steiner in 1916

Daphne's first response to Steiner seems in fact to have been with Margery in mind. Noel received excitable letters from both Daphne and Margaret urging her to meet Steiner, whom they approached at the conference. 'My feeling is that he comprehends anything that psycho-analysts teach – but goes much deeper and further,' Daphne told her. The family was always looking for options. Earlier the same summer, Daphne had travelled to Nancy, in France, to train at Émile Coué's Institute, where the French pharmacist's curative method, based around the fundamental concept of psychology – the importance of the unconscious and the complex acting of the imagination – was taught. (Most famously, Coué offered a daily formula, to be repeated at least twenty times each night: 'Every day, in every way, I am getting better and better.')

Over the years, Margery had been evicted from various nursing homes, forcing Sydney out on frantic searches for places that were affordable and pleasant and willing to take her. Transferring her was never straightforward. In 1921, the year before the Oxford conference, Sydney, armed with a nurse, had tried to lodge Margery at Peckham House. This is likely to have been an emergency measure: Peckham House was a large, grim institution, with a more mixed community of patients than Margery was used to, and nurses who seem to have been harsh and disrespectful. Margery may have been mentally ill but she was also painfully aware of social class and retained all the pride of a governor's daughter. That the nurses at Peckham House teased her about her imaginary romances during a previous stay and were apparently quick to physically restrain her meant that she already hated the place.

It was well into night by the time Sydney, Margery and the nurse even managed to begin the journey to London. Their taxi broke down; they took a bus. Margery refused to travel with her father; he stayed on the open top deck, and then in a separate train carriage. At 1 a.m. they arrived at the asylum. Confronted with her destination, Margery began a violent struggle to escape. Sydney, sixty-two years old, a man whose whole career and outlook on life was informed by a sympathy for the underdog, who was not yet inured to the sight of his oldest child being forcibly restrained, told the staff to let her go. She fled, disappearing into the darkness of the Peckham Road. By the time Margery, under an urgency order this time, was admitted the following day, her father was ill enough to be removed to a nursing home himself. There, suffering with double pneumonia, he hovered on the edge of life, impressing his doctors with his tenacity. Sydney spent four months in hospitals and nursing homes, undergoing surgery in March, before he was able to return to his half-renovated house in Ramsden in the spring of 1922. He had, he told Wells, been carrying within himself a tropical strain of pneumonia for years, which had been lying in wait in his body to strike in Peckham.

In the New Year, Noel wrote to James in an attempt to vouch for her sister as an appealing patient. In some ways, she was most comfortable turning to James, with whom there was no real need to explain. To him, Noel managed to transform Margery's antics into a droll saga, with her family as an accompanying cast of fondly drawn figures of fun. 'Your letter,' James once wrote appreciatively from Vienna, '[...] as usual, was like a chapter of a novel by Wilkie Collins.'

The 'poor Mud is still a most interesting case', she assured him now, 'still very bright & still very much worth while rescuing'. Her hope was that James would ask Freud himself for his opinion. The Professor was not optimistic. Freud dealt largely with neuroses rather than psychosis, and felt anyway that the window of opportunity for having an impact on Margery had long passed. James's own recommendation, the German psychoanalyst Karl Abraham, however, claimed to have had success with similar cases. Abraham was one of Freud's key students and collaborators. In a sad irony, James and Alix were also planning to send him Harry Norton, who had been advised to give up his vocation of mathematics after suffering a breakdown in 1920.

Though Freud may not have felt Margery suitable for him, she was, as a mad, childless feminist, really exactly the kind of woman occupying the two men. He and Abraham were on the cusp of developing their own particular theories about women's deficiencies. Abraham would shortly put forward his famous concept of the Female Castration Complex and Freud would join him in interrogating the psychological fallout for women of lacking a penis. Abraham explained feminists as women struggling with a sublimated desire to be male; Freud suggested that the healthiest way to overcome penis envy was to have a baby. For Margery, her poor German and Abraham's poor English made successful analysis unlikely after all, and she remained in her latest home, Camberwell House, the largest private asylum in London.

Margery was still there when Daphne first met Rudolf Steiner. The Wala, having received a bad report of Margery's condition from Eva Hubback, was finalising plans to move her daughter to a small home in Henley-in-Arden. She feared that moving Margery out of London was moving her away from good doctors; that it was an admission of defeat.

The two women explained Margery's condition to Steiner, who expressed a wish to discuss her case with a doctor. Margaret was insistent that Noel meet him before he departed for the continent, as there was a chance, he had told them, that Margery could be helped by his methods. 'Now we have started another hare!' she announced.

Steiner had offered to show a small party of teachers around the Stuttgart school himself, despite the personal risks he faced when travelling to his native country. Anthroposophy clashed with the far right on a number of issues: its emphasis on individualism, pacifism and internationalist outlook anathema to men like Adolf Hitler, who had recently taken up leadership of the NSDAP, and who criticised Steiner in the press. During a lecture tour the previous year, Steiner's speech in the Nazi stronghold of Munich had been thrown into chaos by right-wing thugs.

Steiner had wanted to establish his own headquarters in Munich but had been denied permission by the authorities. Instead he had designed a brilliant and unusual building in Dornach, a small town not far from Basel. He had named this base the Goetheanum in a tribute to Goethe. It was a double-domed edifice wrought from concrete and seven varieties of wood, which provided a centre for an international movement.

But the welcome was hardly warmer in Switzerland. Steiner's teaching drew on and was tightly bound to Christian dogma (as well as other belief systems) and in Dornach the local Catholic priest condemned the anthroposophists as heretics. On the night of New Year's Eve, just days before the British teachers were due to arrive in Stuttgart, the anthroposophists woke to find the Goetheanum alight. Hampered by the leisurely response of the local fire brigade, Steiner and his acolytes salvaged what they could before watching the two domes fall in and then the entire building, which had stood for less than ten years, collapse under the flames. The arson was attributed by some to local Catholics and by others to fascists; the twin suspicions emblematic of the ideological battleground taking shape in Europe. Reporting on the fire, the *Daily Telegraph* wrote, 'The destruction of this monumental building will be a grave blow to the numerous adherents of one of the new religions which have gained strength from the spiritual chaos left in Europe by the disillusionments of war and peace. [...] The devotion of [Steiner's] admirers was equalled in intensity by the aversion of his enemies.'

*

Ten days after the fire, Daphne arrived in Stuttgart. She had been struggling with teaching for some time. As early as 1920, Noel and the Wala had thought she seemed at a low ebb. When she began to suffer from fainting fits, Noel thought it unlikely that Daphne would be able to 'stand' teaching her unruly pupils much longer. But in Stuttgart, Daphne found her faith restored. She and her companions were welcomed by the Waldorf teachers, who showed them the school and engaged them in long evening discussions after each day's teaching. The director of the Waldorf Astoria factory in Stuttgart was an anthroposophist who had invited Steiner to arrange the curriculum for the children of the factory's workers. Steiner's educational theories, which had sparked Daphne's interest in Oxford, were related to, but distinct from, Anthroposophy. At their centre was the belief that children's creative and spiritual needs should receive as much nurturing as their academic ones, an approach that was deeply appealing to Daphne.

Under Steiner's philosophy, young children were held to learn rhythmically, so that music infused the teaching of a whole range of subjects. Maths, for example, could be taught through foot-stamping and hand-clapping. Steiner had also invented his own art form in Eurhythmy, a type of dance, taught to the children, which intended to express sound through the body. In the classrooms Daphne found children educated without punishments or rewards or textbooks but in long lessons with much discussion. Before the age of seven (a period during which anthroposophists believed that a child's 'etheric body' remained within a protective enclosure) children were not taught to read or memorise facts. The focus was on art, colour and movement. Perhaps most encouraging for the visiting teachers was the palpable pride and enthusiasm of their German counterparts. The school was self-governing, run by a 'college' of teachers. One of the visitors found 'the sympathy between the teachers and pupils very genuine and helpful'. Steiner decreed that a 'child needs teachers with a happy look and above all an honest unaffected love'; this may have been reminiscent of the teaching Daphne and her sisters received from Gertrude Dix and their mother but it remained unorthodox in Germany and Britain. Daphne was impressed by the Waldorf teachers. 'They make one feel it is the most skilled and fascinating profession there is,' she wrote. 'You are an artist and a poet & a musician and a scientist all in one.'

★

In Stuttgart, Daphne was participating in an exhilarating international exchange of ideas and ideals, both a practical and a spiritual generation of hope. Small and determined communities in a devastated Europe, seeking to change the status quo in distinct ways, sought common ground with each other. With their fundamental role in raising the next generation, teachers may well have felt they had the future of the continent in their hands. The conditions in Germany can only have encouraged a sense of urgency.

It seems little wonder that Daphne was in a questing frame of mind in the early 1920s. The war and its aftermath had brought some harsh disillusionments. Daphne was looking for deeper meaning in her life, a philosophy to live by, and she was far from alone in seeking out new answers to old questions. Post-war Europe provided fertile ground for new philosophies, some of them tying in with the new ideas about the human mind and inner life, others simply trying to find new ways to cope with reality. The general scepticism after the war, which no doubt contributed to the declining church attendance in Britain, somehow did not diminish this urge for explanations: credulity found other channels, in the rise of Second Adventism, for example, which became Christabel Pankhurst's new motivating force, and a fashion for Ouija boards. Fairies had even been discovered in Yorkshire.

In a shattered Britain, it was believed that women had the power to fix society but that this power could only be enacted in a curiously passive way: in stepping aside, in soothing angry men and a frightened public, in giving way. For a while after the war women had been the objects of intense attention, both as voters for the first time and as cuckoos in male jobs. It seemed that they had to be corralled back into the home to re-establish peacetime conditions, and they were dispatched by threats, persuasion and downright enforcement.

If the war was supposed to have been a channel for men's natural aggression, it seemed instead to have unleashed it. Warnings about men's capacity for violence abounded. '[A]ll was not right with the spirit of the men who came back,' the war correspondent Philip Gibbs wrote portentously in 1920. 'Something was wrong.' Though outwardly they looked the same – if they were lucky – their behaviour was different. 'They were subject to queer moods, queer tempers, fits of profound depression alternating with a restless desire for pleasure. Many of them were easily moved to passion when they lost control of themselves. Many were bitter in their speech, violent in opinion, frightening.' It was this loss of control that the press dwelt on, and the sexual threat these men represented. Gibbs wrote of their 'homicidal mania and secret lust', many cases of 'murders of young women' and 'outrages upon little girls'. Whether the number of sexual crimes rose or not was almost irrelevant: the papers implied that women were newly menaced. Simultaneously, they fretted on women's behalf that there might not be enough men to go around, reinforcing the idea that an unmarried woman lived a wasted life.

Advertisers played their part as women became consumers, taught what to want by magazines and advertisements: the nice home, the happy husband, the well-fed children. And if they still clung on to work, women found their fingers prised away from salaries. The same Gibbs scolded the 'girls' who 'would not let go of the pocket-money which they had spent on frocks'. In reality, the Restoration of Prewar Practices Act swept 750,000 women out of jobs in munitions in one go; in almost every industry or profession priority was reserved for 'breadwinners', which was synonymous with 'men'. If the suffrage campaign gave women the confidence to step up to the plate during the war, there was little for the majority of them to do with this self-belief now. Among Noel's friends there seemed to be an expectation of solidarity between employed women – a sense of an identity that was under siege, that required defence. Mary Newbery, a talented clothes designer, wrote to Noel to complain about Marie Moralt's attitude to one of her commissions: 'It's not nice if working women behave like that to one another.' It seems possible that, however unconsciously, Noel was reaching for security from this hostile environment when she married in 1920.

In this context, the extension of the vote to five million women in 1918 must have seemed a red herring. It was not presented as a concession to the might and right of the women's movement but as a reward for falling in with the war effort. The post-war years showed women's rights to be one of those fair-weather gifts, nothing inalienable but something only offered when the world was feeling magnanimous, or needed something in return, and the social weather was good enough for women to leave their homes and amass in the outside world. It was not something that survived the retrenchment of post-war depression. British men and women were no longer fighting a common enemy: they had become each other's. When there was less to go around, men had always to have the priority and the women found that the weather in the streets had turned unfriendly enough to send them back inside.

★

In July 1922, shortly before the conference in Oxford, Daphne went to Venice for a holiday. Noel was to follow, and while she waited, Daphne revelled in the city's colours and battled the pounding heat, warning Noel to bring a big hat and a parasol, white and muslin clothes. On holiday in that beautiful place, Daphne was exactly the kind of woman some teachers were railing against at home. The teaching profession was one of the prime battlegrounds in the war over work, and equal pay for female teachers a key campaign in the rearguard action being fought by feminists. Opposition to the principle was strong and its opponents countered that women did not need fair pay: their expenses were frivolous and they were not entitled to them. At a conference called to protest the suggestion of equal salaries for men and women, one teacher used his speech to decry the foreign holidays his female colleagues were able to take on their existing salaries, whilst men like him, he complained, were reduced to spending a measly week in Eastbourne with their families.

The controversy over female teachers' pay had broad resonances, particularly as teaching was one of the few areas of work where educated women had been able to secure a living. (Daphne was among the 80 per cent of female Oxbridge graduates who became teachers – and who typically earned only three-quarters of their male colleagues' wages.) Part of the strain of Daphne's life as a teacher must have been in working alongside better paid colleagues who didn't even feel that she deserved the little she was afforded. All men benefited from the assumption that they would need to support a family, whether they had one or not, whereas the possession of a husband or children was an excuse to exclude women from work. Nor did independent work lives free Noel and Daphne from obligations towards their parents and sick sister. In 1923, the London County Council, which employed Daphne, was being flooded with letters and press reports demanding the dismissal of women teachers who were presumed, despite the existence of 240,000 war widows, to have husbands to provide for them. Within a few years, three-quarters of local authorities would have marriage bars in place, driving married women out of teaching.

The opposition to equal pay seemed more than financial, more than a pragmatic protection of privileges or guarding against competition; as the feminist Rebecca West put it in considering the outraged Eastbourne-sufferer at the conference, 'what is more shocking is that he evidently wants his female colleagues to have neither homes, families, nor a week at lovely Lucerne; to have, in fact, as nearly as possible nothing'. When the President of the Board of Education declared that, even if the government had the funds to pay teachers equally, it would 'spend it on the children instead', it was a statement of the national hierarchy: men, children, women.

Worst of all, at this embattled moment, the woman's movement itself seemed to be fading away. West, a representative of what was now known as 'Old Feminism', took a swipe at the 'modern timidity about mentioning that there is such a thing as sex-antagonism'. In keeping with the times, the idea of 'competing' with men was distinctly out of vogue; egalitarianism gave way to catering instead to what were perceived as women's special needs. The NUWSS had been renamed, becoming the National Union of Societies for Equal Citizenship in 1919, and under the new leadership of Eleanor Rathbone its focus began to change. Rathbone's 'New Feminism' was preoccupied mostly with mothers. The causes of New Feminism were necessary and important, certainly, but shifted the attention away from rights for women and maintained traditional assumptions about a woman's place and potential. Rathbone promised to work for 'what we want for women, not because it is what men have got, but because it is what women need to fulfil the potentialities of their own natures and to adjust themselves to the circumstances of their own lives'.

Many were convinced by this new turn. Eva Hubback became Parliamentary Secretary to NUSEC in 1920, and became one of Rathbone's closest associates. Margery's old friends Dorothy Ostmaston (now Layton) and Amber Blanco White soon joined her on the Executive. In a depressed climate, Eva and her colleagues, identifying women's oppression in economic terms, became convinced that their focus should be on the wives and mothers of the working classes. Fundamental questions had emerged: what actually counted as feminism? What were its hopes for women, and what did it believe about them? Middle-class feminists had liked to see themselves as a vanguard whose achievements would filter out to benefit others but Eva's brand of feminism acknowledged the reality for women unlike herself and shifted focus accordingly. They didn't want to change the structure of society, only to make life bearable for women within it.

Using their new access to Parliament, Eva and her colleagues became targeted lobbyists, practised common cause finders and pragmatic compromisers. There were only two female MPs in 1922 and they had both filled their husband's seats. They weren't about to stage a revolution. A small group of insiders, working almost invisibly at Westminster, and often for causes that must have seemed to have had little relevance to women like Daphne, replaced the mass movement she had once been part of.

Someone like Daphne could be forgiven for thinking that she had no advocates left. When she had stood in the snow, valiantly canvassing in 1910, Daphne had anticipated the beginning of change for women, not a culmination, but the post-enfranchisement world had divided the women's movement and signalled its decline as a political force. Organisations brought to life specifically to agitate for suffrage now seemed obsolete (despite the fact that electoral equality had not been achieved and about a third of adult women remained ineligible to vote) and many of the most energetic campaigners had by now turned their abilities to the cause of pacifism.

In January 1923, when she went to Stuttgart, Daphne was thirty-three. The life of a single, working woman was hard. When the writer and academic C. S. Lewis was introduced to her that year, he judged her to be about forty. In a photo taken of her at a Slade School fancy-dress ball, she looks almost matronly beside her friends, wearing a girlishly sedate dress, whilst next to her sits Joan of Arc and a short-haired beauty in a strapless outfit. Daphne did not cut off her hair like the flappers. She had been born in the Victorian era, had come of age amongst bluestockings. The feminists Daphne knew were in retreat. Newnham, that steadfast haven of female self-determination, had been besieged by a violent mob of male undergraduates less than two years before, when the question of granting women full membership of the University had again been formally defeated in the Senate. For an hour and a half, hundreds of men had clamoured outside, broken windows and battered the college gates with a handcart, trying to break in. The Newnhamite way of life was under attack.

Even the autonomy of spinsterhood, for some a political choice, was out of fashion again. These days, sex had to be reckoned with. Whilst feminists had traditionally voiced outrage against male sexual behaviour and sought to protect women and children from abuse, the increasingly vocal sexology discipline, which included emancipated women like Dora Russell, took them to task for their 'prudery'. Sex was seen as a crucial element of a healthy life, due as much to women as to men. Echoing the defeatism of the twenties, however, sexologists, like anti-feminists, believed male sexual urges to be uncontrollable. They did not, then, seek to change anything fundamental for women; instead, they encouraged them to learn how to enjoy heterosexual sex relations as they already existed, telling women that in doing so they were being liberated. Information about contraception was now more widespread, burnishing the impression of new sexual liberties. Taboos about sex outside of marriage began to loosen, replaced by taboos about abstaining from sex, or 'frigidity'.

These authorities questioned the health of the spinster, pathologising lifestyle choices that had sustained many of the feminists of the previous generation, and, by extension, her fitness as a teacher. '[E]nough is known,' commented the female author of *Motherhood and its Enemies*, 'to make us aware that in entrusting responsibility towards individuals and the state to elderly virgins we may be acting unwisely.' Work with children had once been one of the few occupations considered appropriate for women but the prevalence of singletons like Daphne in the role – women made doubly threatening through their independent salaries and socially untethered position – soon transformed them into a target.

Before she was introduced to Steiner, Daphne had sought comfort in her old love of music. In 1921, she had become a member of London's prestigious Bach Choir, which was at that time conducted by Ralph Vaughan Williams, a man of theatrical irascibility and affability, who was to become a friend. Performing the Bach mass at the great composer's command must have been one of the transporting experiences that sustained Daphne.

Daphne's musical talents were put to good use by her old friends, Evelyn and Maisie Radford. The Radford sisters now lived in St Anthony in Roseland, in Cornwall, in a cottage that could only be reached by boat. Inspired by the popular revival of folk dance over the last few years, they had set up a touring band of musicians and dancers, with a repertoire of traditional European and Elizabethan court dances. The Radfords were the musicians, researchers and organisers. They had a group of four female dancers, to which they had added two male members of the Oxford Folk Dance Society.

In the days before radio had reached much of the country, they toured the villages of Cornwall and Devon, lugging a case of elaborate costumes, music stands, violin cases and a side drum from church halls to schoolrooms through the summer, sharing their enthusiasm with surely perplexed audiences with an almost missionary zeal. In a programme for the concerts of 1922, Daphne is listed as one of the musicians: almost certainly she accompanied the group on the violin. Musical solos were interspersed through the performance, giving the dancers time to change backstage.

It may have seemed an odd and backward-looking pursuit. Certainly the village audiences who found themselves confronted with the stately court dances that opened the 'Roseland concerts' (they included the Pavane, which Margery had mastered for *Comus*) were sometimes unsure how to respond. But this perplexity could work both ways. One entry in the tour log recorded, whilst the group hung curtains in a hall before a performance: 'Enter small boy with mackerel.'

There was a comforting nostalgia (and, for this group, academic curiosity) in reviving these traditional displays. But they also expressed a cultural optimism and internationalism encapsulated in the Prologue that Owen Barfield, one of the Oxford dancers, wrote for their log:

> This we believe: that nations truly live
> Not in the wealth which they from others take
> But in that wealth which to the world they give,
> The songs and dances that their people make.

Owen was joined by his best friend and fellow Oxford student Cecil Harwood: a round-faced, bespectacled character with a scholarly nature. At school in Highgate the pair had been so close that the other boys sometimes referred to them as 'Barwood and Harfield'. Cecil was the youngest son of a Nonconformist minister and had gone up to Oxford in 1919, after active service in France. He was now twenty-four and that summer the pair had moved to London to launch what they hoped would be literary careers. Cecil was, like Owen, an enthusiastic poet and the two shared their attempts with their friend from Oxford, Jack Lewis, critiquing each other's work. Lewis (who would later publish under his initials, C. S.) judged Cecil's poems to be 'original, quaint and catchy'. It was in 1922, whilst he performed courtship dances and she indulged her love of music, that Daphne and Cecil met. It may even have been during that itinerant summer that they fell in love.

3

London, Spring 1923

'I can't believe that any news from this wretched country can interest you,' Noel wrote to James in April. 'Everyone I know is either ill, unhappy or disagreeable. The poor become poorer each week and the humbugs humbugger.' Arthur had a new post at a children's hospital in Surrey, so she and Daphne temporarily moved in together at Cleveland Gardens, near Hyde Park. Brynhild had decided to outstay Hugh in Ventimiglia and would not be home until the end of May. No one quite knew how things would stand when she returned. For now, Margery remained in a nursing home in England; her parents, unlike Daphne, had given up on Steiner, who had not engaged any further since meeting them the previous summer.

In April, Margery turned thirty-seven. She lived at the home in Henley-in-Arden under certification, for which Noel had been the petitioner. Despite all the 'chameleon like' grudges her mind generated – each of which led to violence and upheaval eventually – her subconscious rejected the actual fact of her sister's role in her certification. Of all the friends of her youth, only the widowed Eva Hubback – busier, it seemed, than anyone – had stayed loyally in touch, perhaps still committed to that early, dazzling, image of the Oliviers. For her birthday, Eva sent Margery a copy of *Moby Dick*. 'Aren't we getting old?' she wrote.

In Cleveland Gardens, the leaves had come out on the trees and been promptly covered in soot. The end of the war did not seem to have alleviated the city's bleak aspect. Four and a half years on from the Armistice, they were still living in an aftermath; the future would always be post-war. In November 1920, Noel had gone to meet Sydney at his club, when Margery had driven him from home. It was 11 November, the second anniversary of the Armistice and the day on which the Unknown Warrior was interred. She was late, finding the roads blocked by the funeral. The coffin of the unidentified man had been drawn through the streets on a gun carriage that morning, stopping first in Whitehall for King George's unveiling of the Cenotaph, before arriving at Westminster Abbey for the service. Huge crowds gathered along the route. 'Hour after hour,' the Pathé newsreel recorded, 'an unceasing pilgrimage of bereaved mothers, wives, daughters, sweethearts lay floral offerings on the Cenotaph', adding with restraint that the coffin's progress created a 'memorable scene almost painful in its intensity of feeling'. Banks of flowers and wreaths emerged as long queues – mostly women and children, wrapped up tightly against the cold – continued to add to the tributes.

Around them, grief lingered and even its expression was contentious, provoking arguments about the society that should come next. Of the two-minute silence observed now each November, the writer and former VAD nurse Vera Brittain wrote to a friend, 'I don't require two minutes' silence to think of the dead. They're with me always; it's like putting two minutes aside in which to breathe.' The Women's Guild produced white poppies, protesting the nationalistic tone of commemoration, rejecting the blood-red version. New forms of international cooperation seemed crucial: Noel had joined the League of Nations Union in 1920 and Brynhild helped to set up a local branch in Wiltshire.

When she met Virginia for dinner in 1923, Noel admitted that, two years into her marriage, she still took Rupert's letters out from their hiding place – 'beautiful beautiful love letters – real love letters, she said', Virginia wrote breathlessly in her diary afterwards – and cried and cried.

Virginia was moved by Noel, identifying in her something mournful, something that pinned Noel into the past. 'She looked at me with those strange eyes in which a drop seems to have been spilt,' she wrote after the dinner, 'a pale blue drop, with a large deep centre – romantic eyes, that seem to behold still Rupert bathing in the river [...] eyes pure & wide, & profound it seems.' (This sympathy did not extend to Ka Cox, who claimed to dream of Rupert during the 1920s. 'Why can't she ever wake up from the year 1911?' Virginia asked impatiently.) Yet it was hard to be certain of the Oliviers: perhaps instead there was 'nothing behind [Noel's eyes]'. Virginia seemed to sense melancholy in Noel but it lay beneath a cool, unmoving dignity that made it impossible to verify.

On 21 August 1923, Brynhild checked into the Hotel Great Central by Marylebone station and stayed for two nights. Raymond stayed with her.

On 29 August she posted the hotel bill to her husband, with a covering note that read: 'I do not believe that any satisfactory married life could ever be for you and me.' This was to give Hugh grounds to divorce her.

Not long after Bryn's wedding to Hugh more than a decade before, she and Daphne had walked through the woods in Limpsfield to visit the Garnetts. Daphne recounted their conversation to Rupert Brooke, who was basking in the sun in Samoa:

> Bryn became philosophical ('philosophical' is the word when people are depressing isn't it?) and said how it was only yesterday that Edward & Connie had come as a young couple with their baby and settled in these woods, and now Edward was hoar and Connie was fat and Bunny was a gawky dandy of 22. She didn't think anything adventurous would ever happen now in the Garnetts lives, and she wondered if all married people's lives pass like that, imperceptibly like the sun setting, and yet very quickly. And I told her 'of course'. And we walked on and on kicking the snowy leaves.

Each of the sisters, in their own way, was engaged in a search for answers, for ways to live in an adulthood that was not quite what they had been led to expect; and had to decide on the shape of their lives now that the aberration of war had passed. Brynhild was seeking to establish what she was entitled to from life. Marriage to Hugh had bored her and the legalised power he wielded over her future she experienced as an insult, but it was no longer unimaginable that a woman could simply refuse to accept this, could demand the chance to start again elsewhere. That year the law had been equalised, so that Bryn could, in theory, now divorce Hugh for adultery. In order to protect his job, they had arranged instead that he would divorce her, with Bryn as the guilty party, but the legislative change may have given her the leverage she needed.

For Margery the search for answers was most of all a search for a cure, for an explanation (sought by others on her behalf) of what had corrupted her mind and how she could be brought back, and psychoanalysis had seemed to offer new possibilities in that search. Noel was plotting a way to accommodate marriage and work in her life as the options around both narrowed. In September she moved to Sutton to be with her husband, yet the following month she had secured new work at a clinic in London, alongside a post at the Westminster Hospital for Children, which she had acquired in 1922. Mary Newbery, her friend from Bedales, even believed Noel had picked Arthur with an eye to a good father for her future children.

For Daphne, these years were dominated by the pursuit of meaning. By now she was enraptured with Steiner's teachings and her commitment had gone far beyond the educational principles he espoused. As she was attracted by the Waldorf education system, so Daphne began to be drawn to the ideology it sprang from. Anthroposophy offered something that went beyond the faltering political movements that had occupied her student years, and that tapped into her own suspicions (which had once cost her her liberty) about a world beyond the one she inhabited. The animist elements in Steiner's writings no doubt also appealed to her sense of attachment to the natural world. She was recruited to translate a report on some of Steiner's lectures from German (her translation was published that year).

Anthroposophy offered the chance to be special: to embark on a journey into spiritual fulfilment that few could hope to reach. Steiner had formulated an initiation process that proceeded in straightforward steps. In the early stages, Daphne would have been recommended to cultivate her sense of the beautiful, of sympathy with others, and to work on her powers of observation. Followers then graduated on to forms of meditation, which led towards a state of devotion. Steiner was canny about the needs their times had thrown up. 'It is all too easy for the world to laugh at [Anthroposophy],' he acknowledged. 'But considering the serious tangle in which our civilisation finds itself, one would expect at least some readiness to seek for what cannot be found elsewhere.' His promise of a higher knowledge called for humility and patience. 'Our civilisation tends more towards criticism, judgement and condemnation, and less towards devotion and selfless veneration,' he wrote. Daphne may have felt herself to be too sensitive for such a world; certainly she seemed to find a home in Anthroposophy.

That August, the Wala caused disaster when, left alone with Margery during a visit to her in Henley-in-Arden, she had found herself agreeing to Margery's demands to visit Ramsden. Margaret comforted herself that this could be arranged as a brief holiday for her daughter while Sydney was away. But once Margery was installed, she could not be dislodged.

'I should like to get her away shortly now,' the Wala wrote pitifully to Noel at the end of September, 'as she seems to be getting less good out of it & we also are a little tired.' Margery was being unusually calm with her parents but less so with everybody else. Aside from 'short lapses of slight amiability', the nurse came in for her enmity; Brynhild, who had returned to her house nearby, was also *persona non grata*. As for Noel, Margery simply insisted she was dead, though letters did arrive for her mother from an imposter writing in Noel's name, which Margery insisted on reading.

Much to his annoyance, the Wala pre-emptively hid all of Sydney's tools. Brynhild was a useful resort for them, providing a bed for Sydney when Margery couldn't have him in the house and a refuge for Margery during her episodes. Daphne came to stay over half-term but could do little to help. Finally Margery attacked Brynhild. Margery had often perceived everything Bryn had as something taken from her. She had on at least one occasion caused panic by deciding the infant Philip was her own child and making off with him as he slept in his pram. In this latest altercation, Raymond was also hurt. Mentioning his injury was the first acknowledgement Margaret made in her detailed letters to Noel that he was living at Ramsden with Bryn and the children.

Margery was returned to Henley, against her will. With the house back under their control, Sydney and Margaret established a routine whereby Sydney worked on his new book in the mornings, leaving the rest of the days free for his various building projects, or trips into London for lecturing, seeing his daughters and Fabian meetings. Since his return to Britain, he had re-established his links to the Society, but found himself frustrated by the lack of the vitality he remembered from its early days. It was still dominated by the Webbs and Bernard Shaw, who had so soundly seen off Wells's challenge all those years ago. Sydney was more enlivened by his membership of the Labour Party. The Labour movement was now, more than ever before, truly on the rise as a political force in Britain and in the general election of 1922, Labour overtook the Liberals to become the Conservatives' main opposition. It was a rise that would abruptly derail Sydney's long-awaited retirement.

4

Royal Courts of Justice, Middlesex, February 1924

In January 1924, the Conservatives lost a vote of no confidence. The King summoned Ramsay MacDonald and asked him to form a minority government in their place, making MacDonald the first ever British Labour Prime Minister. He in turn asked Sydney to join his Cabinet as Secretary of State for India. Sydney was raised to the Peerage, becoming Baron Olivier, and quickly came under intense scrutiny. It was a challenging moment to take the helm: Gandhi was in prison, Motilal Nehru had recently signed an election manifesto stating that 'the people of India are resolved to submit no longer to the national humiliation imposed upon them by the autocratic will of their British rulers', and serious unrest erupted within weeks of Sydney's taking office. He, of course, took to the fray, making contact with experts and commentators in India and embarking on a fractious relationship with the Viceroy, a man deeply dubious about working with a Labour Minister. A sympathetic friend who had met Sydney sent perhaps the worst possible advice on him, in solidarity from an embattled establishment: 'I think if you take a firm stand with him you will get your own way. [...] here we are with a socialist government in power and we must do our best to keep them from wrecking the country and the Empire.'

So it was, then, that the news of Brynhild's divorce could hardly have broken at a worse moment for her family, just as they emerged once again into the public eye. The Pophams' case was heard in February and Brynhild's divorce hit the papers five days before her father made his first address to the House of Lords.

'Brynhild Popham, whose maiden name was Olivier', *The Times* reported, was being divorced by her husband 'on the grounds of her adultery with the co-respondent, F.R.J.N. Sherrard'. No mention was made of Hugh's affair with Joan Farjeon. The papers condensed the collapse of the marriage into a few lines: 'Their married life was a happy one until Sherrard, who was engaged in agriculture, appeared on the scene in 1918.' A series of confessions and broken promises were sketched out for the newspaper's readers, culminating in a quotation from Bryn's note with the hotel bill. Even local papers reported on the case, choosing salacious headlines like 'Wife's Confession to Husband', 'Forgiven Wife Returns to Old Lover' and 'Wife Who Fell in Love'. Only three children, 'issue of the marriage', were mentioned. Hugh was granted custody of them.

Brynhild was probably prepared for this custody decision. Andy had by now been sent to a boarding school her parents had seen advertised on the back of the *New Statesman* (Tony already boarded), so that only four-and-a-half-year-old Tristram was with Bryn in Ramsden when the marriage was dissolved. Informally, Hugh and Brynhild had agreed that he would take custody of the boys and Brynhild would take Andy, seeing all three children during the holidays. On this understanding, Brynhild had agreed not to enter an appearance in the suit. But shortly before the case was heard, she took fright on discovering that Hugh had applied for custody of all of their children. He had probably done this to avoid the appearance of collusion with his wife but it was a reminder of her almost powerless position. '[I]t is thought rather remarkable for a guilty wife even to obtain access to the children supposing the husband objects to it,' the lawyer she consulted reminded her. 'You are therefore entirely in your husband's hands.' Though Bryn and Hugh eventually made arrangements to share access to the children, separation from Tristram at this young age was, for Brynhild, an immediate source of anguish.

Until 1920, all divorce cases had been heard at the High Court in London but a rising tide of decree nisis had forced the burden out into the Assize Courts; Hugh's case was one of those now being heard in Middlesex. Brynhild had resolved to face down the humiliation the divorce would bring, drawing on her Olivier hauteur to carry her through, yet this was one of the few areas where social and cultural change was prompting official reform. In the year of her wedding, 586 marriages had ended in divorce; in the year that she sought one herself, hers was one of 2,667 divorces. The equalisation of the divorce law had been one of the few shared goals of the divided post-war women's movement. Eva Hubback had consulted a lawyer on Bryn's behalf and sent on his advice about the children. (This was for Sydney to consult with him, 'as grand-parent interested in custody of his grandchildren' and then arrange matters with Hugh's lawyer. 'He seemed to think there is no need for you to appear in the matter at all.')

Instances of blatant inequity were less tolerated by public opinion, in an age when it was popular to inform women that they had achieved equality. The amendment to the law had been easily passed, yet some solicitors refused to take divorce cases, preferring not to associate their firms with such matters. Divorce remained a scandalous occurrence, far less tolerable than adultery, regardless of social class. The King himself expressed disgust at the reporting of divorce cases in the newspapers.

Even in Bloomsbury, where marriage rarely affected people's love lives, nobody ever divorced. (Bunny only promised his new wife not to 'have love affairs with women without talking to you about it at the time'.) Virginia gossiped gleefully to Jacques Raverat, who was by now dying of multiple sclerosis, about the Oliviers, 'whom I meet about, with their beautiful glass eyes, glazed and fixed and melancholy'. 'Poor Hugh, so I'm told, spent his Sundays making wooden beds, for Sherrard to step into on Monday when he'd gone.'

Brynhild was attempting to arrange her life exactly as she wanted it: in its way this was as radical an act as Margery's suffrage marches had been or Noel's medical degree. To others, Bryn seemed to blithely steamroll through life, pursuing whatever suited her best. Opinions soon arrived. Brynhild was sensitive to people's reactions, accusing Sybil and Ethel's brother, David Pye, of treating her differently after the divorce. He admitted his disapproval:

> I was, and am, made rather gloomy by the fear that your wonderful faculty
> for 'taking things easily' which has enabled you to do things which would
> have crushed 9 people out of 10, has this time betrayed you into drifting
> into a situation without ever facing out what it means for other people.

There was one old friend she could count on for support. 'I'm sorry you've had tangles in your life,' H. G. Wells wrote, '[...] but I understand something of tangles.'

Sydney, Margaret, Noel and Daphne's reactions are not recorded. The Wala, we may safely imagine, was devastated by the divorce but she had borne up bravely under the looming shadow of this disaster for many months. Sydney considered himself a man of the world, generally open-minded when it came to sexual matters. His own sister considered these deficiencies to blame. '[T]he ways of thought in which you have been brought up,' she told Brynhild in response to the news, 'have not in all ways perhaps been such as to guide you best.'

Still, her parents had wanted to avoid the divorce courts. 'Their solution would be that you should go to Canada!' Brynhild had told Raymond. She knew that they were against her decision – their obstinacy on this point had driven her mad – but she could also recognise that, for people of their generation and position especially, the situation was an awful one, and was grateful for their support.

The break-up of her marriage was a loss for the whole family. Her sisters had known Hugh since their youth. Daphne, and particularly Noel, were fond of him and had no such fondness for Sherrard. For Noel, the Popham home on Caroline Place had once been a source of much needed comfort. Bryn's sisters seem, though, to have understood and acknowledged the mismatch of her marriage. Hugh had been doomed by falling in love with someone who had great reserves of hard-headedness, his devotion spent on someone who found it stifling. Neither Daphne nor Noel lost contact with Hugh, and Tony, Andy and Tristram continued to have a full complement of aunts available to them.

5

Torquay, Devon, August 1924

Daphne's third summer in Rudolf Steiner's thrall took place in the seaside town of Torquay. Brynhild was in her decree nisi period, Noel had recently given birth to her first baby, a son called Benedict; Daphne, too, was full of plans. Whilst Bryn prepared for her stay at the Grand Central Hotel in Marylebone, Daphne had been in Ilkley for another course of lectures, accompanied by three other teachers, all of them nurturing the ambition not only to put Steiner's ideas into practice in Britain but to establish an entirely new school in which to do so. Steiner had endorsed their plan and offered to give them a personal course of training the following year. The dedication of the followers at the conference bore fruit when their idea was announced publicly, and three anthroposophists immediately pledged £1,000 between them for the teachers to purchase a house for the school. One of these benefactors was a solicitor who felt that Steiner had 'laid on him the task of helping in the founding and continuance of the school' in a moment of silent communion between them.

The four pioneers were Daphne, Helen Fox, Effie Wilson and Dorothy Martin. Effie Wilson had a long-standing grounding in Anthroposophy. She had lived in the colony at Dornach and trained in Eurhythmy there. Like Daphne, Helen Fox possessed a London teaching diploma and had studied at Oxbridge. Dorothy Martin's experience was as a governess. She also had a colonial background: her father was an army padre and she had spent her early years in India. Dorothy and Helen both came from Quaker backgrounds; Daphne was the only one of the converts not to have had a religious upbringing.

Each of them was single and dedicated to the cause they had chosen. It is tempting to see Daphne forming another kind of sisterhood with these women, a small sorority in the Newnham mould. Steiner, however, had been concerned that the leaders of this new school were all women and insisted they bring a man on board. From the anthroposophist summer school that followed in Wales, Daphne wrote to Cecil Harwood to let him know the news. 'Is there any chance that you would ever [...] feel moved to join us in an education enterprise [?] [...] We are keener than ever to try.'

Now, on 1 August, the Torquay summer school began and Steiner's separate course for the teachers was launched the following day. Daphne was camping outside of town with friends in true Neo-Pagan style: a field exposed to the sun, shared with horses and cows, water collected in pails. Technically, the course was meant to be a dedicated class just for the four women but a few other interested people were allowed, including Cecil, who was one of the campers. Through Daphne, both Owen Barfield and Cecil had been introduced and converted to Anthroposophy. They, too, experienced Steiner's philosophy as an enlightenment. Cecil, partly comforted by Steiner's promise of reincarnation, told C. S. Lewis that Steiner had 'made the burden roll from his back'.

But Daphne's appealing descriptions of teaching had as yet been in vain. Cecil was still planning to work in publishing and, acknowledging this, she had offered to make enquiries about openings at the Nonesuch Press, which Bunny (now – in another unexpected flourishing – a celebrated novelist) had established with Francis Meynell and his partner Vera. They had continued to discuss Anthroposophy together, though, and attend meetings in London with Owen Barfield and even, on one occasion, 'chiefly I think to pull my leg', the deeply sceptical Lewis. Fortunately, and perhaps surprisingly, Lewis liked Daphne, finding her an attractive and skilled conversationalist. On one evening in London, Cecil cooked dinner for them in his flat before the three read *Comus* together and walked Daphne home along the Embankment. Jack told Cecil how much he had liked her. 'I am very fond of her,' came the reply.

As well as lecturing, Steiner had private meetings with each of the intending teachers, guiding them as to the classes he thought they should teach. Daphne and the others had prepared a draft prospectus, with the place-holder name of The New School emblazoned across it. Steiner liked this name so much that the school was duly christened. During one of these talks, the women admitted that they had failed to secure a male teacher. Steiner pointed to Cecil and asked, 'What about him?'

Like others who had come under Steiner's sway, Cecil apparently felt compelled to comply with the Doctor's wishes. By the end of the summer school he had decided to abandon his earlier ambitions and commit himself to teaching. Later he remembered the walks back to camp after days spent in the inspiration of Steiner's lectures, when 'the very stars seemed [...] to shine with the brightness of a new heavenly intelligence'. Wildly enthused, he raced to Torquay station to give Steiner the news of his decision before he left.

The following month, Daphne was staying in Ramsden and planning in earnest. She was working through her own Anthroposophy courses and going over finances ('Finance is an awful business.'). Bryn's divorce had just become absolute and she was living up the hill in cheerful chaos. Daphne seemed to find her manner of life puzzling: she had a sister, she told Cecil, 'who has surrounded herself with almost every known animal [...] babies, and ducks, & hens & sheep & dogs & cats' (she, too, avoided references to Raymond).

In November, Cecil proposed. Though Daphne turned him down, Owen was optimistic about his friend's chances:

> I do not feel much confidence in my opinions on the feminine enigma, or rather I should say that I simply have not got any opinions – but I do feel pretty sure of this – that nine tenths of the ultimately successful proposals that are made by and to serious and sensitive people start off in the way yours has done.

Owen was right. Cecil was an erudite young man, who shared Daphne's love of music and, most importantly, her faith. She had suffered disappointments in love: the abortive affair with Bunny and an infatuation with Charles Ogden towards the end of the war that her mother had feared could trigger another breakdown. But when Cecil tried again, she accepted. When the news of the engagement broke in December, none of their friends were in the least surprised. Evelyn Radford claimed their connection had been perceptible in the very days of the tour on which they had met.

The wedding was scheduled for the following year, which meant that Brynhild got in her second wedding first, marrying Raymond Sherrard quietly in London before 1924 was over. She and Raymond decided to start afresh and to buy a farm in Hertfordshire. As much as any of her sisters, Brynhild loved the countryside. Farming was still personal and local: different regions were known by the specific livestock they produced, horses were in daily use; in the South, much of the land was still divided into petite fields, criss-crossed with ancient hedgerows and studded with great trees, which, together with the arable land they enclosed, sustained a vibrant community of birds. In the early twenties, massive war casualties amongst land-owning families had flooded the market with cheap farmland, as the big estates grappled with huge death duties. Like Daphne, Brynhild's working life would combine directly with family. She and Raymond planned to establish the farm together and it would provide a home for them and their children.

First, however, they had to find the funds to establish themselves. Raymond was without work, Bryn had been crippled by lawyers' fees. She turned to one of the wealthiest of her old friends. 'I've always been a little in love with you and Noel,' H.G. told her, 'and as you want this thing & I can do it I'm very happy indeed to do it. [...] So let the bank go ahead with my love & blessing on you.'

Like her sisters, and many women of their generation, Bryn now had a younger man for her husband. Both Raymond and Cecil were younger than Noel. Cecil was born almost a decade after his fiancé. Noel and Daphne had, in part, postponed marriage through their pursuit of educations and careers and had been matched by a generation of men who had been thrust into maturity early by war.

At Ramsden, Daphne took the opportunity to observe her little nephews at play. She interrogated her sister about what she looked for in a school, though Brynhild's pointed reply may not have been terribly encouraging:

> What I like is an ordinary sort of school which is just sensible. Nobody can really know enough about children not to make mistakes. So the people who make no pretence are the pleasantest. At all events they don't get self-conscious & cranky like people who think they have a mission to reform the world.

Yet watching Philip imitate Tristram while he danced to the gramophone allowed Daphne to see 'the reality of some of these "principles" that we learn so abstractly' in practice. Her own feeling for music, and Steiner's emphasis on rhythmic learning for young children, was validated in seeing Tristram 'illuminated' by dance.

Unlike the original Waldorf School, Daphne and her colleagues would not have a captive audience waiting for them. Daphne felt, instead, that Steiner schooling would have to be 'thrust on an unwilling population' and disliked the self-promotion involved, the necessity of defending a belief system she cherished. She was aware that their little band of anthroposophists would have to find a way to integrate into the community they chose and to introduce Steiner's philosophy. With Cecil she strategised about how to secure invitations to lecture, or establish their own 'drawing room meeting[s]', much as the Fabians had done in their earliest days, in order to spread the word. Steiner would not countenance the idea of a modest school; he was well aware that it would have to make an impact, and be a demonstrable success, if the concept of Waldorf schooling was to flourish in Britain. He had told them to start with a minimum of a hundred children; Daphne estimated that they would need at least fifty to cover teachers' salaries alone.

6

Streatham, London, January 1925

The New School began with seven pupils and five teachers. Just as she had been instrumental in bringing Cecil on board with the school, so Daphne also maintained their zeal through the difficulties of establishing it. '[W]e shall be helped,' she told him when enthusiasm flagged: 'we must believe in our faith.' They found premises in Streatham, in South London, and had hoped to have the school ready to open in the autumn of 1924 but were delayed by difficulty finding pupils. By the end of the year the teachers were all still having to earn incomes elsewhere, whilst the two hundred desks they had ordered sat empty in the school building. The group lectured and wrote articles. They put up notices and waited hopefully for enquiries which rarely came.

When Daphne and Cecil arrived in Streatham it was a still-expanding suburb with an air of fading gentility. The population had grown rapidly in the nineteenth century as London spread into the countryside; by the 1920s there were few open spaces left. Daphne and her colleagues had acquired the lease for a Victorian mansion on Leigham Court Road and for now the teachers lived together at the top of the house, making their way down into the basement when they needed to use the kitchen. The grand old rooms would be turned to new uses: Eurhythmy in the ball-room, meals for the children in the billiard room. Knobs were fixed to the ends of sweeping banisters to prevent children from sliding down them (Andy had the distinction of once destroying a valuable vase that had been ill-advisedly placed at the foot of the staircase she was sliding down at H. G. Wells's house; it's tempting to think Daphne had this escapade in mind). The house had a garden with many trees, which partially shielded an industrial view of the railway line and milk-bottling factory in the distance.

Cecil took the leading class, comprising of two girls of about eleven; Daphne had the class below and took responsibility for the secretarial work that the running of the school required. When it came to the actual teaching, Daphne had the advantage of knowing what to expect. Fortunately, Cecil found that he enjoyed it. He applied himself conscientiously to each subject as it came up, learning knitting at one point so he could keep up with the six-year-olds in his class, and slowly overcame his shyness. They made their way, somewhat erratically, through the first term, looking forward to a visit to the new Goetheanum, then under construction, in the Easter.

Then shattering news arrived from the continent. Weakened by overwork, the endless needs of his followers and the strain of Nazi attacks, Rudolf Steiner died in March at the age of sixty-four. The *New York Times* gave him a front-page obituary. Only one term into the life of the New School, its guiding force was gone. The teachers arrived in Dornach in time for the funeral. This loss, just as they cast off on their journey to put Steiner's ideas into practice, must have shaken Daphne and her colleagues. They had relied on him for advice on almost everything related to the school: from its early funding to the colours they should put on the walls.

The news of Jacques Raverat's death in the same month as Steiner's must have felt like a reminder of a lost world. Jacques had spent the last few years in France, with Gwen and their daughters, losing the ability to live. As Noel embarked on motherhood in this latest great age of maternity, and Bryn worked hard to establish a new life with Raymond, and Daphne marshalled her school through its rocky beginning, the vestiges of their youths were falling away. Friends like Eva Hubback and the Pyes remained within orbit but each sister now had a centre of gravity somewhere between their families and their work, managing to combine the two in different ways and to different degrees.

Daphne and Cecil found a small semi-detached house that barely separated them from the New School grounds but which sat between the end of the school garden and the railway line, and was a short walk from Streatham Common. They had almost no money; at times the school didn't make enough to pay the teachers' salaries. Instead, they kept themselves going with translation and outside teaching work. The sense of struggle was appropriate for the crusading band of teachers, however, and may have helped them to bear their higher purpose in mind throughout the battles for students, control of the students, and funds. By the school's second term, the student body had almost doubled. In the third term, they added a male science teacher, worrying that he barely looked older than his students. By the end of the first academic year they had reached a grand total of thirty pupils. Setting up an entirely new school, one so calculated to appeal directly to so few, one that came with the necessity of much explaining and defending and sacrifice, was undeniably audacious. In the early 1920s, such audacity perhaps felt necessary.

PART FIVE

Brynhild's Bedside:
Christmas Eve, 1934

(Or, Nine Years Later)

I

Brynhild's appetite, fortified by the eggnog sent from the Wala, was returning. She had special yellow crockery and a spot in the best corner of the ward, a ward of polished wooden floorboards and large windows set high into the walls, through which meagre December light cast itself on to a monumental fireplace and Christmas decorations. Around her, doctors and nurses were hanging holly with grave care. After an autumn of self-neglect, of ignoring bad signs, of not raising the alarm, all Brynhild had to do was rest. Her children were being looked after, and so was she. Everything was in the hands of others.

'My dearest Darling Wala,' she wrote to her mother. 'This is just to bring you my love & every best wishes that you will have a happy Christmas – and my dear Father too'. Sydney and Margaret, now in their seventies, had not quite reached a quiet retirement, though Sydney's health often demanded it. They were 'harbour[ing]' the twelve-year-old Philip, whose 'very simple easy nature' Brynhild commended to them, though they knew their grandson well enough to know it already. She hadn't had time to get him a new suit, and so she was writing now to warn the Wala of what he had to wear to Christmas at the Thornycrofts, and to hope helplessly that he would be able to find a clean collar amongst his belongings. 'Really all my children seem to have sorted themselves out very satisfactorily,' she told herself. While her family gathered in her absence, Brynhild cast her thoughts over the people closest to her, recounting their visits to her bedside over the past few days for the Wala.

2

My dearest Darling Wala and
my dear Father too

Bryn's parents had been steadfast in their support of her over these last years. With Margery finally settled in a proper home – a grand country pile of a hospital near Northampton – the Oliviers had all the more space to direct their attention towards themselves and their other daughters. Thinking of them around this time, Beatrice Webb reflected on the five couples who had founded and sustained the Fabian Society, all now well advanced into a venerable old age. 'Has there ever been five more respectable, cultivated and mutually devoted, and be it added, successful couples[?]' she asked herself with matronly self-satisfaction. 'The ultra essence of British bourgeois morality, comfort and enlightenment.' The Oliviers could have been forgiven for looking forward to a period of tranquillity; for holidays and visits with grandchildren; for Sydney to finally work on those books he wanted to finish. They managed all of these things but without the benefit of tranquillity.

Eighteen months before Bryn's letter, on 1 May 1933, Noel was expecting a baby. It is tempting to think that she noticed the date when she wrote to James Strachey that day: in another life she was supposed to be gathering on a platform at Basel station; stamping her feet to keep warm beneath the giant, fanlike windows, greeting a cast of excited and perhaps slightly furtive middle-aged friends: Bill and Eva, Gwen and Jacques, Dudley Ward, Ka, Godwin, Margery, Daphne, Bryn and Rupert. 'It will be fine on Basle platform in 1933,' Margery had promised but Margery now spent much of her time hiding behind the curtains on the window-sill of her room, or lying on the floor partially obscured by blankets, and would never see Basel again. Jacques, Bill and Rupert were dead. The others kept quiet about the Basel Pact, if they remembered it at all, and anyway Noel was barely in touch with most of them, apart from her sisters. On 1 May 1933, Noel was expecting a baby, her fourth. 'Arthur will let you know as soon as it occurs,' she reassured James, who was to be godfather. And that summer, after six weeks with her children in Boswinger in Cornwall, handling 'a great many injuries & diseases on all sides' in the sun, and preparing to return to work in a few days, Noel wrote to reassure him again: 'Your god daughter increases in loveliness.'

It was James she turned to a week later when Sydney caught pneumonia whilst on holiday in Switzerland and had to be hospitalised. Her father's life was despaired of, and so Noel took up her baby daughter and made her way over to Switzerland in the year of the Basel Pact, on a 'terrifying but beautiful' flight arranged by James, landing in that very city, the gateway to France, Italy and Switzerland, which was to have been their gateway out of the future. Sydney had caught a chill climbing the mountains in Hasliberg and spent four weeks in hospital. 'Very hard luck on M[argaret],' he noted, 'for whom I had been projecting a restful holiday.' Instead, the Wala settled into a hotel on a lake with Noel, where she set Sydney up on his balcony once his recovery began. Sydney and his granddaughter came round to the world together, as the baby began 'taking notice' of her surroundings while she was there, and found crowds of nurses and hotel staff ready to coo over her when she did. At the hotel they called her 'Mlle Marguerite' but Noel had named her Isabella. Sydney, of course, recovered. It was in his nature to do so. But the following summer, in 1934, he and Margaret were back in Switzerland, this time with a different patient.

When the doctors told Sydney his daughter's condition was incurable, he refused to believe it. The idea, he insisted, was 'manifest nonsense'. Before him he saw the animated and resilient Brynhild he had always known and he, for one, would never let her down through inaction. For the best doctors, he looked to the continent. ('Our people,' George Bernard Shaw, whom he kept updated on Brynhild's condition, agreed, 'are only highly sophisticated plumbers.') In June, he took Bryn to see Carl Jung, one of the many medical men he had once consulted over Margery, convinced that 'rational methods' would be able to cure her.

Bryn had been diagnosed with Lymphadenoma, or Hodgkin's disease. The diagnosis was of limited aid, as doctors openly admitted that little was known about the illness. '[T]he more that one probes into the condition,' her doctor told the family, 'the more obscure it becomes.' For months Brynhild was treated with X-rays, or radiation therapy, which, as Radiology, was on its way to becoming a specialisation of its own in

British medicine. Giant X-ray machines, with equipment that could be angled over the patient with two levers on either side, were now central to diagnostics in hospitals and advancements in radiation therapy were leading to much greater optimism about the chances of curing cancers of various types. The idea of Bryn's treatment was to target the enlarged lymph nodes in her neck and chest, which had raised unsightly lumps below her face, attacking them so that they eventually shrivelled. Radiation, though itself painless, also damages healthy tissue, leading to tiredness, nausea and other temporary side effects. The body, which had to deal with the effects of the destruction, was weakened, until the glands recovered and swelled up once again. X-ray treatment to her neck and face left Bryn with a sore throat, and difficulty swallowing. In this way, she remained disfigured and yet grew progressively weakened, with only intermittent periods of apparent recovery.

Whilst the possibilities of radiation were explored, one of the first obvious characteristics of the treatment was how sick it could make the patients. Recovery was no longer a straightforward process of getting better. Doctors began to confront the question of the 'price' of the cure, and what an acceptable pay-off might be. Even practitioners were at risk from X-ray and radiation treatment, in ways that were only now being fully understood. That summer, Marie Curie died in France, victim of her own pioneering work. Sydney soon came to the opinion that the methods being used to treat his daughter were 'not only futile but vicious'. Instead, he wanted to try a more traditional remedy: to bolster her constitution with a 'course of hydropathic treatment, hygiene and a restful and restorative regimen of life'.

Brynhild had faith in her doctors and in Noel especially, and the recurrent improvements in her condition made her optimistic. It was Sydney who protested on her behalf, and he decided not to try to persuade Brynhild of a change in treatment but to persuade Noel. As a doctor, Noel had accrued an almost patriarchal authority in a family in constant contact with the medical world. Though she was a paediatrician, she at least understood the principles and terminology applied by Bryn's doctors. Nevertheless, Sydney, unable to identify any logic in a treatment that seemed to make his daughter sicker, never stopped arguing, or trying to make sense of this new world. If Brynhild wasn't well, she couldn't fight the disease at all. He was insulted by a profession that confessed ignorance of her condition and yet scoffed at his suggestion that a course similar to that which had allegedly saved the Irish politician Horace Plunkett – 'going periodically to Battle Creek and being reduced to a functional minimum and then *built up again* on spiritual force and shredded wheat' – could help his daughter. It was, he was sure, only overwork and extreme anxiety, a 'fatigue poison', that had made her ill in the first place and that now left her to spend Christmas in hospital.

3

Raymond, Luly & Clary

Christmas Eve was a Monday. On the Saturday before, Brynhild told the Wala from her bed, Raymond brought their two youngest, Lucilla (known as Luly) and Clarissa (Clary), to visit. The little girls, nine and five, brought presents for their mother, carefully wrapped, and took a great interest in her surroundings at the hospital. As their parents talked about the gift Raymond was tasked with finding for Margaret, the work of decorating the ward was going on captivatingly around them.

Raymond and Brynhild had gone into farming as it teetered on the brink of an apparently terminal decline. They were not the only ones to have done so. The government's wartime protection of agricultural prices and wages was not immediately dismantled, leaving a short and appealing delay before these measures were rescinded and the industry suffered an abrupt collapse. Throughout the 1920s, an average of about four hundred farmers had gone bankrupt per year; in 1932 this figure reached six hundred. Arable land fell into neglect as the prices farmers could expect for their crops slipped to a level that made harvesting them uneconomic. Marketing boards set up by the government in 1931 bought up produce at guaranteed prices but those prices were, the farmers claimed, guaranteed only to rule out profits for the farmers. The papers raised cries about a crisis in England's countryside: a precious landscape, symbolic of Britain's well-being, already eulogised in H. V. Morton's *In Search of England* and J. B. Priestley's *English Journey*. Thousands of urbanites and suburbanites who these days spent their weekends in the green and pleasant parts of the country wanted to see it thrive. Meanwhile, Oswald Mosley's new British Union of Fascists set its sights on currying favour with aggrieved farming communities.

As Raymond himself would write, 'agriculture is an uncertain form of business compared with many other industries. This peculiarity perhaps is the one certainty about it.' The Sherrard farm in Rushden foundered and Brynhild's health suffered a similar decline. After battling through a hot day to finish mowing the lawn, her glands began to swell – around her shoulders and up into her neck – the first outward signs of what her doctors would term a 'mystery disease'.

H. G. Wells had been worrying about his guarantee for years. Having thought in 1924 that he was offering them temporary assistance to acquire the farm, he was alarmed to find that Raymond made no progress in paying off his debts. In the past he had tried demanding that Raymond reduce his overdraft, thereby reducing H.G.'s liability on their behalf, but Bryn had charmed him into giving them more time. 'I'm not so strong as people think,' he grumbled as he backed down, '& sometimes the sound of Harps in the night is quite distinct. And there's such a lot of people to provide for.' When, in the spring of 1934, Sydney discovered, to his horror, that H.G. had indeed had to pay the full sum (when Raymond evidently defaulted), Sydney realised that Raymond had concealed the truly disastrous state of their position from him. Sydney was only now beginning to appreciate that his son-in-law had an 'unlimited capacity for self-deception' when it came to financial matters, and he blamed Margaret's unbending antipathy towards Raymond for preventing him from realising this sooner. The Wala would have nothing to do with Raymond: would not have him in her house nor visit the couple at their ailing farm. Sydney, who was by this time bearing the costs of Brynhild's hospital treatment, had therefore had no idea how bad the Sherrard family finances were.

During the second half of the twenties, Raymond had worked relentlessly at the Rushden farm to try to get it off the ground, leaning on his wife to make sure they could carry on, even instructing her to persuade her older children's new stepmother to order her groceries from them. 'Is there anyone we can get anything from?' he insisted. When Bryn complained to her parents, they were apt to remark that she 'ought to have foreseen all this', which, of course, did little to help. 'The consequence', she told Raymond once, was that 'I had no sleep & no milk for [the infant] Lucilla'.

Luly and Clary, therefore, granddaughters of a peer, daughters of a mother who had grown up in privilege, knew best the hard and dirty life of a farm, their home landscaped by cowsheds and chicken houses. Brynhild had to rely on her elder children to help her keep the younger ones in check, and keeping track of them at all could be a challenge. 'You havn't written to me once yet,' Andy wrote reproachfully from a holiday with her grandmother, 'and this is my third time to you.' Philip could usually be found playing in the dirt. 'The kitten is happy in the barn,' Brynhild informed Tristram on one of his stays with the Wala. 'Our dining room is full of wheat.' It was a stark contrast to the lifestyle she had enjoyed in Bloomsbury (and Brynhild retained the memory of a higher-status life, once dispatching a child to the station with instructions to hold the train for her) but she had thrown herself into the challenge. Even recently, whilst enduring radiation therapy for the swollen glands that had marred her famous appearance and wrecked her vitality, Bryn handled the housework and cooking at Church Farm, managing to feed a brood of children with only a paraffin stove, and washed the milk bottles for Raymond's round. Brynhild relied on the teenage Andy for help and on loans from old friends to keep going. Her family had watched her anxiously – though from a Wala-imposed distance – waiting for a collapse.

When H.G. appealed to him to step in, Sydney had been obliged to outline the sorry state of his own financial affairs. In recent years, any available funds had been obliterated by the costs of Margery's care, as well as the nurses often required by the faltering health of Lord Olivier himself, plus the occasional obligation of bailing out Raymond when loans he could not meet were called in. As Britain weathered the effects of the Wall Street Crash, the Oliviers were not alone in facing hard times. By 1933, a quarter of the workforce was unemployed; extreme poverty blighted Wales and the North, though London and the South came through better. Landing back in a middle-class identity with a discomforting bump was a common experience for returned colonial families but, in the year of his seventy-third birthday, Sydney's income reached its lowest level since 1900. Only when he had received a governor's salary had Sydney ever been able to save money. His pension could now barely stand the pressure of keeping Margery in 'moderate comfort' at St Andrew's, the hospital in Northampton, where she informed doctors that he had been bribed to have her committed. 'Mental care,' he told Wells, 'is damnably costly (and quite impossible for most of the people who need it).'

Margery, at least, was fairly well settled at St Andrew's, a genteel establishment where the superintendents were also administrators of a huge estate. The property included a Welsh mansion with a mile of private beach, Bryn-y-Neuadd Hall, in Llanfairfechan, where patients could spend holidays and Margery was able to take long walks and bathe in the sea.

St Andrew's

By the time she arrived at the hospital, in 1931, Margery was a schizophrenic. It was a relatively new diagnostic option; first attributed at Eugen Bleuler's hospital in Zurich (where Godwin Baynes's mentor Jung worked as a young man) in 1911, when Margery was twenty-five. The term had gradually spread beyond Switzerland but continued to be applied erratically to patients exhibiting a broad range of conditions. Zelda Fitzgerald, suffering from a breakdown in which she heard voices, was judged schizophrenic in 1930; she told her husband, the writer F. Scott Fitzgerald, that 'for months I have been living in vaporous places peopled with one-dimensional figures and tremulous buildings until I can no longer tell an optical illusion from a reality'. In 1934, Lucia Joyce, sufferer of explosive bouts of rage, was being treated by Jung; she had also been diagnosed schizophrenic (though Jung was most concerned about her relationship with her father, James Joyce).

Bleuler's definition included behaviours that did not in themselves indicate illness, among them 'indifference, lack of energy, unsociability, stubbornness, moodiness'; words that carry echoes of Margery. The crucial characteristic, however, was the patient's complete indifference to the world 'outside' them. The violent eruptions of a schizophrenic could look like hysteria but the disconnection was the crucial thing. Though Margery seemed unmoved by her sisters' troubles or her parents' fear of her outbursts, sufferers from schizophrenia were also still able to register these facts on some level. Margery took control of realities to harness them for her delusions. The ideas she expressed no longer conformed to any order that others could understand and if that other world offered facts that didn't align with the tenacious orthodoxies of hers, they were split away and refashioned. Psychologically, she was still bound to her sisters. When she arrived at St Andrew's, she thrust herself into the centre of Brynhild's recent past, telling staff that her sister was trying to involve her as a co-respondent in a divorce case.

On average she was comparatively lucid for between eight and twelve days per month, during which time she would read the papers, spend time in the communal areas of the hospital, discuss poetry and quote German literature. On the bad days, she followed instructions from the voices she hallucinated, could be violent towards staff and fellow patients, and was destructive to property.

In the early 1930s she was treated with Medinal, a barbiturate, and then other sedatives. In those years prominent American psychiatrists like Harry Stack Sullivan had begun to explore the possibility of applying psychoanalytic techniques to psychotic patients – something Margery's family had been wondering about in her case since the 1920s – reporting some notable successes with schizophrenics, but there is no evidence the doctors at St Andrew's considered this for Margery. Those monitoring her condition seemed to find her delusions entertaining – her medical notes were peppered with exclamation marks – but the fantasies were persistent and consistent. She wanted to leave, and calmly assured staff that she was prepared to kill to get away, so that she could finally be free and 'have children'. Her preoccupations developed but essentially remained the same: she was secretly married, the Prince of Wales was in love with her, men waited in her bed.

After years of farming in Rushden, Raymond had found that a good farmer could just about make his money back. 'This,' he pointed out, 'does not help much towards the keeping of children.' Their farm was too small, in any case, to yield anything more than a minimal living. In

1933, he was one of the hundreds of farmers facing bankruptcy. In a characteristic flash of inspiration, however, he had discovered a solution to their troubles during a short family break in West Wittering, a village on the coast in Sussex. There, in conversation with fellow farmers, he was told that the average holding could yield significantly more than his own in Hertfordshire did. As luck would have it, they discovered a farm, called Nunnington, for sale near where they were staying. West Wittering was being developed as a seaside resort: property there seemed an excellent investment. Having exhausted Wells's patience, Bryn now needed to persuade another potential benefactor of the good sense of their plan.

Of the dedicated and conspicuous friends of her parents' youth, few had become more eminent than George Bernard Shaw. An edition of his collected work comprised forty-two plays in 1934, an oeuvre that had earned him renown and a Nobel Prize for Literature. These days he was as venerable as Beatrice Webb could wish, impressed by Hitler and Mussolini, fond of the USSR, and ready to praise all three publicly. He was even married, after his dalliances with some of London's most fearsome socialists, to an independently wealthy woman who generally tried to police his contact with old friends, especially those who came with requests for money. While Sydney, Margaret and Noel were away in Switzerland, Bryn and Raymond appealed to Shaw, borrowed £2,500 from him, and bought Nunnington Farm in a dizzying rush.

In his small, scratchy handwriting, Raymond had handled the correspondence. 'Though we wish it to be on a business footing,' he told Shaw, his help 'would be a great kindness, especially to my wife, whose position for some years has been one of discomfort & anxiety'. But even a cheque from the Nobel Prize winner did nothing for Brynhild's health.

The first warning signs of Hodgkin's disease are usually fatigue, fevers, loss of appetite and weight loss: symptoms that were easily overlooked or explained away in a woman under so much physical stress and worry. Brynhild no longer felt that she could depend on Raymond and the question of how to provide for her children weighed heavily on her.

'B's case is very dreadful,' Sydney told Wells in 1934, 'for she loves life and, for her friends, alleviates it.' Wells suggested treatment at a clinic in Switzerland, and the doctor Jung recommended was based in Zurich, so Brynhild and her parents set off for a break at the Kurhaus Val Sinestra, a health resort in the Swiss Alps, in the summer of 1934. It was arranged that, after the Oliviers' departure, Brynhild would travel home via Zurich, where, in a compromise with the doctors, she would spend some time receiving X-ray treatment at the city's hospital.

In Zurich, Bryn stayed in the quiet, moneyed suburb of Rigiblick. Reached by a funicular, the district looked over the lake and the city. None other than the Switch, the Olivier girls' old Swiss governess, was engaged as her companion. The two women led, Bryn reported, 'a charming lazy life', taking careful walks on which they admired the villas and gardens in the immaculate streets. Bryn rarely ventured into town beyond visits to the hospital (where her face, neck and spleen were subjected to X-ray treatment in a way she feared was excessive) and its shaded garden, where patches of lawn reached into each other past flowerbeds and beneath trees, like rivers and pools. On one appealing day the pair ventured up into the woods on the hill above the city, above even Rigiblick, beyond the recently opened zoo that housed animals in enclosures designed to replicate their native environments. It was hot, and the towering trees filtered the sunlight before it reached them. For Brynhild, illness became another childhood, in which she was watched over by the Switch, who reported home to her mother, and summoned down into the town by doctors who saw no particular reason to keep her informed of their plans for her treatment.

Her respite in Switzerland was nevertheless coloured by ongoing anxiety about money and about her younger children. She was forced to write to her father to ask for cash and to rely on friends to look after Lucilla and Clarissa. Clarissa stayed sometimes in her mother's doctor's household, and sometimes with her mother's cousin Sybille (Laurence Olivier's sister), and sometimes with her aunt Noel, and sometimes with her grandparents. Bryn had long hoped that Raymond would come and 'take charge' of all of them, as he did for the girls' visit to their mother's corner of the ward on Christmas Eve.

4

Andy

Andy, always her mother's right-hand woman, had done Brynhild's Christmas shopping for her, leaving her with one less thing to worry about as she wrote to the Wala. Andy always held the fort whilst her mother was in hospital, a surrogate matriarch for her younger siblings. Out of everyone, it was eighteen-year-old Andy who was on the ground with her mother, supporting her in the day-to-day struggle.

Nunnington had been full of promise. Their home there was a white medieval long house behind an ancient wall, with stone floors and deep walls built to protect. It was north-facing, with potential for dreariness, and had an air peculiar to old farmhouses: of a building hunkering down to withstand hard times and harsh weather. But it was larger than it first seemed, too, with a long attic where a long-lost thatched roof had probably been lifted for space. A staircase installed in the 1700s led you up towards bedrooms where Tudor planks provided floorboards. In the garden they had fig and apple trees, a Victorian vinery that held a great Black Hamburg grapevine, rumoured to have grown from a cutting taken at Hampton Court Palace. An outbuilding held a brewhouse, with a cider press and an old water pump; beyond that lay the farm that would provide for them. The house was less than a mile from the sea. Letters written in pencil on the beach began to arrive from Brynhild at Bognor Regis, where Sydney and Margaret were settling, not far along the coast. Her parents were also migrating coastwards, looking for a climate that could maintain Sydney's health, though what he really dreamed of was returning to Jamaica.

When the Sherrards moved in the spring of 1934, Andy's mother was full of hope. She had secured a new partner to help her run the farm: Mr Grieve, a man who made up in enthusiasm what he lacked in relevant experience (he was, by trade, a bank clerk). Raymond was supposed to provide the theoretical knowledge of agriculture, keeping things on track here as he hadn't been able to in Rushden. He had a new money-making scheme, working for a London milk distributor.

Things were different in Sussex. It was warmer, the farms yielded more, the land was actually worth something. Bryn arrived empowered with a determined optimism; her famous organising energy in evidence. The setting was beautiful and she wanted to make Nunnington a home for her children. She had the skills and the will, if not the resources. The real question would be whether she had the strength.

They got off to a bad start. After packing up Church Farm – a home with no telephone – and moving out, the Sherrards got word that Mrs Grieve, already in place at Nunnington, had come down with the mumps. As this was 'a "catching" thing', as Bryn told Luly, the family was stranded and had to decamp to the Wala's house for the time being. Only Andy, about to head off for skiing and study in Germany, had any clothes with her.

By the time Andy was back from her trip and at Nunnington, it was clear that the whole endeavour was headed for collapse. They had never really stood a chance. Raymond was preoccupied with fending off creditors and trying to earn commission drumming up business for the milk distributors, which was his only real source of income. He had switched sides in a rural battle, as farmers were often at war with milk distributors in these years, resentful of the low prices the companies offered. Before long Raymond took up a post at the Institute of Agricultural Economics in Oxford. Bryn insisted that he accept this prospect of a steady – if small – income, though Oxford was almost seventy miles away. On weekends he came home to see everyone, look over the farm, and tell Mr Grieve off for whatever he had done wrong since the last visit. The rest of the time it was up to Brynhild and Andy to run things, unless Brynhild made one of her periodic trips to hospital, at which point Andy took over.

Over the past few years, Andy's mother had become unrecognisable. She was no longer the beautiful, well-dressed person one could show off to friends. The teenage Andy was embarrassed by Brynhild's spoiled looks, her shabby housewife clothes. She saw a woman weighed down with cooking and cleaning and mending; and the worst of it was that Andy, a tomboy who had grown up with three brothers, was expected to pitch in, to take on the drudgery and risk sinking beneath it too.

Raymond she thought of as her wicked stepfather, with Andy taking the role of Cinderella, the convenient stepdaughter whose presence made it easier for him to disappear and leave them all to it. Andy had taught his children their numbers and letters and washed their nappies; as a child she had accompanied him on his milk-rounds, which, in the worst days, had to be completed before they could afford bread for breakfast, as a way of skipping the 8-mile bicycle ride to school. At the end of the day she sometimes waited hours, or so it seemed to her, for him to come by and collect her, or waited in the float while he ran errands and caught up with neighbours. But Cinderella doesn't have a mother, and the bond between Brynhild and Andy was strong.

In many ways, Brynhild's submersion was replicated around the country. Farming families were under extreme pressure in those days but families in vast swathes of the country were facing destitution. Home was a place to retreat to – a domain possessed of added lustre after the forced separations of the war – and it had quickly re-formed its grip on women. Racks of magazines aimed at women flourished in the 1930s, showing them how to succeed, and take pride, in domestic lives. They had pages and pages of advice on housekeeping, which had become a kind of profession for middle- and upper-middle-class women. An issue of *Woman's Own* in 1933 advised its readers to seek work as private secretaries: 'a short cut to a prosperous marriage'. A reaction to the 'boyish' look of the 1920s had kicked in, with fashionable women now opting for those timeless expressions of harmless femininity: ruffles, frills, floral prints, bows, feathers, extra material in all kinds of impractical places. Domestic appliances – beyond Bryn's means – were tentatively catching on, benefiting from the increased consumer expenditure brought about by the falling prices of the Depression. By 1931 there were 1.3 million electric cookers in use in Britain.

The reality was that these innovations consumed the time of women whose mothers had had staff to undertake such chores. In the same way that middle-class women's lives had been diverted by university, thousands of girls destined for lives in domestic service had instead experienced the independence of work in wartime factories, and in the 1930s they were still proving deeply reluctant to go back. Women who might have been their employers twenty years before simply took on much of the work themselves, aided in some cases by new machines and magazines. Even on holiday, Noel noted, a 'certain amount of fortitude has to be achieved to avoid spending 16 hours or 17 a day in some sort of slavery'.

Andy's aunts, Noel and Daphne, had families almost as big as Brynhild's. In 1934 Andy had four Harwood cousins and four cousins in the Richards family. Daphne, who had waited a long time for hers, rejoiced in her children, the first of whom (a son named John) was born in 1926, when she was thirty-six. 'I havn't told you how lovely, lovely the little one is,' she told her husband about one of their boys. 'I feel he is from the Sun.'

Their homes were happily chaotic. Daphne was charmed by the infant Virginia, Noel's third daughter, who 'waited serenely for [...] supper' at Noel's new house, 'which was an hour late!' Their attention was increasingly distracted, which perhaps explains why Brynhild was able to carry on as she did that autumn without eliciting more sisterly alarm. Like Brynhild trying to keep the farm going, Andy's aunts clung on to work of various kinds. Running the New School required a huge amount of attention; Daphne's husband only met Brynhild on a handful of occasions. 'I havn't been able to get over to see Margery yet,' Daphne admitted to the Wala after one Christmas, 'I'm afraid I'm rather domesticated just now – as I havn't been able to get about & see people for some time.' School life and home life was a finely pitched balance, and if one of the teachers or Daphne's home help went down, the whole thing tilted precariously, and the fewer resources a family had, the more that fell to the wife and mother.

Daphne had been one of the driving forces behind the New School and yet from the birth of her first son she had seen her influence there slip away. In a letter written from her parents' house after John was born she wrote to Cecil, who was managing things in Streatham, with some surprise at the sheer proportion of her time that the baby needed her full attention. Nevertheless she was still trying to work, reading and translating, and keen to remind Cecil of her say in proceedings at the school. 'I'm still on the College of Teachers,' she pointed out on discovering that crucial decisions about staff scheduling had been made in her absence: 'oughtn't I to have an opinion?' But she found that not being there, having her focus shifted, meant that things went on without her. Soon she was sympathising with Cecil instead, acknowledging the hard work he had to put into that term. 'This doesn't mean I sh[oul]dn't heartily endorse all you've done,' she wrote placatingly about the staffing. Dorothy Martin, another of the founding teachers of the school, had also married a New School colleague and had stepped back from management. Effie Wilson had left in 1932 to establish another Steiner school in Derbyshire. For a place founded by women, the New School was quickly taken over by male teachers.

Daphne factored in work where she could. Coming into her bedroom in the mornings, her children would find her surrounded by sheets of paper on the eiderdown as she worked on her translations. Noel bucked the trend of her generation, continuing to work as a doctor, with characteristic determination. Virginia Woolf, in agreeing to be her namesake's godmother in 1931, complained that she couldn't persuade its mother over for dinner (yet when the baby was brought to tea, complained of the 'plague of people' who prevented her from working). After the Richards family moved out of London to the suburban town of Ickenham (Daphne noted the newness and convenience of the house with envy), Noel was known to fall asleep on the train home after a long day of work and miss her stop.

In adulthood, separate families worried gently at the links between the sisters, loosening them imperceptibly; on the political scale a similar – but far more hostile – severance was happening. 'Why in 1934,' the author Winifred Holtby cried, 'are women themselves often the first to repudiate the movements of the past hundred and fifty years, which have gained for them at least the foundations of political, economic, educational and moral equality?' Younger women were no longer moved by these campaigns, regarding 'old' feminists as out-of-touch, elderly, spinsterish figures, whose spare time for meetings and lobbying only indicated how little they understood the realities of life for women: who were either busy earning meagre livings, their ambitions still limited by reality, or busy keeping homes going. The emigration of families into the proliferating suburbs isolated women from the centres of power their husbands now commuted to and from, and often isolated them from each other.

In this way, feminism seemed to disappear entirely, leaving a few lone voices like Holtby's in its wake and mass domesticated organisations like the Women's Institutes in its place. Eva Hubback's work with Eleanor Rathbone focused more and more on women as homebound creatures. In the late 1920s, this had led to a schism within the movement, from which it never really recovered. Rathbone's pet cause was the endowment of motherhood rather than the principle of equal pay for women, a stance she defended in terms that hardly sound feminist but equally spoke to the experiences of women like Brynhild and Daphne. The majority of women workers, she proclaimed, 'are only birds of passage in their trades. Marriage and the bearing and rearing of children are their permanent occupations.'

Bryn never told Andy about the suffrage movement that had animated her generation, and the extension of the vote in 1928 passed them by without comment; a towering pile of mending, precarious on the sofa, was always visible in the corner of their eyes, preventing this kind of conversation.

On one occasion, Andy made her usual trip on the number 2 bus to visit Brynhild in the local hospital and found an unexpected sight at her mother's bedside: another visitor. This mysterious person proved to be a former adjutant of Sydney's from Jamaica, a mythical part of her mother's past. To find this old admirer of her mother's at her bedside had a profound effect: he was a reminder of the attractive and carefree woman Brynhild had once been, a girl taken to dances by this man, once young himself. Andy had thought of her mother as alone for so long; for a moment it seemed that they had not been forgotten.

By the time her family decided to take charge and remove her to Switzerland for the summer, Brynhild was ready to admit defeat at Nunnington. Desperate, she let the farm for a low rate just before her departure, so that when she arrived back – reinvigorated by her retreat and met by Raymond and the children at Southampton – the only home available to them for the rest of the summer was in one of the cottages they had acquired with the purchase of the farm. They were low on furniture and cutlery; really they were camping. Tristram was staying with them but, when Raymond visited, had to sleep outside for lack of space.

The holidays brought the family together. Usually Philip lived with his grandparents to attend a prep school in Bognor; Luly was a 'charity girl' at a school in Woking and they and Tristram left again when term began. Then Andy returned and she, Brynhild and the five-year-old Clary moved back into the newly vacated Nunnington farmhouse, which they now shared with the Grieves. The struggle to keep the farm going did not last much longer, and the hapless Grieves finally fled in October. The farmland was let to a neighbouring farmer, leaving the three of them alone in an isolated house near the sea.

Brynhild had seemed much better when she got back from Zurich but over these weeks she grew sicker and sicker, until she was more or less confined to bed. The doctor visited to administer injections, and his sister gave Brynhild lifts to the hospital when she needed them, and Andy ran the house, tending to little Clary. Raymond's visits became infrequent – he had a new home, and a new lover, in Oxford – and when they were made they were spoiled by ugly scenes with Bryn. Her entrapment in the house, his escape alone: it was a familiar story told in extremes. Bryn did not complain to her family. Even her doctor noted (later and with some regret) that she was 'one of those people who went on simply not wishing to bother people' but this cannot have been how she envisioned the marriage to Raymond, brought about through her own act of will. With him, rows about the poverty of her little abandoned household frequently erupted, the strain proving too much for both of them. 'You cannot get blood from a stone,' Andy once heard Raymond exclaim.

Eventually, Noel arrived to check on her sister for herself. Alarmed by what she found, she had Brynhild admitted to St Bartholomew's Hospital in London. What was left of the Nunnington household broke up. Andy moved back to her father's house in London.

At St Bartholomew's, Brynhild fretted about Andy and the atmosphere in Hugh's household. It seemed to have an influence on her daughter that she didn't trust. 'Andy has gone all flibberty, gibberty again,' she told the Wala in her Christmas letter, 'I wish she had not to live there.' After depending on her for so long, a 'flibberty, gibberty' Andy was not a daughter Brynhild could recognise.

5

Hugh & Tristram

The day after Raymond, Clary and Luly's visit on 22 December, Hugh brought Tristram to the hospital. Hugh came with a Christmas gift for Bryn, Somerset Maugham's short stories, and fifteen-year-old Tristram came with a carefree smile. Hugh had never ceased in his admiration for Brynhild and struggled to conceal his feelings at the hospital. 'Hugh did not look very cheerful poor old thing,' Brynhild told her mother, 'but Tristram was beaming!'

Hugh's home – in St John's Wood, behind Lord's cricket ground, where Noel had lived before she left London – provided the other main setting for Bryn's older children. In September 1925, Beatrice Webb had had a new scandal to relate to her diary. Swapping notes on the shocking sexual morality of modern times with a friend, she heard worrying news about Hugh Popham, whose wife had reportedly gone 'off with another man'. Though they had divorced and both married others, however, the 'late wife' (i.e. Bryn) was now 'flirting with her late husband' (i.e. Hugh), 'much to the dismay of the new wife and new husband!' Beatrice's imagination leapt to her aid: 'Once married they begin to divorce each other, changing partners without hesitation, leave alone remorse for breaking the tie [...] it looks like two other divorces and a re-marriage – all within a few years. [...] Clearly the absence of all "taboos" can't go on?'

The reality behind these salacious rumours was, if anything, more surprising. Apparently unable to wrench himself too far from the Olivier family orbit, Hugh had fallen in love with Rosalind Thornycroft. After Rosalind's divorce from Godwin Baynes, they had reconnected at a party in February (probably held at her sister Joan's house) and the night they spent together had been enough for Hugh to finally extricate himself from his affair with Joan.

Since Rosalind and Hugh had married, they had amassed a household as large as Brynhild's, combining Rosalind's three daughters with Bryn's Tony, Andy and Tristram. After a wary start at Caroline Place, where Rosalind's daughters were confronted with the sight, as the front door opened, of 'three boyish figures sliding swiftly one by one down the banisters to land at our feet', the two groups melded comfortably. Brynhild received rapturous reports of their mass camping holidays in Cornwall. For Philip, spending Christmas with his grandparents this year meant spending it with the Thornycrofts too. It was, by now, a sprawling clan.

Brynhild had taken a dim view of the union between Hugh and Rosalind, feeling that Hugh could have looked a little further afield than her own cousin. After the divorce, Bryn's high expectations of Hugh's financial obligations towards their children had put additional strain on their relationship. She resented the time her children spent in London, away from her, but had found few hearings for her complaints. Sydney was sympathetic to Hugh's yelps of protest on finding loans to Bryn and Raymond go unpaid and requests for funds continue. Despite money worries of his own, Hugh had handled the schooling of Tony (who was skiing in Germany over Christmas), Andy and Tristram. As Sydney put it in his matter-of-fact way, 'Hugh's side of the family may be regarded as a going concern'.

6

Daphne

Daphne arrived at the ward while Hugh and Tristram were visiting. She was, Brynhild reported approvingly to the Wala, glowing; looking to her sister 'very rejuvenated as a result of her last baby', a son. Daphne had been involved in her own way in the family summits over Brynhild's health in the spring and had looked into the possibility of securing her sister treatment at the Steiner clinic which neighboured the Goetheanum at Dornach. Her faith in Steiner's teaching continued to suffuse her life.

This shared belief both sustained her marriage and exposed it to unusual pressures. Daphne and her husband each sought a full spiritual life, alongside the many demands of their material ones, and Daphne lived with a sense of the things she could not provide for her husband. Their separate spiritual quests were in a way isolating. '[A]s far as your own inner spiritual advancement is concerned I am completely unnecessary to you,' she wrote to him in the late twenties, '& neither have you, apparently, any deep concern or interest in mine. But I realised that it was a kind of egoism to wish it were otherwise.'

The couple's faith and related sense of purpose sustained them during difficult years. Even close friends and family remained mystified by their commitment to Anthroposophy. C. S. Lewis, adored by Daphne's children and now godfather to her son Laurence, had not been converted, and vented to his diary that Steiner's philosophy had 'slimed everything over with the trail of its infernal mumbo-jumbo'. Sydney found it absurd that the building bricks he brought out for his grandchildren to play with were rejected by Daphne on the grounds of their hard edges and sharp corners. It seems unlikely he would have appreciated the Waldorf emphasis on imagination and flexibility in early childhood, which also resulted in paper with rounded edges and dolls without faces.

In Streatham the lack of appreciation was a more pressing concern. The Britain of the early 1930s was hardly wholeheartedly open to foreign influences. Concerns about German behaviour, not least the belligerent Chancellor, Adolf Hitler, and his plans to expand the national army, ensured that post-war suspicion persisted. In 1933, Eleanor Rathbone warned her fellow MPs against trusting the new regime. 'No one who has studied the evidence,' she told them, 'can doubt that Germany wants peace just until she has completed the preparations for war.' It was not a good time to be known as 'the German school' but Daphne and her colleagues continued to teach German as well as French and retained foreign customs like the hanging of Advent wreaths in the classrooms before Christmas, things which marked the school out. They also hosted a stream of visitors from abroad, who came to observe Waldorf teaching in action and to offer help. The Vorstand, the executive committee which had run the Society since Steiner's death, even made a special visit from Dornach to see the school in the early days. (Daphne missed the occasion: she was giving birth to her oldest son.)

Nor was a depression the ideal time to interest parents in alternative theories of education. Streatham was a deprived part of the city. Few of the parents who did enrol their children were taken with Steiner's ideas, or the staff's views on teaching, and the New School's openness to pupils from all walks of life (plus an early need for enrolments) led quickly to a reputation as a school for 'troubled' or disabled children, which went beyond the school's resources and contributed to misunderstandings about the nature of the education on offer. Almost twenty years on from Noel's days at Bedales, parents were still wary of a private school where boys and girls were taught together, or where both groups were taught knitting and woodworking. As it was, the school's make-up was heavily weighted towards girls, presumably because parents felt more willing to take risks when it came to their daughters' educations.

Amongst the staff, Daphne was one of the few with formal experience in teaching. Like Cecil, many of the teachers were attracted by Anthroposophy rather than any calling to teach. William Golding, a young graduate from Oxford with aspirations to write but no teaching qualifications (Daphne wrote to Bunny asking for literary advice on his behalf), was apparently given a job on the basis of a recommendation from an anthroposophist friend of his and his supposed prowess at the piano. Discipline problems persisted. Golding kept his classes in line with the promise of stories for the entire second half of each forty-minute lesson, as a reward for good behaviour in the first. Another teacher ended one early lesson with only two children left in the room, both of whom were hitting him over the head with their rulers.

Nine years after the school opened, the Harwoods' circumstances were as difficult as many of their neighbours' in the down-at-heel area. They lived in a tiny, somewhat dilapidated house nearby, which had to fit their expanding family. Though the school was still run by a college of teachers, Cecil was by now the de facto headmaster and, though hardly a 'man of the world', responsible for the business aspects of running it. Daphne handled various secretarial duties, on top of teaching music and some of the younger children. Keen to spread the word, Cecil and many of his colleagues travelled widely lecturing.

Cecil with the children

In 1928, the couple attended the grand opening of the second Goetheanum in Dornach. The building had been constructed faithfully to Steiner's specifications. Around three thousand anthroposophists from around the world made the journey to witness the opening. 'There is no other building like the Goetheanum in the world,' the *New York Times* declared.

After the grand opening, Daphne remained beyond Cecil's stay to attend lectures and demonstrations, and to focus on her own spiritual progress for a while. The Goetheanum was indeed a building unlike any other. Per Steiner's wishes, it was constructed entirely from poured concrete, an edifice that nonetheless existed in conversation with its surroundings, looking almost as if it had emerged from the ground itself. In its form – a crouching, rounded outline – it seemed a younger sibling to the hills surrounding it, taking after them and reflecting its surroundings back out into the world. Steiner was influenced by Goethe's view of nature as rhythm, and elements of the building were based around Goethe's observation of the role of expansion and contraction in the natural world. The seven columns that rippled around the upper parts of the building – varying in size and shape and relating to the seven planetary stages of the earth asserted in Anthroposophical theory – contract and expand in the same way, so that a concrete building is seen to inhale and exhale. Inside there were few closed spaces: if a visitor looked upwards they saw openings and cavities, like being inside one of the nearby mountains; the cooling grey interiors folding over and over themselves. At the front was a huge window that looked out over the parkland surrounding the Goetheanum. Steiner's spirit was everywhere. Having turned to him for guidance in all matters, his followers were now working out how to proceed without him.

It replenished Daphne to retreat to the Goetheanum. 'These are wonderful days,' she told her husband, 'I hope that something of Dornach still is with you like a blessing.' To write to him she sat out on the terrace that ran around the building, facing out over the mottled green and brown forest, an old hermitage just visible among the trees. The atmosphere captivated her, acting almost spiritually on her as the Jamaican mountains once had done. 'I am sitting beneath those great curved walls,' she told Cecil, 'the valley is filled with a transparent warm blue haze, and the air with the sound of cow-bells – and the sun is sinking very gently and softly down into opal coloured mists above the hills.' At the end of the day she walked home to a house in the valley, relishing the setting: 'that walk through the quiet sleeping village is more remarkable than the magic of an enchanter's wand', she wrote.

Coming to the Goetheanum was like returning to the source, giving Daphne the space to focus on her beliefs and reaffirm her commitment. Here she was an eternal pupil, advancing towards that special knowledge that she had often felt her life was missing. Even a single good lecture there, she told Cecil, was 'enough to nourish a life-time', and she left with a renewed sense of the importance of their mission: 'the urgent thing is that the rest of the world should know'. She felt, after this visit, that their work could transcend the challenges of social and economic realities, and the squabbling within the Society itself. 'There will obviously be grievous folly & mistakes made here, but we must not <u>fear</u>, as I think one sometimes does too easily – that the intrigues and pettiness which give Ahriman & Lucifer their opportunity – will really overthrow the purpose of the spirit of the Age.'

So Daphne returned renewed and, by the early 1930s, numbers at the school were creeping up. By 1932 they had 150 pupils and had expanded into the next-door house. When Daphne visited Brynhild at St Bartholomew's, they were nearing the end of a funding drive to enable them to add a further extension.

The school did have a lot to offer. At state schools, classes were large and teachers relied on harsh discipline. (A bill designed to outlaw corporal punishment was rejected by the government in 1932.) By contrast, New School pupils had attentive teachers, who were united in their devotion to their work and a genuine interest in their pupils' welfare (spiritual and otherwise). The school was not a recruitment centre for Anthroposophy and the children were not schooled in Steiner's ideas (which nevertheless governed the way they were taught). The stark difference from other schools was apparent from the moment you entered the building: yellow-gold walls greeted the visitor and a copy of Leonardo's *Head of Christ*.

A special mood permeated the New School, fostered partly by the small scale and the collegial teachers. Each year a Midsummer Festival was celebrated in the garden, marking the summer solstice and the festival of St John, at the end of which staff and pupils would sing to each other around a bonfire. The children performed plays for their parents on these occasions, sometimes Shakespeare, at other times dramas and masques written by Cecil, whose love of traditional English verse influenced the scripts. (Owen Barfield compared them to what some of the Inklings, who had begun assembling in Oxford, were producing.)

Feeling the school had graduated from being 'New', they would soon rename it 'Michael Hall'. Steiner had taught that the Archangel Michael presided over the twentieth century as the guardian of man's freedom – something preserved in an education that focused on developing the individual. 'Hall' was partly a reference to the Parsifal legend, important to anthroposophists, as a place where 'members of all countries might come and be at one'. It was a name that spoke to the Harwoods' values and hopes, ones that were beginning to seem under threat in Europe.

Daphne's new baby, Mark, had arrived rapidly after his brother, Laurence, and she now had two children under the age of eighteen months, as well as a daughter, Lois, who was five and John, eight, who was already a pupil at the school. The demands on Daphne and Cecil were great, but Owen Barfield, visiting their tiny house, was impressed with the 'truly heroic manner in which both of them "coped" domestic-ally as well as occupationally'. Within these confines Daphne managed a warm hospitality for their closest friends. The now balding, rotund and insatiably clever and communicative C. S. Lewis was a regular visitor. He took pleasure in long walks with Cecil and the company of his old friend's brood of children. Thanking Daphne after one visit, he paid tribute to the peculiarities and pleasures their home had to offer:

> It is recorded in the Laxdale Saga that Kjartan Olaffson stood up in the All-Thing and invited the whole of Iceland to his wedding – of which men said that it was 'manfully offered.' Your summoning of the whole clan to Streatham was a delightful revival of these old heroical hospitali-ties. I shall long remember the game of definitions and our later excursion into angelology.

It was difficult for Daphne to get away from her family and school in Streatham, so Brynhild's new presence in London at least meant she could see her. For Christmas, Daphne brought her sister a hyacinth in a pot for her bedside.

7

Noel

One person came every day. 'She is naughty always to insist on coming,' Brynhild wrote in her Christmas missive, 'but she always pretends it is on the way from something or other.' Of course her sister saw through the ruse. Noel visited Bryn's bedside in the evenings, delaying her return home from work. Arthur had set up his GP practice in Ickenham; it was Noel who commuted into the city.

At the Infants Hospital in Westminster, where Noel had been promoted to Physician, the process of excluding female doctors begun in the 1920s was by now almost complete. In 1922, she was one of two female Assistant Physicians hired by the hospital, adding to a staff that included a female anaesthetist, house Physician and Resident Assistant to the Medical Director. By the mid thirties she was the only woman among five Physicians and the only female member of medical staff (beyond nurses) apart from an anaesthetist. She retained a position as an honorary physician to the out-patient department of the Victoria Hospital for Children on Tite Street, and she gave twice-weekly sessions at the Model Welfare Centre on Kingsland Road in Shoreditch. This was a free service, partly run by volunteers, which sought to improve the health of the poorest babies and their mothers in the borough; an early experiment in public healthcare provision and a product of the wartime concern for infant well-being. There were educational talks and demonstrations, a special clinic for breastfeeding, a Light Clinic for the treatment of children with rickets, a dental department catering to the shocking numbers of children suffering from tooth decay, and a dining centre for mothers and children on particularly low incomes, where each child was given a teaspoonful of cod liver oil after dinner. In 1931, an antenatal clinic was added, and there was accommodation for babies suffering from malnutrition or mothers needing help with breastfeeding. These centres catered to a real need among the poor. In 1934, over four thousand children under the age of five visited one of the welfare centres available in Shoreditch.

Noel's base, the Infants Hospital, had a reputation for pioneering work in illnesses related to nutrition. By the mid 1930s, it had space for a hundred cots and was well respected for the research carried out there (amongst its facilities was a 'Milk Laboratory'). Such work was crucial in understanding the interconnectedness of nutrition, maternal health and infant well-being. A floor was set aside as a 'nursing mothers' flat' where seven women could stay with new babies. A delegation from the British College of Nurses was intrigued to discover an 'interesting American invention' there: an 'electrical breast pump for expressing milk, which the mothers can work themselves'. The same delegation was also impressed by 'what is termed Dimmer lighting', which allowed for a subdued glow at night-time, making the wards, well ventilated with balconies facing over the greenery of Vincent Square, into 'a fairyland of light and crystal'. Babies in knitted white outfits, and toddlers in royal blue, slept in white enamelled cots. The celebrity on the ward in the mid 1930s was baby Joseph, who weighed 13 ounces on admission, and lived.

Noel's calm and sensible exterior was perfectly suited to her work. She was quiet and kind; sick children tended to trust her and so their mothers did too. By the time of Brynhild's stay at St Bartholomew's, her expertise was such that she was preparing for the publication of her first (co-authored) book, *Healthy Babies: Their Feeding and Management*. It was part of the Cassell's Health Handbooks series and would be sponsored by the former Physician in Ordinary to George V. In her book Noel offered practical information on caring for, clothing and training babies – the kind of guidance her sisters turned to her for – and non-alarmist advice on when parents should seek medical attention for their children. It would be welcomed as 'a book of facts [...] containing no vague statements and none of the clichés so common in books on the feeding and management of babies'.

Noel's book was protective of new mothers who, it insisted, needed 'peace and protection from worry', and a defence against the 'misleading advice which will often be freely offered to [them]'; but it also had expectations of them. Breastfeeding, for instance, was regarded as a responsibility, whether it appealed to a woman or not. 'Some young mothers', readers were reassured, had little of the usual 'instinctive sympathy for children [...] to guide them' but 'companionship of a baby usually arouses affection and interest very soon'. Few photographs of

Noel looking directly at the camera exist, which may be why the image of her with a new-born Benedict – by now ten years old – seems to show her looking a little vulnerable. She gazes at the photographer with a protective pride, the baby laid out in her lap like an offering. Her own mothering was pragmatic (when in labour with her first daughter, Angela, in 1928, Noel had administered anaesthesia to herself). Fearing that an infant Benedict was not thriving in London, she had sent him, with a nurse, to the Wala in the countryside, leading Bryn to hope she could take him in and gain some income that way. Noel went back to work when Benedict was one. At that stage in her life, Noel told James at the time, she was 'practically completely engulfed'. She spent her first two waking hours with her own baby each day, before travelling around London tending to other people's, not returning home again until 7 p.m. And yet any retreat from work was experienced as a loss. When she stepped back from the Tite Street hospital in the autumn of 1933, not long after returning to work after Virginia's birth, she spoke of being 'broken-hearted'. 'I've never regretted anything so much.'

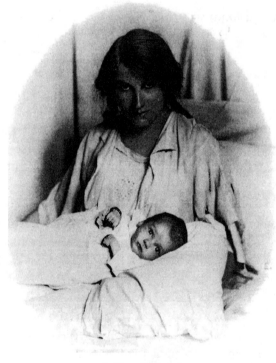

Noel with Benedict

Noel's children had not prevented the continuation of her career, to the chagrin of some of her female colleagues, who had made just that choice, assuming, presumably, that it had to be made. She was aware of the disapproval of other female doctors but carried on as she had done in the face of hostility from nurses and male colleagues in the past. Yet Noel had always struggled with demands made on her by others and the bulky operation of family life sometimes felt oppressive. She preserved a separate life for herself in London, which also gave her space for her relationship with James Strachey.

Not long after Lytton's death in 1932, Noel and James picked up where they had left off more than a decade before. This time, the initiative was all on Noel's side. Perhaps the strength of her concern for James during the torturous final illness of his beloved brother – followed swiftly by Carrington's suicide – forced her to confront her feelings. 'I will come & see you anywhere, if you w[oul]d like it at any time,' she wrote shortly after Lytton died, signing off as 'Your loving Noel'.

By the summer, twelve years after their marriages to other people, Noel and James were lovers again. 'I thank Heaven – HEAVEN Heaven – that what with one thing & another I've woken up in the end,' she told him. As exhilarating as an affair was, there was also something safe in choosing a man so well known, someone who had loved her so well in the past. So much already existed between them and yet this time everything was different.

The Stracheys had returned to London by the mid 1920s and James's career as a psychoanalyst had soon given way to the translation of Freud's writings. James, married but childless, free to travel and work on his great translation project as he pleased, held back, afraid to hurt Alix and no longer needing Noel's love as he once had. He had spent his youth loving first Rupert and then Noel devotedly, with little reward. Now, he had a productive partnership with Alix and, having inherited Lytton's copyrights, was a wealthy man. It was Noel who did the seeking, who was full of need, and the desire for reassurance. Motherhood removes independence, sinks limits into liberty. Noel's life had begun to shrink: space for work, for home, for sick sisters. Even James's wealth affected the balance, as he lent Arthur and Noel substantial sums over the rest of the decade.

James and Alix Strachey in the mid 1930s

Noel also, and characteristically, dreaded causing anyone pain, yet daydreaming of James sustained her when life was too overbearing. Arthur had got used to James, though he still couldn't quite take him seriously, and even invited him to join a family holiday in 1932, unaware of Noel's feelings. But the two met usually in London, or attended the opera at Glyndebourne, and Noel never set foot in the Buckinghamshire home James shared with Alix.

Noel seemed to spend her time waiting for that mothers' miracle, the 'moment's peace' – so that she could use it writing to James. She made contact in snatched moments, time she caught back from her everyday life and used to reach outside of it.

Noel's unflagging persistence when it came to Bryn's treatment gave her sister confidence and hope. Research into Hodgkin's disease had recently been conducted at St Bartholomew's, which was no doubt the reason Noel had had her admitted there, and the two of them had given the doctors a detailed medical history when Bryn arrived. Their old friend Geoffrey Keynes, now doing pioneering work on breast cancer, was on hand on the staff to offer additional support.

Brynhild's spirits were anyway not easily crushed. A postcard she wrote to her mother that year read: 'This is just to let you know I am getting better.' When she returned from Switzerland she had seemed better to everyone. Even Noel was surprised by the positive effects apparent from 'drinking their arsenical waters in the high altitudes', as she conceded grudgingly to James. Brynhild felt that the trip had gone well and on the way home she treated herself to a whole day alone in Paris. The train from Zurich went via Basel, so that she, too, made an unintentional pilgrimage to that emblematic station.

The weather was hot and Bryn's train pulled into Paris on the brink of an exquisite morning. She was worried about her luggage, as she recounted to her mother from the safety of the West Wittering beach later, because she wasn't sure that she had enough money left to pay a porter. She had only 50 francs – and a 10/- note – 'but I was determined not to part with that'. From Paris Brynhild took another train out to Versailles. The palace gardens, vibrant in the summer sunshine, enchanted her, and she committed them to memory for the benefit of the Wala: deep cherry-coloured geraniums, edged with a 'dark purple Verbena-like flower', pear-shaped yew trees surrounding them in a horseshoe. Terraces led to terraces until they reached marble nymphs, shepherds, deities; a top terrace of bright red and white arrangements. Tiny rosemary bushes appeared 'with the utmost regularity', enormous orange trees stood in square pots and Brynhild admired the trees in the woods surrounding the Trianons: 'lovely cedars and huge acacias'.

She could not afford the 2-franc admission fee to go inside the palace so she stayed outside, still unsteady on her feet and stopping frequently to rest, peering in through the windows. Perhaps unsurprisingly, she was more taken with the stables than she was with the palace's magnificent interiors. By the path to Marie Antoinette's Petite Trianon, she found a spot under a fir tree and fell asleep. When the sun began to glare, and the gardens grew busy with visitors and their prams and pet dogs, Brynhild made her halting way back into the city. At the station she did her accounts and had some firm and frank conversations with porters. On the way to Le Havre, she relied on kind strangers, and on the crossing to Southampton, quite in contrast to her outward journey, she slept soundly.

Privately, Noel was frustrated with the care that Brynhild was receiving in London; convinced that the staff were not doing enough, that they saw the case as incurable and took action only to satisfy the sisters. It took her two weeks to persuade them to administer blood transfusions, for which she and Raymond were donors, and, by that point, they had no impact. Brynhild's swellings were gradually subsiding but they still bothered her and prevented sleep. Just before Christmas, though, Noel gave her good news. She had been telephoning Dr Janet Vaughan, a specialist in blood diseases who would shortly establish Britain's first national blood bank, who had proved to be interested in Brynhild's case. Dr Vaughan told Noel that a new professor, expected at the hospital on 1 January, was, as Bryn reported to her mother, 'very, very good indeed'. 'So perhaps they will get some ideas between them. Meanwhile,' she told her on Christmas Eve, 'I am quite peaceful here.'

8

January

Despite Professor Witts's efforts, Bryn died on 13 January. Noel's admiration for her sister lasted to the end. 'She was very magnificent, dying,' she told James.

Losing Brynhild was a kind of orphaning. With Margery incapacitated for so long, and always too erratic to be entirely depended upon, Brynhild had often acted as the eldest sister and an excellent one at that: a brilliant mixture of soothing and yet dazzling, energetic and efficient, as perceptive, full of advice and respectful of privacy as an ideal sibling should be. A twenty-year-old Daphne was convinced that she and Brynhild spoke 'the same language'; Noel had once depended on her intuition above anyone else's. If, as their adult lives and families absorbed them more and more, she hadn't been the close companion she had once been, Brynhild was still an emblem of their sun-filled youth, the star to their wandering barks, an irreplaceable loss. Noel, who had refused to abandon hope, now blamed herself, and tormented herself with thoughts of what might have been done differently, automatically taking responsibility for her sister's health. She still believed that there was a chance that Brynhild could have pulled through – if only through the latest crisis of 'aplastic' anaemia – and dispatched a series of queries to Professor Witts, the highly recommended expert, who answered patiently and in detail.

Daphne and Noel spent their summer holidays that year together, with their children. Daphne kept thinking of herself and her sisters in childhood, alighting on the four of them at different times in their early lives. Not only was Brynhild gone, and Margery now practically unreachable, but that almost mythical time seemed lost with them. 'You gave us all such a beautiful childhood,' she told the Wala. 'All that will live with Bryn [...] and all that was good & beautiful she can take with her on her journey.'

PART SIX

Still Carrying On

(Or, Four Years Later)

BARON OLIVIER'S DAUGHTER

August 1939

Cecil Harwood was playing in the Cornish sea with his children when he saw the telegraph boy approaching the house and knew that the sight meant war. In Streatham one of the younger teachers, new, nervous and feeling out of her depth, had been fielding calls from parents and practising her typing in the office when word arrived that Operation Pied Piper was underway. In Cornwall, Cecil's heart sank. He had 130 children to get to safety. Daphne stayed behind with their own whilst her husband made a swift return to London. Her eldest son was thirteen. Noel's was fifteen. They had nephews, Bryn's sons, who were already of military age.

Anticipating a German onslaught on a massive scale, the government gave schools advance warning of war, hoping to give them a head start out of danger. Across the country, thousands of teachers were returning early from their summer holidays, knowing what their pupils, whose parents hovered anxiously by the radio, did not yet know.

The Luftwaffe had shown what it could do in the Spanish Civil War, the conflict to which Vanessa Bell and Frances Cornford had lost their eldest sons, and which had ended less than six months before. The government was privately expecting 3,500 tons of bombs to fall on London in the first day of conflict, bringing devastation on a scale never seen in Britain before; within two months, it was feared, there would be 1,800,000 casualties. Cinema-goers would in any case have had no difficulty in imagining the carnage. The capabilities of German weapons were the stuff of awestruck rumour but they were also evident in the ten-minute newsreels that played in cinemas. Even before shaky footage of the remains of Guernica, of reports on the German and Italian bombardment of Madrid and Barcelona, they had watched *Things to Come*, a Wellsian warning adapted from H.G.'s 1933 novel *The Shape of Things to Come*. The film showed cacophonous scenes of people caught

in bombardments of city streets: trucks screaming past, humans dropping under tumbling rubble, alarm bells clanging amongst the constant
thunder of guns, the camera resting on the face of a small dead child.
This black-and-white depiction of a fictional world war had shown
people what to expect: a swarm of hostile planes would blacken the
sky above Big Ben, women would scream, children die, landmarks be
blown to smithereens. Psychiatrists warned that the psychological toll
would be even higher than the physical. At the Westminster Children's
Hospital, Noel and her colleagues discussed how to handle influxes of
people harmed by gas attacks. The government's idea was to distribute
the population widely, hoping to at least limit the damage by scattering
the target. It now fell to schoolteachers, and a swiftly mobilised force
of thousands of members of the Women's Voluntary Service, to ferry
groups of children out of harm's way.

On 1 September, when the German army invaded Poland, Britain
mobilised her armed forces and began the evacuation of one and a half
million people from danger zones that had been identified many months
before. In the capital, hundreds of thousands of children, pregnant
women and mothers with babies were put in transit; they followed in
the wake of the treasures of the National Gallery, which had a head start
of several days, and the residents who had already decided to leave.

The Michael Hall evacuees assembled early in the morning, where
they found Mr Darrell, one of the younger teachers, standing on a chair
in the assembly hall, clipboard in hand, directing them into coaches. A
hundred leave-takings had to occur before 8 a.m., when three Royal Blue
coaches pulled away from the school. Inside them, the children clutched
their gas masks and the twenty-four hours' worth of food their mothers
had been told to pack for them. In organising their own transport, the
staff had spared their children the scenes that were unfolding in London's
train stations, where platforms thronged with excited or frightened
minors, labels hanging from their necks, clinging to their bags or their
siblings' hands, seen off by mothers stoical and mothers more frightened
than them. Almost half of London's schoolchildren were leaving, and
would make confused and halting departures. Getting them out was the
priority: where they ended up was far less certain.

The British landscape was newly divided: split into evacuation areas,
reception areas and neutral zones. There were thirteen million people in
the danger zones and eighteen million living in the areas designated to
receive them. Over the next few days, more than 800,000 unaccompanied

schoolchildren arrived in the reception areas. London's minors were scattered across the country from the tip of Cornwall to the coastal corner of Norfolk; an area which encompassed 476 different billeting authorities and seventy-three education authorities. Many schools were broken up and redistributed, separating children from the only familiar faces they had left. Exact destinations for schools were concealed and train journeys were frequently disrupted by the movement of troops, which took precedence. Teachers found themselves trapped for hours in crowded carriages with hoards of hungry, frightened, toilet-needing children. Communication broke down. Well-meaning volunteers in rural villages, armed with tea and treats for schoolchildren, were confronted with weary expectant mothers from the East End; hosts prepared for mothers and toddlers ended up with teenage boys on their hands.

In many places, fired up by circumstance, local communities came out in force to receive their very own refugees. One schoolteacher arriving in Yorkshire with her group was met by 'the police, the Home Guard, the Guides, the Mothers' Union, the Chapel Ladies and all the local council officials'. From the windows of their coaches, the Michael Hall children glimpsed others just like them: bewildered, tired crocodiles of labelled pupils traipsing behind their teachers on their way to new homes. Village halls were transformed into something resembling livestock markets, as hosts haggled over which or how many children to take, and in some places farmers swooped on the oldest boys, bearing off the prize of unpaid labourers. Children lost sight of their siblings, or luggage, or both; abandoned themselves to despair.

Well into a warm afternoon, Cecil and his evacuees, including Daphne's two eldest – John and the ten-year-old Lois – finally arrived in Minehead, a town on the Bristol Channel in Somerset. As they peered from their coach windows, the children might have seen the slow-moving horses on the farms, and as they passed the heathery hill, and then the whitewashed cottages lining steep lanes, they must have realised just how far from South London they had come. They were welcomed by volunteers bearing trays of milk and biscuits. The trusty Captain Field, Michael Hall's own war hero, who had served with Cecil in the last war and had famously overrun a German gun position armed only with his officer's cane, had gone on ahead to arrange billets, so that strangers led them away, singly and in twos, without much fuss. Only some of the teachers found themselves without somewhere to stay, and the atmosphere on that disconcerting day was such that one woman, spotting a young teacher wandering the streets with a billeting officer, ran out of her house to offer her a room.

On 2 September, Cecil telegraphed to a colleague in Streatham to confirm that the school had arrived safely. The following day, Britain declared war.

When war broke out, Noel and her children were in Ireland. It was either a very good or a very bad place to be. There was no immediate reason to think the Irish coast would be bombed but equally no reason to think they would have unlimited opportunities to get back to England.

They had been staying in Ventry, a village on the Dingle peninsula, with Bunny's wife Ray Garnett and their sons, Richard and William, in a pink hotel with a walled garden that ran almost to the sea. The children camped on the grass between the hotel and the craggy coast. They were probably the most comfortable guests. The windows of O'Brien's Hotel offered sea views but also flew open at the slightest provocation. The rooms were generously sized but far less generously furnished. Of the breakfast, Noel reported that the 'porridge is a mixture of lumps of uncooked grain & burnt bits floating in soup. [...] The bacon manages to be oily as well as shriveled and the fried eggs hard.' The day after they arrived, half of the dining-room fireplace fell off. One guest was sleeping on a bed made of packing cases.

But Ventry recommended itself by its isolation. '[E]verything [is] on a generous scale,' she told James, 'so that one sees headland beyond headland & not a suspicion of a resort in any corner.' The children dived from the rocks whilst their mothers basked in the extraordinary weather. '[N]o one expects it to last,' Noel wrote. Though her doctor, Geoffrey Keynes, was lying to her, Ray Garnett knew she was dying of cancer. And less than a week into their stay, Bunny (who was holidaying in England with his twenty-year-old mistress) wrote to warn them that war was said to be imminent.

At first, Noel leaned towards staying put. If there was going to be a war, she wanted to see how it was going to play out before taking her children right to the centre of it. On 31 August, as Michael Hall prepared to evacuate, Noel took her children to the races in Dingle, where there was also a fair, because they had set their hearts on it. The next day, Ray and her sons left to meet Bunny in Mayo. By 2 September, Noel and Arthur had decided to meet in Dublin. He arrived on Monday, the day after Chamberlain's radio broadcast, and that evening the Richards boarded the first boat to leave for Liverpool since the declaration of war.

The wharf was crowded with passengers and the people seeing them off. The Richards had managed to book the last three cabins aboard *The Munster* and, as they left Ireland under a Destroyer escort, Noel worried about being torpedoed. Arthur woke in the early hours of the morning and found them inching their way along a channel marked by buoys, passing through mined waters in a procession of slow-moving ships. Noel slept until they reached the Mersey, where they were greeted by the sight of a flock of barrage balloons – large snub-nosed inflatables designed to obstruct the path of enemy aircraft – which six-year-old Isabella (now nicknamed 'Tazza') mistook for bombs.

Arthur's colleague in Ickenham had already been called up and he was urgently needed back at the practice. As they made their way home, however, Noel changed her mind about taking the children so close to London. Benedict's school was being evacuated to Melksham, in Wiltshire, so he and Arthur went on whilst Noel found rooms for herself and the girls near Oxford. She lodged in the house of a local dentist, whilst the girls slept together in a hotel that had been mostly taken over by officers. All day an orderly sat beside the telephone, preventing anyone else from using it, and a sentry stood in the yard with a fixed bayonet.

Noel was summoned to a committee meeting at the Elizabeth Garrett Anderson Hospital in London but, on the whole, war threatened her with unemployment. All the patients who were sufficiently well had been discharged from the Westminster Infants Hospital on 25 August and Green Line ambulances arrived to evacuate the rest a week later. The hospital was closing for the war. The staff was scattered: nurses to an emergency hospital outside of the city, the Honorary Medical and Surgical staff to other hospitals in London and the resident Medical staff, along with most of the Sisters, to France with the RAMC and Territorial Army Nursing Service. The out-patient department was taken over by the council as a first-aid post and the lecture hall became a depot for hospital supplies; equipment that could be moved was loaned out and the precious portrait of the hospital's President, the Princess Royal, was spirited away to the countryside for safe keeping. Noel decided to take the girls to Nunnington, the farmhouse in West Wittering where Brynhild had wanted to raise her children, but had, in the end, willed to her sister.

The first summer without Brynhild had seen a rift open up between Raymond and the Oliviers – born long before in their dim view of his character and his perceived abandonment of Brynhild – that came to a head over the house. Bryn made a will only at the last moment, leaving her estate to Noel in the hope that something could be salvaged. (Raymond was an undeclared bankrupt so Nunnington would almost certainly have been lost if bequeathed to him.) Noel only just managed to keep the house: it was first let, and then the land sold off, before George Bernard Shaw saved it for them with a final act of generosity towards the sisters. When Noel took possession, Raymond would sometimes turn up unexpectedly, determined to holiday there. It was said that he had climbed on to the roof in an effort to put off the new tenants and he submitted his children to upsetting scenes when police (or bailiffs) eventually arrived to remove him from the house. But by now Nunnington was Noel's beloved second home.

Bryn's family persisted in the bond between the Popham children and their younger siblings, thanks particularly to Andy's matriarchal instincts. For Philip, Lucilla and Clarissa, the holidays from their boarding schools were split between Raymond's new family and Sydney and Margaret's house, and their aunts (and Eva Hubback) stayed in touch with them with as little reference to Raymond as possible.

Like millions of others, Noel had hoped almost to the last minute for peace. Over the last half-decade, public opinion was preoccupied not with preparations for war but with the question of whether it could be avoided. Two days before the Munich Agreement was signed, in September 1938, Noel sent a letter of encouragement to Chamberlain. She had been told he liked to receive them. 'I still think he may manage to prevent war,' she told Ray Garnett, and she was far from alone. But others were already drawing parallels with the past. '*The Times* is taking on that fearful aspect that it had in the last few days of July 1914,' James wrote that summer. For him it added a note of urgency to his relationship with Noel. It was a time for drastic, if hopeless, planning. 'Won't you throw everything to the winds and come away with me to a South Pacific island?' he asked. 'I find myself being gnawed more & more by regrets that we haven't spent the last twenty years so. Time seems now so short and possibilities so narrow.' Noel made only one objection: 'I have my little children to look after.'

By the following autumn, they were used to living at a strange pitch. It was perhaps this atmosphere of heightened emotions that put Noel's marriage under renewed pressure, for though Arthur assured James that he did not question Noel's need for James, he also confided that he was missing 'true companionship' with his wife. With her, his behaviour was bullying. '[T]he tempests seem to rage all around,' she wrote. James was perhaps her truest companion in the mid thirties. 'What I feel all the time – & it practically makes me cry – is that I would like to see you every day & sleep with you every night,' she told him in 1935. The affair left them caught between love and longing. Yet when Noel had a rare sleepless night, 'awake in grief from 3 to 3.30 a.m.' for their separation, she succumbed by reading Rupert's poetry by firelight.

Noel had been anxious about leaving the country in August 1939 and must have been haunted by memories of the last war as she sat on the beach with Ray, watching their fifteen- and sixteen-year-old sons swimming with the girls. There were twenty-one years between the war that dominated Noel and Daphne's youth and the next one: enough time for a baby to grow into a soldier, as indeed Bryn's sons Tony and Tristram, born in 1914 and 1919, had done. Their father had served in the last war, as had Cecil Harwood. The Woolfs' partner in the Hogarth Press, John Lehmann, looked about at young men in September 1939 and was 'haunted by the slightly dazed look that would come over their faces'. For their parents' generation, there could be no such vagueness to their fears: they had known war and would now have to face it again.

2

New Homes

In Minehead, it had been arranged that Michael Hall would share the premises of the County Secondary school, where they arrived on 1 September. Though some parents had made their own evacuation arrangements, the student body had been swelled by refugee children from Steiner schools on the continent (reaching 300 for the 1939–40 school year) and they needed plenty of room. Unfortunately, on the same day, the boys of the Regent Street Polytechnic found themselves on the wrong train. When Cecil rose on 2 September, he discovered that this rival school had been allocated the space instead. Michael Hall was homeless. On their first full day in Minehead, with the weather on their side, the teachers gathered the children and strode out on to the beach and across the moors, keeping them occupied in exploring their new surroundings. Meanwhile, a rigorous search was under way for a proper home.

What Cecil and his colleagues found was Clevelands, the large and gloomy former residence of a Belgian baroness, which had stood empty for years. Positioned high on North Hill, beneath the Minehead Armoured Fighting Vehicle Range, the house had glorious views and a big, steep and overgrown garden. It was also filthy, without electricity and harbouring dry rot. Some of the windows were broken, the wallpaper was peeling, the only water came from a pump and bats circled outside in the warm early evenings. But the house stood on St Michael's Road, close to St Michael's church, which seemed like a sign: the teachers arranged to lease it.

With a renovation crew of unoccupied pupils, work on the house proceeded swiftly. For days, the teachers and older children scrubbed, rearranged, fixed and repurposed. It took a thousand strokes to fill the water tank and in the evenings the rooms were lit by oil lamps. The enormous project was a blessing in disguise, bringing the displaced school together and providing a focus for nervous energies. Supplies began to arrive in containers from Streatham and made surprise appearances throughout the first term, until the sound of tyres on gravel became an excuse to abandon lessons and rush outside to unpack. Daphne brought her three youngest, Laurence (aged six), Mark (four) and Sylvia (three), and settled into the cramped former servants quarters at the west end of the house, a space so small that John had to be billeted in town.

Despite everything, Michael Hall began the new school year only one day late, on 25 September. Term began with typical ceremony, in a ritual dreamed up by Cecil and worthy of anything from the imagination of C. S. Lewis or his colleague at Oxford, J.R.R. Tolkien. First the school body processed through town, up the hill, and to the front door of the school house, where the oldest male pupil, a boy called Harry Bidgood, thumped three times on the door with a staff and requested permission to enter. The house lacked a room large enough to fit all of the children, so they crammed themselves into the dingy hall and spilled along the stairs and across the landing to hear the maiden assembly. The first Minehead term was underway.

Whilst Clevelands was being given a new lease of life, Noel was in West Wittering, at Nunnington, trying to decide what to do. She and Ray Garnett thought about finding a house near Melksham, so that they could live near their sons' school, Beltane. Ralph Partridge, Carrington's widower and now Ray's brother-in-law, had offered to lend them his car so they could explore the area. Noel's daughters Angela, Virginia and Tazza could also have studied at Beltane (it was an experimental and co-educational school, much like Bedales) but she was instead thinking of sending them to Minehead. Though a nerve-racking air raid warning was later exposed as a convincing prank by Virginia and Tazza, the sight of the barrage balloons over Portsmouth from the garden at Nunnington was enough to convince her that they should move. She was worried about Sydney, who appeared to have suffered another stroke, and the Wala, who found him difficult to deal with at the best of times. On top of all this, Noel was suffering from morning sickness.

3

The Twilight War

As the weeks passed, the flight from Nunnington began to seem less urgent. Britons drifted into what Churchill termed 'the Twilight War', a strange and prolonged period in which everything had changed but very little happened. Few of those immediate fears came to pass. Though air raid sirens sounded within moments of Chamberlain's radio address to the nation, they were sounding a false alarm. The cities were not flattened by bombs, nor did the British army engage its enemies. The effect of this anticlimax was oddly unsettling. Instead of a barrage from the air, a torrent of restrictions fell on ordinary people, as well as on the press, which offered only a meagre trickle of information about what was going on. In London, people stopped carrying their gas masks. Parents began to collect their children from the countryside.

Noel started to split her time between Nunnington and Ickenham, using her Ickenham house as a base from which to attend fortnightly committee meetings of 'lady doctors' and a monthly clinic at Westminster. It was already proving harder to see James, who had made a visit to Nunnington soon after she shared the news of her pregnancy, and in place of her usual hospital work, she was generally stuck in West Wittering with three girls under twelve, their au pair and the char lady, having to get to grips with chores like cooking and cleaning, as well as guiltily coming up with lessons for her daughters. 'I'm quite sick of the war, in every way,' she told James. 'Can't we get them to wind it all up now?'

For the Harwoods, the absence of an attack on London put the school in jeopardy. If parents began to remove their children, they would find Michael Hall (and its income) melting away. Billeting had not been an unqualified success. Across the country tensions between hosts and their 'guests' quickly became apparent, arising partly from a culture clash between middle-class hosts and working-class evacuees. A Fabian report on the evacuation outlined some of the problems: 'hosts complained that their guests were verminous, bed-wetters, liars, petty thieves, without respect for property, of unclean habits, ill-equipped, rude and quarrelsome; conversely, that they were stuck up, would give no assistance in the home, and were too expensive to keep'. Miserable children, thus demonised, wet more beds and grew more homesick.

In Minehead, the teachers solved the problem of unsuitable billets by taking over two local houses as boarding hostels for their pupils. But they also had to find a way of maintaining good relations with a local community that showed few signs of including them. More than ever, the school's German links cast suspicion. Worst of all, Michael Hall had actually brought Germans to Minehead. Small-scale warfare erupted between the lower-school boys and local gangs slinging 'Nazi school' taunts. The fact that most of the German children (and staff) at Michael Hall were refugees counted for little. Things got worse when Mr Darrell landed in the local court for failing to observe the blackout properly; he was fined and given a public and humiliating warning of possible imprisonment for future infractions. After that, in a tense and watchful atmosphere, rumours of spying were rife. Minehead's coastal location made the issue particularly sensitive. Restrictions placed on the movements of 'enemy aliens' meant Michael Hall had had to leave some of its teachers behind and even the refugee children were required to report regularly to the local police.

Though the Harwoods had managed to stay together, John's billeting with a smart local family raised its own challenges. The head of that household was the local Master of the Hounds, whose example made Daphne's son look differently upon his own scholarly and unconventional parents. During a visit to the family in December, C. S. Lewis noted the change with some amusement. The teenage John had 'already [...] acquired a new language', Lewis wrote to his brother,

and says that his father ought to get his hair cut! I hardly know which to pity more – a father like Harwood who watches his son being thus 'translated' or a son in the process of such translation who has the embarrassment of a father like Harwood. I think the son: for as some author whom I've forgotten says the anxiety of children that their parents have about children 'being a credit to them' is a mere milk and water affair beside the anxiety of children that their parents should not be an absolute disgrace. Certainly it would not be pleasant to have to explain to a [Master of Foxhounds] that one's father was an Anthroposophist – except that the only impression left on the M.F.H.'s mind w[oul]d probably be that your father was some kind of chemist.

On the other side of this new distinction, John's siblings found his new manners a perplexing surprise.

Lewis's visit found Minehead in the depths of a brutally cold winter. In January, the mains froze in the village, and heavy snow brought down trees and phone lines. In the first weeks of 1940, Hitler promised the British that he would be with them in the spring. Rumours of various high-tech and dastardly German weapons circulated, news spread of atrocities in Poland, sympathy swelled for invaded Finland, battling the Soviets. '[O]h, it's a queer sense of suspense, being led up to the spring of 1940,' Virginia Woolf told her diary.

4

Invasion, Spring 1940

For all the quiet in England, on the continent disaster followed disaster, as the German army overcame Denmark in April before invading the Low Countries. That was on Friday 10 May. The Dutch surrendered the following Tuesday. On the Friday, as German and Allied soldiers raced each other to the French coast, Noel gave birth to her fourth daughter. Within a week of Julia's birth, over 330,000 men of the British Expeditionary Force were trapped on the beaches of Dunkirk with a motley flotilla attempting to rescue them. Two days after that evacuation began, the Belgians surrendered. Almost immediately, Dover was subject to daily bombardments from the air, and before the baby was a month old, Paris had been occupied by the Germans. In the interim, the British acquired a new enemy when Italy declared war.

Around the time of the first air raids on England at the end of May, Noel sent her older daughters to Minehead to join Daphne's school. She stayed behind to give birth in London. The government issued leaflets to every household with instructions for what to do in the event of an invasion. As the Germans made indomitable progress across Europe in the days before Julia's birth, it must have been a terrifying time to be heavily pregnant, one which raised questions about the world into which Noel was bringing her baby. At forty-seven, Noel was relatively old to be having another child. Besides this possibly daunting prospect she also had no safe home to bring the baby to, no way of knowing how long her family would be separated or even if there would be a free Britain for long in which to raise them. As she prepared for this new life, others wondered if theirs were coming to an end. Two days before Julia was born, Ralph and Frances Partridge discussed killing themselves and their young son in the family car. A government minister bought suicide pills for himself and his wife. Adrian Stephen provided Virginia and Leonard Woolf with enough morphia to choose suicide. If the Richards also had such measures in mind, they had easy access to the means in the dispensary attached to their family home.

If the Woolfs had good reason to believe themselves targets for Nazi occupiers, then the Harwoods must also have feared for their future. The German Anthroposophical Society had been banned since 1935 and most of the Waldorf schools in occupied Europe were forced to close. The National Socialists had long hated Anthroposophy and, as an alternative belief system, it was barely tolerated in the early years of their power. Since the beginning of the war there had been deafening silence from the network of Steiner schools that had flourished in the rest of 1930s Europe. Cecil had made a tour of Germany in 1938, in a gesture of goodwill to embattled colleagues. By that time, the schools were banned from accepting new students and staff in them were divided over how far they should assimilate Nazi directives to preserve their existence. Within three years of that trip, there would be no more Steiner schools in Germany, and prominent anthroposophists had been arrested, some of them disappearing into concentration camps. The Harwoods and Michael Hall had harboured enough refugees to understand the reality of life under Nazi rule, and must have known that their beliefs would bring persecution if the United Kingdom fell.

The day after Noel and Julia joined the others in Minehead, the French surrendered, leaving the UK without a single undefeated European ally. Noel and Julia were part of the second wave of evacuations triggered by the spring's events. Sydney and Margaret made a prolonged dash (the journey took twelve hours) to check on Margery at the St Andrew's satellite home in North Wales, where she remained more preoccupied with her 'illegal' detention, and the voice of 'Norton the Murderer', than with the war. The remaining male German teachers at Michael Hall were now rounded up by the British government, who caved in to press hysteria, expressed in a typically restrained 'INTERN THE LOT!' *Daily Mail* headline, and did just that.

There was no space, it seemed, for nuance or common sense. (Even one aristocratic staff member, a German baron, who when interrogated was said to have answered, quite honestly, that his closest relative in Britain was Queen Mary, could not avoid suspicion.) Only the female refugees, such as Inge Beck, a former Waldorf teacher who helped to run one of Michael Hall's hostels, remained. Around the school, road signs were painted over and on the beach stakes were driven into the sand to repel enemy ships. Barricades of wood and wire appeared on the main road; pill boxes and gun mountings emerged. American journalists who arrived in England to get a ringside seat on the invasion of Great Britain – the Germans made their first incursions that month when they overran the Channel Islands – were instead in time to witness the Battle of Britain, which erupted within view of the country's inhabitants that summer, and Churchill's assurances to the world that the nation would 'prove ourselves once more able to defend our island home, to ride out the storm of war, and to outlive the menace of tyranny, if necessary for years, if necessary alone'. 'We shall go on,' he told the House of Commons in June, 'we shall never surrender.'

And, for the most part, the nation agreed with him. His approval rating the following month was an unprecedented 88 per cent. The series of disasters over the spring was, in a way, what everyone had been waiting for. Finally, the ordinary person – primed for eight long months – could spring into action. On the day of the Dutch surrender, the Secretary of State for War issued an appeal for volunteers for local defence forces. A quarter of a million people signed up in a single day; half a million unpaid volunteers had been recruited by the end of June. In the factories, production records were broken; park railings came down; housewives sacrificed saucepans for the building of planes; donations to Spitfire funds flooded in. Bunny's eighty-something mother-in-law volunteered as a fire fighter in London. Alix Strachey pasted a sticker on her car offering 'Lifts for Servicemen'. Cecil Harwood and Arthur Richards, both in reserved occupations, joined the Home Guard. The Harwood children watched their father parade up and down the streets of town and were told stories of his night exercises in the morning. People, a Mass Observation report noted that month, 'were itching for something to do'.

5

The Blitz

Noel, without much company in Minehead, and lonely in the evenings, slipped into a dark frame of mind. '[O]ne adopts,' she told James drily, 'the morbid assumption that one's family is bound to be destroyed fairly soon, in any case, and the question of their future does not arise. Which is all very sad.'

For the summer holidays she took the children to Bunny's house, Hilton Hall, in Cambridgeshire. Ray Garnett had succumbed to cancer in March and her place was taken by Angelica Bell, whose life had been saved by Noel's friend Marie Moralt in 1919 when she was only weeks old. Angelica was raised as Clive Bell's child but in reality her father was Duncan Grant, Bunny's former lover; a fact that Bunny knew and Angelica had only recently been told.

Noel and the children were at Hilton on 7 September when the first air raid hit London's docklands. For the rest of their stay they could hear distant sirens and the sound of enemy bombers flying over their heads after dark. For seventy-six consecutive nights (barring one) after that first raid, the city was bombed and bombed and bombed. Almost ten thousand people were killed and many more thousands injured or made homeless as buildings were blown apart.

In Minehead, a false alarm of invasion was raised, and Cecil spent a tense forty-eight hours on duty, watching the sky and sea for the enemy. Noel returned later in September, in time to see a German bomber brought down over Porlock Bay. She watched the pursuit from her house: transfixed as the planes swept over a nearby field and above the hedge of her garden. 'I saw it being chased,' she wrote afterwards:

it looked as though it was nearly down, flying slowly & very low just above the hedge & the fighter only half a field behind it machine-gunning it; & in less than five minutes the fighter came tearing back, swooping about & showing off over the town.

Most of the time the enemy was only audible: present in the sound of the planes droning over at night, on their way to bomb people somewhere else, explosions rattling the windows and, if one looked, distant flashes and the beams of searchlights.

On the coast at Bognor Regis, Noel and Daphne's parents were subjected to far greater disruption, yet were still refusing to move. Air battles raged above them and bombs fell in the town. Even when they tried to take refuge at Nunnington an air raid shook the house so violently on their arrival that a large corner cupboard crashed down in the dining room, whilst Sydney sat in an armchair and dozed.

In October, Ickenham, on the outskirts of the capital (and linked to it by the Underground), was finally bombed. Arthur and the housekeeper spent the evenings in the air raid shelter in the garden and slept downstairs at night, depending on earplugs to insulate them from the nightly racket of bombs, enemy aircraft and anti-aircraft fire; in his surgery Arthur was kept busy with a stream of minor injuries from broken glass. Over the course of the Blitz, eighteen high explosives fell in the town itself, several close to the Richards' house. The nearby Northolt Aerodrome, a hive of RAF and Polish Air Force activity during the Battle of Britain, also attracted Luftwaffe attention. Suburban landscapes were transformed. Frances Partridge, passing through the suburbs on her way into London the following February, observed

Bomb craters [. . .] fairly frequent among the houses by the line. First there were broken windows, some filled in with cardboard, and then a smashed roof or wall, or a whole house demolished [. . .] The rows and rows of untidy mounds in suburban gardens all along the line presented a disgusting sight; these squalid, mildewed shelters, looking as if pigs or rabbits might inhabit them rather than human beings [. . .] symbols of our fear and degradation.

The Westminster Children's Hospital was hit, damaging almost all of the rooms inside and badly spoiling the exterior. Then the Blitz expanded to other cities. In November, Eva Hubback leapt out of a committee meeting on hearing of a raid on Coventry, where her daughter was living. Eva's daughter was safe but well over a thousand people were killed. In the same month, thousands of explosives fell in Bristol, roughly 40 miles from Minehead, causing more than two hundred fatalities in the first attack.

And winter landed in Minehead again. The town, Noel complained, 'turn[ed] out to be the most bitterly cold place in England. Frightful North easters lash down from the mountains of Wales & fearful howling West winds come raging across the moors or chill mists creep in from the Bristol Channel'. She fell ill and some of the children came down alarmingly with measles; baby Julia, who had started teething, 'fumed & fumed & chewed her knuckles'; at night Noel dreamed of an invasion. At Michael Hall, the staff tried to soothe children whose parents and siblings lived under the Blitz in Streatham, coped with the news of Harry Bidgood's death in the RAF and the internment of a popular gym teacher as a prisoner of war, read the bereavements announced in the school's new journal.

Daphne and Noel's homes were not close and Noel preferred not to leave her house after dark; she anyway struggled to get Julia's perambulator up the hill. During these weeks, though, Cecil and Daphne began to visit her for supper. Sydney and Margaret gave in to their daughters' entreaties in December and moved to Minehead. Noel took in Sydney, who immediately became friends with Julia, and the Wala had a rest from him in lodgings Noel had arranged next door.

There was no travelling for Christmas in 1940 but the family did gather at Michael Hall for what Noel described as 'a great joint feast'. Over the radio, the voices of children evacuated overseas carried festive messages for their parents. London landmarks were being hit: St Paul's at the end of the year, the Bank of England in January. From Minehead they heard a raid on nearby Weston-super-Mare and went tobogganing on the frozen hills. In March or at the beginning of April they would have had news of Virginia Woolf's suicide. It was a sad loss for Noel, who had been close to Virginia in her youth and had maintained links by asking Virginia to be godmother to her namesake. Sydney had written to Leonard only a month before, asking him to tell Virginia 'with my love that her God-child increases in stature and beauty and in laziness and Literary tastes'. Leonard remained a beloved presence in Ginny's life, treating her to days out in London, with visits to museums. In the weeks after Virginia's disappearance and death Leonard received over two hundred letters mourning what was a national loss.

With all the cold and illness and bad news, Minehead in March 'seemed very dark & black & pestilential', Noel told Bunny. Noel and Daphne were thinking about their sons' futures, hoping to put off their enlistment. Philip Sherrard had got a scholarship to Cambridge and Noel was hoping that Benedict, who wanted to be a doctor like his parents, could enrol there early (at seventeen) to read Natural Sciences. She and Arthur, she admitted to James, hoped it would buy him some time and 'prevent his being snapped up at the age of 18'. But later she reconsidered. Cambridge was empty but for medical students and the RAF. It was likely, she thought, that Benedict would have a better time there in peacetime and she decided ultimately to let him 'take his time & put it off [...] till 1942 in the hopes that the war will then be over or drawing to a close'.

6

Hope

In the late 1930s, Noel's love for James had been tremendous and was answered equally in adoration. Theirs managed to be an affair of both intense physical attraction ('I keep imagining you're here with me in the most provocative shapes,' he wrote) and long-standing fondness. To many, James was a charming yet withdrawn figure; in some ways as hard to know as Noel. In 1941 he seemed to Frances Partridge to exist 'in an enclosed world of his own', but with each other he and Noel had a kind of security which enabled passion. In July 1939, trying to take his mind off the likelihood of war, James had looked through his stash of their letters, which ranged over thirty years of friendship. 'The marvellous thing about it was to discover how <u>much</u> we've loved one another, on and off, all through our lives,' he told Noel:

> But it nearly always seemed to be on one side and not the other.
>
> I've only just recently found out – only about three or four weeks ago, I think – that the really most important thing of all is for both of us to love each other at the same time. [...] Though I've also got another idea – which is of our ending up the whole story by being together entirely and inseparably.
>
> Anyhow it's superb to have been mixed up such a terrific lot with you, Noel.
>
> All my love is yours.

They had always spoken as if their relationship had a future, albeit an imprecise and undefined one, but the reality of Noel's family life had obstructed the present. Unable to see her in the summer of 1938, James admitted to his fury 'with you and with all of the various classes of obstacles that you've collected around you – including your husband and your children and your domesticated character and habits'. Noel both engaged in their fantasies of escape and acknowledged the priority of her children. By 1938, her marriage had been stumbling in the face of her distracted love. Arthur was capable of frightening scenes but he also suffered in her emotional absences. 'She is the only one I have ever loved,' he wrote to James, 'and I am completely dependent on her.' At the time of the Sudeten Crisis, in September 1938, Noel was depressed, feeling 'with foreboding', she told James, 'that whatever happens I shall hardly see you again'.

It seemed, finally, that the enforced separation of war would end their affair. In October 1940, James was still her 'darling Love' but shortly after that Noel passed up an offer from him to visit. She didn't write again until Christmas and when she wrote in 1941 she wrote for his help and advice on Benedict's education. The following year she appears not to have written at all.

As the months rolled on towards 1942, the tenor of war changed. In the spring, Westminster Abbey, the British Museum and the Houses of Parliament were all damaged by bombing but with this final surge of wrecking, the Blitz seemed to come to an end, having killed 43,000 people. In June 1941, the Germans invaded the USSR, a huge transfer of resources, and the sense of imminent peril in Great Britain began again to lapse.

The Wala was missing her house and, at the end of October, took Sydney back to Bognor. Late in the year, the Germans were mired in Russian impenetrability. 'Hope is an awkward character to carry about with one,' Frances Partridge noted in November, 'and makes life more agitating and restless than despair or fatalistic resignation.' In December, the Japanese attacked Pearl Harbor and the USA entered the war. The tide truly seemed to be turning. But despite new allies and their victory in the Battle of Britain, the British were still accustomed to bad news, like the losses of Hong Kong, the same month, and Burma, the following year, to the Japanese. It seemed likely that the war itself would linger on, would be hard fought, would require not simply an upswing of courage and energy but sustained stoicism, sustained making-do, sustained struggle.

At home the carrying-on was borne, in large part, by women. For some reason, they proved, an American correspondent informed her readers:

the greatest surprise of the war. Their self-discipline, unselfishness, and determination to win this war is incredible [...] there is work for women to do. It is all hard. Most of it is dangerous, and it is done in the quiet, unspectacular way in which they used to run the village fetes.

Emblematic of women's war effort, alongside the women in munitions factories and the girls working the land, was the Women's Voluntary Service, which had amassed over 920,000 members in 1941. Its headquarters, the same correspondent noted, became 'almost as famous as 10 Downing Street'. Recruits were trained in first aid and fire auxiliary services, deployed in the evacuation, managed refugees, kept play centres and communal kitchens running throughout the Blitz. Self-abnegation, expected of women in peacetime, became a national virtue when the country was at war. Echoing Millicent Fawcett and the Pankhursts in 1914, Eleanor Rathbone had announced early on that wartime 'was no time to speak of women's rights – except one: to give their lives for their country'. Knowing Churchill to be no great feminist, she had been instrumental in establishing the wonderfully named Woman Power Committee, to ensure work was diverted their way. At the end of 1941, with the country now digging in for a long war, conscription was extended to women. Ninety per cent of able-bodied, single women aged between eighteen and forty were engaged in war work over the course of the year.

Nevertheless, among women who survived the First World War there was a new degree of scepticism in the way they went to work in the 1940s. They had not forgotten the lack of inter-war reward. The director of the Women's Royal Naval Service noted frankly that, though her recruits proved 'that women can do anything', she feared that they would be 'disappointed as they were in many ways after the last war'. (Even their lives were not valued as highly as men's, and female civilian victims of enemy action received a lower rate of injury compensation than men.)

Age and domestic commitments exempted both Noel and Daphne from having to register for war work. The government was extremely reluctant to encourage the mothers of young children away from the home, afraid of challenging the Ministry of Health's firm views on maternal responsibilities. Despite the huge mobilisation of women, which exceeded the previous war, their primary employment remained as housewives. Daphne and Noel were middle-aged: fifty-four and forty-nine respectively when conscription was first introduced. This was not their generation's war and though affected daily by the conflict, they must have felt in some ways incidental to the war effort. Neither succumbed to the deep psychological anguish they had suffered during the First

World War, no doubt partly because they were not directly bereaved by it, but perhaps also because of this sidelining effect of age. Both sisters were grey-haired by 1941, mothers of all the children they would have, rooted into place where they were apparently most needed. When Noel and Virginia Woolf posed for a photograph beside Ginny by the shed where Virginia wrote at Monk's House, the little girl, on best behaviour, appeared between two women who were beginning to look elderly. Noel's clothes are smart and unshowy: a dark skirt suit to the pretty dresses of both Virginias. Her gaze resolutely denies the photographer and looks fixedly into the garden instead. Her hair is completely white, her figure thicker, but all of the features of her youth are still there in her face: her good fortune in cheekbones, her skin clear and firm. In person she had a calm and unassuming air – an air that concealed the desires and rebellion and fear that once found expression in her letters to James – that spoke instead of capability, understated authority; a practised ability to inspire trust that was no doubt honed in the children's wards at Westminster.

This, in many ways, was a woman for wartime. In a BBC Radio broadcast at the beginning of the Blitz, J. B. Priestley praised the women of London for their resolution, for 'still carrying on', for appearing each morning 'neat as ever, rather pink about the eyes perhaps, and smiling rather tremulously, but still smiling'. One could be forgiven for thinking that women's greatest contribution to the war was symbolic: women's faces could not admit to its strain. 'Let us face the future bravely and honour the subtle bond between good looks and good morale,' a wartime Yardley advert trilled. But around the country, people did hang on to their solidarity by refusing to show their fear: both supporting and buoyed up by the many others who were managing to keep a brave face on things.

Noel wrote gamely to friends about being 'extraordinarily free from menaces' in Minehead, whilst Daphne filled her letters to their mother with descriptions of the children's antics and the surrounding countryside. This was what middle-aged mothers were expected to contribute to the war effort. They did not have to stay beautifully made up to bring succour to soldiers' spirits (or to find that delicate balance in this beauty so that it still promised patient fidelity), they did not even have to work in an office during the day and traverse London on a motorbike in a volunteer despatch team for the Ministry of Information at night as their grown-up niece, Andy, did. They just had to carry on. By doing so, they would help others in more important work to do the same.

*Noel and Ginny with Virginia Woolf in front of the writing
lodge at Monk's House*

It was perhaps less easy for Daphne to maintain her equilibrium during
the war than for Noel. There was something in the outside world that
she met with fear. The Harwood siblings were sheltered children. There
were many things that their mother deemed a risk to them: certain
reading material, films (Laurence did not set foot in a cinema until his
late teens), the plays put on in the village, the news of the war. Instead
of magazines and movies, Daphne entertained her children with music.
They visited Noel's house in part to read the *Picture Post*, which they
were not allowed at home. Daphne wanted to protect them from the
world, which had become all the darker since 1939. For her, evil was
more than an abstract concept: it was a real and present threat to the
people she loved most.

It is hard to say whether the belief system of Anthroposophy, which
undoubtedly aligned with Daphne's sense of the world, may have in
some ways exacerbated her fears, or whether it simply offered comfort.
Anthroposophists understood history in terms of an ongoing struggle
between Christ and the forces of evil. Noel, in commenting on other

anthroposophists she met in Minehead, felt that it attracted people who had suffered in life. Daphne belonged to a small outsider community in Britain, especially here on the fringes of village life, and may have struggled to feel part of the patriotic solidarity that others could seek comfort in. She was still a pacifist.

Daphne was sincere and tenacious in her faith, though marriage and motherhood had enabled another retreat. Of his three close friends who were anthroposophists (Daphne, Cecil and Owen Barfield) C. S. Lewis identified Daphne as the most ardent. Though he respected her, his admiration was for her role as 'an excellent mother of five children'. Her involvement at Michael Hall was by now limited to the occasional teaching of music. Cecil ran the school and was heavily involved, too, in the Anthroposophical Society on a national (and international) stage. Daphne's commitment remained far more private. During their time in Minehead she was translating two Anthroposophical books: work that she could do in isolation, without leaving her home.

Noel's matter-of-factness left her with little patience for Daphne's peculiarities but it did not stop her from worrying. The difference in their outlooks was exasperating and yet, beneath her impatience, Noel appreciated something of what lay behind (what seemed to her to be) Daphne's infirmity. On arriving at Minehead, she told James, she found her sister to be 'more or less an invalid suffering from chronic fatigue & a cough & thinness, all brought on by keeping her windows shut day & night to keep out the bad spirits. She calls it a cold. It has gone on for over six months.'

'The lightless middle of the tunnel'

Both Daphne and Noel were delighted to leave the enclosed spaces of London and its suburbs, and emerge into the kind of landscape they both deeply appreciated. 'I often bless the beauty of this place,' Daphne wrote, 'and am most humbly grateful to have been able to live in it through these terrible years – and for the children to be having it.' They made sure that the children made the most of it. There was a whole tribe of Olivier children in Minehead during the war, unexpectedly enjoying a childhood not unlike their mothers' in Limpsfield. Daphne's were John (turning sixteen in 1942); Lois (now thirteen), a keen violinist; Laurence (nine), sweet-natured and helpful; the most precocious of her brood, Mark (eight), and little Sylvia, who was six. Lois had a near contemporary in Noel's oldest daughter, Angela, who had a dark beauty that hinted at her Welsh (and Huguenot) heritage. Together with her three younger sisters – Virginia (now eleven), known as Ginny; Tazza (nine) and the youngest, Julia, who in 1942 could say 'Bub', 'Da' and 'Mum' but was steadfastly refusing to graduate on to proper speech – she would come to remind Bunny of the young Olivier girls he had once known.

Julia, at home all day with her mother, bore the brunt of Noel's excursions – wedged into a back seat on Noel's bicycle as she plunged up and down the Minehead hills – but she had her revenge in a tendency to totter off by herself whenever the opportunity arose. Noel was fascinated with Minehead. 'It is a curious place,' she told Bunny, 'no two days are alike – terrific winds & then calms & then mists & then a bright dry day – all in about a week. The air can be extraordinarily clear. I think I have never seen the stars & the moon brighter.' A flock of Harwoods on bicycles was also a common sight, and Daphne took her children on great walks across Exmoor, gathering snowdrops, or for horse rides across the neighbouring hills. The boys were a little afraid of the ponies but

Daphne had remained an accomplished horsewoman and her two daughters shared her passion. Lois had her own pony but when North Hill was taken over by the Americans she was left with fewer places to ride. Worst of all, when the horse injured itself on the barbed wire at the boundary and developed tetanus, he had to be put down, as there were no medical supplies spare for ponies.

Noel with her daughters

The cousins were in and out of each other's homes: Angela and Lois and Tazza and Laurence were most closely matched in age; Sylvia played nicely with her littlest cousin and John was on hand for babysitting. If Noel had to return to Ickenham or London, Daphne stayed over or deputised one of her children to take care of the girls. Sydney, hard to understand after his strokes and a little intimidating (except to Julia), and the Wala were regular presences. Bryn's son Tristram also made visits to see them, tempted away from what the children were certain was a 'hush hush' war job. Andy might well be found on a visit to their grandparents in Bognor.

There were mass picnics on the beach at Minehead, or Cecil would take the children to nearby Horner to play in the stream, whilst the Olivier sisters prepared lunch and followed by bus with the baby. The Harwoods learned to swim in the pools in the river there, which also provided a setting for Laurence and Mark's small electric boats and a harbour their elder brother built for them. On one occasion, while Cecil snoozed and the children played, Daphne and Noel took themselves on a walk, climbing steeply above the picnic glade and pausing to watch the scene of their combined families below them. This, perhaps, was their personal triumph of the war: the provision of a family life for their children, against many odds. Somehow the war had brought the Oliviers together.

Daphne with Laurence, Sylvia and Mark

Noel's hopes for an end to the conflict in 1942 were not met. Instead, the country soldiered on into what the novelist Elizabeth Bowen would call 'the lightless middle of the tunnel'. This meant that the deprivations of wartime continued and extended. Both sisters remained in cramped and insufficient housing. Some of the Michael Hall teachers ran the hostels, the rest were squeezed into Clevelands where they could find space; one teacher made his home in an old hayloft. These ramshackle arrangements could be dangerous: Mr and Mrs Darrell were almost killed by carbon monoxide poisoning when their boiler malfunctioned. In the old servants' quarters, Daphne shared her room with Sylvia. Until Laurence helped his father to wire the house – looping unsightly lengths of flex through brackets along the walls – the family relied on oil lamps, and the children each went to bed with a candle. Both Daphne and Noel struggled to find domestic help during the war years, as women who typically did this work were diverted into factories and other, better paid, wartime employment. Noel complained drily about 'living the life of a housewife': a housekeeper in Ickenham and a busy career had so far insulated her from such day-to-day labour. She did not have the skill for it, nor did she enjoy it. A thank-you note to the Wala for a knitting pattern read: 'I will now get on with my knitting, as I have no excuse not to.'

Noel and the girls moved to another house in the spring of 1942 but it was hard to settle into a temporary home. '[W]e are crowded with suitcases, & cardboard boxes & piles of books & toys & so on,' she told friends. 'Very terrible.' Noel's new domesticity was a change for her daughters, too. As Arthur's surgery was attached to the family home, they were more used to his presence than their mother's. Noel had always brought her work home in the stories she told her children about her patients and their progress, and if they joined their parents in bed as they drank their morning tea they would be likely to hear them discussing cases. When Noel was with them, however, she made the children feel that she was truly present; she had an ability to focus on them that Arthur's coming and going inevitably lacked, and in Minehead, Angela, Ginny and Tazza had her undivided attention.

Daphne tried to be more buoyant about the drudgery, boasting of an 'economical' washing method she devised: 'a combined wash of clothes & floors [...] you use your soapy water each time its too black for the clothes – it never seems quite too black for the floor!' But she did not relish domestic life any more than Noel did. One colleague felt that she 'found it hard to suffer the constraints of daily life. [...] though the mother heart was much engaged, there was discordance between the will that lived in her and the demands life made on her'.

Daphne's inspiration was spiritual; she was by nature a retiring person but was animated about Anthroposophy. She engaged in friendly debates with C. S. Lewis that left him frustrated at her unbendingness, her application of Steiner's ideas to all aspects of life. 'When you have heard half as many sentences beginning "Christianity teaches" from me as I have heard ones beginning "Steiner says" from you and Cecil [...] – why then we'll start talking about authoritarianism!' he wrote during one disagreement over love and marriage. But there was little scope for this energy in the domestic struggle.

Even for those who were used to housework, the work was harder than ever before. Food was not perilously scarce but it was extremely limited in variety. Shops did not have much to offer but when they did, the queues were daunting. Both Noel and Daphne raised their children on tales of Jamaica: an impossibly exotic imaginative leap for young people growing up in a country where bananas sometimes appeared as raffle prizes.

There was very little in the way of dairy products like milk or cheese, nor was there much meat, sugar, tea or coffee; citrus fruits, apples and sweets were barely available. Instead of white bread, they had to feed their children the grey alternative, 'utility loaf'; the Food Ministry recommended making marmalade out of carrots, or eating crow rather than chicken, or drinking 'Victory coffee' made of ground-up acorns. 'Don't just serve potatoes once a day,' one advert suggested merrily: they could appear in almost every meal. Beside potatoes on a child's plate was most likely to be turnips and swedes from local Minehead farms, parsnips, carrots, perhaps some fish. Eggs came as a powder, which had to be reconstituted with water. One boarding school in 1942 advertised 'Eggs' alongside its 'Moderate fees' to recommend itself.

The pressure on women to make do with less was relentless: not only less contact with family and less freedom of movement and less security than they were used to but also to fashion ordinary daily life with fewer and fewer resources. To read government posters was to believe that wasteful housewives were as much to blame for the drowning of merchant seamen as German U-boats. Coal shortages meant that keeping their homes warm (particularly during the harsh first three winters of the war) was a lost cause. There were numerous shortages that made raising very small children – or running a school – especially difficult: feeding bottles and rubber teats were hard to come by, as were cots and their bedding, prams, baby baths, blankets, soap, medicine and toothbrushes. Even pencils now came without paint or varnish. It was hard to celebrate the children's birthdays when one couldn't get hold of sugar or balloons or toys. Noel and her children sought escape in the cinema, seeing Noel's cousin Laurence Olivier in *Pride and Prejudice* and the film version of Bernard Shaw's play *Major Barbara*.

Though the war summoned women into work with an urgency never witnessed in peacetime, for women like Daphne and Noel it battened down the hatches of domestic life. Noel had returned to work after each of her pregnancies but, without adequate childcare (and with the hospital that employed her anyway closed for the duration), her maternity, as it were, caught up with her. Daphne's children had reached an age of comparative self-sufficiency just as daily life became more burdensome. The government was slow to include married women, and especially mothers of young children, in the calls to war work; reluctant, too, to distribute the burden of housework or childcare to free them up for factories and ministries. Even at a time of great peril, few were prepared to suggest that a woman's home and family were anyone's responsibility but her own.

Batches of children in blue blazers and caps or berets charging up and down the steep cobbled streets were now a fixture in Minehead. The teachers, conscious that the school needed to make a good impression, tried to discourage the running and have the boys raise their caps to passers-by. But it had always been a school that favoured pastoral care over discipline and this character now came to the fore.

As one educational sociologist observed, 'The importance of the school, considerable as it is in peace, becomes paramount in wartime.' The Harwoods and their colleagues had taken on enormous responsibility with the evacuation, undertaking to provide a surrogate family for over a hundred displaced children in deeply uncertain times. Fortunately, most of the Streatham teachers, including Cecil, were above the call-up age (teaching was a reserved occupation, so the conscription of some younger colleagues would also have been delayed), and they were able to offer a degree of continuity.

Over a period when there were over sixty million changes of address (in a civilian population of only thirty-eight million), the stability Michael Hall offered was precious. Many of the teachers lived in Minehead with their own families, and other parents had by now moved to the vicinity as Noel had, contributing to a domestic atmosphere. But this was still offset by the unease and anxiety of separation for many of the pupils. Medical professionals were already warning that evacuation was having greater psychological effects on children than bombing. When the younger children cried as their beds shook in the Michael Hall hostels during intense bombardments on nearby cities, they were crying for the family members they knew to be sheltering in London as much as for themselves. Ballads expressing the pain of separation, of longing for reunion, Vera Lynn's 'We'll Meet Again' and 'It's a Lovely Day Tomorrow', were emblematic in their popularity.

Daphne and Noel were largely spared the fear of the postman's approach but Noel and her children did suffer the separation from Arthur and Benedict. Arthur now had no partner at the practice so could rarely get away. As petrol became more intensely rationed, the only way he could reach Minehead was by arduous train journey; without the car he also couldn't collect Benedict from school to see his mother. Visits were few and far between. The strain of work and noise in Ickenham told on him and the time apart told on his marriage. He was not entirely faithful to Noel during those years, a situation she took in her stride; even arranging a dinner with one interloper, about whom their housekeeper, Anne, had tipped her off, to stake her position.

As the prominent (and first) Steiner school in one of the few free countries left in Europe, Michael Hall was a standard bearer for Steiner's ideas on education, and the teachers were more than ever motivated by the hope that their work might preserve an impulse that would outlast them. The school's distinguishing features remained: German continued to be taught, music and the creative arts were a focus rather than an extra-curricular, control of the children could be shaky. Even Noel's daughters joined their classmates in sometimes giving Cecil the slip. In the summer, Eurhythmy classes would silently diminish as one by one pupils slipped out of the classroom's open doors on to the terrace and away into the garden where, at other times of year, a pitched battle fought with giant pinecones might be underway.

At a time when almost all schools were operating with disruption and staff shortages, the school's reputation for laxity in intellectual rigour must have seemed less of a concern. As well as Eurhythmy, the children played mixed hockey on the beach at low tide and a yearly football match with the usurping Polytechnic school. The stables at Clevelands were converted into a makeshift gym and theatre. The school continued its tradition of huge theatrical productions, in which roles were found for everyone. Pupils ranged across the surrounding countryside, exploring Dunster and its castle, swimming at Greenleight Farm, collecting alabaster at Blue Anchor which they carved into candle holders.

They made the best of what they had. Someone donated an old Morris to the school, a car quickly nicknamed 'Old Jo' for its number plate that began JO, in which Miss Russell – the teacher who had manned the phones on that fateful day in August 1939 – ferried groups of children (twelve at a time) from billets to lessons. The elderly vehicle struggled to master the hills even more than Julia's perambulator, and Miss Russell's passengers were often ejected to climb it themselves anyway. On one occasion she gave up and let Old Jo roll gently down the hill, backwards, to the nearest garage.

War also brought plenty of excitements. When a plane crashed into a nearby beach, the boys set off to explore the remains, returning with relics that were examined reverently by the younger children. Italian prisoners of war – a curious sight in their distinctive yellow-flecked uniforms – made their way into town to worship at the Catholic church in Minehead. In Ickenham and in Minehead, the Richards and Harwood children's fathers paraded through town on practice marches with the Home Guard, an opportunity Arthur used to chat with old friends and patients, who would all then have to run to catch up with the others. Cecil's enthusiastic impulse to teach found expression in long nights stationed at pill boxes up on Exmoor, where he kept his fellows entertained with the ancient myths and legends he loved. His courage was tested one night when footsteps were heard out on the dark moor, and, raising his rifle, Cecil found himself the only man brave enough to confront what turned out to be a lost cow.

Perhaps more glamorous were the American troops who began to arrive in earnest in 1943 (even taking over Noel's hospital in London). The children became used to the noisy clatter of army boots on the cobbles and, though the stark contrast of American provisions did not go unnoticed in the village, found the new soldiers generous with treats. 'Say, have you any gum to spare?' they learned to ask. For an out-of-the-way town, war was never very distant from Minehead. From the sandbags piled high in the streets, and the coastal defences on the beach, to the apparently endless batter of firing from the training grounds on North Hill, the antenna of the RADAR station emerging from its masts, and the roads torn up by American tanks as they arrived at the station and drove in noisy, stately procession along the seafront and up the hill, the evidence surrounded them daily, had become part of life.

8

Bereavement

In February, Sydney died. For his daughters the shock was intense. He may have been ailing for years but Sydney's vitality had held them in a false sense of security. 'I hoped he would pull through & survive for another two or three years,' Noel confessed to James, who wrote to console her after months of silence between them. 'He was extraordinarily bright & in contact with us all.' Old age was a great inconvenience to Sydney. The war, and the last years of his life, in which he failed to focus the British on the mistreatment of colonial subjects, left him deeply pessimistic. He worked only intermittently on a book on Africa, knowing that paper shortages would make its publication unlikely. Instead, he passed the time watching his grandchildren at play and exercised his autonomy by ignoring directives from his daughters and stubbornly subverting the Wala's attempts to care for him. Neither Daphne nor Noel would have claimed their father was an easy man to deal with – 'wilful & contrary' were terms Noel used, 'a naughty fellow' in Daphne's way of putting things – but they also believed him to be a great man and his death triggered months of work for them and their mother in sorting and preparing his work for a posthumous collection.

Margaret insisted on visiting Margery not long after Sydney's death. Noel didn't like the idea. Feeling that her presence provoked Margery, she had for some years distanced herself from her sister and resented the stresses that visiting her imposed on their parents. Though Daphne and Noel both occasionally received letters from their sister, part of the 'masses of incoherent rubbish' her doctors recorded her as writing, their contact with her was limited. Noel hadn't seen her for years. 'It will be very tiring and depressing,' Noel wrote to her mother. 'But I suppose it is better to go soon if you must go. Poor Mudie. I wonder how she feels.'

Sydney looking perplexed by a grandchild

Margery was deeply disturbed by Sydney's death and redoubled her demands for release, convinced that her father had been buried alive and that she had to go home and disinter him. Margaret's visit calmed her considerably but she remained one of the patients at St Andrew's who had to be watched constantly because of her obsession with escape. Only a few weeks before Sydney's final illness, she had fractured her neck trying to climb a tree out of the grounds at Bryn-y-Neuadd.

The staff diligently observed and recorded her. In September 1941, she was 'A tall pale grey haired woman, rather thin' whose 'mental condition remain[ed] unchanged'. She didn't take care of herself, could be destructive to property and aggressive towards other patients, she still heard voices. Her family were apparently in the dark about some of her more serious excesses – which included, in 1939, an attempt to strangle a nurse – as Noel and Eva Hubback both acted as emissaries in Margaret's (failed) attempts to have Margery released into her care. Noel and Eva also actively tracked developments in the field that might offer new options for Margery's treatment. In the 1940s, Noel raised the question of insulin and electric shock therapy with the Medical Superintendent of St Andrew's, Dr Tennent, to find that they had not been extended to Margery.

Noel had good reason to ask. Reports of beneficial results from both treatments had led Dr Tennent to introduce insulin treatment to St Andrew's in 1938, engaging a Swiss expert to train the staff in its administration, though by the 1940s he was prioritising ECT. Both treatments were premised on the idea that the provocation of a fit in a schizophrenic produced calming effects. (Prevailing thought held that epileptics did not develop schizophrenia, which led to associations being made between an epileptic-style fit and potential treatment.)

Insulin treatment began with a course of injections that lowered the blood sugar levels, sending the patient into hypoglycaemic shock and then into convulsions or a coma, from which the patient allegedly emerged soothed. A year after its introduction at St Andrew's, *TIME* magazine exposed the effects of induced fitting on schizophrenics (in this case using metrazol), a treatment it deemed 'so horrible [...] that practically no patients ever willingly submit'. Its victims saw flashes of 'blinding light', experienced terror and sustained physical injuries: 'During their violent convulsions, patients arch their backs with such force that sometimes they literally crush their vertebrae.' Electric shock therapy cut out the physical dosing but aimed at the same results. Nevertheless, early signs were apparently encouraging: the hospital reported that since their introduction, the number of patients they were able to discharge as recovered had tripled.

In some ways the interventions for women like Margery had not advanced much beyond the principles of the rest cure and 'stuffing': the idea was still to immobilise and pacify the patient. Insulin treatment resulted in substantial weight gain and the recipients of both methods could emerge from their fitting mentally disoriented, their memories disturbed, their moods and appearances curiously blank. In the life of a large institution like St Andrew's, patients took their cues from each other as much as the doctors. Those returning from insulin comas and ECT spread fear in the wards.

It was not, then, that these treatments were not applied at St Andrew's but rather that Margery's most disruptive behaviour conveniently tailed off in time for her to evade them. When he met Noel to discuss Margery's case, Dr Tennent also described an additional treatment the hospital used in 'distressed cases': the prefrontal leucotomy (or lobotomy). This surgical invention involved severing the nerves in the prefrontal lobes of the brain. The operation, he acknowledged and Noel reported to the Wala, could sometimes have the effect of making the patient 'somewhat dull' but was justifiable in the case of restless and unhappy people. '[I]f she had gone on being as excited & restless as she had been for a time – I gather a year or two ago – he might have thought it advisable to try it,' Noel told Margaret. Instead, Margery had modified her behaviour in time to be overlooked.

9

Appraisals

It was not a good time to die, because everyone was busy or away. But *The Times* acknowledged Sydney as 'one of the foster-parents of the Labour Party', noting his condemnation of racial discrimination and remembering him as a 'handsome, distinguished-looking man'. Hearing of his death on the radio, the elderly Beatrice Webb recalled the last time she and her husband had seen the Oliviers. 'I remember I felt sorry for poor Lady Olivier who had to look after him. His four daughters had not been a success in life; except one who was medical – and I think married a fellow medical man.'

It was a bleak and, for Beatrice Webb, typically judgemental dismissal. The Olivier girls had of course never met with Beatrice Webb's approval. Success is often measured against early promise. Margery, a talented student, marcher for suffrage, gatherer of friends, had fallen by the wayside of real life. Her sisters ploughed on without her, as the world did. Her own dramas and conspiracies at St Andrew's were the drastic flutterings of a moth trapped in a glass – she moved urgently in no direction. The medical profession had as yet innovated nothing that could retrieve normal life for her.

Unlike their father and Mrs Webb, the sisters had all chosen decidedly private lives. There was no inkling of a need for recognition and acclaim among them. And by the standards of the thirties and forties, leaving aside Brynhild's faux pas of divorce, their private lives were successful: husbands, each of them, and a brood of sixteen children between them. Nor were they disinterested in the world: they were of their time and engaged with it. The League of Nations, anti-slavery, public health; campaigns for socialism, suffrage, birth control, and for Feed Europe Now at the end of the war – these all elicited their interest and energy, as they did for many women of their generation and education.

Sydney wanted them to have success and yet had never doubted the inescapable destiny of their gender. Margery's had, for him, been a contributing factor in her breakdowns and, as Brynhild faced bankruptcy and sickness, he had coolly noted a certain 'shrillness' in her voice. But he had also taken note of Noel's childhood interest in science and encouraged her career in medicine. Brynhild had found him hard to reach: unsympathetic about her personal choices and yet instinctively kindly to her about the consequences. Noel felt her world irrevocably changed without him.

If success can be judged against early promise, it can perhaps also be judged against what has been promised. A few days after Sydney's death, a twenty-fifth birthday party was held for women's suffrage, the Suffragette Fellowship being now more engaged in commemoration than campaign. For girls born into the world of 'the Advanced', who came of age at the height of the women's movement and socialised with the idealistic students of Edwardian Cambridge, it must have seemed as though the world was preparing to grant them far more than had hitherto been allowed. 'Hope is Strong', read one of the giant suffrage banners at a procession on St James's Street, in the year that Margery turned twenty-four and Noel eighteen. And the struggles of the suffrage movement were just that – struggles, framed in terms of battle and conflict. Being a modern woman was not, perhaps, going to be easy – there was no suggestion of having it all or achieving everything they set their minds to – but it might be worthwhile. The great struggles that did arrive for their generation, however, also altered its possibilities. Post-war conservatism instigated a long period of settling and sheltering, not something the Newnhamites had wanted to expect. Daphne might be said to have retreated into a different realm of goals, to seek her fulfilment in spiritual terms instead. Yet there were practical achievements, too: Michael Hall was an act of will and her translation work was instrumental in spreading Steiner's ideas in the English-speaking world. Brynhild had made full use of the limited social and legal progress for women to pursue the personal life she wanted. Noel had surely come closest to the early (and middle-class) feminist ideal, contrary to the trends of her generation. She had built a life, now interrupted by the Second World War, that allowed her a home with children and a career that continued to interest her. Even the young Eva Spielman (now Hubback), energetic and hugely optimistic for her sex, had doubted, in 1909, that a life combining motherhood and work was feasible. In these terms, Noel, singled out by Beatrice Webb, was a quiet and extraordinary success.

The End

In the spring of 1944, John, almost eighteen, returned home from visiting the Wala in Bognor Regis to find a summons for a medical examination waiting for him. The notice filled his mother with foreboding. At his examination, John was passed as fit for service and it was confirmed that he would serve in the Royal Navy, which he had wanted. Daphne couldn't help but be affronted by his good cheer: 'the little wretch himself is rather bucked & proud [...] his face when he told us [was] pleased as punch. They <u>are</u> queer.'

John would not be called up until his school certificate exams ended in July but he also wanted to go to Oxford, and if his exams went well enough, she hoped he could get a further deferment in order to take a scholarship exam in October. Tension reigned in the Harwood house over the next weeks, as John revised for tests that had taken on a whole new significance for his future. Daphne worried about how he would suit the Navy – 'It's so <u>rough</u>,' she wrote to the Wala, '& they have to be so <u>tough</u>. And John isn't tough' – but in the meantime contented herself with arranging preferential treatment for him in the family home, moving Lois into her own room, and the three youngest into a shared bedroom, so that John could have some space to himself in what might be his last weeks there.

As those weeks passed, there were signs that he might just escape the conflict altogether. The Normandy landings were underway before his exams were, and their significance was generally understood. John's exams went well enough for him to be granted deferment. The Allies pushed on through France. In August, Paris was liberated. By the end of the year, the Home Guard stood down; the beach near the Wala's house at Bognor Regis reopened and holiday-makers appeared amongst the collapsing sandbags and rolled-up tangles of rusty barbed wire; Noel and Arthur went to the theatre in London together. People began to plan for 'after the war'. Noel and James made tentative overtures to one another but when he did propose to visit Minehead, she was away. Daphne and Cecil searched for a permanent, rural, home for Michael Hall. Noel asked Bunny, who for much of the war had an important role at the Political Warfare Executive working on British propaganda, if he could help her trace the Polish Jewish relatives of a friend she had made among the teachers at the school.

Christmas that year, then, was an inevitable disappointment for the many who had hoped for victory in 1944. Rather than ending the war, the D-Day landings had unleashed the V-weapons on Britain. Bognor and Ickenham came under fire again, this time from frightening pilot-less missiles. The V-1, quickly dubbed the 'doodlebug' for the hum, building to a loud rattle, that it emitted, chillingly lapsed into silence moments before detonating and had an intense psychological impact, as well as, with the V-2s, causing carnage. In 1943, the Richards had spent a month in Ickenham over the festive period but the following Christmas they had again been banned by their father because of the danger. They had lived in Minehead for over four years, time for Julia, born as the family's evacuation began, to grow into a little girl with 'bluish eyes & fair hair with pretension to curls'.

Over nine thousand people were killed by these new weapons; Streatham, part of a slice of South London directly under their flight path from France, joined a region known as 'Doodlebug Alley'. Philip Sherrard, who had been called up, was posted to India. As the year turned, Daphne struggled. She was glad to have Noel nearby. Her children and her surroundings, she confided in her mother, helped her to go on. Life was 'interspersed with the fascinating conversation of Sylvia & Mark – & the friendliness of Laurence – & the music of Lois. And out of the window are those hills, with their ever varying light & colour – and soft scents of the earth – and bird calls which thrill of spring'. She and Noel were always begging the Wala to come and stay with them but early in 1945 Daphne made a renewed plea: 'I am badly needing you,' she wrote, 'feeling very low to-day after seeing John off to Skegness yesterday.'

Watching as he departed for training, she felt as though she were witnessing the end of her son's childhood. She and Cecil spent the following day assailed with memories of him throughout his life. From now until the end of the war Daphne lived in a state of internal distress and worry, fears she shielded her younger children from. Daphne knew that she was lucky to have kept John at home for so long. 'But hearts aren't reasonable,' she allowed. 'And it is at such times that one is reminded of their intense reality – & feels what heart-ache means.'

In April, the hated blackout was lifted. John was probably still in training in a requisitioned Butlin's holiday camp in Skegness. Victory in Europe Day, on 8 May, saw him yet to leave the UK. He was still there in September, when Japan surrendered and the war was finally over.

Afterlives

(Or, Seventeen Years Later)

'I'll not let you forget some things till you die.'
Rupert Brooke to Noel, 1911

'But once you are in a biography all is different.'
Virginia Woolf, 1930

When Christopher Hassall met Noel Olivier Richards on 7 September 1962, in a house on Kensington Park Road, she was a retired paediatrician, weeks away from her seventieth birthday. Despite knowing her to have been a consultant, Hassall had imagined Noel as 'a sort of Matron' and prepared himself to confront someone 'competent, formidably sane, rather intimidating'. It was not that she was not all of these things but rather that she was not any of these things in the way that Hassall had expected. Instead, Noel was greatly aged by grief.

Noel had taken early retirement to care for Arthur, who in later life suffered from Paget's disease, a painful condition affecting the bones. This had not prepared her for his death, which came as a shock that shattered her. '[T]he present moment might be unfavourable,' James wrote belatedly to warn Hassall, 'as I think she's in rather a state.'

'He was a dim little man,' Geoffrey Keynes, the most active of the Brooke trustees and Hassall's chief cheerleader, ruminated, 'no one could ever understand why the clever & so attractive Noel married him when she had so many to choose from.' He was upset that Arthur's death would delay Noel and Hassall's meeting. Hassall gave Noel three and a half weeks from the date of the funeral in West Wittering, where Arthur was buried near Brynhild, before contacting her to arrange the dinner at Joan's house.

It took Noel several weeks to muster the courage to look at the pages Hassall gave her at that dinner. She knew it would hurt. She had tried to communicate this distress to Mr Hassall, as she insisted on referring to him, but he had met her reservations with jovial, surely wilful, misapprehension. It was not only that returning to the story of that early, tortuous, experience of love – so soon after the loss of her husband, on whose memory she might just then have preferred to dwell – was painful. She knew, too, that despite Hassall's command 'I must have the Truth', she would not find the truth there. When the publication of Rupert's letters had first been mooted, she considered the project pointless because she felt that any image of him that emerged could only be a false one. 'Writers think the truth is either black or white,' she told Hassall in his sister's house. He accused her of confusing writers with journalists. But she had seen an idealised portrait of Rupert emerge almost instantaneously from his death, watched others burnish it (and scrap over it) in the intervening years. She had long ago decided not to take part in the legend.

In maintaining her obstructive stance, Noel at least knew that she had Daphne's backing. Daphne had died, far too early, of cancer, in 1950, telling Cecil on her last day of life that she was about to embark on a long journey but that she just had to see Noel, who arrived soon afterwards, before she went. In Daphne, Noel had lost both an altruistic and talented sister and a thoughtful sounding board. On the question of publishing Rupert's letters, though, the two sisters had been in agreement. Bryn had been more relaxed about letting close friends read her own letters from Rupert but she, too, had refrained from making them available for publication. 'You know my attitude,' Noel wrote to Keynes shortly before the project was abandoned late in 1955. 'I think it is a bad thing to publish Rupert's letters whilest the people involved are still alive.'

Her position derived, too, from admiration for Rupert. She felt he deserved the kind of detailed appraisal that could not be accomplished while those involved were still living. Details of his life's journey, she told one would-be biographer, were 'so elaborate, so subtle, so strange & also so fine; that it is not possible to do them justice yet & it would be a great pity to do them less than justice'.

Noel was well versed in negotiations over posthumous legacies. After Sydney's death, she and Daphne helped the Wala collect his writings for publication. Daphne had sought to acknowledge the importance of faith in Sydney's life, feeling that his words on 'essential humanity' were of particular value in the 1940s, 'when the question of the treatment of Germany [...] & the Germans is getting discussed so confusedly'. The Wala considered him a man preoccupied principally with 'practical affairs', who ought to be allowed, after death, to 'speak for himself'. She did not want him appropriated for new causes or to see his legacy presented according to Daphne's worldview. 'But please realise,' Daphne had argued, well aware of the responsibility of their position, 'it is you who are deciding which of the things he has spoken shall now be heard, & which shall not.'

Hassall tracked Noel down at Nunnington and rang her up on 1 October. She told him she hadn't started reading. On the tenth she admitted to Bunny that she was 'trying to induce [her]self to look at certain passages sellected by Christopher Hassall in his manuscript'. Ginny and her family had been staying with her but they had now gone off to Somerset, 'to try & find a valley with a beautiful stream [that] Ginny remembers from 1942', so she had no more excuses. In reality she had started reading the book a few days before, starting with the Cambridge chapters. 'Unfortunately I have begun to regard him, Christopher, as an enemy.'

Two days later Hassall tried again. On the fourteenth she replied telling him she needed more time. After four days she repeated the message. He issued an ultimatum, giving her a deadline. A few minutes before it expired (i.e., a few minutes before midnight) his phone rang. It was Noel, suggesting they meet. Hassall once again offered to come to her. Once again she suggested London. Joan was called upon.

On 16 November 1962, Noel arrived punctually at Joan's house at 10.30 a.m. She had told Hassall they would need about two hours to go through her notes, so Joan was ready to provide lunch. In the event, they talked and argued for a total of nine hours. At lunchtime, Joan unobtrusively laid out the meal. In the afternoon, she gave them tea. Eventually she cooked them dinner as well. As the day drew on, she offered Noel a bed upstairs on which to rest. Noel declined, leaving the exhausted Hassall to battle on.

'My God, we did "go at it"!' he told Geoffrey afterwards. 'She was tireless.' Noel had obviously decided to cooperate but she continued to withhold the letters, which was what Hassall was really lusting after. Noel's version of compliance was oddly obstructive, her method of cooperation indicative, perhaps, of duress. She began by asking for Hassall's patience, describing herself, somewhat disingenuously, as 'uneducated', perhaps seeking to pre-empt his frustration. Then she produced pages and pages of hand-scrawled notes written both horizontally and vertically across scrap paper of various sizes. These she insisted on reading aloud, submitting Hassall to a verbal précis of his own book, which just then was sitting finished in typescript in his house, waiting only for what he and the Keyneses hoped would be the 'crowning touch' of Noel's contribution. Repeatedly she lost her place and began again from some way back. Her criticisms made regular reference to photographs and documents she had no intention of allowing him to see. Hassall, seated beside her at the table, manfully summoned 'the patience of a lifetime'. Each time she raised a point that they agreed should change, he made his own note. Sometimes they argued for an hour over the alteration of a single assertion.

Hassall was determined not to let Noel simply have her way with his book: 'I had to be convinced first that a larger issue than her personal wish was being served.' That day they disagreed most violently on the circumstances surrounding Rupert's breakdown at the end of 1911. Hassall's view was that, in falling in love with Ka, Rupert came into conflict with his own conscience, because of the declaration of love he had already made to Noel at Buckler's Hard. Noel firstly clarified that there had never been a proposal at that camp but that Rupert had simply made his feelings for her known. She also denied that there was any emotional or moral conflict when Rupert fell in love with Ka but struggled to make Hassall understand this attitude. In the book, Hassall had described Rupert calling on Noel to tell her about his entanglement with Ka. 'It was hard to explain,' Hassall had written, adding (to 'enlist sympathy' for Noel, he explained): 'and must have been even harder to understand.'

'It wasn't hard to understand at all!' said Noel now. Ka 'was never disloyal' to her and Noel had felt anyway that 'she could take nothing from me, for my relationship with [Rupert] was of quite a different order'. This Bloomsbury-esque putting aside of sexual jealousy, this refusal to claim another (and thereby leaving one's own self equally free) was apparently impossible for Hassall to comprehend; instead he passed judgement on the teenaged Noel's behaviour in describing the 'normal' response against which she had fallen short. 'I explained,' he told Geoffrey afterwards, that

> To the reader, a young man having to tell girl A that he was head-over-heels in love with girl B within a few months of having declared his undying love to A, and at the same time assuring A that his feelings for

A were unaffected – <u>was</u> both 'hard to explain' and '<u>harder</u> to understand', because, such is human nature, a girl does not see herself as 'one of a crowd' where love is concerned, unless she's a trollope [sic], but rather is she either jealous and fights for her man, or is outraged and tells the man to go to blazes, or is firmly on her dignity and says 'make up your mind which of us two it is, because I'm not going to be one of a pair. If', I went on, 'you did <u>none</u> of these things, then you were <u>very</u> exceptional.'

On the other hand, he told Noel, Rupert's 'attitude was that of a normal man in his position; he could not but feel he was, inevitably, betraying his relationship with <u>you</u>, and <u>that</u> contributed to the inner stresses which caused his breakdown'. Noel asked for Hassall's evidence for this claim, only to learn that evidence for an assertion of that kind was quite unnecessary. Besides, Hassall went on, Noel was 'not a man' and Hassall himself was a man and was therefore qualified to interpret a fellow man's state of mind. Then they argued interminably about Margery and whether she could be assigned culpability for 'interference', with Noel defending her against Hassall's charges. 'I've <u>rarely</u> been so exhausted,' he admitted afterwards.

After this gruelling encounter, Hassall came to a shattering realisation. Noel was to blame for everything. Rupert's vacillations between Noel and Ka had caused the breakdown: that he had already established. Why hadn't Noel put a stop to it and thereby saved Rupert from so much suffering? Where until now, he and others had tended to view Ka as the guilty party because of her failure to resist Henry Lamb's sexual appeal, he now realised that if Noel had just staked her claim to Rupert like a normal woman, she might have prevented him from betraying her with Ka in the first place. It was in fact her inability to succumb that was the problem. Noel, he seemed to think, had tried to deceive them all in ever letting anyone believe she may have had genuine feelings for Rupert. When Rupert and Jacques turned up at Bedales, hadn't she refused to break the rules and take tea with them? Didn't she ask Rupert not to tell the others about his first declaration of love? Why was she so 'understanding' about Rupert's feelings for, and travel with, Ka if she really cared about him? If only Noel had

had her own normal share of possessiveness, or pride, or even jealousy – it would, I believe [...] have been of vital help to R[upert]. [...] All along Noel had 'evaded definition.' If she had openly stood by R[upert]'s decision at Buckler's Hard, or in any way taken a stand, or accepted the position as R[upert]'s girl, R[upert] would have known where he was from the first [...] Noel was either abominably weak, vague, timid, or endowed with super-sexual wisdom. Both R[upert] and Ka were normal young people. So the <u>real</u> misfortune at the back of the whole affair was not Ka and her character, nor R[upert] and his passions, but <u>Noel</u>, whose 'understanding' gave him the <u>wrong</u> sort of support – in fact it was <u>no</u> support.

The more he dwelt on this revelation, the more he realised that he and Geoffrey (whose project the collected Letters had been) were victims of Noel's outrageous evasiveness; a malicious timidity which really just made life difficult for them. 'I think she lacks the nerve to fall in love at <u>all</u>,' was his final assessment.

Noel, from Nunnington, promised Bunny a visit soon. 'I should like to grumble to you about "memoirs" and "biographies",' she told him.

Whilst Noel had been urging herself to read Hassall's book, a copy of Bunny Garnett's latest arrived. *Familiar Faces* was the third volume of Bunny's memoirs. The first, *The Golden Echo*, published shortly after the Wala died in 1953, had painted a vivid picture of the Oliviers' shared childhood in Limpsfield and had followed the Neo-Pagans and their friends up to the First World War. *The Golden Echo* must have made poignant reading for Noel, coming so soon after the loss of her mother and only three years after Daphne's death. In a book such as Bunny's, her life became something recognisable and yet curiously separated from her stewardship; her self artistically re-wrought and the new image left to stand in her place, a representation made for public consumption.

That Bunny, whose book was swiftly rechristened *The Golden Eggo* in Noel's household, had been enthralled by his exquisite and formidable playmates was clear. 'The four girls dominated my youth,' he told his readers. 'Usually rather serious and always noble in looks and manners and in attitude of mind, they could be as unthinkingly cruel as savages. Sometimes they were savages.'

'You let me off lightly in that volume,' she told him at the time, 'so I shouldn't complain. I enjoyed reading it, it was very good entertainment.' But she did not claim that it represented The Truth, and Bunny's assumption of power frightened her:

I liked best the parts about people I didn't know, or hardly knew [...] But here and there, in the parts about people I knew well, I was shocked at your indiscretion and at some of the more vindictive attacks you made. That can't be helped now. But I wish you would get someone to read through the next volume and edit it, before it is too late. Some freind you know, who is sensible & imaginative.

As children in Limspfield, Bunny and the Oliviers had been suspicious of outsiders; Bunny had now invited them in; worse, he had laid himself and his friends on as entertainment for them. In Bunny's book Noel saw only how she had been seen. It was clear that the sisters had projected an aura of self-assurance that they had not always felt; Bunny had never imagined Daphne's shyness at the nude bathing at Penshurst, or Brynhild's disapproval of Noel's swimming with the young men. He could only see them as the noble savages of his imagination. They were, in a sense, as invented as the 'savages' he compared them to.

This was all part of the danger of having interesting friends. Cecil cropped up in C. S. Lewis's memoir, *Surprised by Joy*, in 1955; various Bloomsbury archives were disappearing over the Atlantic to American libraries as old friends monetised their histories in sales, brokered, often, by Bunny. The Wala had sold Margery's letters from Rupert to the Berg library in New York in an attempt to meet the ongoing costs of Margery's care at St Andrew's.

Part of the reason that Noel agreed to meet Hassall was, it seems, because a biography had already been published which made imaginative use of her memories. In the late 1920s she had met an American adventurer, Richard Halliburton, who idolised Brooke and wanted to write a book about him. Halliburton's infatuation alarmed Noel and she was provoked into disbelieving scorn when the man arrived at her house dressed as if he wanted to *be* Rupert. But she was open to, and perhaps enjoyed, speaking with an admirer of his. Nevertheless she did not provide any of the documents Halliburton asked about and was clear that she didn't approve of the project, asking that she be omitted or at least not mentioned by name. 'It seems to me nothing but desirable that your own acquaintance with what you admire should be improved,' she told him, 'but why should there be biographies?'

In 1939, Halliburton drowned on one of his expeditions and the material he had collected was taken up by another writer, the Canadian journalist and novelist Arthur Stringer, and worked into a poorly written romance entitled *Red Wine of Youth*, in which Noel appeared as an image of 'girlish loveliness [with] a small sun-tanned face [and] an extraordinarily friendly smile'. Her relationship with Rupert became a proto-1950s ideal of an artistic romance: 'Noel read and praised the early scripts of Rupert's poems, and he made fun of her Latin and pleaded with her not to turn into a bluestocking.' Geoffrey had managed to prevent the book's publication in England for the time being but Hassall pointed out that he had had no trouble getting hold of a copy. If she could no longer count on preserving the Oliviers' privacy, Noel may have thought, she might as well try to influence what was written about them.

Noel must also have been alarmed by the ease with which the record could be tweaked. In 1919, Marie Moralt, dispatched by Noel to help care for Vanessa Bell's baby Angelica (now Bunny's wife), had stayed at Charleston for a few weeks. In his second memoir, Bunny recalled that she 'had been ill and depressed' when she arrived but that the stay had '[done] her good'. He had chopped wood for the fire and sat up with her in the evenings, talking. Yet Moralt had given Noel rather a different report, which she had passed on in detail to James at the time:

> Bunny took her for a series of walks on the downs, he amused her occasionally & bored her repeatedly. [...] The last night, Duncan deliberately left her alone with Bunny in the drawing room. He began by praising her a great deal for her grand character & telling her all the speeches which Vanessa & Duncan had made in her praise. Then he held one hand until she withdrew it unobtrusively; then the other. She said 'Don't be so silly, Bunny' & he said he would like to kiss her – placing himself on the arm of her chair & his arm around her waist. This made her feel uneasy so she tried to wither him [...] However he took no notice, but with increasing self confidence swept the lamp off the table & sent it crashing to the floor & in the darkness proceeded to make further advances.
>
> Poor Moralt was siezed with terror at the thought of his gigantic size & strength & determination but luckily she had no inclination to submit to any one she found so repulsive so after a melèe in which (apparently) her hands only were covered with slobber – she fled from the room, leaving him amazed.

It was an alternative (female) perspective on the uninhibited sexuality that Bunny had celebrated in his life and writing that did not make it into history.

*

Once, visiting her son Benedict in Cambridge, Noel had been introduced to some of the sons of people she had known in her youth and had found herself overwhelmed. '[T]here was a whirl & tumult of social contacts,' she told her mother afterwards, 'I became quite bewildered.' She found refuge in the still and silence of the more distant past, slipping into the Zoology museum, where 'among the skeletons of whales & porpoises & great antbears & primeval horses & gorillas & homo sapiens' she found a place 'to rest & recuperate. It was quiet & peaceful & remote in the museum & I found the silence & immobility of the old bones & fossils marvellously refreshing.'

As a shy teenager, the small and self-involved Cambridge world had often caused her similarly to withdraw, shielding herself from the many precocious friends of Rupert's and her sisters', who expected to have their say during the difficult process of her relationship with Rupert, which coincided so awkwardly with her own coming of age. She had held her own counsel then, rather than allow her story to become shared property. Now, decades later, she was facing a lack of comprehension all over again.

Hassall sent a lengthy report on his encounter with Noel to the Keyneses, who reacted with jubilation. He had apparently pulled off the impossible. Lady Keynes congratulated him on having 'caught & pinned down the evasive Noel at last!' Old friends, denied confidences at the time, found satisfaction for curiosity that had waited half a century, and an opportunity to air their own opinions. Taking Hassall's cue, Lady Keynes wrote:

> Don't you think some of the explanation of the extreme 'understanding-ness' she showed Rupert may have been that she wasn't really in love with him, so that she wasn't jealous or possessive etc etc about him, because her emotions weren't really aroused deeply? That w[oul]d also explain her refusal to marry him – that, & the Olivier vagueness. (Margery was very vague always I think & so was Daphne I rather believe: Bryn was the only decisive one.)

Geoffrey agreed with Hassall that it was difficult to put their suspicions across too explicitly in the book. 'Readers will have to form their own conclusions,' he allowed reluctantly.

The Keyneses shared Hassall's letter with the seventy-seven-year-old Justin Brooke, who responded in gleeful outrage to confirm his old friend's inability to love. He also singled out Brynhild amongst the sisters – but her perceived sexual availability did not commend her above Noel's 'remoteness': 'Strange, that while Bryn was a [...] woman who spent her life in indulging her sexual feelings to excess, Noel was unable to get any interest in sex.' No one gave any sign of finding Noel's insistence on privacy permissible. Geoffrey had been wildly disappointed when Hassall's interview was postponed in the summer – 'just when she was coming to heel!' Even James, just then embroiled in a similar situation, had helped establish contact between them.

That year, a biographer named Michael Holroyd had arrived at the Stracheys' home in Buckinghamshire with the intention of writing a Life of Lytton, whose memory James revered and protected. James's usual method of dealing with such people – introducing them to the mass of papers he and Alix kept in a freezing outbuilding in the garden and waiting for them to give up – had so far failed to discourage the young man, implying to James that society could be nearing a time when it would be able to cope with the (mostly sexual) revelations in Lytton's papers.

Frances Partridge, who became a key source of Holroyd's (she had married Ralph Partridge, with whom Lytton had lived in a tempestuous ménage à trois with Carrington), found Noel's position unforgivable. She understood very well the pain of sorting through letters from lost loved ones and faced many of the questions that Noel must have asked herself; in fact, her judgement of Noel's decision ultimately influenced her own. Revisiting her correspondence at Holroyd's request, and reading the letters between Ralph and his first wife, had felt to Frances like 'grovelling in the past'. These grovellings, she wrote in her diary,

> raked up a substratum of confused feelings. Do I want this young man to have access to any of it? Should people in no way concerned with feelings that were private, tender or painful have access to them? I'm aware of such conflicting motives in myself that I don't trust my own judgement and am seized at moments with a desire to burn all the papers I have. Yet the obstinacy of Noel Olivier in refusing to show Rupert Brooke's letters to his biographer has always seemed to me irrational and selfish.

Justin and the Keyneses were the remnants of Rupert's Grantchester bevy (Margaret Keynes was Gwen Raverat's younger sister). Ka Cox had died suddenly in the 1930s, Gwen Raverat in 1957, Dudley Ward and

Frances Cornford, who had energetically quashed the publication of the Letters, neither of them feeling it represented Rupert properly, had by now both passed away too. Death was clearing the field of influencers when it came to Rupert's memory.

Noel and James had been partial outsiders to the Neo-Pagans since the days of Rupert's breakdown, if not before, and their perspective on him made the others uneasy. The icon of the flawless youth presented by Eddie Marsh had largely persisted, chiming with Rupert as a symbol of Britain's sacrifice during the First World War. In the first twenty years after publication, his *Poems 1911* went through thirty-seven editions, amounting to almost 100,000 copies, and when the *New Numbers* sonnets were published in *1914 and Other Poems* after his death, the collection sold in the tens (eventually hundreds) of thousands. Decades after 1915, the anniversary of his death was still marked commemoratively in newspapers.

Geoffrey Keynes – whose abortive attempt to collect Rupert Brooke's letters for publication was an episode so explosive that it culminated in the indefinite postponement of the book's release and Keynes threatening to resign his trusteeship – was determined to overturn the 'Golden Apollo' image erected by Eddie Marsh's memoir, which had been markedly altered by edits insisted on by Mrs Brooke. The book was nothing but an 'elegantly written trifle', Keynes wrote, a 'pretty sketch [that] should never have been printed'. But what he found most worrying was the persistent public impression that Rupert was homosexual, something Keynes partly blamed on the 'equivocal aura [that] pervaded the memoir' and he was concerned, as he wrote later, 'to establish a truer valuation of [Rupert's] wholly masculine character and mind'.

Despite his and Christopher Hassall's campaign for the Truth, he was an ardent censor and the Faber editor's responses to his typescript of the Letters was littered with phrases like, 'Why bowdlerize this?' It was this instinct of the trustees to suppress what were, to Keynes, unpalatable facets of Rupert's life and character that informed James's decision to keep his letters from Rupert (which included Rupert's account of losing his virginity to another man) to himself. Geoffrey was quite comfortable with this omission. That correspondence would appear in print only, he said, 'over [his] dead body'.

Hassall had assured Noel, through James, that it was better to let him handle her letters from Rupert with 'discretion' than to have them 'blurted out without excisions at some remote future date'. His personal priority was not a balanced account of Rupert's life. 'If anything I did were to reflect unsympathetically or in any way adversely, on R.B.,' he wrote, 'I would never forgive myself.'

Back at Nunnington, Noel was regretting having given any comments at all. She asked Hassall to let her have the remaining chapters – he had only shown her the sections of the book that concerned her directly – fastidiously determined to follow the story to the end. When she finished, she returned the manuscript to Hassall without a covering letter. She also declined his offer to mention her in the acknowledgements of the book, maintaining an extra-limelight stance that had seen her refuse the dedication of Rupert's *Poems* (a choice Hassall regarded as 'inverted vanity') but also obliquely refusing to convey approval of his book. She did have further questions for him, however, and made several requests for his evidence for claims in the book that suggest she was still trying to decipher Rupert's feelings decades after his death.

Hassall made some small changes to the text. His editor found the descriptions of Rupert's love life 'a little obscure'. The author's prejudice was perhaps showing in the text, for the description of Noel left him, he told Hassall, 'the tiniest bit disappointed [...] I found it difficult to see her as the very attractive girl we are told Rupert always found her to be. It is a pity that she has to be so shadowy here.'

Noel was probably in Paris with her youngest daughter, Julia, when Christopher Hassall died suddenly of a heart attack the following spring. In England, Geoffrey Keynes was left to see the biography through to publication. Noel and Julia had arranged to spend a month in France together, while Bunny and his youngest daughters looked after Noel's cat at Hilton Hall. Noel had not been looking forward to 'horrible peace' at home. Benedict was kept busy working as a doctor; Angela was kept busy by James Strachey, whom she assisted in his ongoing translation of Freud's oeuvre; Ginny had a young family and periodically lived abroad; Tazza had left home and moved north. Julia, twenty-three, remained. Theirs had not always been the easiest relationship. Julia was younger than her closest sister by seven years and Noel had found herself parenting a teenager in her sixties. This also meant, however, that Julia enjoyed (or endured) the most of her mother's attention. While her older sisters complained of childhood neglect, Noel had later reduced her work at the Westminster hospital to part time, and Julia was still at home when Noel retired.

Julia was a child of what the *Daily Mirror* called 'The Beanstalk Generation'. These were post-war children, beneficiaries of that era's affluence; taller and healthier than any cohort before them, with spending money, leisure time and activities; expectations of state-provided healthcare and education. They had everything going for them. The last thing they wanted was to be like their parents, those oppressive representatives of a bleak and conservative generation – old people overtaken by war and depression.

Parental authority went slowly into retreat and Julia, a sometimes-lonely teenager who found company with friends her mother disapproved of, had been a handful. Arthur had left the girls to Noel, intervening only once when Julia flung a knife at one of her sisters (her aim was good but fortunately not fatally so). When Julia was younger, Noel had taken her on ward rounds at the hospital, where she had been fussed over and had learned to admire her mother through the respect her colleagues and patients showed her; but as she grew older she was bored by her birdwatching, long-walk-enjoying, medicine-obsessed parents. A day of work might end, for Noel, with a search for a wayward daughter.

Post-war parenting experts such as Dr Benjamin Spock and the psychologist John Bowlby would have encouraged Noel to blame herself. They had warned that constant maternal attention was of paramount importance for the development of well-adjusted children, an argument no doubt helpful in ushering mobilised mothers back into the home in the late 1940s. The risks of its absence were so severe, Spock warned in a book published in Britain when Julia was seven, that, 'It doesn't make sense to let mothers go to work.' Noel, however, had gone back to the hospital as soon as the war was over. Julia was what the popular press enduringly termed a 'latchkey kid', with all the risks of juvenile delinquency and pre-marital sex that went with it. Convent school had been tried and had failed but Julia finally followed in her sisters' footsteps to Michael Hall and calmed down there. By now, she and Noel were friends.

Now was the sixties. The Beanstalk Generation were originators of a culture all their own. They had Mary Quant and the Beatles, whose first single was released shortly after Noel met Christopher Hassall for the first time. They had the Pill. They had radical politics; a penchant for demonstrations; an antipathy towards authority, conservative morality, dogma.

Not since the Basel Pact had youth been so worshipped. And just as Rupert Brooke's elders, men like the aged Henry James, had looked upon him as a promise – broken by the first war – so this new sub-culture of the young began to have an unprecedented influence on wider society. The old represented a loss of spirit; the young attained a cultural influence that was startlingly new.

Quant dressed women like Julia in miniskirts, worn with tights and long boots. The Beatles, as one fan wrote in 1964, allowed one to 'lose oneself in the unconscious hypnotic euphoria of the music'. There were other ways to lose oneself too. '[W]e took drugs to see the world entirely differently,' the writer Jenny Diski said later, and took the drugs 'very seriously'. The aim was to alter consciousness, to see beyond the 'straight' world around them. It was part of a broader questioning of accepted norms and established authority. Normality, one influential writer posited, was really just an 'adjusted state' and 'the betrayal of our true potentialities'.

This put those who markedly did *not* conform to 'normality' in a different light. The writer was R. D. Laing, whose bestselling study of schizophrenia, *The Divided Self*, became a sensation of the sixties. Laing began with the surprisingly radical idea of attempting to 'make madness, and the process of going mad, comprehensible'. Rather than see the schizophrenic as an 'other' to be incarcerated, he wanted to meet them on their own terms.

Laing was a controversial psychiatrist with a global reputation, who treated and influenced icons of the sixties from Jim Morrison and Sean Connery to Sylvia Plath, Ted Hughes and Doris Lessing, and who became an icon of the counter-culture in the process. Together with Erving Goffman's 1961 *Asylums*, written after a year's fieldwork in an American mental hospital, Laing brought existing concerns about the asylum model into the mainstream, as a prominent advocate for community care (as opposed to separation and isolation) for the mentally ill.

After two world conflicts, and from the midst of the Cold War, Laing was more inclined to question who got to decide what madness was than those early doctors of Margery's (and Daphne's and Virginia Woolf's) who had judged women's grasp on reason so deficient. 'The statesmen of the world who boast and threaten that they have Doomsday weapons are far more dangerous, and far more estranged from "reality",' Laing wrote, 'than many of the people on whom the label "psychotic" is affixed.'

Laing saw the insane as victims of a broader system that imposed the rules of normality. There are echoes of Daphne's riposte to her confinement in 1915, as well as her belief in the under-explored potential of human consciousness, in his statement that society repressed 'any form of transcendence', punishing those with 'experience of other dimensions, that [they] cannot entirely deny or forget'.

Could schizophrenia be nothing more than a label, a status conferred by others, rather than an existential fact? Might, even, the children of the sixties have something to learn from people like Margery?

It was no innovation to take an arguably romantic view of madness. (In the late forties, Bunny commented that a description of Margery given to him by Noel 'made [Margery] sound rather magnificent [...] getting great pleasure from immense walks over the mountains of N[orth] Wales, bathing in streams, quite mad, like some creature in a Wordsworth poem'.) Yet some people like Margery began to benefit.

The grand influences of changing social attitudes and debates on the level of theory, philosophy and science are not always easy to track in the lives of ordinary people. In the life of a mentally ill person like Margery, however, held in stasis by forces beyond her control – divested of the pretensions to autonomy that others have – they are more visible. Margery's life plotted the liaisons between the medical community and society at large in the very notes kept on it.

In all likelihood, by now Margery was too institutionalised to live anywhere but St Andrew's. Still, by the late 1950s she no longer lived in the hospital but was housed at the 'Ladies House' at Moulton Park, a farm in its grounds where a small number of patients lived with an even smaller complement of nurses. And in 1960, she was 'regraded' to 'informal status'. Though she never left the care of St Andrew's, the influence of the debates within psychiatry (to which Margery was never invited), which entered the mainstream in the 1960s, were translated into her changed abode and status.

By 1964, when Laing wrote a new preface to *The Divided Self*, Margery had been incarcerated on and off for forty-seven years; permanently for forty-two. Forty years after she was first committed, her doctors noted at the time, she was still 'harp[ing] back to what happened in 1917'. That first compulsory incarceration was indeed the defining moment of her adult life and set the pattern for what came after. Her behaviour had settled down considerably, sparing her some of the favourite treatments of the 1930s, '40s and '50s, so that in the early 1960s the staff noted that

'Despite frequent demands to be set free she appears to be quite contented'. In the sixties she was treated with some of the first generation antipsychotics which were then poised to revolutionise the treatment of the mentally ill but they apparently had little impact and eventually she refused them altogether.

While Erving Goffman saw the ward system as a 'method for disciplining unruly persons through punishment and reward', the staff at St Andrew's had never quite made a compliant patient out of Margery. If hospital life dulled her reactions, she yet never gave up her bids for freedom, was careless with her hygiene and clothes, never ceased to barricade her door at night – never ceased to believe in her male predator – refused medication, upset the other patients and refused to 'join in' when the 1960s nurses encouraged ward games in the day room. She was not a success story by anyone's measure and she never admitted anyone else's reality, but stuck to her own, which, though it varied in detail, was markedly persistent in its core themes of threat, injustice and her own desirability. Her doctors' notes grew gradually shorter, repeated themselves obsessively.

By the time Noel and Julia got back from France, the cat had disappeared. It had been foisted on Noel by her son over seven years before and so she declined Bunny's guilty offer of a replacement kitten: if her cat didn't return, she told him, it would 'be the greatest possible mercy & convenience'.

Julia was planning more travel. '[S]he has fixed herself up a course at the Universidad de Valencia,' Noel told Bunny. When it came to seeing her daughters off into the world, Noel couldn't help viewing the place with suspicion: 'I hope [the university] actually exists. One can't feel quite certain.' It seemed to her that the modern world was fraught with danger. There was little in the sexual liberation of the sixties that Noel hadn't seen before. Where the Neo-Pagans had prized youth and innocence, Noel had been just as influenced by precocious Bloomsbury: a minority that had been well ahead of its time. In her insistence to Hassall of her own version of her feelings about Ka – her lack of possessiveness towards her 'lover' – she was advocating values that were only now coming into vogue. Nevertheless, she was alarmed when permissiveness entered the mainstream and Julia disappeared to late-night parties or took off abroad by herself. When an Italian man propositioned one of her young daughters on a family holiday, Noel intervened with a painful twist of his arm. She supported her daughters' activism, particularly in the CND (the first person Julia saw when she joined one Aldermaston march was her eldest sister, Angela, at its head) but she saw, perhaps, as the feminists of the twenties had feared, that sexual revolution might not straightforwardly mean liberation for women, and she worried about unwanted pregnancies, safety; wanted the security of marriage for her girls.

Noel (far right) at Tazza's wedding. Arthur is standing next to the bride, with Julia on the other side of him

Of her own youth, they knew very little. Noel had a curated list of stories: free-spirited days in Jamaica, early friendships with Virginia Woolf, Ferenc Békássy, Rupert Brooke. She was not above historical gossip (Augustus John's lifestyle) or sharing ancient confidences (Virginia's accusations of childhood sexual interference against her half-brothers) but this candidness stopped short at her own past. Julia's older sisters knew there were letters from the famous poet Rupert Brooke locked away somewhere in the house but they were never allowed to see them.

There had been hints of secrets, perhaps. Tazza's husband, a literature student, had once asked to borrow Noel's treasured copy of John Donne's poetry, a request she declined, she explained reluctantly, because Rupert had given it to her. He knew that she had cried for two days when the poet died because she had told him, but she hadn't told more than that. Women with unspoken histories were hardly uncommon in Noel's generation. Post-war children were often the children of second chances, raised by mothers bearing silent losses. So when Christopher Hassall's book appeared posthumously in 1964 it contained revelations. Julia could tell that her mother despised the book. Publications about Rupert and his love for her took away the distance and control Noel preferred in her interactions with the world. Despite the biography, which she didn't read straight away, Julia chose not to pry.

The book encouraged people to talk about Brooke again. Well before publication, the press had been in touch with Keynes, hoping for confirmation of 'sensational' revelations. When it did appear, the *Times Literary Supplement* ran a front-page article discussing the biography and its subject. 'How many eyes still glisten as they gaze on the famous profile?' an advert for the issue asked. 'How many people still bow down and adore Rupert Brooke as their image of the poet-hero?' For those who had known him, the allure lingered. 'If the impossible were to happen and he were to ring up and ask me to go and see him now,' Bunny told a friend that spring, 'I should be off like a shot.'

Ka's son had cooperated with Hassall and Keynes without reservation, shipping off her cache of letters without even looking at them. The depiction of Ka's relationship with Rupert, which was indeed significant and complicated, was then inevitably fuller in the book than that of Noel's. 'His longest and most frustrating relation was with Ka Cox,' ran one review, 'which passed through every phase of mutual torment. Earlier, there was Noel Olivier.' This can hardly have been regretted by Noel yet it must still have been an odd sensation to find herself a secondary character in what was, after all, also Noel's own story, despite all the exposure she had endured. Appearing in someone else's biography is an experience in relegation. The interest in Rupert must, at times, have seemed to reduce the bulk of Noel's life to insignificance, once it was no longer illuminated by the young Apollo.

In 1967, Margery, her condition deteriorating with the onset of dementia, was transferred from Moulton Park to the hospital's geriatric wing. After the war, Noel had resumed occasional visits to Northampton (perhaps in the Wala's stead) but, since she did not drive, each one was an offputtingly exhausting undertaking. In the same year, James Strachey died.

With the loss of James, one of her oldest and closest friends, 1967 must have felt like the close of an era to Noel. It also proved a kind of culmination of Bloomsbury, or rather a final test of the Bloomsbury project. Though he did not live to see publication, James survived long enough to witness the storm provoked by Michael Holroyd's biography of Lytton.

While Bunny surpassed the others in sheer blustering fury, all of the surviving members of Bloomsbury met Holroyd's book with a degree of discomfort. It hid nothing. Duncan Grant's affair with Lytton and the ménage à trois between Lytton, Carrington and Ralph Partridge were described in detail; an abortion of Carrington's was also included. In the summer of 1966, a year before gay sex was legalised, Duncan feared arrest. More than that, he expressed reservations probably very close to Noel's own four years previously: 'I cannot help feeling very averse,' he told Holroyd, 'to having my most private feelings of so long ago openly described.'

There had been Bloomsbury memoirs by now, but the usual way of expressing the truth of those old and unashamed affairs had been to make them obvious enough to those in the know, whilst taking measures to obscure the reality from those who were not. 'The rocks and shoals are immense,' Bunny told a friend while writing the second volume of *The Golden Echo*. 'I shall have to be extremely adroit if I am to succeed in saying anything worth saying.' When someone else was telling his story (for he appeared, naturally, in Holroyd's biography) Bunny's opinion was fairly close to Noel's. He believed, he told James, that biographers 'should not go into other people's love affairs'. He himself was 'on the whole in favour of truth in biography – but not at the expense of the happiness of the living and their security'.

'What the Hell is to be done about it?' James retorted. He had been through the manuscript forensically ('I was extremely abusive,' he assured Bunny) and was against suppression, feeling that Lytton's commitment to candour and to personal freedom behooved him to allow publication. The question was whether the rest of them were prepared to acknowledge publicly the way of life they had insisted on for themselves in private; to stand by the freedoms they had seized long ago just as social attitudes might finally be catching up with them. Holroyd assured Duncan that attitudes had changed; Bunny assured him they had not.

But they were changing. Not long after the Brooke trustees were ponderously denying any hint of homosexuality in Rupert's make-up, James was determined to support a biographer who openly acknowledged his brother's sexuality. He also planned to publish *Ermyntrude and Esmeralda*: Lytton's short, epistolary tale, written in 1913, that follows two teenage girls as they share their investigations into the mysteries of sex. It is irreverent, silly and very funny. But as Lytton's biographer would note, 'Implicit throughout the lightly written satire is a scathing criticism of the taboos under which [Lytton] himself suffered, and the repressive procedures that governed the upbringing of adolescents, especially young girls.'

At the time that Lytton read it aloud, in his distinctive high-pitched voice, to his brother, Bunny, Daphne and Noel at Christmas in 1914, to publish would have been unthinkable (a representative sentence: 'By-the-bye, my new theory is that being in love is merely a more polite way of saying that your pussy's pouting'). But in the last year of his life, James wryly suspected that 'it ought to be a best seller in these debauched days'. Alix arranged publication and found that its publishers went so far as to have the story serialised in *Playboy*. Noel's daughter Angela described Alix setting off to the local WHSmith to secure a copy for herself, and worrying 'what her old friends will say', expecting 'a rocket (or an icy silence) from Leonard [Woolf] for one!' Noel had already had her say. Hearing Lytton read from two of his works that evening, she wrote in 1915, 'impressed us all immensely & proved Lytton a Genius'.

Hassall's biography glossed over much of the reality of Rupert's life – his fluid sexuality, his breakdown, a great deal of his viciousness and volatility. It was published at a time of crusading battles over public morality; a year after Profumo's fall and only months after Mrs Whitehouse launched her campaign to 'clean up' national television with a manifesto appealing to the 'women of Britain'. Given Noel's desire for privacy, she was fortunate that Hassall belonged to the old guard who obscured as much as they described. By 1967, when Holroyd's book was published, the laws on homosexuality and abortion were reformed. It had taken more than fifty years for legislation to catch up with the lives he described. The sixties mood of permissiveness, of shedding inhibitions, was bearing fruit.

It was not shame that put Noel off tell-all biography. It was more a belief in showing consideration to those left behind, and a sense of her own right to unknowability, as well as a duty, perhaps, to protecting that of her sisters, who all now depended on her to protect their stories. She was the keeper of their shared past (in some sense literally, as, for instance, the possessor of Daphne's youthful journals). Surely, too, a life-long habit of not giving way, of holding true to her own convictions without feeling the need to explain them to dissenters, guided her still.

When Geoffrey Keynes published his own memoirs he would accuse Noel of viewing him as a 'publishing rascal' in the mould of the unscrupulous academic in Henry James's *The Aspern Papers*. In that novella, the protagonist inveigles his way into the home of a 'subtle old witch' once beloved of a great man, who now jealously guards his letters to her and ultimately arranges their destruction rather than hand them over. Yet Noel's instinct was never to obliterate the record of her past. She could easily have destroyed her letters but she didn't. They mattered too much. At the height of her affair with James, too, she sent a batch of James's missives back to him to avoid their discovery by Arthur. 'I can't possibly have them burnt,' she told him. 'You must keep them for me where the others I sent you are. One day, when everything seems perfectly safe or nothing matters anyhow, I will call for them all.' She never did.

By 1967 Noel was more resigned to being a source of information for people researching Rupert but she did not stop resenting those who questioned her. Michael Hastings interviewed her that year for his book about Brooke and his notes suggest that she was surprisingly candid with him. She seems to have been one of the few people who harboured no illusions about Rupert, raising, for instance, the possibility that he could have contracted a strain of gonorrhea that would have made him more susceptible to the infection that killed him. She also seems to have discussed her own sense of disillusionment when, early in Rupert's courtship of her, she read the letters between him and Brynhild. Despite this, or perhaps because of it, she complained to Bunny that she felt Hastings 'was out to pick my brains, if not to suck my blood'. By now perhaps resistance seemed futile – Hastings called and wrote to her repeatedly, twice showing up at her house unannounced – and yet the record was important to her on some level too. Of Hastings's forthcoming documentary about Rupert one of the Pyes asked, 'After all, what does it matter'? 'I believe it does matter a bit,' Noel responded.

She is known to have annotated her copy of Hassall's biography. For whom were these notes made? She couldn't transmit them to Hassall himself and does not appear to have sent them to Geoffrey Keynes; she did not intend to discuss the story with her daughters, her husband was dead. James was beyond her reach and she did not go into detail in her exchanges with Bunny. And yet the impulse to set the record – or at least what she knew of it – straight was there. Even if she committed it only to the care of her own bookshelves, Noel was having her say.

When Geoffrey Keynes went ahead and published the Brooke letters in 1968, *The Times* remarked that his mission of stripping the myth from Rupert Brooke seemed complete, though not, perhaps, in the ways that he had intended: 'The mask and the make-up are off, the classical drapery has been wrenched aside and the god is undoubtedly dead'. The world had moved on from Rupert Brooke. Men like Wilfred Owen and Siegfried Sassoon were now regarded as the true war poets: Brooke's sonnets stood for the establishment.

The review was published as the Parisian mayhem of May 1968 dissipated, and only months before American feminists publicly discarded the 'instruments of torture to women', like bras and hair curlers, outside the Miss America contest. British feminists took up the protest in 1970, disrupting the Miss World competition in London and triumphantly signalling the return of spectacle to the women's movement, a phenomenon not seen since the days of the suffragettes. Radical though the mood of the sixties was, it took a long time to get round to sexism. Jenny Diski realised later that women had been 'mostly of ornamental, sexual, domestic or secretarial value to the men striking out for radical shores'. Eventually, often amongst those who had been campaigning for nuclear disarmament, or against the Vietnam War, or for the Radical Left, it occurred to women to campaign for themselves.

In 1968, the academic Sheila Rowbotham wrote an article for the *New Left Review* that began, 'The first question is why do we stand for it?' Consciousness-raising groups emerged across the country, in which women began to ask themselves just that question. These discussions were crucial. It was the coming together that mattered. Many women, realising that they had been separated from, and set against, their natural allies by the patriarchy, were seeking re-entry into the kind of hallowed gang that the Olivier sisters had enjoyed since childhood. They were looking for sisters.

Rowbotham spoke of the 'yearning for sisterhood'. Sisterhood became the equivalent of class-consciousness for women, the promise of a support network that celebrated, protected and furthered them and their cause. Noel welcomed the emergence of Women's Lib. Much as she hoped her youngest daughter would get married, she had also been determined that Julia should go to university. Whilst Margery, Daphne and Noel had been the beneficiaries of those first women who had established higher education as a possibility for women, they were also among the first for whom the university certificate's insufficiency became clear. By 1965, it was still the case that only a quarter of university students were female. It had taken until 1961, more than a decade after Daphne's death, for the principle of equal pay in teaching to be established and only in the sixties did women writers like Hannah Gavron and Betty Friedan begin, in public discourse, to worry at the entrapment of housewives.

Nevertheless, the liberal feminists of the sixties now again felt certain that work – or rather, careers – would emancipate them. It was, after all, the home that had isolated women, separating them from their sisters and removing them from the public realms of power and significance. In these terms, Noel, who had earned her own living for most of her adult life, was a model feminist. But Brynhild, the only Olivier sister not to study at university, had never seen herself as disempowered in quite those terms. Raymond Sherrard, before he became her husband, had once offended her with an offer to buy her clothes. She had her own funds, she assured him. This was because she saw her day-to-day activities as work for which she was due a share of Hugh Popham's income. 'I don't feel dishonoured,' she told him firmly, 'buying myself "decorations" [...] with money I consider quite well earned from Hugh for house-keeping & looking after the children & attempting, not very successfully, to make him a comfortable home.'

In some ways, being ahead of your time is a curse. There is nowhere to wait while the rest of the world catches up: life has to be lived and often it is lived within the boundaries established by others. On the eve of her wedding, Daphne smarted at the injustice of losing her surname, signing off her letter to her fiancé that evening as 'Daphne Olivier', as if to relish the identity one last time. Still, she became Mrs Harwood in the morning. Her sisters found their own ways to keep the name with them – Noel was known intermittently as Dr Olivier Richards throughout her career, Brynhild bequeathed it to her oldest daughter, Anne Olivier. For consciousness to survive, a group of like-minded supporters is needed. The Oliviers' personal circumstances had offered them this but the society in which they existed still set the parameters for their opportunities; the structure within which their advantages had to operate. In 1973, Sheila Rowbotham published a seminal work, *Hidden from History*, which sought to rediscover women's experiences. '[I]n what conditions have women produced and reproduced their lives,' Rowbotham asked, and 'how has the free expression of this activity been distorted and blocked by the circumstances of society?'

As the momentum of the Edwardian suffrage movement faded away, some of the Oliviers' friends began to disavow those optimistic Newnhamites that they had known before the war. Being 'Advanced' became a misguided pretension of youth – what else could all those ideas have been, when they were never ratified by the society that came after? Later in life, Frances Cornford looked back on 'the futility of young people who think they are "advanced"', looking with pity on women like Ka Cox who had thought they were 'clever' but had suffered, in her opinion, precisely because they had never lived in 'strict home[s]' or been courted by 'conventional young men'. As histories of Anthroposophy began to be written, the assumption that Cecil Harwood (who, in the 1960s, was still Chairman of the British Anthroposophy Society) and other brilliant young men had been the moving force behind Steiner schooling in Britain quietly became fact. In the 1950s, the anthroposophist George Adams commended Daphne in his memoir for her contribution to the cause: 'Several very talented young men, who [...] have since become the bearers of the Anthroposophy Movement in this country, became acquainted with it in the first place through her.' When the feminists of the 1960s began to look for fore-mothers, they had to look hard to find them.

In the spring of 1969, Noel was at Nunnington, the beloved home that Brynhild had left her, with her son, two of her daughters and six grandchildren. She was in good spirits: well and happy because her daughter Ginny had just moved home after a spell abroad, and because a pregnant Julia had recently married. It was warm and leaves were coming out in the garden. Dressed in an old pair of blue jeans and an even older windbreaker jacket, she was tending to the great vine in the conservatory when she suffered a stroke. She died in hospital the next day. 'I know it is the most marvellous luck really,' Angela wrote, reflecting on her mother's swift passing, 'but I have the most terrible pain in the guts.'

Noel tending to the vine at Nunnington

When Bunny was called to the phone to receive news of Noel's death, his daughter heard him let out a wail of pain. It was a loss that reverberated back to the very beginning of his life. Four years later he was still wondering, characteristically, how differently their lives might have turned out if he had only asked Noel to come to bed with him, but chiefly he suffered because there was no one, he complained, apart perhaps from Harold Hobson, 'to whom I can talk about the past without explanations now'.

But there was someone who remembered. The year after she was transferred to the geriatric ward, Margery Olivier was given a check-up. She was not sure where she was, how long she had been where she was, or why she was there at all. She did not know her age, the date or even the month. All she could tell her questioner was that she had been at Cambridge University for a time, and that she hoped to go home soon.

Her time at Newnham may well have been the high point of Margery's
life. It coincided with a kind of political sisterhood for women, which
did not fully reappear until shortly before her death at St Andrew's
Hospital in 1974. The eldest Olivier, she had outlived all of her sisters.

Postscript

More than a century after Bunny's search through the Limpsfield woods, the Olivier sisters gained another pursuer. For the success of my own pursuit it was important that I didn't consider my presumption in the matter. For it was quite clear that the Oliviers didn't want to be found. They had no interest in the people who tried to understand them, to pin them down into one definition or another, and they had made efforts to avoid posterity. They had no need of us. The relationship – the fascination – was inevitably and terribly one-sided. And yet, as the biographer Richard Holmes has said, biography is 'the story of the relationship between the subject and biographer, even if that's never consciously expressed'.

The more I thought about Noel's resistance to biographers of Rupert, her discomfort about her friends' memoirs, the more I realised how vulnerable one's story is in the hands of others. Political sisterhood, especially in the sixties and seventies, in the form of women's history, was an act of making use of women, salvaging their stories from a history written by men and making them part of a historical tradition that would belong to women of the present and future. They could be icons, warnings, heroes and models. They restored something to the women who came after them: they were rescued and sacrificed. I began to feel the need to take responsibility for this book explicitly, and to be honest about the fact that almost everything in it came at least in part from my imagination. The Olivier sisters lived. They were fascinating and complicated. But in writing this book, I had also invented them.

This book is more than an accumulation of facts. It was written by someone – me – who always took the sisters' side (even when they were fighting each other), who wanted to see them as special, who believed in the existence and importance of a distinct women's history of the twentieth century. It was written by someone who admired the Oliviers, who benefited hugely from writing about them, who was seeking to learn something both from the experience and from the story.

In her old age, Noel no longer had her sisters around to back her up, but she still invoked their views for support. Researching this book, I started to notice how the Olivier descendants who helped me referred me to each other, knowing what the others would be able to tell me, or how they would remember things distinctly, or what – in terms of inheritance and authority – they had divided up between them; I noticed, too, the way Noel's granddaughter conferred swiftly and electronically with her own sister when I presented her with a permission document from my publisher. Sisters were back-up, sharers of responsibility, references for life stories.

The sociologist David Bouchier described the solidarity of sisterhood as a 'concept arising from feminism'. Sisterhood, he wrote, 'expresses a feeling or a value universally shared by feminists, and carries the same deep meaning for them as does the notion of the unity of the oppressed classes for Marxists'.

I have my own sister and, though I spent much of her early childhood railing against our mother for allowing her into our (perfectly sufficient) lives, I had come to understand very well what my mother (one of three girls) had always insisted: that a sister is a gift. My concept of sisterhood is inevitably influenced by those relationships, yet I felt sure that sisterhood was an identifiable and distinct form of relationship, and a way of emerging into the world that would colour one's experience of it.

Four years after Margery Olivier's death, at the fiftieth anniversary of the equalisation of suffrage, British feminists addressed the women who had gained them the vote in an open letter which read, 'Dear sisters, we are writing to you because you will understand how angry we are. [. . .] women are still not free.'

Thirty years after that, I went to Newnham College, where some of the Oliviers studied. I believed that education was liberating. I lived and worked in twenty-first-century Britain, so I also knew that access to education was not enough. I identified with what I knew were middle-class-focused ambitions for women and I still believed in their validity. I had read biographies of Rupert Brooke and the Neo-Pagans published after all the sisters were dead and I was angry. (Angry that a male biographer in 1999 would refer to Margery as the 'less fanciable sister' or that the men who wrote of Rupert Brooke took up, in brotherly solidarity with their subject, a story of sexual competition – even among sisters – to explain her opposition to Rupert's pursuit of Noel.) I compared the hopes of women in their generation with the hopes of mine and I was angry. When I read about the ideas that held women back a hundred years ago, I did not reflect on how far we had come. I thought that women were still labouring with a legacy they may not even fully know, that there was still so much to change. That the same pressures and excuses could hold us back. Reader, you should know that I did not come to this story unburdened. My admiration for, and fascination with, the Oliviers is a true thing. But I did not think in writing this book that I was writing only of them. I knew that the Oliviers – Daphne and Noel, at least – did not like being written about. So though I see this book as a tribute to the sisters, I can't honestly say I wrote it in service to them or with their imagined blessing. But if I acknowledge my presumption in writing about them, I should acknowledge what I gained from them, and acknowledge that I am here, marshalling four vast and private lives into seven curated fragments.

Acknowledgements

The author gratefully acknowledges the kind permission of the heirs of Anne Olivier Bell to quote from the private papers of Brynhild Olivier, Anne Olivier Bell and Hugh Popham; of the heirs of Dr Noel Olivier Richards and Dr Arthur Richards to quote from the Harris/Richards papers and from Margery Olivier's papers; of the heirs of Brynhild Olivier and Raymond Sherrard to quote from private papers; quotations from Gwen and Jacques Raverat's letters appear courtesy of the Raverat Archive.

This book would not have been possible without the support, patience, hospitality, understanding and enthusiasm of many descendants of the Olivier sisters. It was an honour to meet and talk with Anne Olivier Bell, whose memories, personal archive and kind welcome were crucial to the book. I would also like to thank Virginia Nicholson for her kind help and advice. For the welcome, the conversations, the delicious lunches, and for permission to quote from the papers of Daphne and Cecil Harwood, very grateful thanks to Laurence Harwood, OBE and Melissa Harwood, and also to Matthew Harwood for Jamaican directions. For letting me spread old letters all over her floor during a house renovation, to Dr Tamsin Armour. For her early support and advice, to Dame Pippa Harris. For the frank conversations and many enlightening notes, to the intrepid Julia Rendall, who topped off the experience of writing this book by meeting me for a smoothie in Jamaica.

I am grateful for the time, conversations and help offered by: Tazza and Keith Ramsay, the late Virginia Allen and Michael Allen, Lois Olivier and Fiona Athanassaki, Sarah Shand and Laurence Shand, Liadain Sherrard, Sophie Popham, Andrea Linell, Carolyn Hanbury, Emma Campbell, Elizabeth Pye, Sally and David Hopson, and Katharine Eldridge.

I would also like to thank the staff and librarians at the King's College Archive, Eton College, Morley College, St Andrew's Healthcare, the Bodleian Library, Newnham College Archives, the Royal College of Art Archives, University of Liverpool Archives, the UCL Records Office, the Charles Deering McCormick Library of Special Collections at Northwestern University, the Royal College of Music, the Simon Fraser University Archives, ETH-Bibliothek, Hochschularchiv der ETH Zürich, Princeton University Library, the Williams College Special Collections, the LSE Library, King's House in Kingston, Jamaica, and the Master and Fellows of St John's College Library and the Syndics of Cambridge University Library.

Thank you to the lovely Bea Hemming and her colleagues at Jonathan Cape, including Daisy Watt and Alison Davies; to Tim Bent, Mariah White and their colleagues at Oxford University Press; for their invaluable support and encouragement, to Sarah Chalfant, Tracy Bohan, Jennifer Bernstein, Kristina Moore, Hannah Townsend, and others at The Wylie Agency.

I would also like to thank the Biographers' Club and the 2016 judges of the Tony Lothian Prize for their early encouragement.

Thanks also to reader extraordinaire E(lla) G(riffiths); Dr Debbie Falconer for fielding my obscure medical queries; to Sally Walton for letting me turn her new summer house into a 'writing shed'; to the cherished Cat and Tom Watling, and to John Watling. It is a matter of deep personal regret that this book was not finished in time to be offered up to Tom Watling (senior) in tribute and for discussion; to him and the dearly missed Audrey May Watling: This book was written at your table. Thank you to Sara Willis, my co-conspirator on this book, who read every page before it was readable. And, of course, to Julian Walton, for everything.

SELECTED BIBLIOGRAPHY

Appignanesi, Lisa, *Mad, Bad and Sad: A history of women and the mind doctors from 1800 to the present* (Virago, 2008)

Barfield, Owen (ed.), *The Voice of Cecil Harwood: A miscellany* (Rudolf Steiner Press, 1979)

Baynes Jansen, Diana, *Jung's Apprentice: A biography of Helton Godwin Baynes* (Daimon Verlag, 2003)

Bearman, C. J., 'An Examination of Suffragette Violence', *The English Historical Review*, vol. 120, no. 486 (April, 2005), pp. 365–97

Bell, Anne Olivier (ed.), *The Diary of Virginia Woolf Vol. 1, 1915–1919* (Hogarth Press, 1977)

Bell, Anne Olivier (ed.), *The Diary of Virginia Woolf Vol. 2, 1920–1924* (Hogarth Press, 1978)

Bell, Anne Olivier (ed.), *The Diary of Virginia Woolf Vol. 3, 1925–1930* (Hogarth Press, 1980)

Bell, Anne Olivier (ed.), *The Diary of Virginia Woolf Vol. 4, 1931–1935* (Hogarth Press, 1982)

Bell, Anne Olivier (ed.), *The Diary of Virginia Woolf Vol. 5, 1936–1941* (Hogarth Press, 1984)

Bell, Quentin, *Virginia Woolf: A biography* (Pimlico edition, 1996)

Blom, Philipp, *The Vertigo Years* (Phoenix, 2009)

Bouchier, David, *The Feminist Challenge: The movement for women's liberation in Britain and the USA* (Macmillan, 1983)

Brookes, Barbara, *Abortion in England, 1900–1967* (Croom Helm, 1988)

Caine, Barbara, *Bombay to Bloomsbury: A biography of the Strachey family* (Oxford University Press, 2005)

Clemen, Carl, 'Anthroposophy', *The Journal of Religion*, vol. 4, no. 3 (May 1924), pp. 281–92

Crawford, Elizabeth, 'Women and the First World War: The work of women doctors', *Ancestors* (2006)

de Lisser, Herbert George, *Twentieth Century Jamaica* (Jamaica Times, 1913)

Delany, Paul, *The Neo-pagans: Friendship and love in the Rupert Brooke Circle* (Macmillan, 1987)

Diski, Jenny, *The Sixties* (Profile, 2009)

Dwork, Deborah, *War is Good for Babies and Other Young Children: A history of the infant and child welfare movement in England, 1898–1918* (Tavistock Publications, 1987)

Dyhouse, Carol, 'Driving ambitions: women in pursuit of a medical education, 1890–1939', *Women's History Review*, vol. 7, issue no. 3 (1998), pp. 321–43

Dyhouse, Carol, *Girl Trouble: Panic and progress in the history of young women* (Zed Books, 2013)

Elston, Mary Ann C., *Women Doctors in British Health Services: A sociological study of their careers and opportunities* [unpublished Ph.D. thesis, University of Leeds] (1986)

Garnett, David, *The Golden Echo* (Chatto & Windus, 1953)

Garnett, David, *The Golden Echo: The flowers of the forest* (Chatto & Windus, 1955)

Garnett, David, *The Golden Echo: The familiar faces* (Chatto & Windus, 1962)

Goffman, Erving, *Asylums: Essays on the social situation of mental patients and other inmates* (Penguin, 1961)

Gömöri, George & Mari (eds.), *The Alien in the Chapel: Ferenc Békássy, Rupert Brooke's unknown rival, poems & letters* (Skyscraper Publications, 2016)

Hale, Keith (ed.), *Friends and Apostles: The correspondence of Rupert Brooke and James Strachey, 1905–1914* (Yale University Press, 1998)

Harrison, Brian, *Prudent Revolutionaries: Portraits of British feminists between the wars* (Clarendon Press, 1987)

Harwood, Laurence, *C.S. Lewis, My Godfather* (InterVarsity Press, 2007)

Hassall, Christopher, *Rupert Brooke* (Faber & Faber, 1964)

Hastings, Michael, *The Handsomest Young Man in England: Rupert Brooke* (Michael Joseph, 1967)

Higonnet, Margaret R. et al. (eds.), *Behind the Lines: Gender and the two world wars* (Yale University Press, 1987)

Hinely, Susan, 'Charlotte Wilson, the "Woman Question" and the Meanings of Anarchist Socialism in Late Victorian Radicalism', *International Review of Social History*, vol. 57, no. 1 (April, 2012), pp. 3–36

Holroyd, Michael, *Lytton Strachey: A new biography* (Chatto & Windus, 1994)

Hooper, Walter (ed.), *All My Road Before Me: The diary of C.S. Lewis, 1922–1927* (Harcourt Brace Jovanovich, 1991)

Hopkinson, Diana, *Family Inheritance: A life of Eva Hubback* (Staples Press, 1954)

Jackson, Holbrook, *The Eighteen Nineties* (Penguin, 1913, 1950)

Jalland, Pat, *Death in War and Peace: Loss and grief in England, 1914–1970* (Oxford University Press, 2010)

Jeffreys, Sheila, *The Spinster and her Enemies: Feminism and sexuality 1880–1930* (Pandora, 1985)

Johnson, B. S. (ed.), *The Evacuees* (Gollancz, 1968)

Kent, Susan Kingsley, 'The Politics of Sexual Difference: World War I and the Demise of British Feminism', *Journal of British Studies*, vol. 27, no. 3 (July 1988), pp. 232–53

Keynes, Geoffrey, *The Gates of Memory* (Clarendon Press, 1981)

Knights, Sarah, *Bloomsbury's Outsider* (Bloomsbury, 2015)

Laing, R. D., *The Divided Self: An existential study in sanity and madness* (Penguin Books, 1960, 1965)

Lee, Francis, *Fabianism and Colonialism: The life and political thought of Lord Sydney Olivier* (Defiant Books, 1988)

Lee, Hermione, *Virginia Woolf* (Chatto & Windus, 1996)

Mackay, Robert, *Half the Battle: Civilian morale in Britain during the Second World War* (Manchester University Press, 2002)

MacKenzie, Norman and Jean, *The First Fabians* (Quartet, 1979)

Mansfield, Joy, *A Good School: A history of Michael Hall: a Steiner Waldorf School* (Blue Filter, 2014)

Marwick, Arthur, *The Sixties: Cultural revolution in Britain, France, Italy, and the United States c.1958–c.1974* (Bloomsbury, 2012)

McLaren, Angus, 'Illegal Operations: Women, doctors, and abortion, 1886–1939', *Journal of Social History*, vol. 26, no. 4 (Summer, 1993), pp. 797–816

McNally, Kieran, *A Critical History of Schizophrenia* (Palgrave Macmillan, 2016)

McWilliams Tullberg, Rita, *Women at Cambridge* (Cambridge University Press, 1998)

Nicolson, Nigel (ed.), *The Letters of Virginia Woolf Vol. 1, 1888 –1912* (Chatto & Windus, 1975)

Nicolson, Nigel (ed.), *The Letters of Virginia Woolf Vol. 2, 1912–1922* (Chatto & Windus, 1976)

Nicolson, Nigel (ed.), *The Letters of Virginia Woolf Vol. 3, 1923–1928* (Chatto & Windus, 1977)

Nicolson, Nigel (ed.), *The Letters of Virginia Woolf Vol. 4, 1929–1931* (Chatto & Windus, 1978)

Nicolson, Nigel (ed.), *The Letters of Virginia Woolf Vol. 5, 1932–1935* (Chatto & Windus, 1979)

Nicolson, Nigel (ed.), *The Letters of Virginia Woolf Vol. 6, 1936–1941* (Chatto & Windus, 1980)

Olivier, Margaret (ed.), *Sydney Olivier: Letters and selected writings* (George Allen & Unwin, 1948)

Partridge, Frances, *A Pacifist's War* (Hogarth Press, 1975; Phoenix, 1996)

Partridge, Frances, *Everything to Lose: Diaries, 1945–1960* (Victor Gollancz, 1985; Phoenix, 1997)

Partridge, Frances, *Hanging On: Diaries, 1960–1963* (William Collins, 1990; Phoenix, 1998)

Partridge, Frances, *Other People: Diaries, 1963–1966* (HarperCollins, 1993; Phoenix, 1999)

Partridge, Frances, *Good Company: Diaries, 1967–1970* (HarperCollins, 1994)

Pederson, Susan, *Eleanor Rathbone and the Politics of Conscience* (Yale, 2004)

Phillips, Ann (ed.), *A Newnham Anthology* (Cambridge University Press, 1979)

Pugh, Martin, *We Danced All Night: A social history of Britain between the wars* (Bodley Head, 2008)

Radford, Maisie and Radford, Evelyn, *Musical Adventures in Cornwall* (Macdonald, 1965)

Robbins, Keith, 'The British Experience of Conscientious Objection', in Cecil, Hugh and Liddle, Peter, *Facing Armageddon: the First World War experienced* (Leo Cooper, 1996), pp. 691–708

Rowbotham, Sheila, *The Past is Before Us: Feminism in action since the 1960s* (Pandora, 1989)

Rubinstein, David, *Before the Suffragettes: Women's emancipation in the 1890s* (Harvester, 1986)

Sargant Florence, P. and Anderson, J.R.L. (eds.), *C.K. Ogden: A Collective Memoir* (Pemberton, 1977)

Satre, Lowell J., 'After the Match Girls' Strike: Bryant and May in the 1890s', *Victorian Studies*, Vol. 26, No. 1 (Autumn, 1982), pp. 7–31

Savage, Gail, 'Erotic Stories and Public Decency: Newspaper reporting of divorce proceedings in England', *The Historical Journal*, vol. 41, issue 2 (June 1998), pp. 511–28

Seddon, Richard, *Rudolf Steiner: Essential readings* (Crucible, 1988)

Showalter, Elaine, *The Female Malady: Women, madness, and English culture, 1830–1980* (Virago, 1987)

Smith, Harold L. (ed.), *War and Social Change: British society in the Second World War* (Manchester University Press, 1986)

Spalding, Frances, *Duncan Grant: A biography* (Pimlico, 1998)

Spalding, Frances, *Gwen Raverat: Friends, family and affections* (Harvill, 2001)

Taylor, Anne, *Annie Besant: A biography* (Oxford University Press, 1992)

Thornycroft, Rosalind and Baynes, Chloe, *Time Which Spaces Us Apart* (privately published, 1991)

Uhrmacher, P. Bruce, 'Uncommon Schooling: A historical look at Rudolf Steiner, Anthroposophy, and Waldorf Education', *Curriculum Inquiry*, vol. 25, no. 4 (Winter, 1995), pp. 381–406

Villeneuve, Crispian, *Rudolf Steiner in Britain: A documentation of his ten visits*, vol. 2 (Temple Lodge, 2004)

Wells, H. G., *Ann Veronica* (1909; Virago, 1980)

Williams, Stephanie, *Running the Show: Governors of the British Empire* (Viking, 2011)

Winter, J. M., *The Great War and the British People* (Macmillan, 1986)

NOTES

Unless otherwise noted, quotations are from letters or other documents held in private collections. Quotations from the correspondence between Christopher Hassall and the Keyneses are taken from the Christopher Hassall Papers and the Sir Geoffrey Langdon Keynes Papers: MS Add.8905 and MS Add.8633 respectively at the Cambridge University Library, Department of Manuscripts and University Archives.

Abbreviations

AR: Arthur Richards
BL: British Library
BO: Brynhild Olivier
Bod.: Oxford, Bodleian Library, Sydney Olivier Papers
CH: Cecil Harwood
CHL: Christopher Hassall
CSL: C. S. Lewis
CUL: Cambridge University Library
DG: David (Bunny) Garnett
DO: Daphne Olivier
ECA: Eton College Archives, Rupert Brooke Collection (Reference: MS 586)
EG: Edward Garnett
GBS: George Bernard Shaw
GK: Geoffrey Keynes
HGW: H. G. Wells
HP: Hugh Popham
JR: Jacques Raverat
KCA: King's College Archives
LRB: Keynes, Geoffrey (ed.), *Letters of Rupert Brooke* (Faber & Faber, 1968)
MaO: Margaret Olivier
MO: Margery Olivier
NO: Noel Olivier
NW: Charles Deering McCormick Library of Special Collections, Northwestern University Libraries
PM: postmarked
POP: The Papers of Hugh and Brynhild (Olivier) Popham, King's College Archive Centre, Cambridge (Reference: GBR/0272/PP/POP)
RB: Rupert Brooke
RCB: The Papers of Rupert Chawner Brooke, King's College Archive Centre, Cambridge (Reference: GBR/0272/PP/RCB)

RS: Raymond Sherrard

SO: Sydney Olivier

SoL: Harris, Pippa (ed.), *Song of Love: the letters of Rupert Brooke and Noel Olivier: 1909–1915* (Bloomsbury, 1991)

Idiosyncrasies of spelling and punctuation in the sisters' letters have been preserved in quotation.

Introduction

xi   *Words* NO to MaO, 31 January 1942, Bod.

x   *psychological resistance* GK to CHL, 12 September 1962, CUL.

x   *gravely incomplete* CHL to Lord Dalton, 22 June 1960, RCB, KCA.

x   Hassall's descriptions of the meeting are taken from CHL to GK, 10 September 1962, CUL.

xii   To be precise, Margaret Olivier recorded that Wells taught her daughters 'a new sort of croquet which he had invented', SO Letters, p. 93.

xiii   *dim background figures* VW Diary, II, p. 6.

xiii   Quite possibly the admiring Neo-Pagan talk of uncivilised creatures might have sounded differently to the sisters, with their colonial background. It was not so different from terminology that had had distinctly unliberating repercussions for colonial subjects.

xiv   *Biography sets out* Lee, *Virginia Woolf*, p. 4.

xiv   See 'Did Women Have a Renaissance?' Joan Kelly-Gadol in *Becoming Visible: Women in European History* (Houghton Mifflin, 1977).

xiv   *Very little is known* Quoted in Lee, *Virginia Woolf*, p. 13.

Part One

4   *in white jerseys* Garnett, *The Golden Echo*, p. 98.

5   Shaw on Sydney: 'Some impressions', SO Letters, p. 9.

5   *Heart – hard* SoL, p. 201.

5   *looks and manners … cruel as savages* Garnett, *The Golden Echo*, p. 99 & p. 98.

6   *inoffensive service* SO Letters, p. 72.

6   *wanton burning* Ibid., p. 56.

7   *sat up till* SO Letters, p. 64.

8   *the wonder* Jan Marsh, *Jane and May Morris: a biographical story 1839–1938* (Pandora Press, 1986), p. 181.

9   *Someone read* SO Letters, p. 77.

10   *read into* Quoted in Hinely, p. 21.

10   *Let us pretend* 'Misogyny in Excelsis', *Today*, August 1887.

10   *a woman who* Hinely, p. 25.

10   *I always* SO Letters, p. 71.

10   *expeditionary force* Michael Holroyd, *Bernard Shaw: The One-Volume Definitive Edition* (Vintage, 1998), p. 103.

11   *If we prepare* Quoted in Mackenzie, p. 81.

12   *Three people* Figures disputed. These are taken from Lisa Keller, *Triumph of Order: Democracy and Public Space in New York and London* (Columbia University Press, 2009).

12   Margaret Olivier's descriptions of Bloody Sunday are taken from SO Letters.

12   *like smoke* Holroyd, *Bernard Shaw*, p. 107.

12   Fabian membership figures from Reva Pollack Greenburg, *Fabian Couples, Feminist Issues* (Garland Publishing, 1987), p. 11.

13   *very jolly* SO Letters, p. 88.

13   *My dear* SO to MO, [undated], Bod.
13   *pleasant outlook* SO Letters, p. 78.
14   *London has* E. Nesbit, *Five Children and It* (Wordsworth, 1993), p.10.
14   *enchanting country* SO Letters, pp. 92–3.
16   *extra-urban headquarters* Ford Madox Ford, *Return to Yesterday* (Victor Gollancz, 1931), p. 33.
16   *firebrand* SO Letters, p. 94.
16   *country parish* Mackenzie, p. 190.
18   *That bear* Garnett, *The Golden Echo*, p. 14.
18   Gertrude Dix on the Oliviers: 'Our Fabian Circle Book of Letters' (1892), pp. 141–3, Glasier Papers, University of Liverpool.
19   *a little girl* Garnett, *The Golden Echo*, p. 30.
19   *through the mist* Ibid., p. 98.
19   *stoats' skulls* Ibid., p. 98.
20   *I have ordered* SO Letters, p. 105.
21   *It is alive* SO to MaO, 2 January 1895, Bod.
21   Henry Maudsley, *Sex in the Mind and in Education*.
22   *dragging at* Ford, p. 55.
22   *the porch* Hinely, p. 9.
27   *seething indignation* Garnett, *The Golden Echo*, p. 55.
27   *fundamental absurdity* Quoted in Francis Lee, *Fabianism and Colonialism*, p. 78.
27   *suffered a sudden* Jackson, p. 52.
28   Figures: Fransjohan Pretorius, 'The Boer Wars', BBC History.

Part Two

33   *splendid lives … new world together* LRB, pp. 191–5.
34   *Basle platform* Ibid., p. 199.
35   *a Heaven* Ibid., p. 195.
36   *topmost leaves* Sybil Pye, *Life and Letters*, May 1929.
37   *think of* Gwen Raverat to Frances Cornford, August 1910, quoted in Delany, pp. 93–4.
37   *copious, rebellious* Hassall, p. 118.
38   *intellect personified* F. M. Wilson in *A Newnham Anthology*, p. 67.
39   *I even* LRB, p. 154.
40   *You are* MO to RB, 12 September 1908, ECA.
42   *a huge* Mackenzie, p. 334.
43   *days of* H.G. *Wells in Love*, quoted in Michael Sherbourne, *H.G. Wells: Another Kind of Life* (Peter Owen, 2012). This break from studying didn't prevent Amber from scoring a Double First, though her gender did prevent her from actually receiving a degree.
44   *gleaming silence* LRB, p. 256.
45   *damnable system* 'Our Fabian Circle Book of Letters', p. 149.
45   *afraid of* SO Letters, p. 134.
46   *unconventional and care-free* Hopkinson, p. 41.
46   *enormous books* NO to MaO, 27 April [1909], Bod.
47   *Actor-Manager's* LRB, p. 131.
47   *There is One* Ibid., p. 118.
47   *Switzerland fair* Ibid., p. 155.
48   *You must* Ibid., p. 161.
48   *I turned … singing* Ibid., p. 164.
48   *golden Bryn* Ibid., p. 143.
48   *came to* Ibid., p. 164.
50   *I had on* NO to MaO, 27 April [1909], Bod.
51   *Lay down* SoL, p. 3.

51   *kind advice* Ibid., p. 6.
51   *very long* Ibid., p. 3.
52   *Regard the* Ibid., p. 8.
52   *She wishes* Ibid., p. 10.
52   *Don't you* LRB, p. 171.
52   *I didn't* SoL, p. 12.
54   *I am quite* NO to MaO, 27 June [1909], Bod.
55   *Brigade hopeless* Williams, p. 335.
57   *Half the joy* de Lisser, p. 75.
58   *Here I am* BO to Eva Spielman, 7 November 1910, ECA.
58   *steadfast exclusion* SO Letters, p. 194.
63   *unselfconscious paganism* The Oliviers were also to some extent unencumbered by the weight of a Victorian family background. As Daphne noted in 1924, Sydney and Margaret had 'made a clean sweep of everything'.
63   *fall asleep* Garnett, *The Golden Echo*, p. 179.
64   *friendliness* Ibid., p. 169.
64   *a house* Quoted in Sherbourne, p. 204.
65   *I won't* Garnett, *The Golden Echo*, p. 164.
66   *I told* LRB, p. 140.
65   *they'd do* Ibid., p. 135.
66   *I can't* Hassall, p. 196.
66   *nightly anti-Olivier* LRB, p. 180.
67   *up mountains* RB to Ka Cox, 4 September 1909, RCB, KCA.
67   *romance reaches* Baynes Jansen, p. 47.
68   *not disturbed* Ibid.
69   *You must not* MO to RB, undated, ECA.
69   *Are you sure* LRB, p. 181.
70   *sanctimonious people* RB to BO, 27 April [1910], ECA.
70   *What can I* MO to RB, 24 November 1909, ECA.
70   *such a responsibility* Delany, p. 70.
70   *If you were older* MO to RB, 24 November 1909, ECA.
72   *You unnatural* April 1910, Bod.
75   *undercurrent* MaO diary, Bod.
75   *curious to hear* Ibid.
76   *suspended* Ibid.
79   *Daphne seems* NO to MaO, 23 October [1910], Bod.
79   *Mammy dear … more human* DO to MaO, 13 October [1910], Bod.
80   *I dont think* BO to MaO, 1 September 1910, Bod.
81   *I hate* LRB, p. 212.
81   *He always* SoL, p. 32.
81   *If you ever* NO to RB, 27 March 1910, ECA.
82   *dangerous & vitally … the goodness* NO to DG, [March], NW.
82   *splendid landing stage* BO to RB, 27 June 1910, ECA.
85   *intelligent as well as* JS to LS, 18 August 1910, BL.
85   *what happened … the first* SoL, p. 46.
85   *Other people* Ibid., p. 45.
87   *Apparently* DO to Maynard Keynes, undated, JMK/PP/45, KCA.
88   *If we* SoL, p. 50.
88   *I adore* Ibid., p. 56.
88   *I dont think* Ibid., p. 59.
88   *Margery is* Ibid., p. 67.
88   *I want to* Ibid., p. 70.
88   *idiotic and wicked* Ibid., pp. 71–2.
89   *grave quiet voice* DO to MaO, 21 October [1910], Bod.

89 *extremely original* Hopkinson, p. 62.
89 *hinges* BO to RB, 1 October 1910, ECA.
90 *infinitely the nicest* JS to Ka Cox, 18 September 1911, ECA.
90 *without heart* HP to BO, 13 October 1910, POP, KCA.
90 *minx like* Gwen Raverat to Frances Cornford, [1912], BL, Add MS 58398.
90 *encouraging ... unbearably difficult* BO to HP, [c. 15 October 1910], POP, KCA.
92 *very puzzling* HP to Doris Popham, 10 December 1910, POP, KCA.
93 *all that business* SoL, p. 62.
93 *One cant* BO to RB, 13 May [1911], ECA.
94 *For goodness sake* SoL, p. 75.
95 *So much simpler* NO to MaO, 27 December 1910, Bod.
95 *astonishingly good* SO to Graham Wallas, 6 May 1910, Bod.
95 *Write yourself ... wondrous proud ... a lover* SoL, pp. 80–2.
96 *very names* Ibid., p. 86.
97 *When you're not* Gömöri, p. 66.
97 *terrible little pagan* Beatrice Webb Diary, LSE.
98 *We have inherited* Quoted in Hassall, p. 208.
98 *pretty chit* VW Letters, I, p. 466.
99 *How incredible* JS to Ka Cox, 18 September 1911, ECA.
100 *We just tingled* BO to MaO, 'Sunday', Bod.
101 *'Noel'* JS to Ka Cox, 2 July 1912, ECA.
101 *so very peculiar ... I dont want* SoL, pp. 90–1.
101 *Wherever I am* Gömöri, p. 66.
102 *the exquisite* SoL, p. 101.
102 *a Cushion* LRB, pp. 308–9.
103 *'The Olivier'* SoL, p. 111.
104 *the heights* Ibid., p. 148.
104 *the awful difference* Ibid., p. 151.
105 *horrible business* Ibid., pp. 154–5.
106 *I've treated* Ibid., p. 156.
106 It is possible that Ka fell pregnant in February but later miscarried; see Delany.
106 *You seem* LRB, p. 363.
107 *most modern and advanced* Delany, p. 89. JR described his friends in an unpublished novel in which they all appeared under pseudonyms. (Noel became Yseult.)
107 *she has a glass eye* VW Letters, I, pp. 494–5.
109 After one of her first meetings with Rupert, Margaret Olivier noted his shyness around the young women in the group. Comparing him to Justin Brooke, who had been to Bedales, she put this shyness down to Rupert's not having been educated alongside girls.
110 *Friend of my* LRB, p. 372.
110 *The future seems* SoL, p. 165.
110 *an old fraud* BO to RB, 13 May 1911, ECA.
111 *more terrible* SoL, p. 118.
111 *terribly mad* Ibid., p. 174.
112 *pale as tallow* Ibid., p. 194.
113 *she is happy* Ibid., p. 211.
113 *almost impossibly much* HP to BO, [c. 15 July 1912], POP, KCA.
113 *slip away* BO to HP, [PM 19 July 1912], POP, KCA.
113 *quite simple* HP to BO, 23 July, POP, KCA.
114 In fact, at the end of the stay, Maynard found himself with a £40 fine from his landlady, who had objected to the shocking behaviour of his guests.
114 *doomed men* DO to MaO, 'Tuesday', Bod.
114 *eye of responsibility* LRB, p. 380.
114 *an off chance* Hale, p. 247.
114 *decency* Ibid., p. 208.

115   *I feel so* RB to BO, June 1912, ECA.
115   *Do you know* BO to HP, August 1912, POP, KCA.
115   *a comprehensive statement* BO to HP, 27 July 1912, POP, KCA.
116   *dreadfully conventional* LRB, p. 402.
116   *I think if* Ka Cox to NO, 'Saturday', ECA.
117   *silly sorryness* SoL p. 192.
117   *too disgusting* Ibid., p. 203.
117   *Time fairly rushes* BO to JS, August 1912, BL.
117   *perfect conjugal harmony* BO to RB, 19 August 1912, ECA.
117   *You must'nt* BO to HP, 19 August [1912], KCA.
118   *smash up altogether* SoL, p. 212.
118   *for marrying you* RB to BO, September 1912, ECA.
120   *a characteristic scrawl* HP to BO, 19 August 1912, POP, KCA.
120   *feasts & riots* SoL, p. 211.

Part Three

124   *she only rouses* SoL, p. 263.
124   *We three aunts* SoL, p. 272.
124   *Living in the* NO to JS, 9 October 1914, BL.
124   *dotty with* SoL, p. 270.
124   *quite unique* MO to JS, 30 March 1914, BL.
124   *neo-pagan mothers* Frances Spalding, *Vanessa Bell* (Tauris, 2016), p. 140.
125   *A DOG!* Holroyd, p. 97.
125   *incredibly firm* Delany, p. 130.
125   *You must* DO to LS, 6 January 1915, BL.
125   *tones of* Garnett, *The Golden Echo*, p. 17.
125   *a thing to* DG Diary, 1 January 1915, NW.
125   *We walk about* NO to JS, [PM 26 October 1914], BL.
126   Caroline Place was later renamed Mecklenburgh Place.
126   *plays by* NO to Maitland Radford, 9 January 1915, BL.
128   *Isn't it luck?* Hassall, p. 489.
128   *lock jaw* NO to JS, October 1914, BL.
129   *the whole country* Godwin Baynes to Maitland Radford, September 1914, BL.
129   *I'm even sorry* SoL, p. 240.
129   *My dear* Ibid., p. 244.
129   *envious admiration* NO to JS, 3 April, BL.
130   *pure and elevated* Hassall, pp. 502–3.
130   *the mood* M. E. Waterhouse in *A Newnham Anthology*, p. 105.
130   *If message of love* Hassall, p. 509. The message ended pathetically, 'waiting anxiously
       for the news'.
132   *I think* SO to MaO, 26 April 1915, Bod.
132   *King David* Hassall, p. 521.
132   *He did his duty* Harold Monro in *The Cambridge Magazine*.
133   *I can't tell you* Gömöri, p. 183.
134   *Dreadful if* SoL, p. 278.
134   *he was always* Gömöri, p. 186.
134   *I wonder did you* Ibid., pp. 179–80.
135   *I still thought* Ibid., pp. 184–6.
136   *I spew* Garnett, *The Flowers of the Forest*, p. 119.
137   *a patriot* BO to HP, 13 May 1917, POP, KCA.
138   *ruthless Valkyries* Garnett, *The Golden Echo*, p. 258.
138   *You must* NO to JS, undated, BL.

138   *almost dead* JS to LS, 8 September, BL.

139   *Is the lull* Enid Bagnold, *A Diary Without Dates* (William Morrow, 1935), p. 104.

139   Figures from Winter, p. 93.

139   *huge & grey* NO to JS, [PM 31 August 1914], BL.

140   *Twenty years* Joyce Marlow (ed.), *The Virago Book of Women and the Great War* (Virago, 1998), p. 46.

141   *I feel I* Godwin Baynes to Maitland Radford, 22 July 1915, BL.

142   *more & more miserable* NO to JS, 16 September 1916, BL.

142   *has to get up* SO to JS, 6 July 1915, BL.

142   *more like* DG Diary, 2 February 1915, NW.

142   *deadly slight* (this was her description to Rupert, however, to whom she may have wished to down-play her feelings for James) SoL, p. 250.

142   *more patient* NO to JS, 3 December [1915], BL.

142   *adorable* NO to JS, 30 December [1915], BL.

143   *overpoweringly sensible* SoL, p. 49.

143   *improper* JS to LS, 5 October 1915, BL. When James took Noel to the coast to recuperate in June 1915, wartime laws meant that they had to register in their real names wherever they stayed. In a suspicious atmosphere, and unable to pose as a married couple as they usually did, they had struggled to find hosts willing to rent them a room.

143   *appeared in the bath room* NO to JS, 24 May, BL.

144   *very jolly ... spoil her week-end* NO to JS, 22 July 1916, BL.

144   *wretched remains* NO to JS, November [1916], BL.

146   There is no record of the substances Daphne was given but it is worth noting that several of the most popular sedatives used at the time (chloral, veronal, paraldehyde) could have the opposite of the intended effect when given in large doses to an already over-excited patient. Talkativeness, rage, impaired judgement and even delirium could result; i.e. the treatment could in fact cause the symptoms of madness the patient exhibited. See Hermione Lee, p. 185.

147   *jolly sitting* DG Diary, 26 January 1915, NW.

147   *wool & pink* NO to JS, 23 October, BL.; NO to JS, 5 September, BL.

147   *The Oliviers* Garnett, *The Flowers of the Forest*, pp. 53–4.

148   *never want* DG Diary, 6 February 1915, NW.

148   *very dangerous* Knights, p. 83.

150   *practically nothing* Leonard Woolf, *Beginning Again: An autobiography of the years 1911 to 1918* (Hogarth Press, 1964), p. 160.

152   *innumerable people* SO Letters, p. 145.

152   *Mudie is magnificent* NO to JS, [PM 22 May], BL.

156   *It is enough* Marlow, p. 191.

157   *enlightened virgins* VW Letters, II, pp. 137–8.

158   *queerer* NO to JS, 8 September 1915, BL.

159   *the real Margery* Garnett, *The Golden Echo*, p. 262. (Though this observation was made with the benefit of hindsight.)

159   *I do feel* JS to BO, 22 April 1914, POP, KCA.

160   *Margery Olivier* VW Letters, II, pp. 82–3.

160   *People don't* Ibid., p. 84.

160   *more experience* Delany, p. 253.

161   *I feel more* NO to JS, [PM 5 September 1916 & PM 8 September 1916], BL.

162   *the cruellest disaster* Alix Sargant-Florence to Mary Sargant-Florence, 3 March 1917, BL.

165   Chiswick House casebook, Wellcome Library, MS5725/6222/6226.

166   *excessive sexual probing* Quoted in Daniel Pick, 'The id comes to Bloomsbury', *Guardian*, 16 August 2003.

166   *most terrible* NO to JS, 24 May, BL.

169   *Mrs So & So* NO to JS, [PM 13 September 1916], BL.

170   *an absolute penance* BO to MaO, 1 December [1916], Bod.

170   *You've never known* BO to HP, [PM 24 July 1912], POP, KCA.

170   *very rampageous* BO to MaO, 1 December [1916], Bod.

171   *almost continuous* BO to HP, 13 May 1917, POP, KCA.

172   *cut her out* BO to HP, 30 January 1918, POP, KCA.

172   *about three* BO to HP, 13 May 1917, POP, KCA.

174   Descriptions of Tatsfield, and the journey there: BO to HP, 13 May 1917 (and later), POP, KCA.

174   *I cling on* Ibid.

175   *I wish to God* BO to HP, 24 September [1917], POP, KCA.

176   *The dear old Mud* NO to JS, 'Thursday evening', BL.

178   *get thoroughly* BO to HP, 2 September [1917], POP, KCA.

178   *evil fascinations ... overwhelmed with gloom* Ibid.

180   *party at Bryn's* JS to LS, undated, BL.

180   *Dear, dear* LS to JS, 20 April 1918, BL.

180   *Its as bad* NO to JS, 19 July 1917, BL.

180   Figures for early 1918 from Winter.

181   *ultimate issue* Dwork, p. 209.

181   *Darling* NO to JS, [PM 20 April], BL.

181   *Perhaps she may* BO to HP, 13 May 1917, KCA.

182   *tiny white* JS to LS, 2 October 1917, BL.

182   *air of* VW Diary, I, p. 60.

182   The Raverats' antipathy was partly explained by their anti-Semitism, a prejudice they applied to anyone of whom they didn't approve, regardless of whether they were actually Jewish (the Stracheys were not). Noel, in one of several defences she made of the Stracheys against Rupert's attacks, wrote in 1912: 'You need have no fear of slug-like influences from the people Jacques calls "the Jews" (they comprise the Bloomsbury household & the Stracheys, I believe).' SoL, p. 216.

183   *melancholy haunt* Woolf, *Beginning Again*, p. 216.

183   *someone I took* VW Diary, I, p. 143.

184   *The two babies* BO to HP, 4 December 1917, POP, KCA.

185   *It's too late* BO to HP, 9 December 1917, POP, KCA.

185   *I agree* SoL, p. 251.

185   *I shall be* Ibid., p. 274.

185   *Bryn says* NO to JS, 11 September 1916, BL.

Part Four

189   *Mussolini* SO Letters, p. 152.

199   *Why didn't you* VW Diary, II, p. 229.

200   *So we thought* NO to MaO, 21 August, Bod.

200   *We 3* NO to JS, 3 September 1919, BL.

202   *unattainable romance* VW Diary, II, p. 136.

203   *I find no* Ibid., p. 39.

203   *I do so* Caine, p. 177.

204   Figures from Dyhouse, p. 321.

204   *There never* Emily Forster, *How to Become a Woman Doctor* (C. Griffin & Co., 1918), p. 48.

205   *We need hardly* Elston, p. 300.

205   *hated like poison* Patricia Fara, *A Lab of One's Own: Science and suffrage in the First World War* (Oxford University Press, 2018), p. 224.

206   *I still wish* NO to MaO, 29 September 1920, Bod.

207 The story of Noel refusing to perform an abortion for Alix was gossip DG heard from Vanessa Bell and recorded in his diary, noting that Alix ultimately turned out not to be pregnant.

207 *restore regularity* Brookes, p. 5.

207 *unsavoury cases* quoted in Brookes, p. 28.

209 *absolutely shattering* Holroyd, p. 481.

209 *altogether broken* VW Diary, II, p. 242.

209 *You can't think* VW Letters, III, p. 180.

212 *a great teacher* quoted in Villeneuve, p. 772.

212 *be classified* in Blom, p. 215.

212 *the future* quoted in Villeneuve, pp. 755–6.

212 *Steiner's devoted* George Adams quoted in Villeneuve, p. 806.

213 *You may* Villeneuve, p. 792.

215 *poor Mud* NO to JS, 25 January 1922, BL.

217 *the sympathy* quoted in Villeneuve, p. 841.

217 *child needs* Seddon, p. 186.

218 *All was not* Philip Gibbs, *Now It Can Be Told* (Harper & Brothers, 1920), pp. 547–8; p. 551.

220 Teaching figures from Fara, p. 268.

220 *240,000 war widows* Winter.

220 *more shocking* Rebecca West in *Time and Tide*, 9 February 1923.

221 Eleanor Rathbone quoted in Kent, p. 240.

223 *Enough is known* Jeffreys, p. 174.

224 Tour log: Radford & Radford, pp. 44–5.

224 *original, quaint* CSL Diary, p. 53.

225 *I can't believe* NO to JS, 21 April 1923, BL.

226 *I don't require* Vera Brittain (ed.), *Selected Letters of Winifred Holtby and Vera Brittain 1920–1935* (A. Brown & Sons, 1960), 11 November 1921, p. 18.

226 *beautiful beautiful* VW Diary, II, p. 229.

226 *Why can't* VW to Vanessa Bell, VW Letters, III, p. 415.

228 *It is all* Uhrmacher, p. 389.

228 *Our civilization* Seddon, p. 16.

230 *take a firm stand* Francis Lee, p. 150.

231 Divorce figures from Office for National Statistics.

232 *have love affairs* quoted in Knights, p. 193.

232 *whom I meet* VW Letters, III, pp. 92–3.

235 *made the burden* CSL Diary, p. 253.

235 *chiefly* Ibid., p. 338.

235 *very fond* Ibid., p. 275.

236 *very stars* Barfield, p. 287.

240 After Steiner's death it was discovered that he had given two conflicting sets of advice on the best colours for the schoolrooms, an anomaly that was never explained.

Part Five

245 *My dearest Darling* BO to MaO, 'Christmas Eve 1934', Bod.

246 *Has there ever* BW Diary, 16 July 1935, LSE.

247 *Arthur will* NO to JS, 1 May 1933, BL.

247 *a great many* NO to JS, 11 August 1933, BL.

247 *terrifying but beautiful* NO to JS, 21 August 1933, BL.

247 *Very hard* SO Letters, p. 169.

247 *manifest nonsense* SO to GBS, undated copy enclosed in correspondence with Carl Jung, ETH Zurich University Archives.

247 *Our people* GBS to SO, Ibid.

247 *one probes* Dr Thomas Nelson to SO, 22 January 1935, Bod.

248 *not only futile ... fatigue poison* SO to N and AR (copy), 9 April 1934, Bod.

249 *going periodically* SO to HGW, 17 April 1934, Bod.

250 'Luly' was sometimes spelled 'Lulie'.

250 Bankruptcy figures from Pugh, p. 264.

250 *an uncertain form* 'The certainty of farming', *The Farm Economist*, January 1935, p. 185.

251 *mystery disease* SO to N and AR (copy), 9 April 1934, Bod.

251 *unlimited capacity* SO to GBS, 23 [February?] 1935, BL.

252 *Mental care* SO to HGW, 16 April 1933, Bod.

253 *for months* Appignanesi, p. 228.

253 Lucia Joyce in fact spent the last decades of her life at St Andrew's, coinciding with Margery.

253 *Bleuler's definition* Appignanesi, p. 206.

254 Harry Stack Sullivan, 'The Modified Psychoanalytic Treatment of Schizophrenia', *American Journal of Psychiatry*, November 1931.

254 *the keeping of children ... business footing* RS to GBS, 25 September 1933, BL.

255 *B's case* SO to HGW, 17 April 1934, Bod.

256 *a charming* BO to MaO, 'Sunday' postcard, Bod.

256 *take charge* BO to MaO, 'Saturday' postcard, Bod.

258 *catching thing* BO to Lucilla, 19 March 1934, [incomplete letter], Bod.

259 *a short cut* Pugh, p. 126.

259 *certain amount of fortitude* NO to JS, 13 August 1935, BL.

260 *waited serenely ... rather domesticated* DO to MaO, 18 January [1931], Bod.

261 *plague of people* VW Letters, V, p. 74.

261 *Why in 1934* Kent, pp. 236–7.

261 *only birds* Ibid., p. 241.

263 *one of those people* Dr Thomas Nelson to SO, 22 January 1935, Bod.

263 *You cannot get* Anne Olivier Bell to Paul Delany, 5 June 1988, RCB, KCA.

264 *off with another man* BW Diary, 27 September 1925, LSE.

265 *three boyish figures* Thornycroft and Baynes.

265 *Hugh's side* SO to GBS, 28 [January?] 1935, BL.

266 *slimed everything* CSL Diary, p. 449.

267 *studied the evidence* Pederson, p. 272.

267 *a recommendation* John Carey, *William Golding: The Man Who Wrote Lord of the Flies* (Faber & Faber, 2009).

270 *members of all countries* Mansfield, p. 27.

271 *truly heroic* Owen Barfield on CH, *Anthroposophical Quarterly*, 1976.

271 *It is recorded* Harwood, p. 65.

272 *over four thousand children* Report of the Medical Officer of Health for Shoreditch for 1934, Wellcome Library.

273 *interesting American invention* The British Journal of Nursing, vol. 84 (February 1936), p. 40.

273 *a book of facts* Public Health, vol. 49 (October 1935–September 1936), p. 399.

273 *peace and protection* Noel Olivier Richards & Amy Dorothea Baker, *Healthy Babies: Their Feeding and Management* (Cassell's Health Handbooks, 1935), pp. 7–8.

274 *practically completely engulfed* NO to JS, 4 November 1927, BL.

274 *broken-hearted* NO to JS, [PM 6 October 1933], BL.

275 *I will come* NO to JS, [PM 23 January 1932], BL.

275 *I thank Heaven* NO to JS, [PM 1 August 1935], BL.

277 *This is just* BO to MaO, undated postcard, Bod.

277 *drinking their* NO to JS, 22 January 1935, BL.

277   Brynhild's description of Versailles from BO to MaO, undated, Bod.

279   *very magnificent* NO to JS, 22 January 1935, BL.

279   *You gave us* DO to MaO, 'Tuesday', Bod.

Part Six

283   *privately expecting* figures from Mackay, p. 20.

285   *London's minors* figures from Smith, p. 6.

285   *the police* Mary Custance in *The Evacuees*, p. 56.

286   *porridge … No one expects* NO to JS, 22 August 1939, BL.

288   *I still think* NO to Ray Garnett, 28 September 1938, NW.

288   *fearful aspect* JS to NO, 29 August 1938, BL.

288   *I have my* NO to JS, 30 August 1938, BL.

289   *true companionship* AR to JS, 13 September 1938, BL.

289   *The tempests* NO to JS, 26 August [1938], BL.

289   *What I feel* NO to JS, [PM 7 October 1935], BL.

289   *awake in grief* NO to JS, [January] 1936, BL.

289   *haunted by* 'I Am My Brother', quoted in Andrew Sinclair (ed.), *The War Decade* (Hamilton, 1989).

292   *quite sick* NO to JS, 9 October [1939], BL.

293   *hosts complained* Richard Padley and Margaret Cole, *Evacuation Survey: A Report to the Fabian Society* (Routledge, 1940), p.72.

293   *acquired a new language* Harwood, p. 56.

294   *a queer sense* VW Diary, V, pp. 264–5.

296   Steiner's ideas about a hierarchy of races were arguably in line with Nazi thought, however.

296   At least one teacher, Ernst Lehr, a German Jew who had been at the school with his wife for less than two years, is recorded as having been interned on the Isle of Man.

297   Churchill's approval rating and volunteer figures from Mackay, pp. 60–1.

297   *itching for something* Ibid

298   *one adopts* NO to JS, 12 July 1940, BL.

298   *I saw it* NO to JS, 3 October 1940, BL.

299   *Bomb craters* Partridge, *Pacifist's War*, pp. 80–81.

300   *most bitterly cold* NO to JS, 23 December 1940, BL.

300   *fumed & fumed* NO to DG, [December 1940], NW.

300   *joint feast* NO to JS, 23 December 1940, BL.

300   *with my love* SO to Leonard Woolf [copy], 21 February 1941, Bod.

301   *seemed very dark* NO to DG, 16 March 1941, NW.

301   *prevent his being* NO to JS, 16 March 1941, BL.

301   *take his time* NO to DG, 15 May 1941, NW.

302   *I keep imagining* JS to NO, 3 August 1938, BL.

302   *enclosed world* Partridge, *Pacifist's War*, p. 93.

302   *The marvellous thing* JS to NO, 1 July 1939, BL.

302   *with you* JS to NO, 10 August 1938, BL.

303   *She is the only* AR to JS, 9 September 1938, BL.

303   *with foreboding* NO to JS, 26 September 1938, BL.

303   *Hope is* Partridge, *Pacifist's War*, p. 112.

303   *the greatest surprise* Anne Stewart Higham, 'Women in Defence of Britain: An Informal Report', *Journal of Educational Sociology* (January 1942), p. 293.

304   *no time to speak* Partridge, *Pacifist's War*, p. 49.

304   *women can do anything* quoted in Susan Gubar, '"This is My Rifle, This is My Gun", World War Two and the Blitz on Women', *Behind the Lines*, pp. 228–9.

304   *injury compensation* Harold L. Smith, 'The Womanpower Problem in Britain during the Second World War,' *Historical Journal*, XXVII (1984), p. 926.

304   *primary employment* Smith, p. 210.

305   *Yardley advert* quoted in Janice Winship, 'Women's magazines: times of war and management of the self in *Woman's Own*' in *Nationalising Femininity*, p. 138.

305   *extraordinarily free* NO to DG, [December 1940], NW.

307   *an excellent mother* quoted in Harwood, p. 78.

307   *more or less* NO to JS, 12 July 1940, BL.

308   *I often bless* DO to MaO, 24 May [1944], Bod.

308   *It is a curious* NO to DG, [December 1940], NW.

311   *the lightless middle* Elizabeth Bowen, *The Heat of the Day* (Vintage, 1948, 1998), p. 93.

311   *living the life* NO to DG, [December 1940], NW.

311   *I will now* NO to MaO, 17 July 1943, Bod.

311   *We are crowded* NO to JS, 23 December 1940, BL.

311   *a combined wash* DO to MaO, [March 1943], Bod.

312   *When you have* quoted in Harwood, p. 93.

313   *The importance* Louise, J. Despert, 'School Children in Wartime', *The Journal of Educational Sociology*, vol. 16, no. 4 (December, 1942), pp. 219–30.

317   *I hoped* NO to JS, 1 April 1943, BL.

317   *wilful* NO to JS, 14 August 1939, BL.

317   MO case notes, St Andrew's Healthcare archives.

317   *It will be very tiring* NO to MaO, 26 February 1943, Bod.

319   *so horrible* McNally, p. 2.

319   *discharge as recovered* Arthur Foss & Kerith Trick, *St Andrew's Hospital, Northampton: The first 150 years* (Granta, 1989), p. 249.

320   *If she had* NO to MaO, [December 1944], Bod.

321   *I remember I* BW Diary, 20 February 1943, LSE.

322   *shrillness* SO to GBS, 23 [February?] 1935, BL.

323   *the little wretch* DO to MaO, [March or April 1944], Bod.

324   *bluish eyes* NO to DG, 30 August 1944, NW.

324   *interspersed with* DO to MaO, undated partial letter, Bod.

324   *I am badly … hearts aren't* DO to MaO, undated, Bod.

Afterlives

329   *I'll not* SoL, p. 113.

329   *But once* Leonard Woolf (ed.), *Collected Essays vol. 4* (Hogarth Press, 1967), p. 54.

329   *a sort of* CHL to GK, 10 September 1962, CUL.

329   *The present moment* JS to CHL, 9 August 1962, CUL.

329   *dim little man* GK to CHL, 8 August 1962, CUL.

330   *I must have … Writers think* CHL to GK, 10 September 1962, CUL.

330   *You know my attitude* NO to GK, 30 November 1955, RCB, KCA.

330   *so elaborate* NO to Richard Halliburton, 27 September 1927, Richard Halliburton Papers (C0247); Manuscripts Division, Department of Rare Books and Special Collections, Princeton University Library.

331   *But please realise* DO to MaO, 22 October [1944], Bod.

331   *trying to induce* NO to DG, 10 October 1962, NW.

331   Hassall's descriptions of their November meeting are from CHL to GK, 8 December 1962, CUL.

332   *crowning touch* Lady Margaret Keynes to CHL, 7 August 1962, CUL.

333   *her own normal* CHL to GK, 8 December 1962, CUL.

334   *I think she lacks* CHL to Lady Margaret Keynes, 10 December 1962, CUL. Rupert's own belief that Noel had, at least at one time, been in love with him was apparently irrel-

evant. Rupert, in fact, seemed to understand that Noel had 'her own method with love', as he put it, in a way that later commentators never did.

334   *I should like* NO to DG, 25 November 1962, Illinois, NW.

334   *The four girls* Garnett, *The Golden Echo*, p. 99.

334   *You let me off* NO to DG, 5 April 1954, NW.

335   *It seems to me* NO to Halliburton, 8 September 1927, Halliburton papers, Princeton.

336   *girlish loveliness* Stringer, Arthur, *The Red Wine of Youth* (Bobbs-Merrill, 1948), pp. 137–9. The story of Noel dropping a cup during the dinner at which she first met Rupert, and his leaping to her aid, was here lingered over and embellished in a way that annoyed Noel when she found it replicated elsewhere. Noel's name is spelled 'Noël' in the book.

336   *had been ill* Garnett, *The Flowers of the Forest*, p. 196.

336   *Bunny took her* NO to JS, [PM 14 February 1919], BL.

337   *a whirl & tumult* NO to MaO, [December 1944], Bod.

337   *Don't you think* Margaret Keynes to CHL, 10 December 1962, CUL.

337   *Readers will* GK to CHL, 11 December 1962, CUL.

338   *Strange, that while* Justin Brooke to GK, December 1962, CUL.

338   *coming to heel!* GK to CHL, 8 August 1962, CUL.

338   *grovelling in the past* Partridge, *Other People*, p. 111.

339   *Rupert Brooke* sales figures from John Lehmann, *Rupert Brooke: His Life and Legend* (Weidenfeld & Nicolson, 1980), p. 55 and p. 165.

339   *elegantly written trifle* Keynes, p. 165.

339   *equivocal aura* Ibid., p. 170.

339   *why bowdlerize* Hale, p. x.

339   *dead body* Ibid. A similar concern about sexuality had set Geoffrey firmly against the publication of his brother Maynard's indiscreet exchanges with Lytton Strachey. When Lytton's biographer Michael Holroyd came across the correspondence in the 1960s, he got the distinct impression that its fate was in limbo whilst James (in favour of publication) and Geoffrey (pro-suppression) each waited for the other to die.

339   *blurted out* CHL to JS [copy], 17 November 1960, CUL.

340   *If anything I did* CHL to GK [copy], undated, CUL.

340   *inverted vanity* CHL to GK, 8 December 1962, CUL.

340   *a little obscure* Richard de la Mare to CHL, 20 July 1962, CUL.

341   *Beanstalk Generation* Marwick, p. 61.

341   *Julia flung a knife* The author is assured that the resulting scar is only small.

341   *It doesn't make sense* Bouchier, p. 30.

342   *lose oneself* quoted in Marwick, p. 71.

342   *took drugs* Diski, p. 37 and p.35.

342   Laing, pp. 9–12.

343   *sound rather magnificent* DG to GK, 6 March 1948, CUL.

344   *method for disciplining* Goffman, p. 150.

344   *greatest possible mercy* NO to DG, 6 April 1963, NW.

344   *I hope* NO to DG, 2 July 1963, NW.

346   *sensational* GK to CHL, 30 May 1962, CUL.

346   *If the impossible* Partridge, *Other People*, p. 57.

347   *I cannot help* Spalding, *Duncan Grant*, p. 456.

347   *The rocks and shoals* Knights, p. 407.

347   *should not* DG to JS, 29 June 1966, BL.

347   *What the Hell* JS to DG, 2 July 1966, NW.

347   *extremely abusive* JS to DG, 12 March 1967, NW.

348   *Implicit throughout* Michael Holroyd, Introduction to *Ermyntrude and Esmeralda: An entertainment* (Blond, 1969), p. 6.

348   *it ought* JS to DG, 12 March 1967, NW.

348   *what her old friends* Angela Harris to DG, 6 July 1969, NW.

348   *impressed us all* NO to Maitland Radford, 9 January 1915, BL.

349   *publishing rascal* Keynes, p. 168.

349   *subtle old witch* Henry James, *The Aspern Papers and Other Stories* (Oxford University Press, 2013), p. 57.

349   *I can't possibly* NO to JS, [PM July 1939], BL. Brynhild was far less sentimental when it came to her love letters from Raymond. 'I dont really believe in keeping more than one can remember or anyhow put in a very small drawer,' she told him.

349   *was out to* NO to DG, 10 April 1967, NW.

350   *The mask* The Times, 8 June 1968.

350   *mostly of ornamental* Diski, p. 90.

350   *The first question* quoted in Diski, p. 92.

350   *yearning for sisterhood* Rowbotham, *The Past is Before Us*, p. 157.

352   *In what conditions* Sheila Rowbotham, *Hidden from History* (Pluto Press, 1973, 1977), p. ix.

352   *the futility* Frances Cornford to CHL, CUL.

352   *Several very talented* quoted in Villeneuve, p. 806.

352   *I know it is* Angela Harris to DG, 12 April 1969, NW.

353   *to whom I can* Knights, p. 508.

Postscript

355   *the story of* Interview: The Art of Biography No. 7, *The Paris Review*, issue 223 (Winter 2017).

356   *concept arising from feminism* Bouchier, p. 63.

CREDITS

Images: **p.1** Sisters in tree, used by permission of the heirs of Anne Olivier Bell; **p.14** Margaret Olivier, from the Harris / Richards Papers, used by permission of the heirs of Angela Harris; **p.14** Sydney in Antigua, 1895, from the Harris / Richards Papers, used by permission of the heirs of Angela Harris; **p.20** Daphne, Margery, Brynhild, Noel, used by permission of the heirs of Anne Olivier Bell; **p.25** The cast of *The Usurping Baron*, used by permission of the heirs of Anne Olivier Bell; **p.30** The Oliviers in Kingston, Jamaica, from the Harris / Richards Papers, used by permission of the heirs of Angela Harris; **p.31** Photograph of Margery, used by permission of the heirs of Anne Olivier Bell; **p.31** Photograph of Brynhild, used by permission of Laurence Harwood, OBE; **p.31** Photographs of Daphne and Noel, from the Harris / Richards Papers, used by permission of the heirs of Angela Harris; **p.36** Rupert Brooke in 1913 © National Portrait Gallery, London; **p.39** A Fabian summer school, King's College Library, Cambridge. RCB/Ph/61; **p.42** Margery at Newnham, from the Harris / Richards Papers, used by permission of the heirs of Angela Harris; **p.44** Suffrage parade, c. 1908, Women's Library, LSE / Flickr; **p.49** Noel, Margery and Evelyn Radford at Bank, used by permission of the heirs of Anne Olivier Bell; **p.54** Noel as seen by Noel, 1909, Bodleian Library; **p.61** Brynhild and Sydney with guests, from the Harris / Richards Papers, used by permission of the heirs of Angela Harris; **p.62** Daphne with a polo team, from the Harris / Richards Papers, used by permission of the heirs of Angela Harris; **p.71** A skiing party in 1908, King's College Library, Cambridge. RCB/Ph/62–5; **p.77** Margery, probably in King's House, from the Harris / Richards Papers, used by permission of the heirs of Angela Harris; **p.79** The sisters with Sydney at a picnic, used by permission of Laurence Harwood, OBE; **p.84** Brynhild as Helen of Troy, King's College Library, Cambridge. RCB/Ph/58; **p.86** Noel at Buckler's Hard, used by permission of the heirs of Anne Olivier Bell; **p.100** Noel, Maitland Radford, Virginia Woolf and Rupert at Clifford Bridge © National Portrait Gallery, London; **p.100** Daphne with Geoffrey Keynes at Clifford Bridge, used by permission of the heirs of Anne Olivier Bell; **p.100** Ka Cox beside Rupert at Clifford Bridge, King's College Library, Cambridge. RCB/Ph/155; **p.102** Brynhild and Margery climbing, used by permission of the heirs of Anne Olivier Bell; **p.109** The Coronation Procession, 1911, Women's Library, LSE / Flickr; **p.112** Margery, from the Harris / Richards Papers, used by permission of the heirs of Angela Harris; **p.115** Hugh diving, used by permission of the heirs of Anne Olivier Bell; **p.119** Noel at camp, used by permission of the heirs of Anne Olivier Bell; **p.121** Noel cutting James Strachey's hair, used by permission of the heirs of Anne Olivier Bell; **p.127** Brynhild and Tony at camp, 1914, used by permission of the heirs of Anne Olivier Bell; **p.135**

Ferenc Békássy, Wikimedia Commons; **p.138** Bunny, Hugh and Frankie Birrell with three Oliviers, used by permission of the heirs of Anne Olivier Bell; **p.148** Bunny and Daphne in 1914, used by permission of the heirs of Anne Olivier Bell; **p.154** Brynhild and Tony in Lyme Regis, used by permission of the heirs of Anne Olivier Bell; **p.171** Hugh, used by permission of the heirs of Anne Olivier Bell; **p.179** Margery and Brynhild in Tatsfield, used by permission of the heirs of Anne Olivier Bell; **p.187** Noel, from the Harris / Richards Papers, used by permission of the heirs of Angela Harris; **p.190** Hugh with the children in Draycott Fitzpayne, 1919, used by permission of the heirs of Anne Olivier Bell; **p.193** Raymond Sherrard, used by permission of the heirs of Anne Olivier Bell; **p.196** The Hanbury Gardens, author's own; **p.199** Andy at La Mortola Inferiore, used by permission of the heirs of Anne Olivier Bell; **p.202** Arthur Richards (third from left) with colleagues, from the Harris / Richards Papers; **p.206** Noel (standing) with colleagues, from the Harris / Richards Papers, used by permission of the heirs of Angela Harris; **p.213** Rudolf Steiner in 1916 © akg-images; **p.243** Brynhild with baby, used by permission of the heirs of Anne Olivier Bell; **p.253** St Andrew's © Popperfoto / Getty Images; **p.268** Cecil with the children, used by permission of Laurence Harwood, OBE; **p.274** Noel with Benedict, from the Harris / Richards Papers; **p.276** James and Alix Strachey in the mid 1930s © National Portrait Gallery, London; **p.281** Daphne, used by permission of Laurence Harwood, OBE; **p.306** Noel and Ginny with Virginia Woolf, Houghton Library, Harvard University. MS Thr 562 (0184); **p.309** Noel with her daughters, from the Harris / Richards Papers, used by permission of the heirs of Angela Harris; **p.310** Daphne with Laurence, Sylvia and Mark, used by permission of Laurence Harwood, OBE; **p.318** Sydney looking perplexed by a grandchild, used by permission of Laurence Harwood, OBE; **p.327** Noel and Arthur birdwatching, used by permission of Julia Rendall; **p.345** Noel at Tazza's wedding, used by permission of Julia Rendall; **p.353** Noel tending to a vine at Nunnington, used by permission of Julia Rendall; **p.354** The sisters in Cornwall in 1914, used by permission of the heirs of Anne Olivier Bell

Quotations: The excerpts from Rupert Brooke's letters are reproduced by permission of Andrew Motion; James Strachey's letters by permission of The Society of Authors as agent to the Strachey Trust; Christopher Hassall's letters by permission of David Higham Associates. The quotations from *The Letters of Virginia Woolf: The Flight of the Mind, 1888–1912 Volume 1* by Virginia Woolf edited by Nigel Nicolson published by Chatto & Windus are reproduced by permission of The Random House Group Ltd. © 1975; *The Letters of Virginia Woolf: The Question of Things Happening, 1912–1922 Volume 2* by Virginia Woolf edited by Nigel Nicolson published by Chatto & Windus by permission of The Random House Group Ltd. © 1976. The quotations from Owen Barfield are reproduced by permission of the Owen Barfield Literary Estate. The excerpts from H. G. Wells's letters are reproduced by permission of AP Watt *at* United Agents LLP on behalf of The Literary Executors of the Estate of H. G. Wells; C. S. Lewis's *All My Road Before Me* © CS Lewis Pte Ltd 1991.

INDEX